THE CHANGING CANADIAN
METROPOLIS

VOLUME TWO

THE CHANGING CANADIAN METROPOLIS:
A Public Policy Perspective

Frances Frisken, Editor

VOLUME TWO

Institute of Governmental Studies Press,
University of California, Berkeley, and the
Canadian Urban Institute, Toronto
1994

Library of Congress Cataloging-In-Publication Data

The changing Canadian metropolis : a public policy perspective / Frances Frisken,
   editor.
            p.   cm.
        Includes bibliographical references.
        ISBN 0-87772-344-3
        1. Urban policy--Canada. 2. Metropolitan government--Canada. I. Frisken,
   Frances.
HT127.C48 1993
307.76'0971--dc20   93-43356
                                                                                        CIP

Contents

VOLUME ONE

Preface

VOLUME TWO

Politics and Public Policy

The Federal Government

Provincial Governments

Municipal Governments

Contributors

Politics and Public Policy

Chapter 11

The Federal Government and the Metropolitan Housing Problem

George Fallis
York University

An understanding of the changing Canadian metropolis requires an understanding of the political context in which metropolitan areas develop. It requires analysis of the roles of local, regional, provincial, and federal governments, and of their many policies and programs. This chapter analyzes the federal role in one policy field: housing policy.

Many activities of the federal government have significant impacts on Canadian urban areas, from immigration and trade policy, to decisions about railway cutbacks and airport expansions, to closing a military base or opening a museum. But perhaps the most important and direct impact comes from federal housing programs. Ever since the first National Housing Act (NHA) was passed by the government of Canada in 1938 and followed in 1945 by an act to create Central Mortgage and Housing Corporation, CMHC, (now Canada Mortgage and Housing Corporation) as a crown corporation to administer the NHA, the federal government has been the dominant level of government in Canadian housing policy. It remains dominant, although the provinces are now more and more important partners, and some cities have developed housing policies.[1]

This chapter begins by surveying the evolution of federal housing policy over the last two decades and then poses the question: can the changes in federal housing programs be understood as part of the state's response to urban growth and change? Because housing programs so

---

[1]The municipal role in housing is surveyed in Carter and McAfee (1990).

directly influence urban housing conditions, many analysts have implicitly assumed, quite understandably, that federal housing policy has developed and changed in response to the housing problems accompanying urban growth and change. The thesis of the chapter is that the level and shape of federal housing involvement is not *primarily* influenced by urban growth and change; rather it is most fundamentally shaped by federal macro-economic policy. It is also shaped by federal attitudes to federal-provincial relations and by the redistributive politics of the welfare state, which are only distantly connected to urban change. Therefore, federal housing policy is best analyzed as part of the externally determined environment of cities and city governments, rather than the federal portion of the entire public sector's urban policy.

The following discussion of federal housing programs does not distinguish between programs directed at housing problems in Canadian metropolis as opposed to those directed at smaller cities or towns, because there are no specifically metropolitan programs.[2] There are a group of programs for native people and for rural areas; these are not considered here. Therefore the focus is on urban housing programs.

FEDERAL HOUSING POLICY FROM THE 1970s TO THE 1990s

During the early to mid 1970s, CMHC had more extensive involvement in housing markets than ever before, or since. This period was the full extension of what I have termed the second era of housing policy (1964-1977). In the first era (1954-1963), the primary federal concern was economic growth and stabilization of the economy. During the second era, "governments were confident that the economy could be stabilized and would grow. There was affluence, the prospect of increasing affluence, and governments intervened to ensure a fairer distribution of the pie. The emphasis shifted from stabilization and efficiency to distribution" (Fallis 1985, 170). In 1973, the federal minister responsible for CMHC made the most explicit statement ever regarding the housing norms of Canada: "it is a fundamental right of Canadians, regardless of their economic circumstances, to enjoy adequate

---

[2]The absence of specifically metropolitan programs perhaps indirectly supports the thesis of the chapter: housing programs were for cities of all sizes and all situations and not specifically responses to the conditions of metropolitan areas.

shelter at reasonable cost" (Hansard 1973). Things began to change in the late 1970s, leading to a third era (1978-present) of housing policy. The era began with concern about stagflation and now continues with increasing emphasis on fiscal restraint. In some ways we have returned to the worries of the early postwar period: worries about economic growth and stabilization of the economy.

The task of this section is to characterize the broad themes in the evolution of federal housing policy from the period of extensive involvement to the present. Then the question can be addressed of whether this evolution should be understood as part of the state's response to urban growth and change. Not all the details of each program and how the program changed over time can be presented, there is simply not space in a short chapter.[3] CMHC has summarized its orientation and programs under a list of headings at various times over the last 20 years. The list of headings has often changed because the range and focus of CMHC's programs has often changed. I will look at its programs under two headings: rental assistance programs and ownership assistance programs. This by no means includes all CMHC programs; but limited space prevents a more comprehensive treatment.

Rental Assistance Programs

Rental assistance programs are the principal policy instruments used by CMHC in pursuit of its stated goal of assisting "households who are unable to obtain suitable, adequate and affordable shelter in the private market" (CMHC 1985, 11). The programs charge rents that are below the cost of providing the housing. Some rents are set according to the tenant's ability to pay, usually between 25 and 30 percent of household income. Such units are called rent-geared-to-income (RGI) units and provide a deep subsidy. Admission to them is rationed using an elaborate screening mechanism. There is always a waiting list. Almost all RGI tenants have low incomes. Other rents are set according to the inevitably complex terms of the programs; most often a government or government-assisted mortgage with attractive terms permits rents that are slightly to moderately below the true costs of providing the housing. Admission to such units is most often on a first-come, first-served basis.

---

[3]A more detailed summary of the programs into the early 1980s is available in Fallis (1985) and a short report of the rest of the 1980s in Fallis (1990). See also Pomeroy (1989).

Tenants in these units are usually moderate-income households. There is a constant, unresolved debate in rental housing policy about whether moderate-income households should be assisted; if so, how large should the subsidy be; and how should the limited housing assistance budget be divided between moderate- and low-income households.[4] On some occasions rental assistance has been extended to housing available to people regardless of income.

In 1971, there were three main rental housing programs: public housing, entrepreneurial housing, and nonprofit housing. Public housing was available under two sets of terms: Federal-Provincial Rental Housing (Section 40) favoured by smaller, poorer provinces, and Public Housing (Section 43) favoured by the larger, richer provinces.[5] Both programs offered CMHC mortgages to finance construction of government-owned buildings (federal, provincial, or local government) occupied entirely by RGI tenants. Subsidies to cover the gap between operating costs and rents were cost-shared by the three levels of government. The entrepreneurial and nonprofit programs, both using the same (Section 15) arrangements offered high-ratio (usually 90 percent) CMHC mortgage loans at slightly less than market rates, which enabled landlords to charge rents that were slightly lower than equivalent private-sector housing built without government assistance. These programs provided units with relatively shallow subsidies and therefore could only be occupied by moderate-income households. The subsidy meant rents were about five to ten percent below the cost of providing the housing (Dennis and Fish 1972).[6]

Thus, in 1971, social housing had one public sector, one private sector, and one third sector program. Each operated independently of the

---

[4]The above quotation (CMHC 1985, 11), actually defined the purpose of social housing as being to assist "low-income households. . . . " This reflects current CMHC policy. The adjective "low-income" was not included in the text because CMHC subsidy monies still go to moderate-income households in existing projects.

[5]The sections of the National Housing Act have since been renumbered. The text uses the numbering of the time when the programs were implemented. This numbering is used in most of the literature.

[6]This paragraph, and the chapter, uses the term "subsidy" to refer both to government payments to cover the difference between revenues and costs and to program terms—for example, mortgages at reduced interest rates—that allow rents to be lower than otherwise.

other. All used CMHC mortgages. The public-sector buildings were occupied 100 percent by RGI tenants receiving deep subsidies. The private- and third-sector buildings were usually 100 percent moderate-income tenants receiving quite shallow subsidies. About 60 percent of the assisted rental housing units added annually were public housing, 32 percent were entrepreneurial, and about 8 percent were nonprofit (Table 11.1). These rental housing programs averaged 26,060 units per year from 1971-1974, which represented about 13 percent of all housing starts, and well over 20 percent of rental starts.

In 1973, nonprofit groups and cooperatives were recognized explicitly in the National Housing Act and could obtain more favourable arrangements than entrepreneurs. Nonprofits and coops could receive 100 percent mortgage loans and capital grants for up to 10 percent of capital costs. Also, the program could be combined with the rent supplement program that allowed units to be offered on an RGI basis, with the costs shared as under public housing. Many nonprofit projects had 25 percent RGI units. The nonprofit sector expanded considerably in the following years, while the entrepreneurial program waned and was terminated in 1975 (Table 11.1).

During the early and mid 1970s, the purview of federal housing policy expanded considerably. The Residential Rehabilitation Assistance Program (RRAP) was begun in 1973, offering loans to private and nonprofit landlords (also to homeowners) to finance rehabilitation of existing substandard housing. The loans were at attractive interest rates, and a portion of the loan could be forgiven. Private landlords had to agree to rent regulation to ensure that the improvements were not fully matched by increased rents. The Income Tax Act was changed in 1974 to allow the capital cost allowance on multiple unit residential buildings (MURBs) to be deducted against other income. This made real estate investment an attractive tax shelter and was designed to encourage construction of rental buildings. In 1975, as part of the Federal Housing Action Program, the Assisted Rental Program (ARP) was initiated. Interest-free loans were available up to $1,200 per unit; further loans were available for 10 years reduced by one-tenth of the original amount each year. The combination of government loans and a private-sector mortgage created a graduated payment mortgage. Units were to be modest in size and priced at or below an established maximum unit price. With these programs, especially the latter two programs, the federal government was assisting rental housing intended not just for low- and modest-income groups but for all renters.

Table 11.1.   *Annual Authorized Rental Assistance Units, 1971-1991*

	Public Housing		Entrepreneurs	Third Sector		Total
	Federal-Provincial Section 40	Section 43		Non-profit	Coop	
1971	2,120	19,360	11,507	3,280		36,267
1972	1,875	14,609	8,797	2,040		27,321
1973	2,536	10,944	4,526	1,228	193	19,427
1974	2,501	10,003	2,544	5,195	1,000	21,243
1975	892	12,582	10,895	4,421	1,469	30,259
1976	1,706	12,199		8,434	1,623	23,962
1977	1,562	5,454		4,417	1,812	13,245
1978	1,923	5,974		1,338	1,247	12,696
1979	1,661	143		15,487	1,883	18,174
1980	1,354	237		14,981	4,788	21,360
1981	1,390	2		13,496	5,560	20,448
1982	1,216			13,872	6,578	21,666
1983	1,305			13,934	6,164	21,403
1984	1,261			13,137	3,877	18,275
1985	1,061			13,080	4,732	18,873
1986				13,791	3,196	16,987
1987				16,866	3,945	20,811
1988				15,672	3,060	18,732
1989				14,127	2,039	16,166
1990				12,548	1,642	14,190
1991				12,615	1,785	14,400

Source: CMHC (various years).

But things began to change in the late 1970s; expansion turned into contraction, and the adjustment process continues to this day. Most activities under public housing (Section 43), nonprofit and coop programs were wound-up and replaced by the new Nonprofit Program (Section 56.1). All groups would receive assistance on the same terms. (The Section 40 terms were still available to provinces that used them heavily.) No longer would CMHC make the mortgage loans; all groups had to obtain private-sector mortgage financing, but could obtain NHA mortgage insurance. CMHC provided an annual interest reduction subsidy, reducing financing costs to a mortgage interest rate of two percent. The rents on some units were set at the low end of comparable market units, and some rents were RGI. The overall effect of the financing and rent-setting arrangements was that there was a considerable mix of income groups in the buildings; but a substantial portion of the assistance went to modest-income rather than low-income households.

The new nonprofit terms led to a substantial increase in the annual number of units approved until the early 1980s (Table 11.1). However, other programs were curtailed. ARP was gradually wound up in the late 1970s. MURBs were ended in 1981. The purview of rental housing policy was shrinking. There was one new program in the early 1980s, the Canada Rental Supply Plan (CRSP), but this was short lived, intended as part of fiscal stimulus to fight the recession rather than a housing policy initiative.

Following the election of the Conservative government in 1984, there was an extensive review of government housing programs and lengthy federal-provincial consultations culminating in a new policy direction at the federal level. (Pomeroy (1989) reviews this in more detail.) The basic programs remained the same, but the funding mechanisms were changed to target assistance at those most in need. Under the Nonprofit Program, CMHC will only share the operating deficit of households in core housing need. These households are primarily low-income households.[7] RRAP became an explicit social housing program targeted at households in inadequate or crowded housing. The delivery mechanisms also changed. Each province and territory negotiated a global and an operating agreement with CMHC. All the provinces except PEI became the delivery agents for nonprofit housing, and several took over

---

[7] A household is in core housing need if it lives in either inadequate, unsuitable, or unaffordable housing *and* it cannot obtain adequate suitable housing in its community without spending 30 percent or more of its income on housing (CMHC 1991).

RRAP. Both delivery and cost-sharing arrangements now differ significantly by province.

Coops could still use the nonprofit terms, but a unilateral federal coop program was introduced to provide security of tenure to households not in core need but who could not become homeowners. Provisions were also available to mix core need households at RGI rents in these projects. The program also introduced a new mortgage instrument—the index linked mortgage (ILM).

Simultaneous with the move to targeting assistance was a gradual decline in annual new commitments under the nonprofit and coop programs (Table 11.1). The federal budget of February 1990 established an Expenditure Control Plan. Rental RRAP was discontinued. That budget scaled back planned annual social housing commitments by 15 percent in 1990-91 and 1991-92. The next budget extended this to 1995-96. The 1992 budget curtailed the annual growth of all social housing spending to three percent until 1996-97; which implied a further cut in annual new commitments. The federal coop housing program was terminated. There seems little doubt that this restraint will continue for the foreseeable future.

Although much detail has been presented, all the many programs and their changes since 1971 have not been reported. Nevertheless most of the main themes in the evolution of federal rental housing policy can be identified.

An early theme is the disenchantment with public housing that had entirely RGI tenants, leading to a new orientation toward social mix (more exactly, income mix) within buildings. The public housing and nonprofit programs therefore could be combined in 1978 because they had the same mandate. No longer was one responsible for buildings with deep subsidy RGI units and the other for buildings with shallow subsidy units; buildings would include both and only one program was needed. There was a continuing controversy about the appropriate fractions of RGI and other units in a building, about how large the public subsidy ought to be on these other units, and about how these subsidies should be shared between the federal and provincial governments. In the late 1970s, the questions were implicitly answered by provincial responses to the complex provisions of the Section 56.1 Nonprofit Program. By 1986, the federal government had adopted a new approach: it would not contribute to subsidizing non-RGI units (more precisely to subsidizing households not in core need). Some provinces remain committed to assisting substantial numbers of non-RGI units (for example, Ontario), but others are less inclined, and their nonprofit buildings now tend to have 100 percent RGI units. It remains to be seen whether the original public housing critique will reappear.

A mixture of incomes in a building can be achieved in different ways, for example it can be achieved by using a rent supplement program to house RGI tenants in privately owned buildings. Such an approach was explored but never adopted as the dominant policy instrument. This reveals a second major theme: the decline in importance of private sector landlords in housing socially assisted tenants and the rising importance of the third sector. The Entrepreneurial Program was cancelled in 1975, and with the 1973 and 1978 nonprofit programs, nonprofit groups (including coops) became major vehicles for delivering both RGI and moderate subsidy units.

A third theme is the shift in financing rental assistance projects from public-sector mortgages to private-sector mortgages that are publicly insured under the NHA. This shift occurred in 1978 with the 56.1 Nonprofit Program and remains. Also there has been increasing use of innovative mortgage designs as a way of easing the problems of financing rental housing during periods of high interest rates. When interest rates are high, annual mortgage payments are high, and so rents must be high; under a standard level-payment mortgage, these high mortgage payments continue during the entire 35- to 50-year amortization period of the mortgage. But presumably tenant incomes will grow over this period so the mortgage burden in the rent will be heavy in the early years and light in the later years. New mortgage designs such as the coop ILM (and the graduated payment mortgage of the Assisted Rental Program) allow mortgage payments to rise over time and therefore allow rents to be lower in early years and then rise in keeping with tenant incomes. The usage of these new mortgage designs will likely become more widespread over time.

Table 11.1 reports the annual number of housing units authorized by CMHC under many of the rental housing programs discussed so far. The table documents a fourth theme: a gradual decline in the annual number of rental assistance units authorized. Annual commitments averaged over 25,000 during the mid 1970s; from 1981 to 1983 they averaged 21,170; whereas from 1989 to 1991 they averaged 14,920.

We sometimes hear reference to massive cut-backs in federal commitment to social housing, but a comprehensive assessment yields a mixed picture. Annual commitments of units are 45 percent below their historic highs and about 25 percent below a longer-run average. Assisted rental approvals were about eight percent of all housing starts from 1989-91, compared to 13 percent in the early 1970s. But assisted rental was 23 percent of apartment, semi-detached, and row starts, slightly above the percentage of the early 1970s. And annual federal subsidies, which are payments to support both current and past commitments, continue to grow strongly (Table 11.2). This growth is both nominal and real—for example, since 1984 when the Progressive Conservatives formed the government, annual rental subsidies have grown 55 percent in nominal terms compared to a 37 percent increase in the Consumer Price Index.

The fifth theme is that available assistance has been more and more targeted at lower-income households. All of the programs that were not well targeted have been cancelled—beginning with ARP, MURB, and CRSP and followed by RRAP rental and the coop program. Even more important, since 1985 CMHC will only share the cost of assistance for households in core housing need.

Ownership Assistance Programs

In 1971, CMHC had no ownership assistance programs and in 1991 had only one: the Residential Rehabilitation Assistance Program (RRAP) for owners. At both times, the federal attitude to home ownership was approximately the same: the role of CMHC would be to facilitate and support the smooth functioning of private housing and mortgage markets, rather than to provide subsidies to home buyers. CMHC provides mortgage insurance on mortgage loans by approved private lending institutions and is more willing than private insurers to insure new mortgage instruments. CMHC sometimes provides direct mortgage loans, but this is intended to be residual, if for some reason the private market fails to lend to credit-worthy customers especially in rural areas. CMHC supports research on housing design and building technology and encourages all governments to recognize that the gains from land-use and housing regulation must be traded off against higher housing prices;and from time to time an ownership program may be part of macro-economic stimulus. In the main, however, home owners are expected to secure their housing in the private market without direct public subsidy.

The income tax laws, of course, have always given assistance to owners by treating savings placed in home equity more favourably than savings placed in other investments such as stocks or bonds: the imputed income from home equity is not taxed whereas the dividends from stocks

Table 11.2. *Annual Rental Assistance Subsidies, 1971-1991, ($ million)*

	Public Housing Subsidies[1]	Interest Reduction Contributions[2]	Subtotal	Residential Rehabilitation Assistance[3]	Total
1971	17		17		17
1972	30		30		30
1973	46		46		46
1974	63		63	1	64
1975	87		87	10	97
1976	117		117	29	146
1977	141		141	63	204
1978	179		179	88	267
1979	266	1	267	97	364
1980	267	17	284	107	391
1981	323	61	384	126	510
1982	399	183	582	135	717
1983	393	363	756	183	939
1984	453	465	918	202	1,120
1985	595	579	1,174	159	1,333
1986	498	637	1,135	103	1,238
1987	527	663	1,190	131	1,321
1988	548	670	1,218	146	1,364
1989	650	727	1,377	148	1,525
1990	785	814	1,599	140	1,739
1991	698	912	1,610	128	1,738

[1]Data include Federal-Provincial Housing, Section 43 Public Housing and Rent Supplement.

[2]Data include Nonprofit and Coop Housing.

[3]Data include both landlord and homeowner RRAP.

Source: CMHC (various years).

Table 11.3.   *Other Rental and Ownership Programs, 1971-1989,*
($ million)

	Assisted Home Ownership Program		Assisted Rental Program	
	Loans	Grants	Loans	Grants
1971				
1972				
1973	133			
1974	435	5		
1975	458	10		
1976	80	21	138	3
1977	24	29	321	10
1978	2	35	96	18
1979	-	32	-	20
1980	-	25	-	26
1981		16	36	30
1982		14	47	32
1983		7	30	37
1984		6	40	46
1985		2	15	35
1986		1	7	47
1987		1	9	52
1988		-	-	48
1989		-	-	40

Source: CMHC (various years).

and the interest on bonds are taxed; the realized capital gains on a
principal residence are not taxed whereas the realized capital gains on
stock or bond trading are taxable (above the $100,000 lifetime exemp-
tion).   But the federal government continues to resist extending this
favourable treatment further by allowing the deduction of mortgage
interest—an often-called-for provision, which is permitted in many
countries.

	Canadian Home Ownership Stimulation Plan		Canada Rental Supply Plan		Canada Home Renovation Plan	
	Loans	Grants	Loans	Grants	Loans	Grants
1971						
1972						
1973						
1974						
1975						
1976						
1977						
1978						
1979						
1980						
1981	-	-	-		-	-
1982	291	362	118		64	37
1983	373	417	110		162	174
1984	9	21	242		-	25
1985	-	-	5	15	-	-
1986	-	-	-	23	-	-
1987	-			24		
1988	-			24		
1989	-			23		

However, this federal attitude to home ownership assistance did not always prevail over the last 20 years. In 1973, CMHC offered assistance to first-time home buyers under the Assisted Home Ownership Program (AHOP). The program began with both public loans and ongoing subsidies (Table 11.3) then was altered several times until the combination of government and private loans on a house was like a graduated payment mortgage. AHOP subsidies were removed on new commitments in 1978. Also during the 1970s, the federal income tax law had a special provision to assist first-time home buyers called the Registered Home Ownership Savings Plan (RHOSP). A taxpayer was allowed to deduct up to $1,000 per year, to a lifetime maximum of $10,000, of contributions to a savings plan; when the money was withdrawn to buy a house, it was not subject to income tax. There was also an ownership program as part of a fiscal stimulus in 1982—the Canadian Home Ownership Stimulation Plan (CHOSP). Both the RHOSP and CHOSP are now terminated.

The one ownership assistance program that remains is the Residential Rehabilitation Assistance Program (RRAP), which was begun in 1973. Owners may obtain loans to renovate substandard housing to ensure that the housing will have a further 15 years of usable life. Owners' loans are partially forgivable; forgiveness is "earned" over a five-year period by the owner continuing to occupy the dwelling. Maximum forgiveness is available for households earning less than $13,000; forgiveness decreases to zero at an income of $23,000. The benefits of RRAP flow mainly to low- and moderate-income owners, and therefore the continuation of the program is consistent with the theme of targeting federal funds at needy households. Also, the program does not assist households to become owners but rather assists existing low-income owners.

For most of the time between 1973 and the present, RRAP assistance was also available to private and nonprofit landlords. (Landlord RRAP was cancelled in 1989.) Partially forgivable loans were available to repair dilapidated housing and in return landlords would agree to controls on rents. Another theme of federal policy over this time is the increased emphasis on renovation of existing housing rather than construction of new housing. Providing a needy household with a renovated unit does not improve their housing conditions as much as a new unit; but the cost of the assistance is correspondingly less, and the available dollars can help more people. The nonprofit program also will finance the purchase and renovation of existing housing, although it is primarily a new construction program.

FEDERAL RESPONSE TO URBAN GROWTH AND CHANGE

The evolution of federal housing policy over the last 20 years has been sketched and the main themes identified. The question may now be posed: can the evolution of federal housing policy be understood as the federal response to urban growth and change?

Let us begin by trying to examine what would be necessary for federal housing activities to be deemed a federal urban housing policy. If federal housing programs were systematically altering in response to urban growth and change, this would constitute a federal urban housing policy, either implicit or explicit. I would argue that a necessary condition for a federal urban housing policy is that the federal government's own analysis of its activities within the civil service, at least on occasion, utilize an urban framework. An urban framework or paradigm has a *spatial* orientation and emphasizes how the demographic, social and economic forces in society interact to allocate people and activities *in space*—how they are allocated to separate cities in a system of cities and how they are allocated within each city. Housing problems within an urban framework would be seen as problems *of* the city, rather than simply as problems *in* the city (Lithwick 1970). For example, if the housing problems of certain low-income households were seen as the result of an expanding central business district and of inner-city gentrification, then federal rental assistance could be regarded as part of an urban policy. (And federal responses might be directed at the causes of low-income housing problems rather than the outcome.) But federal analysis does not adopt such a framework, with a few exceptions discussed below. To expect such a framework is not to be a naive academic looking for analytical abstraction in the practical world of policy, because city housing departments do use this framework and, to a certain extent, provincial housing ministries do so as well.

Analysis at the federal level using the framework of a system of cities is probably the least likely to occur. It would have to displace a long-established and constitutionally entrenched framework of regional and provincial analysis. The federal government is committed to regional equalization and at least implicitly acts to smooth the uneven regional patterns of economic activity over the business cycle. It is unclear how the federal government would (or should) react to the housing market outcomes that result from the uneven rates of economic growth in cities that are so much a part of the Canadian experience. For example when the rapid growth of Toronto, or Calgary or Vancouver, causes rents and house prices to rise, should (or would) the federal government intervene to dampen growth and housing demand, or should it provide more housing assistance in these cities,[8] which would help the beneficiaries of the programs but also further stimulate housing demand? Also, perhaps social science is not sufficiently advanced to permit the system of cities as the fundamental framework; we certainly have not had enough data organized on this basis to permit the development of a sophisticated social science. One thrust of the Ministry of State for Urban Affairs (MSUA) was to develop an empirically based model of the Canadian system of cities, and to make the system of cities framework a part of federal policy thinking. Neither the model nor the policy approach advanced very far. The federal government experimented with this urban framework, but it died with the demise of MSUA. I do not wish to argue whether this is a desirable or undesirable outcome; only that federal housing policy cannot be regarded as a national response to urban growth and change in a national system of cities. In any event, many scholars would argue the appropriate starting framework should be the regional economy, not the system of cities; regional economies will influence the cities within them but the starting point should be the region. Certainly this view is implicit in a staples explanation of differential urban growth rates.

It is perhaps more realistic to expect that federal housing thinking might utilize that part of an urban framework that focuses on the internal spatial structure of cities. Our social science is much more developed here, and the framework is widely used by other levels of government. The federal government seems to have used such a framework for a time but now seems to have abandoned it. An urban framework is most clearly revealed when rental and ownership programs, giving assistance to an individual household or individual building, are implemented in the context of ideas about neighbourhood, community, or city structure. From time to time, CMHC has had neighbourhood, community, and urban infrastructure programs in conjunction with housing programs. For example, the first era of housing policy used the urban framework to a certain extent, when direct lending and mortgage insurance to finance single detached houses were combined with assistance for new sewage and water treatment plants. Land banking also had an urban orientation. The framework was even more evident in the development of the Neighbourhood Improvement Program in conjunction with RRAP.

---

[8]This did occur in 1980-81, when additional nonprofit units were directed to B.C. (Vancouver).

Again, MSUA was important in making the framework part of federal thinking. Of course MSUA has been abolished long since. However, these programs were never the organizing framework for housing policy and, apart from RRAP, have all been terminated. Nevertheless, it should be acknowledged that this group of programs was urban oriented and can be regarded as part of the state's response to urban growth and change.

There have also been specific initiatives within an explicit urban framework. One example is the Winnipeg Core Area Initiative. It incorporates housing programs and expenditures from all three levels of government as part of a more holistic approach that addresses social, economic, and physical concerns in central Winnipeg. Urban redevelopment projects such as False Creek in Vancouver and St. Lawrence neighbourhood in Toronto are other examples.

Although not necessarily reflected in the design of housing programs, CMHC has always been deeply involved with the development of urban planning, urban design, and residential architecture in Canada. Major contributions have come from its own staff, through building projects it supported, and from research it has funded. In recent years, as "urban context" programs have stopped, CMHC has focused more on a role of encouraging innovation, research, and information dissemination.

Thus, although CMHC has always been a major centre of thinking in Canada about the internal spatial structure of cities, and sometimes the analysis of its programs has used this thinking, the urban framework never has been the principal paradigm for developing, analyzing, or evaluating housing programs. The barrier, in part of course, is constitutional: the federal government cannot speak directly to city governments, the formal route must be to approach the province first and then to draw in the cities. The fundamental point of contact for the federal government is the province.

Another condition necessary for federal housing policy to be considered as urban oriented is that it be responsive to the different situations in different cities. Even this condition is barely met. Certainly the federal government cannot unilaterally respond to a city's differentness. Most of the rental assistance programs are delivered within federal-provincial agreements, and CMHC has only minor influence over the allocation of assistance across cities. CMHC allocates assistance to provinces on the basis of housing need, measured using the concept of core need. To the extent that an increase in core need in a city leads to an increased provincial allocation, it might be said that federal policy is sensitive to the needs of individual cities. The Coop Program, which after 1985 was unilaterally delivered by the federal government, contains no explicit provisions for responding to the specific situation of a city.

Therefore there is nothing in the broad design of federal housing programs, nor is there anything in the main housing policy debates and controversies over the last 20 years to suggest that an urban framework *significantly* informed the analysis and therefore that housing policy is a federal response to urban growth and change. And any influence of an urban framework has diminished over the last 20 years.

Although not using an urban framework, it might be that federal housing policy has evolved in response to changing housing needs in cities. It is difficult to assemble data to measure housing need specifically in urban or in metropolitan Canada. Frequently, we must use national data or nonfarm data. (A point to consider, although it is beyond the scope of this chapter, is whether we require metropolitan or urban data on housing need because all areas have become so much alike that national data are sufficiently accurate.) A crude indicator of housing need among renters is the percentage that are spending 30 percent or more of their income on rent. From 1971 to 1981, the percentage rose slightly from 21.5 to 22.6 in nonfarm areas (Table 11.4). During the period, many new rental assistance programs were begun, then terminated; annual new commitments moved up and down but declined over the decade. From 1981 to 1988, the percentage rose sharply from 22.6 to 29.3 (Table 11.4). However, no new rental assistance programs were mounted, and annual new commitments declined (although annual subsidies continued to rise). Changes in the level of federal rental assistance do not seem to be responses to the changing needs of urban renters.

There is no widely accepted measure of need for homeowners or first-time home buyers, or indeed no consensus about whether the public sector ought to subsidize owners. But a crude proxy for changing need might be changes in the average real house price. New house prices rose dramatically in the 1970s, and CMHC initiated ownership assistance programs. Prices rose again in the late 1980s, but this time no assistance was offered. There has been a mixed response to this housing needs indicator.

The themes in the evolution of federal housing policy have already been discussed: the disenchantment with public housing; the shift toward income mix in buildings; the decline in the role of private sector landlords in social housing, and the increase in the third sector's role; controversy over the appropriate income mix in buildings; how much to

Table 11.4. *Percentage Distribution of Nonfarm Tenant Occupied Dwellings By Cash Rent as a Percentage of Income*

Percentage of Income	1971-72[1]	1981-82	1988-89
< 15	40.1	37.4	31.0
15 - 19	19.4	17.9	17.1
20 - 24	9.3	13.8	11.7
25 - 29	9.2	8.5	10.8
30 - 34	2.7 ⎤	5.5 ⎤	7.1 ⎤
35 - 39	6.2	3.4	5.1
40 - 49	0.1 ⎬ 21.5	4.8 ⎬ 22.6	6.0 ⎬ 29.3
50+	12.5 ⎦	8.9 ⎦	11.1 ⎦
Average Percentage	16.2	16.0	17.6

[1]Income data are for first indicated year; rent data are for May of second indicated year. *Source*: For 1971-72, Canada (1975) computed from Table 5. For 1981-82 Canada (1983) Table 15. For 1988-89 Canada (1990) Table 13.

subsidize moderate-income people and who should pay for it; the decline in public mortgage lending and the emphasis on new mortgage instruments; the increased emphasis on renovation; the continued use of housing programs and the housing sector in macro-economic policy; the cancellation of certain programs—rental programs not targeted at low-income people, ownership assistance programs, and community infrastructure programs; and the improved targeting of federal housing subsidies. None of the policy debates or program design changes accompanying these themes could be said to reflect an urban framework or a response to changing housing need.[9] The housing policy of CMHC is not explainable as a state response to urban growth and change. What, then, does explain these themes in housing policy?

MACRO-ECONOMIC POLICY

I would argue that the dominating forces shaping federal housing policy are federal decisions regarding monetary and fiscal policy. In a way, this is hardly surprising. The conduct of macro-economic policy is a preeminent responsibility of the federal government. And of course, housing expenditure like any other expenditure must be fitted within the budget. But the influence of macro-economic policy bears more on housing than on most other expenditure areas and was especially important over the last 15 years. Federal housing policy is better analyzed as part of the state's response to changes in unemployment and inflation than as part of the state's response to urban growth and change.

The federal government has always used housing programs as instruments of fiscal policy: when stimulus is desired new programs are begun and more funds are allocated to existing programs; when restraint is desired housing programs are cancelled and allocations to existing programs are reduced. New construction programs are most commonly used, but renovation programs and special tax provisions have been used as well. Housing programs are well suited for the fiscal task. When a new construction incentive is announced, resources can move into this sector quickly and at relatively low transactions costs. Unemployment is often relatively high in the construction sector. There is a fairly immediate increase in employment. The bricks, lumber, mortar, and construction labour come mainly from Canada, and therefore there is a relatively low leakage of the stimulus into imports. There are further spinoffs in the home furnishing and home appliance sectors. There is always public support for housing assistance, and the assistance can be effectively targeted at specific households or regions and can be limited in time. Most of the characteristics that make a housing program a good candidate as an instrument of stimulus also make it a good candidate to be cut in times of restraint. The hardest cuts to make, politically, are those programs on which people have come to rely. It is very hard to cut

---

[9]CMHC has developed the concept of core housing need and uses it in allocating available assistance across provinces. However, the measure of need appears to have little influence on the annual level of new commitments.

the old age pension or unemployment insurance, or to close an air base or remove postal service from a neighbourhood. And the federal government has never cut its assistance to tenants in already-constructed buildings. What it does cut, and this is much easier politically, is annual federal commitments to finance additional units. It is always easier to cancel something you are going to build, than to close down something already built. Commitments to fund new units are ideal instruments of discretionary fiscal policy.

In order to examine more carefully how fiscal policy shaped housing policy, the budget speeches of the Ministers of Finance over the last 20 years were examined. The link between macro-economic fiscal policy and housing programs is clear and explicit. In almost every budget, housing programs were mentioned, and in the context of either stimulus or restraint. In almost no other policy field would major changes be so often announced as part of the budget.

The budgets in 1971, '72, and early '73 were clearly expansionary. Unemployment was high and rising; the rate was 6.2 percent in 1971, high by the standards of the late 1960s but low by our present standard. The speeches opened by declaring the urgent priority to create jobs; the commitment was to "a substantial reduction in unemployment." However, the housing sector was expanding, rising to record levels of new starts in 1971 and 1972. Total CMHC lending was actually cut back in the early 1970s, despite the need for fiscal stimulus. During 1973, 1974, and 1975, unemployment remained persistently high, but the annual inflation rate rose to 10.9 percent. The government faced a difficult macro-economic dilemma: reducing either inflation or unemployment would likely push the other one higher. The Minister of Finance attempted the delicate balancing act of trying to curb inflation within a moderately expansionary fiscal policy. Housing starts were falling in response to high interest rates, and new home buyers faced affordability problems. During this period there was a great expansion of housing programs for renters, owners, and for community infrastructure. The budgets contained specific discussions of the housing sector and announced the RHOSP and MURB provisions in the income tax. CMHC's total lending rose to $1.6 billion in 1975, the highest level ever reached, before or since (Table 11.5). The delicate balancing act enjoyed some success in 1976, but over 1977 and 1978 both inflation and unemployment were rising again. The right balance seemed impossible to strike, and the budgets began to mention the rising federal deficit and the need to curb government expenditure growth and reduce public borrowing as long-term solution to our macro-economic problems. The major revision in 1978 of the rental assistance programs (creating the 56.1 Nonprofit Program) was a direct result of the need to reduce public sector borrowings. From 1978 to 1979, CMHC direct lending fell $700 million to only $350 million (Table 11.5). Similar pressures changed AHOP and ARP from programs trying to meet the problems of high mortgage interest rates through direct subsidies, into programs meeting the problems through graduated payment mortgages. Many of the housing policy changes of the 1970s were influenced by federal government attempts to work out a macro-economic policy in the face of simultaneous high unemployment and high inflation.

Worries about public sector deficits and inflation were increasingly dominating the budget speeches, and then came the deep recession of 1981-82. The need for fiscal stimulus was clear, and new housing programs, of limited duration, were mounted. CMHC direct lending increased to over $1 billion in 1983 and fell back to $440 in 1984 (Table 11.5).

In September 1984, the Progressive Conservatives were elected, and in November the Minister of Finance published his *Agenda for Economic Renewal*. The themes set out there would be re-iterated and adhered to, with surprising consistency, through all subsequent budgets. The *Agenda* had three primary points: the best way to create permanent jobs is not through government initiative but through private initiative; good government is not more government but more efficient government; long-run prosperity depends upon reducing the federal deficit and reducing the accumulated national debt. The last point was more and more highlighted. Deficit reduction would be achieved by a combination of expenditure restraint and tax increases. The Conservatives had adopted much of the neo-conservative critique but did not attempt a wholesale rollback of the public sector. They chose the path that Mishra (1990) has termed "the mixed economy of welfare." Budget deficits are to be reduced; tax rates are to be reduced to encourage investment; there is moderate deregulation and privatization; but social justice remains important, and the government retains a role in health, education, housing, transportation, regional development, and income security. This is the climate that has shaped federal housing policy since 1984. There were no new housing programs, and many were curtailed. There was a gradual reduction in annual new commitments for assisted rental units, and the available federal subsidies were targeted at the most needy households. New initiatives were confined to exploring new mortgage designs; they did not involve new

Table 11.5.   *Public Funds Authorized Under the National Housing Act, 1971-1991, ($ million)*

	Loans	Grants and Subsidies	Total Borrowings from Government
1971	1,009	62	901
1972	742	82	742
1973	933	111	678
1974	1,225	144	984
1975	1,605	251	1,203
1976	1,585	313	1,235
1977	1,366	524	913
1978	1,185	694	1,224
1979	350	840	724
1980	327	997	698
1981	326	1,007	563
1982	824	1,390	431
1983	1,027	1,740	424
1984	440	1,700	374
1985	310	1,648	271
1986	267	1,368	222
1987	266	1,480	270
1988	281	1,522	269
1989	261	1,687	280
1990	230	1,886	230
1991	334	1,962	260

Source: CMHC (various years).

loans or subsidies. As already noted, the 1990 budget introduced an expenditure control plan that was tightened in each subsequent budget; housing programs were constrained more and more in each iteration. Despite all the restraint, annual housing subsidies continued to grow, simply to service previous commitments. The restraint of the budget deficit was similarly moderate.

FEDERAL-PROVINCIAL RELATIONS

A second dominating influence on federal housing policy is the interplay of federal and provincial attitudes to each other. The Constitution Act does not clearly assign housing policy to either, or any, level of government. The federal government has general authority to pass laws for the peace, order, and good government of Canada and has the residual power. It has as well specific authority for public debt, currency and coinage, and banking. All of these provisions have been used to justify housing initiatives (as well as to assign the responsibility for macro-economic policy). The provinces have authority to pass laws concerning all matters of a purely local or private nature in the province, and more specifically laws concerning incorporation of companies with provincial objects and concerning property and civil rights. Given this vague constitutional assignment of responsibility, the constantly shifting relationship between federal and provincial governments in housing matters is to be expected. Albert Rose in his major study of Canadian housing policy concluded that "the most important background fact in the Canadian housing experience is that Canada is a federal state" (Rose 1980, 16).

The constitution also forces federal housing policy into the framework of federal-provincial relations for another reason. Local governments have no constitutional standing, rather they are created by the provinces. As a result, the federal government cannot directly contact cities, it must first make contact with the province.

After the Second World War, the federal government was dominant in almost all social policy areas, largely because it was financially dominant. This position was embodied in the doctrine of the federal spending power. "The spending power lies at the heart of much of Canadian social policy, including the field of social housing. According to the traditional doctrine, the spending power allows the federal government to make payments to individuals, institutions, and other levels of government for purposes that Parliament does not necessarily have the power to regulate. That is, the federal government claims the right to give money away, and attach conditions to it if it wishes, even if the purposes fall entirely within provincial jurisdiction. The spending power served as the basis of payments to individuals and private organizations, including direct assistance to nonprofit groups and cooperatives in the field of social housing. . . . It supported payments to the provinces, including conditional grants for health insurance, post-secondary education, social assistance, and, most important for our purposes, social housing" (Banting 1990, 117).[10] During times when the federal government sought to expand its domain and aggressively asserted the spending power doctrine, it was more likely to expand housing programs and to act unilaterally. And when the reverse was true, federal housing policy would contract. The long-run trend is toward less use of the federal spending power doctrine, and correspondingly the trend is toward less federal involvement in housing policy.

In the early 1970s, the major federal housing programs were shared-cost rental programs, delivered jointly by CMHC and the provincial housing corporations that had been created to deliver public housing. However, the provinces resented the shared-cost format, claiming it was inefficient and distorted provincial priorities. Moreover, Quebec's constant claim for more autonomy was repeated in other provinces during the regional discontents of the 1970s. Housing programs became weapons in the federal-provincial battles.

The federal government was determined to resist the provincial demands in the mid 1970s. In the housing area, the federal and provincial governments engaged in "competitive unilateralism" (Banting 1990, 126). The proliferation of federal housing programs from 1973 to 1976 was part of the federal strategy of resistance. The increasing role of the third sector in rental assistance emerged at this time, in part because CMHC preferred to assist directly nonprofit groups and coops rather than send money to provincial or municipal housing agencies. Assistance to the third sector produced more federal visibility and public support.

The acrimony in federal-provincial relations grew, then gradually the federal government began a grudging accommodation, recognizing the merits of some provincial demands and, at least as important, acknowledging the need to control its own spending. The new Nonprofit Program, created under Section 56.1 of the NHA in 1978, reflected this change in federal-provincial relations. Although the previous public housing program was cost-shared, the new program involved an unconditional federal contribution. The provinces could add on further subsidies, but they were not required. At the same time, the federal government announced a policy of "disentanglement" in housing matters.

---

[10]This section on federal-provincial relations draws heavily on Banting (1990).

The Ministry of State for Urban Affairs was abolished. CMHC withdrew from detailed supervision of assisted housing projects. And not surprisingly, there were no federal housing initiatives over the next few years, and the use of an urban-oriented framework in policy design waned.

When the Liberals returned to Ottawa after the brief Clark government, they stopped the process of accommodating the provinces. Instead, they sought to raise the visibility of the federal government and to bring it directly into contact with Canadians, illustrating the federal role in Canadian life. Their term was dominated by adjustment to the recession, but it is significant that the housing programs in the fiscal stimulus package were all unilateral federal programs delivered through CMHC branch offices. The provinces could have been involved, but the federal government decided against it.

A Progressive Conservative government was elected in 1984, with a commitment to national reconciliation and federal-provincial consensus. The minister responsible for CMHC embarked on a tour of provincial capitals and by 1986 created a structure of global and annual operating agreements with the provinces. CMHC retained control of the broad directions of social housing policy but accepted the principle that provinces should deliver all rental assistance programs, except the coop program. This approach to federal-provincial relations surely helps to explain the lack of new federal housing programs in the late 1980s. Political scientists have often argued that more decentralized government means more limited government.

The lack of federal unilateralism also helps to explain the decline of an urban orientation in federal policy thinking. If the federal government has little contact with municipalities or city-based groups, and all federal assistance must pass through the provincial capitals, then the federal urban perspective will wane as the need for it diminishes. If this argument is correct, it suggests the central governments of unitary states would be more likely to use an urban framework of analysis than the central government of a federal state.

No discussion of Canadian policy and politics continues for long without introducing the issue of federal-provincial relations. Housing policy is no exception. Federal initiatives and involvement in housing are more likely to be caused by changing strategies with respect to the provinces than by the changing demographic, social, and economic conditions of cities.

REDISTRIBUTIVE POLITICS IN THE WELFARE STATE

In the United States, the politics of housing policy are framed by the politics of race. In the United Kingdom, the politics of housing policy are framed by the politics of class. In Canada, the redistributive politics of the welfare state frame the politics of housing policy. Certain questions are raised in any policy field within the welfare state. The questions are most obvious when new fields are being considered, for example such as day care or denticare. Should it be a universal program or limited? Should the goal be a similar standard of service for everyone or a minimum level for the needy? If the program is not universal, how do we ensure that the beneficiaries are not stigmatized, and how do we maintain the consensus in support of the redistribution? Should assistance be extended to moderate-income households? How large should subsidies be for low-income people as opposed to moderate-income people? Should the public sector provide the service, or the private sector under government regulation, or the nonprofit sector? How are the salaries of the service providers to be established? Is it inevitable that governments will try to control costs by depressing the salaries of service providers? These are questions about redistribution, and most of them are asked in housing policy discussions. The answers change from time to time as the elected governments change and as the balance of competing interests—nonprofit and coop associations, advocacy groups, builders and developers, civil servants, the general public, politicians—changes in the political process. The evolution of housing policy in Canada is in many ways like the evolution of the welfare state in Canada.

The welfare state had a core of universal programs in education, health, unemployment insurance, and old age security; these were joined by an array of complementary programs that were not universal but targeted at areas of residual distress. Public housing was one such program. Many of these complementary programs began to expand to consider the problems of moderate-income households, supported by a confidence in social engineering to resolve pressing social problems. This expansion occurred in housing toward the end of the second era of housing policy. AHOP, ARP, RHOSP, and MURBs were intended to assist middle-income people. NIP and RRAP were an attempt at comprehensive policy to shape the development of inner-city neighbourhoods. The disenchantment with public housing reflected a desire to reduce the stigma and isolation of beneficiaries. The subsidies to middle-income people in income-mixed buildings were a way to sustain the political consensus supporting housing assistance. The income mix helped to combat the not-in-my-backyard syndrome and to convince the middle class that governments were sensitive to their housing problems. The housing debates about income mix and whether to assist less needy households are the echoes in housing policy of more general debates about universality and taxing back benefits, such as old age pensions or family allowances, received by high-income households. And changes in housing programs owe more to changes in this larger debate than to changes in the urban conditions.

The consensus supporting an expanding welfare state collapsed in the middle to late 1970s. The need for expenditure restraint was more and more widely accepted. More and more skeptics spoke out against the record of our social engineering. The government providers of services were seen as bureaucratic and distant from the needs of people they were intended to serve. General debates about the scope of the welfare state and the efficacy of its programs were repeated as specific debates in each policy field, including housing. In Canada at the federal level, the housing debate was resolved in favour of a gradually reduced involvement. The main cuts were to programs for middle-income owners and renters and for community infrastructure. The available federal dollars were redirected to assist needier households.

URBAN POLITICS AND POLICY:
SOME CONCLUDING REMARKS

This chapter began by asserting that housing programs are one of the most direct and important influences of the federal government on urban areas. It then asked: are changes in housing programs a federal response to urban growth and change? If the answer were yes, federal housing policy would then be part of the entire (federal, provincial, regional, and local) state's response to the changing demographic, social, and economic structure of our cities. The federal government might even articulate urban goals and objectives and utilize housing programs as instruments to pursue them. The fundamental purpose of the Ministry of State for Urban Affairs was to do just this. This chapter has argued that federal housing programs are not a response to urban growth and change but are most fundamentally shaped by the dictates of macro-economic policy, of federal-provincial relations, and by the redistributive politics of the welfare state. Housing programs have never been universal and have always left many needs unmet. A new initiative always finds a strong constituency to support it. But shifts and changes in housing policy are not *primarily* caused by shifts and changes in the nature of our urban housing problems.

Recently, there have been several books re-examining the study of local government and local politics, most notably Paul Peterson's *City Limits* and Paul Kantor's *The Dependent City*. Both books criticize traditional urban political science because it presumes cities are relatively autonomous political units with a full range of policy instruments at their disposal and are unconstrained by fundamental external forces. Cities were studied in the same way as nation states. (I think it is more correct to say "large nation states not dependent on international trade," i.e., nation states like the United States in the 1950s and 1960s. Urban political scientists studied cities in the same way as political scientists studied the United States. Small nation states reliant on international trade, like Canada, have a full range of policy instruments, but political scientists have recognized that Canada faces fundamental external forces beyond its influence.) Both authors argue that the limits on city policy instruments and the external socio-economic and political context determine the structure of urban politics and policy.

This study of federal housing policy is consistent with that literature, although starting from a different perspective. That literature begins from an examination of urban politics; this chapter begins at the federal level, but concludes that federal housing policy, which one might have expected to be responsive to changes within the urban area, is best considered part of the externally determined environment of the city. This chapter's conclusion highlights a limit and constraint on urban governments.

The chapter is consistent in other ways. That literature emphasizes the federal system in which cities operate. Peterson and Kantor contend that the limits to city governments imply that cities will be very concerned with economic development programs to increase their income and wealth and less concerned with redistributive policies. Implicitly, they argue that central governments will be concerned with macro-economic policy and income redistribution policy. This chapter supports this view of federal concerns. It has argued that the federal government did focus on macro-economic policy and on the redistributive questions of the welfare state, and this focus was so strong that it structured the evolution of housing policy. Little extension is needed to show that a central government in a decentralized federation like Canada, confronted with a small number of regionally based provinces, will be preoccupied with federal-provincial relations. This too will shape housing policy.

Both authors contend that the limits to urban government are inherent in local government within a federal system. Peterson goes further and argues that if the federal government tries to implement programs in its policy domain using state and local governments, the attempt is bound to fail. Kantor is more sanguine about the prospects for a national urban policy and, by implication, about the prospect for making federal housing policy more responsive to urban changes and concerns. Kantor believes the most promising solution to the dilemma is a national urban policy to reduce competition among local governments for development, thereby reducing their economic dependency. In other words, diminished local competition would alter the nature of central-local relations.

I do not think this solution holds promise in Canada, certainly if it is extended to suggesting that federal housing policy could become a federal urban-oriented housing policy. The dominance of federal macro-economic concerns will remain. Canadian provinces are much stronger than American states and will block (indeed have blocked) the development of federal-local connections. Federal intergovernmental relations can only be federal-provincial relations. In the domain of redistributive social policy, "Canada has increasingly edged towards a bifurcated welfare state, in which the income-security system remains relatively centralized while social services have become decentralized" (Banting 1990, 120). The discussion of this section makes this understandable. Income security involves direct payments to people and is suited to central control. Social services are provided using social workers, counsellors, and the like. They involve establishing a bureaucracy in close contact with its clients. This is more suited to provincial and local government. Housing programs are closer to social services than income security payments. Federal housing programs delivered through city governments and responsive to urban concerns would be resisted by the provinces and subverted by city governments, because city governments are unsuited to redistributive politics due to the limits and constraints within which they operate. The gradual withdrawal of the federal government from the delivery of housing programs and from detailed consideration of the allocation of units among competing locations, which has occurred in Canada over the last 20 years, is probably inevitable.

I would argue that the increased provincial role has the possibility of creating a housing policy that is more responsive to urban concerns in Canada. A provincial urban housing policy is more likely when some of the city limits are removed. Canadian cities are less limited than American cities, because we have stronger metropolitan and regional governments.   American metropolitan areas tend to have many small autonomous municipalities and weak metropolitan structures.   The individual municipalities are especially limited by the intense competition for the economic development that will occur in that metropolitan area.[11] Canadian metropolitan structures are stronger because they are less limited, and therefore their politics and policy will be more amenable to the redistributive issues of housing policy. Many Canadian cities have now grown physically beyond the boundaries of the metropolitan structures established in the 1960s and 1970s. The success in establishing enlarged institutions of metropolitan governance will enhance the prospects of making housing policy responsive to urban growth and change. However, there seems little interest at the present time among provinces for creating enlarged, stronger institutions of metropolitan governance

---

[11]Some residential municipalities also compete to resist growth pressures and to escape high-density redevelopment.

REFERENCES

Banting, Keith G. 1990. "Social Housing in a Divided State." In *Housing the Homeless and Poor: New Partnerships among the Private, Public and Third Sectors*, ed. George Fallis and Alex Murray, Toronto: University of Toronto Press, 115-163.

Canada. 1975. *Household Facilities by Income and Other Characteristics, 1972.* Ottawa: Statistics Canada, 13-560.

_____. 1983. *Household Facilities by Income and Other Characteristics, 1982.* Ottawa: Statistics Canada, 13-567.

_____. 1990. *Household Facilities by Income and Other Characteristics, 1989.* Ottawa: Statistics Canada, 13-218.

CMHC. Various years. *Canadian Housing Statistics.* Ottawa: Canada Mortgage and Housing Corporation.

_____. 1985. *Basic Facts.* Ottawa: Canada Mortgage and Housing Corporation.

_____. 1991. *Core Housing Need in Canada.* Ottawa: Canada Mortgage and Housing Corporation.

Carter, Tom, and Ann McAfee. 1990. "The Municipal Role in Housing the Homeless and Poor." In *Housing the Homeless and Poor: New Partnerships among the Private, Public and Third Sectors*, ed. George Fallis and Alex Murray, Toronto: University of Toronto Press, 227-262.

Dennis, Michael, and Susan Fish. 1972. *Programs in Search of a Policy: Low Income Housing in Canada.* Toronto: Hakkert Press.

Fallis, George. 1985. *Housing Economics.* Toronto: Butterworths.

_____. 1990. "Housing Finance and Housing Subsidies in Canada." *Urban Studies* 27: 877-903.

Hansard. 1973. "Speech by the Hon. Ron Basford." *Hansard.* Ottawa: Queen's Printer.

Kantor, Paul, with Stephen David. 1988. *The Dependent City.* Glenview, Ill.: Scott Foresman/Little, Brown College Division.

Lithwick, Harvey. 1970. *Urban Canada: Problems and Prospects.* Ottawa: Central Mortgage and Housing Corporation.

Mishra, Ramesh. 1990. "The Collapse of the Welfare Consensus? The Welfare State in the 1980s." In *Housing the Homeless and Poor: New Partnerships among the Private, Public and Third Sectors*, ed. George Fallis and Alex Murray, Toronto: University of Toronto Press, 82-114.

Peterson, Paul. 1981. *City Limits.* Chicago: The University of Chicago Press.

Pomeroy, S. 1989. "The Recent Evolution of Social Housing in Canada." *Canadian Housing* 6: 6-12.

Rose, Albert. 1980. *Canadian Housing Policies: 1935-1980.* Toronto: Butterworths.

Chapter 12

The State's Response to Homelessness:
A View of Three Countries

Gerald Daly
York University

Until recent years, homelessness was considered a third world phenomenon. Even now, in postindustrial societies like Britain, Canada, and the United States, many public officials deny its existence; others acknowledge the problem only in large urban centres. This chapter examines the state's response to homelessness in three countries. It explores (1) the relationships between central and local governments, (2) the effectiveness of public policies, (3) the nature of innovative and successful projects, (4) apparent gaps between policy and implementation, and (5) the advantages and disadvantages of the respective responses to homelessness. In looking at approaches to a common problem in the three countries, this study assumes, as Seymour Lipset observed, that nations can be best understood in comparative perspective (Lipset 1990, xiii).

Homelessness as defined here encompasses those who are absolutely, periodically, or temporarily without shelter, as well as those who are at risk of being on the streets in the immediate future. This typology of homeless conditions is shown in Figure 12.1. Differentiating between causes and precipitating factors, the model suggests that the types of homelessness may be seen as a continuum from absolute to being at risk. It is important to recognize that effects and needs differ among groups. The model is based on an assumption that aid can be rendered early, in order to preclude homelessness, particularly among those who require only housing or short-term financial assistance. It also presumes that a continuum of needs can be matched with support services to help people become independent.

Figure 12.1. *Conceptual Model of Homelessness*

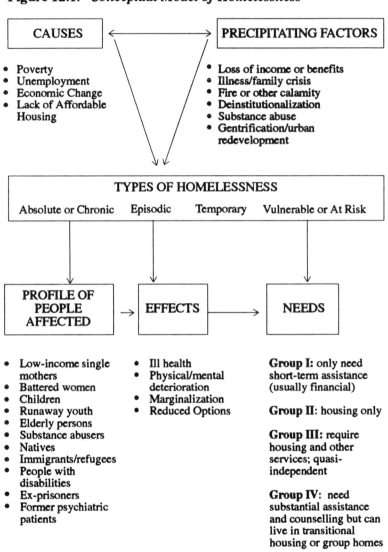

THE NATURE OF HOMELESSNESS

Who are "the homeless?" They are a heterogeneous population ranging from people who require temporary financial assistance to those in need of long-term care. Most of those who are homeless are somewhere in between: they need several forms of support, counselling, and training. A key point, often overlooked, is that a substantial percentage of homeless people can become independent if provided with appropriate, timely assistance.

The social, economic, and political causes of homelessness are similar in Britain, Canada, and the United States. Government responses, as well as the role of the third sector, have been dictated by historical trends, by precedent, and by the ideological positions taken by politicians and public officials. All three countries are postindustrial societies grappling with such issues as deindustrialization, shortages of affordable, adequate housing, and growing disparities between deprived inner-city districts and wealthy urban or suburban areas. In the 1980s all three pursued strategies aimed at reducing the national government's role in the provision of housing and witnessed substantial increases in the number of homeless people. A comparison of these countries is useful; while similar in some respects, they have different traditions, governmental systems, and histories with respect to the role of the public and private sectors in dealing with housing and welfare issues. Not surprisingly, they have followed different paths in dealing with homelessness.

A framework for comparing the three approaches to social problems is provided in Table 12.1. Because of differences in the laws and the social safety nets in the three countries, the profile of people classified as homeless varies. In Britain almost two-thirds of those certified as homeless are in households with dependent children. In Canada over 60 percent of shelter occupants are single men because social policy and practices dictate that women and children must be provided with the necessities of life. The definitions of homelessness used in Britain and Canada are broader than those generally used in the United States. The concept of vulnerability to homelessness has been more widely adopted in Britain and Canada, so that people are accepted as "priority need cases" who would not receive government assistance in the American system. It appears that about seven persons in a thousand, or a total of more than 400,000 in Britain, are accepted annually as being homeless by local authorities (Department of Environment 1990). In Canada about 5 persons in a thousand, or a total of more than 100,000, use the emergency

Table 12.1.   *Contextual Framework for Comparing the Three Countries*

	U.S.	Britain	Canada
Government	Federal system; concentrated government power is mistrusted; *Laissez-faire* and home rule important. Politics heavily influenced by race and parochialism.	Centralized; no constitution; legislature and executive very close; voting along party lines; local authorities have significant housing powers, but seriously weakened since 1979.	Federal system; significant role for the provinces; necessary to effect compromises among provinces and between provinces and the federal government in order to make major changes.
Approach to Social Problems	Individualistic; collectivism suspect; self-help important; weak welfare system; no socialist party.	Collectivism evolved over 100 years and is deeply entrenched; recent trend toward privatization.	Leans to British approach; collectivism and protection of group rights more important than in U.S.
Status of Social Safety Net In all 3 countries cost containment is a major issue.	Concern about long-term dependency on welfare; AFDC has grown dramatically; heavy reliance on private	Established system of dole and hostels works to maintain people but only at very minimal level.	Function shared by provincial and local governments (with senior govt. funding) and voluntary sector; govt.

	charity; welfare seen as disincentive to work.		still assumes voluntary sector will carry major part of the load.
Health In all 3 countries health problems are surprisingly pervasive. Few have publicly acknowledged the inequalities of their systems.	Those who can afford it get good care. Those unprotected by employers or by private insurance (1/3 of population) are vulnerable to catastrophe, often leading to homelessness.	NHS still operating; cost problems; care generally good once people are admitted; tiered system: middle and upper classes opt for private care.	Good national system. Regional disparities. Difficult for some homeless people, natives and rural residents to get good care.
Economy/ Employment One of the weakest areas in all 3 countries; lack of imaginative schemes for job training and skills development especially in preparing for beyond the year 2000.	Deindustrialization; low-paid employees being left behind; low pay, part-time, few benefits; U.S. attempted workfare: results mixed.	One of the U.K.'s major problems; unemployment over 2.5 m; some on dole for years; difficulty in maintaining productivity and competitiveness; concern about U.K. being left behind.	Struggling to remain competitive as it moves toward service economy; little done in terms of job training; widespread anxiety about effects of Free Trade agreement.

shelter system (Canadian Council on Social Development 1987). In the United States, according to HUD (U.S. Department of Housing and Urban Development, 1984) and to more recent studies in a number of states, about three persons per thousand (600,000 to 750,000 people) are judged to be homeless (Momeni 1990, Vol. II, 165-83).

In all three countries the extent of homelessness is growing, aggravated by social and economic changes and by government policy. Much of the responsibility for social issues has been devolved from central to local government and to the voluntary sector.

HOUSING TRENDS

During the 1980s substantial changes occurred in national housing policy, in budget allocations for social housing, in the nature and scope of subsidies or benefits, in supply and tenure, and in the roles of local authorities, private firms, and the third sector. These changes and other factors affecting housing opportunity are summarized in Table 12.2.

Britain

Public attitudes and policies toward homeless people in Britain have deep historical roots. Traditionally, those without homes were dealt with under the Vagrancy Acts. This Poor Law mentality persists in some quarters as homeless individuals are seen as "work shy." Although homelessness was identified as a public concern in the National Assistance Act of 1948, central government was reluctant to take responsibility until voluntary groups forced the issue in the 1970s. Eventually, the concept of housing as of right was widely acknowledged, and substantive legislation to deal with homelessness was enacted in 1977. The Housing (Homeless Persons) Act of 1977 had an immediate impact. The total number of *households* accepted as being homeless in England and Wales rose from 33,000 in 1976 to 53,100 in 1978, the first year after passage. By the late 1980s this number doubled again, to more than 128,000 households (Department of Environment 1990).

During the 1980s the poverty gap in Britain increased. While the richest quintile's share of household income rose from 45 to 49 percent (1979-1985), the share of the poorest 40 percent of the population fell from 9.5 to 5.3 percent. Unemployment among women tripled from 1979 to 1985. The number of jobless under age 25 was over 1 million in 1987. Some of the young people on the dole have never worked. One-half of

Table 12.2. *Housing Trends in the 1980s*

	U.S.	Britain	Canada
National Housing Policy	Housing near bottom of political agenda because of deficit, HUD scandals, and S & L crisis. Housing policy made by all 3 government levels; federal role circumscribed; government provides tax relief to homeowners; privatized public housing (shelters less than 2 percent). Reduced support for rental housing.	Much stronger central government role than in U.S. or Canada; Housing near top of political agenda; Thatcher government encouraged homeownership through tax relief, privatized council housing, deregulated building societies, and reduced the role of municipalities.	Housing not high on federal agenda; but CMHC has pursued policy of public-private joint efforts to create social housing. Housing an important political factor in some provinces and cities. Government favors homeownership; provides capital gains tax relief to owners.
Public Spending and Construction	President Reagan cut housing expenditures by 80 percent; HUD budget was $32b in 1981; $6b in 1989; Public housing needs $20b repairs; waiting list for public housing over 5 years in many cities.	Major cutbacks. Government sold 1.25m council dwellings on discount. £30b required to repair existing housing stock.	Main vehicle for social housing is co-ops and nonprofit housing. Decline in number of social housing units produced, but government financial burden increases because of previous commitments. Long waiting lists for public housing units built prior to 1980.

	U.S.	Britain	Canada
Housing Benefits	14 percent of renters receive subsidies; 4m renters receive welfare assistance. Less than 1/3 of poor receive any housing subsidy. Major housing benefit is tax relief for homeowners.	Total public expenditures on all forms of housing construction and benefits is exceeded by the amount of mortgage interest tax relief given to homeowners.	Rental subsidies declined by over 70 percent in 1980s. Federal subsidies limited to "households in core need." Provides subsidies so that tenants pay no more than 30 percent of income for housing.
Supply Changes	Homeownership declined substantially in 1980s especially among young families. Loss of low-cost urban housing to gentrification; 700,000 units of subsidized rentals are in danger of disappearing as federal subsidies expire. (Apgar 1988, 24) Supply of low-cost rentals declining as result of 1986 Tax Reform Act.	2/3 of population are homeowners. Only 3 percent of units overcrowded; but 5m households underoccupy their homes. 750,000 empty dwellings. 1982-1988: 87 percent increase in house prices while retail prices rose only 37 percent; developable land very costly. Private rental sector declined to 7 percent of total stock in 1990.	Loss of low-cost units to gentrification and condominium conversions. Toronto, for example, lost 11,000 units in 10 years; Ottawa lost 40 percent of rooming houses in 4 years. Rate of social housing production slowed during the 1980s.

Local Government Role	Has large *potential* role but actual involvement varies substantially from place to place. Local governments in some areas have been forced by court action to provide low-cost housing and shelters for homeless people. Local regulations, codes, and processing procedures often inhibit or delay the construction of low-cost housing.	Municipality has substantial role in social housing, but this was consciously reduced in 1980s; spending caps and variety of penalties imposed by central government. Local planning and development controls undermined.	Municipality can (if it wishes) have substantial role in social housing provision. During the 1980s the municipal role grew dramatically. Many municipalities now assume a direct role in the provision of social housing, the establishment of nonprofit housing corporations for low-income people, and joint ventures with private groups.
Public-Private Interaction	Federal government encouraged increased private role; some cities (e.g., Boston and Chicago) established public-private joint ventures to build or renovate housing. About 200 cities and counties regulate rents in an attempt to control housing costs.	Much closer link than in the past; government seeks U.S.-type privatization. Thatcher deregulated building societies and loosened financial controls, fueling a housing boom.	Not as much as in U.S.; considerable interaction between governments and third sector for the provision of social housing. Some local governments use rent control as a way of ensuring a supply of affordable housing.
Private Rentals	Low-rent housing has declined; 10 percent of housing stock covered by some form of rent control (Appelbaum et al. 1991, 154).	Deregulated in 1988; result was price increases.	Moribund sector; developers/landlords prefer condominiums.

	U.S.	Britain	Canada
Factors Affecting Housing Opportunity	Racial discrimination; cities are highly segregated. Poor housing tends to be concentrated in black and Hispanic neighbourhoods. For poor households, housing costs rose faster than incomes since 1975; 11 million households pay over 1/3 income on rent; 5 million pay over half. Most new jobs are in the service sector; many pay only the minimum wage, which is too low to allow people to obtain decent housing; 1/4 of homeless people work but do not earn enough to afford permanent housing.	Poorest rental stock requires upgrading; most poor housing is occupied by elderly, unemployed, and ethnic minority households. Almost 1m homes unfit for habitation; 1/2 million units lack standard amenities.	14 percent of all households and 28 percent of renting households are in core housing need; rate is over 50 percent for single mothers (renters) with young children and for natives, and 41 percent for single women over age 65 and unattached youths under 25. Three times as many involuntary part-time workers in 1990 as in 1980. During 1980s minimum wage worker's purchasing power declined by 1/3; more than 1/2 households are working poor.

the recipients of unemployment benefits in 1987 had been out of work for more than 39 weeks; over 40 percent of the total had been jobless for longer than one year (Department of Health and Social Services l987). A 1987 study by the British Economic and Social Research Council reported "an exceptionally high incidence of unemployment among the young, the less-skilled, and the black population" (Buck, Gordon, and Young 1987, l22).

Government's Response to Homelessness

The story of the public sector response to homelessness in Britain takes place at the local level, primarily in cities. The National Assistance Act of 1948 directed local authorities to provide temporary accommodation only to people who were homeless "in circumstances which could not reasonably have been foreseen." Over the next three decades, central government's role was limited to occasional surveys of local authority practices. These were essentially arm's length reports on what was perceived as a local issue. In the mid-seventies the government finally accepted the need to clarify responsibilities toward the homeless. It was still assumed, though, that the issue should be dealt with by voluntary agencies and local authorities. Passage of the Housing (Homeless Persons) Act in 1977 and its subsequent amplification by a Code of Guidance was due in large measure to the cooperative relationship between voluntary organizations and the Department of the Environment (DoE) (Raynsford 1986).

The 1977 legislation charges authorities with the duty to prevent homelessness or to secure rehousing for those in priority groups, provided that these individuals do not have a "local connection" in another district and have not made themselves "intentionally homeless." The law specifies that priority must be given to households with dependent children or pregnant women and that consideration should be given to those who are vulnerable because of old age, physical or mental disability, or some other "special reason." For those not in priority groups, but who are homeless or threatened with homelessness, the authority must offer "advice and appropriate assistance." Those with priority but without the necessary local connection must be put in contact with the appropriate local authority and must be offered temporary housing if they require it.

Donnison and Ungerson found that the central issue, once the act was passed in 1977, was its implementation by a diverse array of local authorities (Donnison and Ungerson 1982, 276-77). The key to implementation is the Code of Guidance (Department of Environment 1977). Developed at the time of the act's passage in 1977, the code represents a genuine commitment on the part of the government of the day to ensure that the growing problem of homelessness could not be ignored. In practice, however, the expectations implicit in the code have not been fulfilled.

Implementation of the act varied widely from place to place. Unsympathetic to the needs of homeless families, the Thatcher government (1979-1990) limited the power of local authorities to provide housing (Her Majesty's Stationery Office, White Paper 1983; Cochrane 1985). Government cutbacks in housing expenditures during the eighties eroded the ability of local authorities to provide permanent dwellings. Government housing expenditures (including new construction, subsidies, improvement grants, and loans) declined from £6,101 million in 1979-80 to £2,860 million in 1988-89 and housing subsidies to local authorities dropped by 72 percent in real terms. The number of dwellings completed for local authorities declined from 112,340 in 1978 to less than 20,000 in 1988 (Central Statistical Office 1990, Tables 3.6 and 3.10). Housing's share of public expenditure fell from about seven percent in 1979-80 to less than three percent in the late 1980s. The best council housing stock (1.5 million homes) was sold at discounts averaging 48 percent of market value in 1987-88, and local authorities were fined if they defied government orders to reduce housing expenditures. Faced with falling subsidies and rising costs, councils were forced to raise rents or to make transfers from the general rate fund to their Housing Revenue Accounts. The major government housing program continues to be mortgage interest tax relief for 8.6 million homeowners, amounting to more than £5.2 billion in 1988-89. During the 1980s low-income homeowners encountered significant problems in keeping up with house payments. Among poorer homeowners there was a five-fold increase in mortgage arrears and repossessions from 1979 to 1986 (MacLennan and Gibb 1990, 908; MacLennan, Gibb, and More 29).

The Response of British Local Authorities to Homelessness

There are considerable variations among authorities in their policies and procedures for complying with the homelessness statute. Those found to be homeless and in priority need (as a percent of total applications) varied from 26 to 84 percent in different cities and boroughs (Niner 1989, 81). The household composition of homeless people accepted by local authorities is shown in Table 12.3. Disparities among local authorities cannot be explained by financial capacity because local authorities in poor boroughs or regions are more likely to certify applicants as homeless. A better indicator is ideology or political beliefs. Labour-controlled councils have been more generous than their Liberal or Conservative counterparts. London boroughs are more likely to certify as homeless unattached singles and childless applicants who are pregnant. As shown in Table 12.3, non-London authorities prefer households with dependent children. Other variables that apparently affect the local authority's decision are the magnitude of housing shortages, the availability of temporary accommodation, vacancy rates, the level of in-migration and immigration, and language or cultural factors (Evans and Duncan 1988; Niner 1989).

The British approach to homelessness is summarized below in relation to the five key questions raised at the beginning of this chapter.

1. *Relationships between central and local governments*: Britain's political economy is characterized by class divisions and regional disparities; increasingly political matters also depend on ethnicity and ideological conflicts. The roles of each level of government during the 1980s were dictated in part by economic restraint and in part by the Thatcherite policy of reining in local authorities (Hambleton 1990, 75).

2. *Effectiveness of public policy*: The government's policy, reflected in the 1977 Act and the Code of Guidance, appears to be effective when there is a genuine local commitment to house homeless households and to assist those in priority need who are at risk.

3. *Innovative and successful projects*:

a. Information: All major British cities now have information and advocacy centres that provide one-stop assistance to homeless people with housing, legal, health, and employment problems.

b. Health: London's Hungerford Drug Project offers "on-the-street" advice, counselling, and referrals for drug abusers and people with AIDS, many of whom are homeless.

c. Education and Training: The North London Education Project, in operation since 1980, has successfully integrated life skills and job training, formal and informal education, and transitional as well as permanent housing for homeless young people and ex-prisoners (North London Education Project 1987, 1-3).

d. Housing: Intended to preclude homelessness, self-build and community architecture projects have enabled entire neighbourhoods in major cities to renovate homes and to construct new units. Loans and

Table 12.3. *Household Composition of Applicants Accepted as Homeless*

	London Authorities	Metropolitan Authorities	All Local Authorities
Households with 1 dependent child	30%	28%	36%
2-3 dependent children	18	29	31
4 or more dependent children	7	6	4
Applicant pregnant (no children)	17	11	12
Childless (no one pregnant)	28	22	16

housing grants are available to low-income homeowners, most of whom are elderly, to enable them to have repairs completed while they remain in their homes (Ospina 1987, 41, 59).

4. *Gaps between policy and implementation*: This is the key issue. The significant differences among authorities indicate that national policy is substantially altered and, in some cases, ignored by unsympathetic local officials. The capacity of councils to respond is sometimes hampered by their lack of resources.

5. *Advantages of the British approach*: Homeless people are being housed, in part because there is an enormous stock of empty dwellings. Because the law includes those at risk, there is a great deal of attention focused (mainly by voluntary agencies) on vulnerable groups, including low-income single mothers. A number of agencies have established links between housing and education, training, health and employment programs.

6. *Disadvantages of the British approach*:

a. Without a committed local authority it is difficult for homeless people to secure their rights.

b. Immigrants have difficulty with the highly bureaucratized system.

c. The housing provided is frequently the worst available (Donnison and Ungerson 1982, 278-79).

d. A great deal of reliance is placed on voluntarism.

e. Housing alone may be insufficient to address the problems of very poor households.

The United States

In American cities homelessness increased rapidly in the 1980s (between 20-25 percent annually, according to the U.S. Conference of Mayors) as a result of several trends (U.S. Conference of Mayors 1989, 2).

1. *Reduced government spending on public housing*: The number of low-income public housing units under construction declined from 126,800 in 1970, to 20,900 in 1980, to 9,700 in 1988 (U.S. Bureau of the Census 1990a, Table 1287). The rate of production of moderately priced housing equalled only about one-third of the loss of affordable units through demolition, conversion, or rental increases.

2. *Decreasing supply of low-cost rental units*: Less than 7.5 percent of private multifamily stock is within the reach of poorer rental households. There has been an irreparable loss of rooming houses and single room occupancy (SRO) units (Marcuse 1987, 426). About five million units were removed from the nation's housing stock as a result of fire, demolition, or conversion.

3. *Rising price of rental housing*: In the 1970s and 1980s median rents increased at about twice the rate of median incomes. Poor households were forced into overcrowded and substandard housing, and many found themselves on the street. From 1974 to 1987 the income of young (age 25-34) single-parent renters fell by 34 percent, while their rent (as a proportion of total income) rose from 35 to 58 percent. The number of renter households with extremely low incomes (under $5,000 in 1986 dollars) almost doubled, from 2.7 to 4.7 million (U.S. Bureau of the Census 1989).

4. *Declining incomes*: During the period 1977-1987 the average after-tax family income of the richest decile of Americans increased by more than 27 percent while the poorest decile's income dropped by more than 10 percent. In 1988, 31.9 million Americans lived below the national poverty line, which in terms of money income ranged from $6,024 for one person to $12,092 for a four-person household (U.S. Bureau of the Census 1990b, No. 166). In 1980, 42 percent of the poor received no welfare, food stamps, Medicaid, school lunches, or public housing (Hopper and Hamberg 1986, 20). One-quarter of all full-time jobs, 24

million positions, did not pay enough to raise a family of four above the poverty line.

In the United States, public policy during the 1980s consisted of stopgap measures or attempts to shift the burden of social responsibility (U.S. General Accounting Office 1985). Both public and voluntary sectors concentrated on such expedients as emergency shelters and welfare hotels. The number of shelters in the United States grew from 1,900 (with 100,000 beds) in 1984 to 5,400 (with 275,000 beds) in 1988 (U.S. Department of Housing and Urban Development 1989). During the 1980s the federal government significantly reduced expenditures on housing (by 80 percent), employment, and training programs (by 70 percent), block grants for child care (30 percent), and grants to state and local governments (33 percent) (Wolch and Akita 1989, 62-85).

By 1983 it was clear to many that the issues of homelessness required federal attention. The government response consisted of a limited number of actions. In 1983 the Secretary of Health and Human Services established the Federal Task Force on the Homeless to coordinate efforts directed at assisting homeless people. At the end of 1983 Congress appropriated emergency funds (through the Federal Emergency Management Agency) for food and shelter on a temporary basis. The Reagan administration, however, declined to seek funding to extend this initiative. HUD issued a report in 1984 that concluded that 250,000 to 350,000 people were homeless (U.S. Department of Housing and Urban Development 1984). In 1984 the Department of Defense was authorized to use certain military facilities as emergency shelters (U.S. General Accounting Office 1985).

While Congress passed The Homeless Eligibility Clarification Act (Public Law 99-570) in 1986, it was not until 1987 that it enacted significant legislation. The Stewart B. McKinney Homeless Assistance Act (Public Law 100-77) represented a major policy shift by the Reagan administration (U.S. Congress 1987). In response to pressure from advocacy groups and supporters in Congress, the act acknowledged the need for federal intervention.

Subsequent events confirmed that the Reagan administration's commitment to aid for homeless people was lukewarm at best. While initial funding authorizations were $442 million in 1987 and $616 million in 1988, actual appropriations were substantially lower: $365 million for 1987 and $356 million for 1988. In 1987, $46 million was appropriated to offer health care for homeless people; in 1988 this was reduced to an appropriation of $14 million. Similarly, the act created a new mental health block grant with an initial appropriation of $43 million; in the following two years the appropriation was reduced to less than $5 million annually. In 1989 the administration requested no new funds for the adult literacy program established by the act, nor for the mental health demonstration program, nor for the special alcohol and drug abuse program. Congress appropriated new funds for the McKinney programs, over the objections of the White House. A review of the McKinney Act found that the legislation "does not address the economic and social-welfare-policy roots of the homelessness crisis" (Wolch and Akita 1989, 78). The government's response was widely criticized because it did not replace severe budget cuts in social programs, nor did it include mandated programs. Moreover, the McKinney "programs were mostly targeted toward emergency needs rather than long-term solutions," and they "seriously underestimated the real resource costs of solving the crisis in an efficient and humane way" (Wolch and Akita 1989, 85).

The Response of State and Local Governments in the United States

The political system in the United States is considerably more complex than in either Britain or Canada. In America there are more tiers of government and quasi-governmental organizations, a variety of different public management models, a wide diversity among cities and regions in terms of history, location, climate, ethnicity or race, and economic well-being. In particular, city-suburban disparities are more apparent in the United States than in Canada or Britain, though a number of British inner cities show evidence of very substantial deprivation. Dramatic differences between American inner cities and suburbs exist in terms of housing, income, employment, and family structure. The issue of homelessness in America is generally perceived as an inner-city problem. Not surprisingly, then, substantial differences are evident in the responses of local government to this phenomenon.

Some state and municipal agencies have chosen to deal with homeless people by adopting a comprehensive array of innovative programs. Others have ignored the issue. Most state governments are not directly involved in providing services to homeless people. Generally they pass through federal block grants and other funds to local governments. The exceptions to this generalization are major states with significant homeless populations or with administrations that have made a public commitment to assist the homeless (notably Connecticut, Massachusetts, New Jersey, and New York) (Momeni 1989, Vol. I).

The principal roles of local governments include operating public shelters, providing funding for shelters run by private or voluntary groups, distributing vouchers to homeless individuals for use in motels, hotels, or apartments, and leasing or rehabilitating buildings for private shelter operators. Public housing authorities are not involved with homelessness because they are obliged to deal with existing waiting lists.

The American approach to homelessness is summarized below:

1. *Relationships among the levels of government*: Intergovernmental politics in the United States are pluralistic, often dominated by race or parochialism, or both. Even though cities, as creatures of the states, do not possess significant legal powers they have considerable latitude in determining how, where, and to whom federal dollars are dispensed. The American system is based on a presumption of local autonomy in what many regard as a local issue (i.e., homelessness) and is frequently characterized by an aversion to federal interference. There is no apparent desire on the part of the federal government to provide either carrots or sticks to local government in order to preclude homelessness.

2. *Effectiveness of public policy*: Prior to 1987 no comprehensive public policy with respect to homelessness existed at the national level. The McKinney Act of 1987 incorporated a number of useful programmatic concepts and acknowledged the need for federal intervention; its record to date, however, has been disappointing.

3. *Innovative and successful projects*:

a.   Information: A number of organizations in the United States have continuously publicized the problems of homeless people and lobbied on their behalf in order to inform legislators and citizens and to ensure that funding is provided to deal with the most pressing issues. These groups range from grass-roots advocates like the Coalition for the Homeless to quasi-public bodies like the U.S. Conference of Mayors Task Force on Hunger and Homelessness (U.S. Conference of Mayors 1989, 1).

b.   Health: One of the most significant initiatives has been the use of foundation grants to establish Health Care for the Homeless clinics in 20 cities. As a result, a great deal is known about homeless people, their health problems, and the links between health and other issues (Wright and Weber 1987, 17).

c.   Education and Training: A number of projects, including the Massachusetts Employment and Training Choices Program, offer job training, counselling, and referrals, along with free transportation and day care for single mothers and others who are receiving welfare assistance (Kaufman 1984, 21-25).

d. Housing: Several cities (notably Los Angeles, San Diego, and Portland, Oregon) have organized public-private joint ventures to preserve rooming houses and to create single-room occupancy hotels. Others, notably Boston, Chicago and San Francisco, have developed new and renovated units through joint ventures with private groups (Suchman 1990). Transitional housing for women has been developed by groups like the Women's Institute for Housing and Economic Development in Boston and the Women's Development Corporation in Providence, Rhode Island (Sprague 1986, 18). Self-help initiatives have been sponsored by groups ranging from the Navajo nation to The Enterprise Foundation (Daly 1990, 138). A recent project in Orlando, Florida, attempts to deal with the problem of delays in obtaining planning and building approvals, which lead to higher housing costs. The demonstration project uses public funds to provide down payment loans to low-income people. This concept is combined with procedural changes: density flexibility, smaller setbacks, reduced on-site infrastructure costs, and faster permit processing. In the initial project households with incomes as low as $17,000 were able to purchase homes (York 1991, 493).

4. *Gaps between policy and implementation*: Implementation has been fragmented. It is difficult to develop comprehensive long-term responses when the problem of homelessness is seen by many public officials as a short-term local phenomenon.

5. *Advantages of the American approach*: Most of the progressive initiatives addressing homelessness have been at the city level. Usually these involve nongovernment groups or public-private joint ventures (Suchman 1990, 117).

6. *Disadvantages of the American approach*: Without a national commitment to deal with homelessness it is inevitable that the measures adopted will be stopgap, fragmented, or misdirected. The American experience demonstrates both the effectiveness of charitable or voluntary endeavors and their inherent limitations.

Canada

On the night of January 22, 1987, the Canadian Council for Social Development conducted a "snapshot survey" of shelters and reported that Canada had "472 facilities (with 13,797 beds) that exist primarily to serve the homeless and destitute" (Canadian Council on Social Development

1987, 1-4). More than 100,000 different people used these shelters at some time throughout the year, representing about five persons per thousand in Canada. The average length of stay in shelters was found to be about 19 days. On the night of the survey, 61 percent of the shelter occupants were men, 27.5 percent were women, with children (age 15 and under) making up the remaining 11.5 percent. Table 12.4 describes their characteristics.

In Toronto, which has the highest incidence of homelessness in the country, more than 25,000 different individuals use emergency shelters annually. Approximately one person in a thousand in Toronto is housed in an emergency shelter. This is one-fourth of the rate in New York City, where the comparable ratio is approximately 1:235 (Municipality of Metropolitan Toronto 1987).

The safety net in Canada is significantly more refined and extensive than in the United States. Universal health care is provided at a reasonable standard in most parts of the country. For certain segments of the population, however, access to quality health care and adequate housing continues to be problematic. Natives, for example, have poorer housing, more health problems, higher morbidity rates, and considerably shorter life spans than other Canadians (Irwin 1988). Even in cities like Toronto, where there are many hospitals, homeless people have difficulty in obtaining treatment (City of Toronto 1987, 6).

Some social policy critics assert that the social security system in Canada has not kept pace with social and economic trends. Those who depend on social assistance do not receive enough to reach the poverty lines set by Statistics Canada. While real incomes and purchasing power rose during the 1960s and 1970s, both indices dropped during the 1980s. Though the gap between the top and bottom quintiles did not increase, by the end of the 1980s the bottom 20 percent of the population earned only 4.7 percent of national income, while the top quintile received 43.2 percent (Ross and Shillington 1989, 29; Hulchanski et al. 1991, 11).

The poverty rate for families in Canada hovered around 13 percent during the 1970s and 1980s, but the total number of families below the poverty line set by Statistics Canada grew from 701,000 in 1973 to 895,000 in 1987, an increase of 28 percent, compared to a total population increase of approximately 16 percent. Moreover, the number of low-income, unattached individuals grew from 766,000 in 1973 to 1.14 million in 1987, a growth rate of 48 percent. By the end of the 1980s well over two million households (families plus unattached individuals) were in poverty (Ross and Shillington 1989, 21-22).

Table 12.4. *Characteristics of Emergency Shelter Residents in Canada*

Situation	Percent of Sample
Unemployed	54.7
Receiving social assistance	51.5
Alcohol abuser	33.3
Current or ex-psychiatric patient	20.1
Drug abuser	15.0
Evicted	9.4
Physically handicapped	3.1

Given the harsh winter climate in Canada, the number of visible street people is not necessarily a good indicator of the extent of homelessness. Advocacy groups and some government officials are concerned about growing numbers of people without adequate or secure shelter. They are particularly disturbed about the problem of hidden homelessness among battered women and abused children or youths.

Perhaps the most striking characteristic of homelessness in Canada is the dramatic variation among cities. Certain regions had substantial increases in the number of homeless people as a result of recessions in the eighties. Southern Ontario enjoyed a buoyant economy during most of the eighties, and the Toronto region attracted thousands of unemployed individuals hopeful of finding work. Doubling up and overcrowding resulted. Toronto's vacancy rate in the late 1980s was the lowest in North America. The city lost more than 10,000 rental units from the mid-seventies to mid-eighties to condominium conversion and gentrification (City of Toronto, Department of Planning and Development 1986, 42-46). Similarly, Ottawa's stock of rooming house units declined by 40 percent during a four-year period (1976-1979). Dramatic losses of low-cost rental dwellings and rooming houses have also been documented in Vancouver's downtown from 1971 to the mid- eighties (Ley 1985). These losses exacerbated the housing problems of low-income households. In 1988 about 1.7 million Canadians in renter households (including 411,000 children) were in core housing need as defined by CMHC. Over 800,000 renter households in core need spent 30 percent or more of their income on shelter. On average they spent almost half their household income on rent (Engeland 1990-91, 7-8). While government policy cannot be held responsible for homelessness, many housing advocates feel that more can be done at the federal, provincial, and municipal levels to meet the shelter needs of all Canadians.

CMHC made a conscious effort, starting in 1984, to devolve responsibility for housing delivery to the provincial and territorial governments. Nevertheless, CMHC still funds housing programs. It also attempts to uphold the principles of equal access to housing, reduce regional disparities, and continue to influence social housing production. The 1986 Federal/Provincial/Global Agreements on Social Housing, which set out cost-sharing arrangements for nonprofit, rent supplement, and residential rehabilitation programs, offer incentives to increase provincial participation. These agreements allow the provinces and territories to sponsor nonprofit housing programs and to fund projects initiated by third-sector nonprofit organizations (Pomeroy 1989, 9) If a nonprofit group's proposal is accepted by the provincial government, CMHC has committed itself to sharing the difference between the project's operating costs (mortgage, utilities, maintenance, and taxes) and the amount paid by tenants (based on a rent-geared-to-income formula).

In Canada the attention given to social housing and homelessness varies dramatically from one region to another. Some provinces have taken little action. Others, like Ontario, after considerable prodding by housing activists, have demonstrated that a great deal can be accomplished when all three levels of government cooperate. The province of Ontario, which has been involved in the provision of public housing since the 1960s, introduced several new measures in the mid-1980s. It passed the Rental Housing Protection Act to control the demolition and conversion of rental housing when the supply of affordable units is threatened. It conducted an inquiry into the housing situation of roomers, boarders, and lodgers that resulted in the inclusion of rooming houses and SRO units under the Landlord and Tenant Act. Ontario also implemented a housing policy requiring all municipalities and planning boards to allocate at least 25 percent of new developments and redevelopments for affordable housing (Ontario Ministry of Housing 1989).

The provincial government's main thrust has been to produce permanent housing for low-income households by providing grants to municipal nonprofit and private nonprofit housing corporations, as well as to housing cooperatives. Approximately 80 percent of these units are subsidized. Within a particular building or district developed under these guidelines there is no differentiation between subsidized and nonsubsidized dwellings (Daly et al. 1989, 30-31).

Municipal Housing Initiatives to Assist the Poor and Homeless in Canada

Responsibility for implementation of housing programs rests with the provinces, who, in turn, have delegated to municipalities the power to zone, regulate land use, and establish building development standards. During the 1970s and 1980s, it became clear that the private sector was unable or unwilling to provide rental housing for low-income groups and that no more large, monolithic public housing projects, accommodating only very low-income households, would be built. Some municipalities and provinces attempted to fill this void by developing, facilitating, and/or funding social housing (Carter and McAfee 1990, 228-33).

There are several models for municipal involvement in the production of social housing: one is the municipal nonprofit housing corporation, like Cityhome in Toronto, which develops about 400-500 units per year and now has an inventory in excess of 5,000 units. Projects are occupied by a mix of residents: about 35-40 percent "deep core" households requiring a substantial or full subsidy, about 40 percent "shallow core" households receiving a smaller subsidy, and the remainder paying full market rents. Cityhome's guidelines (reflecting CMHC's definition of "core housing need") describe those in need as low-income households in crowded, inadequate, or unsuitable dwellings, or those low-income people who are paying more than 30 percent of their income in rent.

A second approach is employed when the city assumes a facilitator role to support the development of social housing. Vancouver used this model to assist developers through the provision of land and subsidies, by offering assistance in permit processing, and by lobbying with the provincial and federal governments for funding (Carter and McAfee 1990, 233).

Another approach, where there is an active third sector, is for the municipality (with assistance from senior governments) to provide funding for nonprofit housing corporations and cooperatives that develop social housing. These efforts are supported by federal and provincial funding.

Other municipal efforts to increase or maintain the stock of affordable housing include:

1.   Residential intensification: e.g., Toronto's proposed Main Streets project, a joint public-private initiative to upgrade infrastructure, to develop additional housing along transportation arteries, and to encourage more people to live downtown.

2.   Liberalized regulations: e.g., the legalization of accessory apartments and the use of variances that permit the construction of bachelor units.

3.   Renovation: e.g., Winnipeg's Main Street hostel and the efforts of the Downtown Eastside Residents' Association in Vancouver to preserve and improve the existing stock of rooming houses.

4.   The provision of social housing through density bonusing or transfer of development rights.

5.   Attempts to maintain affordable housing through downzoning and the exercise of development controls (Daly 1988, I-12 to I-19; Carter and McAfee 1990, 244-57).

The Canadian approach to homelessness may be summarized as follows:

1.   *Relationships among the levels of government*:   As a federal state there are tensions among the three levels of government with respect to the provision of shelter. Debates are commonplace over who will provide the funds and who will receive the credit for creating new dwellings. Although the federal government has devolved authority for housing provision to the provinces there has been a great deal of variation in social housing production in different areas of the country. The provinces have given municipalities substantial room to develop locally devised schemes to produce social housing. Thus, the results are mixed, depending on perceived needs and the political leverage exercised by housing advocates.

2.   *Effectiveness of public policy*:   Federal policy has been to encourage the development of social housing by other levels of government and by the third sector. This policy has been effective when provincial and municipal (or regional) governments feel motivated to mount an aggressive housing program. Without this local commitment the policy goals cannot be realized. Moreover, there is no comprehensive national policy to link housing and supportive services to address the issues associated with homelessness.

3. *Innovative and successful projects*:

a.   Information: An example of a successful neighbourhood advice centre is the Downtown Eastside Residents' Association in Vancouver, which has operated as a nonprofit society since 1973. It acts as a clearinghouse and advocacy organization for area residents (mostly low-income single men) on such issues as housing, welfare assistance, pensions, unemployment insurance, and legal aid (Hulchanski et al. 1991, 34. See also Ley, this volume.). A nationwide group, The Housing Networking Project, involves church and community activists in disseminating information on nonprofit and cooperative housing projects for homeless people (Housing Networking Project 1986).

b.   Health: Streetfront health clinics, like those provided by nurses at Streethealth in Toronto, have proven effective in assisting street people to obtain first-aid, counselling, and access to hospitals. Other initiatives are aimed at community care for disabled individuals who have been deinstitutionalized. An example is Quebec City's Centre François-Charon, which has been operating apartments and group homes and providing the services of a multidisciplinary health team since 1979 (Plamondon 1985).

c.   Education and Training: A variety of advocacy groups, like Réseau d'aide in Montréal, the Single Displaced Persons' Project, and the Supportive Housing Coalition in Toronto, provide education and training for community workers interested in developing housing for lower-income single people (Single Displaced Persons' Project 1983). At the national level, educational services are offered by Canada Mortgage and Housing Corporation, acting as a clearinghouse for information on self-help and cooperative housing, homelessness, and related topics.

d.   Housing: Supportive housing projects developed by the Association for Women's Residential Facilities in Halifax offer child care and child development programs, referrals to health, welfare, employment, and community agencies, as well as permanent housing. Self-help housing units have been built in significant numbers in Canada, particularly in the Atlantic Provinces, for many years. A great deal of progress has been made in the systematic provision of social housing by a variety of nonprofit groups.

4. *Gaps between policy and implementation*: While Canadian housing policy is designed to create social housing for those in "deep core need," production in recent years has only been about one-half the level of the early 1970s. Policy implementation depends upon the political will of provinces and municipalities.

5. *Advantages of the Canadian approach*: Perhaps the single most important characteristic of the Canadian approach is the existence of a relatively comprehensive social safety net and the provision of free health care for poor people. Another element of the Canadian system (at least in Ontario and Quebec) is that single people may receive welfare assistance even if they have no fixed address. Moreover, in some jurisdictions, residents of lodging and rooming houses are given the same legal protection as other renters.

In some Canadian cities, notably Vancouver, Winnipeg, Toronto, Montreal, and Halifax, public and private agencies are moving away from the traditional model of large shelters and giving more attention to small group homes, transitional housing, and permanent dwellings.

CMHC's decision to devolve delivery authority to the provinces has resulted in an increase in the production of social housing by municipal nonprofit housing corporations and third-sector groups. The mixed-income projects they have developed appear to be working reasonably well and represent a major improvement over monolithic public housing projects of earlier decades.

By sponsoring or funding third-sector nonprofit housing CMHC and provincial governments have allowed the development of some projects that are planned, designed, and managed by users. Post-occupancy evaluations reveal that these developments have achieved most of their objectives and are functioning reasonably well (Daly 1988, 46-48).

6. *Disadvantages of the Canadian approach*:   While federal subsidies are limited to the "core needy," provincial and municipal housing subsidies are sometimes directed at moderate-income households as well as those who are classified as "deep core." This has the effect of "de-ghettoizing" new developments but also reduces the amount of assistance available for the poorest households. There is constant tension between the need to erect new units and the need to win community acceptance for subsidized housing. The experience in the United States has been that public authorities and third-sector providers frequently opt for the path of least resistance and build social housing in poor inner-city areas where residents have little political power (Dear and Wolch 1987, 8). In certain Canadian cities (notably Toronto and Vancouver), however, gentrification and residential intensification have caused inner-city land values to escalate, making suitable sites for social housing more difficult to acquire. Suburban municipalities, where land is less costly, have generally been unreceptive to arguments that they should assume their fair share of the regional social housing burden. In addition, delays

inherent in the processing of planning and development applications inhibit the production of social housing and make it more difficult to deliver low-cost units.

SUMMARY

The definition of homelessness frames the response. In the United States a narrow definition is used, at least by public agencies, and the numbers thought to be homeless (about three per 1,000 population) are low relative to Canada and Britain. Local authorities in Britain are obliged by law to house people who are found to be homeless; as a result, the numbers certified as homeless are rather high (seven per 1,000 population), and the nature of those sheltered are different. British law specifies that older people, pregnant women, psychiatrically ill individuals, and some singles are in the vulnerable category. Homeless people in American cities, on the other hand, are primarily singles and young mothers with children. Canada is located somewhere between the American and British approaches. The customary use of the term "homelessness" in Canada usually includes some people (particularly battered women and youths) who are considered to be at risk or vulnerable to homelessness. Some tentative efforts are being made to catch people before they become homeless.

Table 12.5 summarizes the approaches taken in the three countries surveyed. Certain aspects of homelessness are common to Britain, Canada, and the United States. All three have experienced a shortage of affordable housing, a policy of deinstitutionalization, and economic changes that have contributed to the continued marginalization of low-income single women, youth, and visible minorities. During the 1980s a retreat from the Welfare State was evident in social spending cutbacks. In all three countries the response of government to the growing problems of homelessness has been to devolve responsibility to local authorities and to the voluntary sector.

Despite these similarities there are striking differences among the three countries. A specific statute relating to homelessness has been used since 1977 in Britain, while the United States did not adopt any meaningful legislation on this subject until 1987, and the McKinney Homeless Relief Act has been implemented only on a spotty or tentative basis. In Canada there is no legislation specifically dealing with homelessness. Moreover, the notion of "housing as of right," which is

Table 12.5. *Summary of Approaches to Homelessness in the Three Countries*

	U.S.	Britain	Canada
Definition of Homelessness	Narrow; usually limited to absolute homelessness. Housing as of right generally not accepted.	Broad; includes those at risk (some singles, psychiatrically ill, pregnant women, older people.) Housing as a right widely accepted.	Located in between the American and British approaches. Includes some who are at risk (battered women).
Number of Homeless People	3/1,000 (HUD estimate).	7/1,000 (official figure); 25/1,000 inner London.	5+/1,000 (based on National shelter survey).
% in Poverty (using official poverty line in each country)	13.1 percent	14.0 percent	13.5 percent
National Legislation	Stewart McKinney Homeless Relief Act of 1987	Housing (Homeless Persons) Act of 1977	None on homelessness; National Housing Act makes funds available for nonprofit and coop housing.
Central Government Role	Virtually none; limited funding to state and local agencies who may choose to deal with problems or ignore them.	DoE oversees local authorities, establishes policy; DHSS provides benefits.	Authority devolved to province; CMHC provides some housing aid; promotes creation of non9profit housing by cities and third sector.

Local Government Roles	Concentration on emergency shelters; assist people after they become homeless; some cities deal with homelessness only when courts required it.	Legally obligated to certify homeless and provide housing; substantial variation among authorities depending on degree of ideological commitment.	Different in each province. Municipal nonprofit housing corporations develop and renovate housing and assist private (3rd sector) nonprofits.
NGO/Third-Sector Roles	Operate shelters, missions, and food banks. Some now developing/renovating housing.	Responsible for 1977 Act. 3rd sector involved in information and advocacy/lobbying. Development of self-help and shared housing.	Development of self-help and coop housing. Use of facilitative management model. Women's housing groups active.
Principal Actors	City governments; NGOs; philanthropic groups.	DoE; Local authority housing officers; Advocates for homeless people.	Provincial/municipal governments; 3rd-sector nonprofit housing groups; Housing cooperatives.
Nature of Programs	Some innovative housing, including transitional homes for women; health outreach programs; useful model of public-private joint ventures.	Many hostels archaic; Emphasis on shared, short-life, and transitional housing. Housing, education, health, employment schemes often linked.	Emphasis on coop and nonprofit housing with income mix. User design and planning of group homes.

generally accepted in Britain, is not universally acknowledged in North America.

There are also important differences in the roles assumed by governments to deal with homelessness. In Britain local authorities are obliged to provide housing for homeless people but there is substantial variation among authorities and regions in terms of the enthusiasm that housing officers bring to their task of sheltering homeless households. Central government has devolved authority to the local level. Nevertheless, Whitehall continues to establish policy, provide benefits, set spending limits, and to reward or punish local councils in response to their perceived degree of cooperation. In the United States, on the other hand, the role of the federal government was extremely limited during the 1980s. Local and state governments are for the most part free to deal with homelessness or to ignore the problem (except when ordered by courts to provide shelter). In many American cities the principal response from the public sector has been to open emergency shelters or to pay for the use of welfare hotels and motels. Canada has moved away from reliance on emergency shelters to some extent and has attempted to develop permanent social housing. While devolving delivery authority to the provinces, Canada Mortgage and Housing Corporation has remained involved in funding, in disseminating information, in promoting the creation of nonprofit housing by municipalities and by the third sector, in joint planning and monitoring, as well as in direct delivery of a few programs in certain provinces.

In Britain the third sector has been active for decades in lobbying, advocacy, and information gathering and dissemination. Voluntary groups act as effective watchdogs on government. In the United States this sector has been heavily involved in the operation of emergency shelters, missions and food banks, often with partial funding from government. Some groups are now using public-private joint ventures to develop housing. In Canada the voluntary sector has been engrossed, throughout the 1980s, in the development of transitional and permanent housing through various mechanisms, including self-help and cooperatives. Women's housing groups have been particularly active.

Because of the different approaches taken, the nature of the principal actors changes from place to place. In Britain the lead roles have been played by the Department of Environment, local authorities (particularly the housing officers), and by advocacy groups. In the United States most of the action is at the city level, where municipal governments, NGOs, and philanthropic groups have carried the load. In Canada, all three levels of government are generally involved, as are third-sector nonprofit and cooperative housing organizations. As a result, there are several important differences among the three countries in the programs utilized to deal with homelessness. Britain has emphasized the provision of shelter, even though the housing provided is frequently substandard. Emphasis has also been placed on links between housing, education, health, and employment programs. The most noteworthy features of the American approach have been an unfortunate concentration on expedients like emergency shelters or welfare hotels, and a commendable use of creative models of public-private joint ventures to produce housing. The approach taken in Canada has resulted in substantial production of social housing, using a mixed-income model and employing a variety of public and private nonprofit producers.

CONCLUSION

Cross-national comparisons are a useful way to check our progress and learn from the experiences of others, perhaps to avoid their mistakes. This review of three countries, while revealing similar problems in terms of homelessness, has shown that there are significant variations among the approaches taken and the results achieved.

In the case of Britain, relations between governments have been dictated by economic restraint and ideology; thus, public policy is most effective when there is a genuine local commitment to shelter homeless households. The effectiveness of public policy in the United States is difficult to measure because the federal policy and role are not readily apparent. Moreover, because of an aversion to federal interference in what are seen as local matters, there is little incentive for cash-strapped federal officials to become enmeshed in conflicts at the city or state levels. In Canada federal policy has been to encourage the development of social housing by other levels of government and by the third sector. This policy has been effective when provincial and municipal governments feel motivated to mount an aggressive housing program. Without enthusiastic local participation the policy goals are not likely to be realized.

A key issue in all three countries is the gap between policy and implementation. Results are predicated on political will. In Britain local officials often alter or ignore policy directives from above, but they are subject to punishment because central government controls the purse strings. In the United States homelessness is seen as a short-term, local problem. Accordingly, it is often ignored or dealt with by means of expedient measures. In Canada policy implementation depends upon the willingness of provincial and municipal authorities to put effort and funds behind social housing initiatives.

Certain advantages and disadvantages are apparent in the approaches taken. In Britain people are sometimes assisted before they become homeless because the concepts of vulnerability and housing as of right are generally acknowledged. But this does not mean that housing provided to homeless people will be of acceptable quality. The British experience demonstrates the importance of a local commitment to deal with homelessness. In the United States, because the federal government remained on the sidelines for so long, local agencies and private groups were compelled to join forces. The results were often innovative, successful joint ventures to produce housing for low-income and homeless people. The American experience, however, points out both the effectiveness of charitable or voluntary endeavors and their inherent limitations. In Canada the existence of a social safety net has been an important factor in containing homelessness, though the concept of vulnerability has not yet been universally accepted. The Canadian approach to production of mixed-income social housing provides a useful model for others, particularly when users are allowed to participate in the planning, design, and management of their own housing. The difficulties evident in the Canadian approach are limited resources and the obstacles to development of social housing for homeless people in areas where it is needed and where land is affordable. In all three countries public authorities, private developers, and third-sector housing advocates have been confronted with high urban land costs and processing delays in the planning system that have constrained their ability to deal with the housing needs of homeless people.

REFERENCES

Buck, N., I. Gordon, and K. Young. 1987. "London: Employment Problems and Prospects." In *Urban Economic Change: Five City Studies*, ed. V. A. Hausner, Oxford: Clarendon Press, 88-131.

Canadian Council on Social Development. 1987. "Homelessness in Canada: The Report of the National Inquiry." *Social Development Overview* 5(1). Ottawa: CCSD.

Carter, T., and A. McAfee. 1990. "The Municipal Role in Housing the Homeless and Poor." In *Housing the Homeless and Poor: New Partnerships Among the Private, Public and Third Sectors*, ed. G. Fallis and A. Murray, Toronto: University of Toronto Press, 227-62.

Central Statistical Office (U.K.). 1990. *Annual Abstract of Statistics*, No. 126. London: HMSO.

City of Toronto Department of Planning and Development. 1986. "Housing in the Toronto Region." *City Planning* (Fall): 42-46.

City of Toronto. 1987. *Report of the Inquiry into the Effects of Homelessness on Health*. Toronto: Department of the City Clerk.

Cochrane, A. 1985. "The Attack on Local Government: What it is and What it isn't." *Critical Social Policy* 4 (Spring): 44-61.

Daly, G. 1988. *A Comparative Assessment of Programs Dealing with the Homeless Population in the United States, Canada, and Britain.* Ottawa: Canada Mortgage and Housing Corporation.

_____. 1990. "Programs Dealing with Homelessness in the United States, Canada, and Britain." In *Homelessness in the United States. Vol. II: Data and Issues*, ed. J. A. Momeni, New York: Greenwood Press, 133-52.

_____, V. Helfand, and D. Thornley. 1989. *Social Structure Analysis Study for Ataratiri.* Toronto: City of Toronto Housing Department.

Dear, M., and J. R. Wolch. 1987. *Landscapes of Despair: From Deinstitutionalization to Homelessness.* Princeton: Princeton University Press.

Department of Environment (U.K.). 1977. *Code of Guidance to England and Wales Housing [Homeless Persons] Act 1977.*

_____. 1990. "HIP Returns from Local Authorities." London: HMSO.

Department of Health and Social Services (U.K.). 1987. "Duration of Spell of Unemployment." *Unemployment Benefit Summary Sheets.* London: HMSO.

Donnison, D., and C. Ungerson. 1982. *Housing Policy.* Harmondsworth: Penguin.

Engeland, J. 1990-91. "Canadian Renters in Core Housing Need." *Canadian Housing* 7 (Winter): 6-10.

Evans, A., and S. Duncan. 1988. *Responding to Homelessness: Local Authority Policy and Practice.* London: HMSO.

Hambleton, R. 1990. "Future Directions for Urban Government in Britain and America." *Journal of Urban Affairs* 12(1): 75-94.

Her Majesty's Stationary Office. 1983. *Streamlining the Cities, Government Proposals for Reorganizing Local Government in Greater London and the Metropolitan Counties.* London: Cmnd 9063 (White Paper).

Hopper, K., and J. Hamberg. 1986. "The Making of America's Homeless: From Skid Row to New Poor, 1945-1984." In *Critical Perspectives on Housing,* ed. R. Bratt, C. Hartman, and A. Meyerson, Philadelphia: Temple University Press, 12-40.

Housing Networking Project. 1986. *People, Projects & Issues.* Toronto: Housing Networking Project.

Hulchanski, J. D., M. Eberle, K. Olds, and D. Stewart. 1991. *Solutions to Homelessness: Vancouver Case Studies.* A report prepared by the Centre for Human Settlements, University of British Columbia, for the Canada Mortgage and Housing Corporation.

Irwin, C. 1988. "Lords of the Arctic, Wards of the State: The Growing Inuit population, Arctic Resettlement and Their Effects on Social and Economic Change." Ottawa: Health and Welfare Canada.

Kaufman, N. K. 1984. "Homelessness: A Comprehensive Policy Approach." *The Urban and Social Change Review* 17(1): 21-25.

Ley, D. 1985. *Gentrification in Canadian Cities: Patterns, Analysis, Impact and Policy.* Vancouver: University of British Columbia, Department of Geography.

Lipset, S. 1990. *Continental Divide: The Values and Institutions of the United States and Canada.* New York: Routledge.

MacLennan, D., and K. Gibb. 1990. "Housing Finance and Subsidies in Britain after a Decade of 'Thatcherism.'" *Urban Studies* 27 (6): 905-18.

_____, and A. More. 1991. *Fairer Subsidies, Faster Growth: Housing, Government and the Economy.* York: Joseph Rowntree Foundation.

Marcuse, P. 1987. "Why Are They Homeless?" *The Nation,* April 4.

Momeni, J. A., ed. 1989. *Homelessness in the United States*. Vol. I: *State Surveys*. New York: Greenwood Press.

_____. 1990. *Homelessness in the United States*. Vol. II: *Data and Issues*. New York: Greenwood Press.

Municipality of Metropolitan Toronto. 1987. "Emergency Shelters for the Homeless." Community Services Department, Hostel Operations, September 25.

Niner, P. 1989. *Homelessness in Nine Local Authorities: Case Studies of Policy and Practice*. London: HMSO.

North London Education Project. 1987. *Report, 1984-86*. London: North London Education Project.

Ontario Ministry of Housing. 1989. "Housing Policy Statement." Toronto.

_____, Social Housing Wing. 1990. *Social Housing Inventory*. (Printout)

Ospina, J. 1987. *Housing Ourselves*. London: Hilary Shipman.

Plamondon, J. 1985. "Deinstitutionalization: Its Implications and Requirements." *Deinstitutionalization: Costs and Effects*. Ottawa: Canadian Council on Social Development.

Pomeroy, S. 1989. "The Recent Evolution of Social Housing in Canada." *Canadian Housing* 6 (Winter) 6-13.

Raynsford, N. 1986. "The 1977 Housing (Homeless Persons) Act." In *Policy Change in Government*, ed. N. Deakin, London: RIPA, 35-51.

Ross, D., and R. Shillington. 1989. *Canadian Fact Book on Poverty*. Ottawa: Canadian Council on Social Development.

Single Displaced Persons' Project. 1983. *The Case for Long-Term Supportive Housing*. Toronto.

Sprague, J. F. 1986. *Transitional Housing*. Boston: Women's Institute for Housing and Economic Development.

Suchman, D. 1990. *Public/Private Housing Partnerships*. Washington, D.C.: The Urban Land Institute.

U.S. Bureau of the Census. 1989. "A Status Report on Hunger and Homelessness in America's Cities, 1988." Washington, D.C.: USGPO

_____. 1990a. *Statistical Abstract of the United States, 1990*. (110th edition). Washington, D.C.: USGPO.

_____. 1990b. *Current Population Reports*. Series P-60. Washington, D.C: USGPO.

U.S. Conference of Mayors. 1989. *A Status Report on Hunger and Homelessness in America's Cities: 1988*. Washington, D.C.: U.S. Conference of Mayors.

U.S. Congress. 1987. *Public Law l00-77: Stewart B. McKinney Homeless Assistance Act.* Washington, D.C.: USGPO.

U.S. Department of Housing and Urban Development. 1984. "A Report to the Secretary on the Homeless and Emergency Shelters." Washington, D.C.: The Office of Policy Development and Research.

_____. 1989. *A Report on the 1988 National Survey of Shelters for the Homeless.* Washington, D.C.: The Office of Policy Development and Research, Division of Policy Studies.

U.S. General Accounting Office. 1985. *Homelessness—A Complex Problem and Government's Response.* Washington, D.C.: USGPO.

Wolch, J. R. and A. Akita. 1989. "The Federal Response to Homelessness and its Implications for American Cities." *Urban Geography* 10(1): 62-85.

Wright, J. D., and E. Weber. 1987. *Homelessness and Health.* Washington, D.C.: McGraw-Hill.

York, M. L. 1991. "The Orlando Affordable Housing Demonstration Project." *Journal of the American Planning Association* 57 (Autumn)33: 490-93.

Chapter 13

Federal Urban Activity:
Intergovernmental Relations in an Age of Restraint

Caroline Andrew
University of Ottawa

Intergovernmental relations can safely be described as one of the undertheorized areas of social science research. Numerous descriptions exist of the relations between different governments at different points in time, but little has been produced in the way of theory to explain these relations. This has been particularly true for tri-level relations in the Canadian context. The strongly defended provincial government claim to complete jurisdiction over municipal government has structured, at least in part, the perspective of the academic community, which primarily describes federal urban activity as a minor aspect of federal-provincial relations rather than as something to be explained on its own terms. Nonetheless, recent studies of intergovernmental relations raise a number of analytical suggestions that may provide us with ways of looking at current trends in federal activity relating to the managing of urban centres.

Gelfand's description of the emergence of urban issues on the national political agenda in the United States offers a classificatory framework for evaluating the importance of different factors. He categorizes the important factors as "constitutional, political and demographic" (1980, 28) and in his analysis describes how federal activity can be seen as a reaction to changing demography, filtered through constitutional-legal structures and political organization. Demographic changes represent the bottom line, but the translation of these into federal activity is framed by political-legal structures and by the patterns of organization of political forces. An example of this can be seen by comparing ways in which the interests of suburbs are mobilized at the federal level in the United States and Canada. The basic change is demographic—the twentieth century has seen the massive spread of suburban development. In terms of both population and land use, the shift has been dramatic. In the United States suburbs have sought a political voice through the creation of national lobbying organizations that exert political pressure directly on the federal government. This is much less true in Canada because of the creation of regional governments and the consequent amalgamation of suburban and centre city interests at the regional level. The representation of these interests is more site-specific and is channelled, to a large extent, through provincial governments. Federal-local ties in the American case are reinforced by political alliances—national party politics being well established in the major urban areas. In Canada the regional cleavages of the party system and the very weak formal role of established parties at the municipal level tend to reinforce the provincial-regional ties and to weaken federal-local links.

Gurr and King (1987) look at state activity in relation to cities, and their analysis can be seen as an elaboration of the constitutional and legal factors raised by Gelfand. They argue in terms of the relative autonomy of the state: "the economic processes which reshape cities and the contending private interests which influence urban policies are limits or constraints on the state's policies, not determinants of those policies" (p. 9). For Gurr and King, the state's basic interests are threefold: "in maintaining public order and authority in urban populations, in securing public revenues, and the interests of officials in the pursuit of their programmatic goals with respect to urban welfare."

The third factor opens up an avenue of investigation into the way both elected and appointed officials, through their efforts to develop particular programs directed at some specific policy area, influence the thrust of federal urban activity and the kind of tri-level links established. This focus indicates that the definition of program activity relevant to federal-urban concerns should be drawn widely in order to see the way in which specific program concerns lead, or do not lead, to federal intervention in urban areas. It also allows for consideration of different periods of activity, because programmatic activities add up to a vision of the public sector and its legitimacy at a particular time. Ashford (1986), in his analysis of the emergence of welfare states, clearly links the development of the welfare state to a subordination of local governments to central decisions.

The welfare state could not develop unless national governments were able to nationalize the social policies dispensed among local governments, assigned to localized charities and left to local religious institutions. The struggle between levels of government began some decades before national governments agreed to take on social responsibilities, and so both the duration and the intensity of the struggle are important clues to the political development of the welfare state (1986, 121).

Following the same logic, other authors now reverse this link in what they see as a postwelfare state era. If the construction of the welfare state required centralization, with federal supervision and/or control over municipal actions, postwelfare state intergovernmental relations are decentralizing.

The rethinking of intergovernmental relations which is taking place cannot be distanced from the general rethinking of the role of government which is occurring in OECD economies as a whole. . . . Decentralization, in a general sense, to markets and to local actors, has been a key issue running through these reforms. But in keeping with the argument of this chapter, decentralization can be understood only with respect to how the previous position was conceptualized. For exposition purposes it is useful to depict the dominant previous position as one dominated by a "welfarist" paradigm (Bennett 1990, 3).

This very selective reading of recent studies does not, at this stage, enable the formulation of a theory of intergovernmental relations, but it does suggest questions to ask about current reality. It alerts us to the importance of looking at intergovernmental relations as an indicator of the role of government and of debates over this role. Both Bennett (1990) and Gurr and King (1987) discuss the dual dimension of local autonomy, both from local civil society and from other levels of the state. Analyses must therefore situate federal urban activity in the larger context of the role of the state.

Within this context, the study of officials' programmatic concerns is one important focus for understanding the concrete processes by which intergovernmental activity develops and evolves. But these concerns can be seen in turn as elements that structure or frame the more fundamental influence, that of demographic change. The political and institutional factors are then useful in explaining how demographic shifts get factored into the political system.

FEDERAL URBAN ACTIVITY IN CANADA

Even looking at federal urban activity in Canada could be considered rash because anything resembling a "federal urban policy" has disappeared as a project, and as a category, since the 1970s. The short-lived experience of the Ministry of State for Urban Affairs (MSUA) from 1971 to 1979 led to a number of evaluations,[1] but since then the idea of the federal government having a policy, or even a number of policies, that could be described as urban has not been studied, nor even really considered. However, there are signs that it is time to reevaluate the question of federal urban activity. The intention of this chapter is to provide some preliminary comments for this reevaluation.

One reason for this reevaluation is the recognition that the federal government has continued to influence the development of Canada's major urban centres despite the abolition of the MSUA. Indeed, one could claim that federal influence was more profound in the 1980s than in previous periods. Two recent studies describe the major urban projects that have marked the centre-cities of almost all of Canada's major metropolitan areas (Leo and Fenton 1990; Artibise and Kiernan 1989). Vancouver, Winnipeg, Toronto, Montreal, [2] Quebec, and Halifax have all seen major development projects in which the federal government has played a central role.

This reevaluation seems due not only because of the reinterpretation of past federal urban impact but also because there would seem to be a modest increase in federal interest in things urban. Peter Spurr signalled this in his paper for the 1988 Canadian Housing and Urban Studies Conference when he wrote "in Canada, a reawakening of interest in urban matters in recent months could be the beginning of a more fundamental change" (Spurr 1988). The naming of a federal Minister of State for Housing in September 1988 would appear to be one indication that the federal government saw as politically attractive a more visible presence in the housing field. The evaluation of this increased federal activity will be one of the major concerns of this chapter.

---

[1] Among others, Feldman and Milch 1981; Gertler 1979 and 1982; Oberlander and Fallick 1987; Andrew 1988.

[2] Montreal is perhaps a partial exception, but this is more because the Waterfront development project has not really got off the ground. We have included it because the federal government has had a major project there but, in terms of real impact, Montreal should not be on the list.

In order to situate the present context for federal policymaking, it is useful to compare it to that of the 1960s, the period from which the MSUA emerged. The comparisons are striking, in terms of the demographic challenge, in terms of federal government policymaking objectives, and more generally, in terms of the role of the state. An examination of these dimensions indicates how very different is the policymaking context of the two periods. From a period of optimism about the possibilities of public action and public solutions to the challenges of urbanization, we have moved to a period of pessimism about the possibilities of public action both on the practical level (fiscal considerations) and on the theoretical level (questioning of the role of the state).

The background to the creation of MSUA can be found in the very rapid urban growth of the 1950s and 1960s. This led to debates and concerns about the direction of urban growth. These concerns found political expression at the federal level with the electoral victory of the Liberal Party, led by Pierre-Elliott Trudeau, in 1968. In this election almost all the ridings in Vancouver, Toronto, and Montreal were won by the Liberals, and this concentration of urban members increased the likelihood that voters' concerns would be translated into government action.

Not only were influential urban members of Parliament urging the federal cabinet to act, but also this political pressure coincided with more administrative pressures to improve federal decision-making procedures. The government was preoccupied with finding ways to improve the pro-active capacity of the federal cabinet and its own capacity to act in coordinated fashion on issues involving a number of departments. The creation of MSUA was part of an attempt to improve the rationality of public decision making.

The ministry was set up in 1971 with essentially three objectives: the coordination of federal activities related to urban issues; the establishment of tripartite links among governments; and the building up of a research and information base. The abolition of MSUA can be explained in terms of these goals. The ministry was not able to coordinate federal activities, and the major line departments continued to plan and implement policy related to urban areas without coordination with MSUA. Second, and perhaps inevitably, the federal policy irritated the provinces, and they became increasingly vocal in their opposition. Finally, the research and information activities did not succeed in creating a clientele or a political base for the ministry. This research had not established clear policy directions, nor had it succeeded for the most part in altering definitions or ways of looking at reality. Therefore it had not shaped the policy agenda in either practical or theoretical terms.

In some cases, the large urban projects that have influenced major urban areas had their origins in the MSUA period or involved MSUA in their planning. In other cases the projects began after the demise of the ministry. In all cases, these large projects were very "political" in nature, emerging as election promises (Harbourfront in Toronto, the Rideau Centre in Ottawa), as responses to the local power base of a federal cabinet minister (Ron Basford's role in Granville Island, Vancouver; Lloyd Axworthy and the Winnipeg Core Area Initiative) or as part of the ongoing competition between federal and Quebec governments for political visibility (the projects in both Quebec and Montreal). This is not just to say that political considerations were involved but rather that fundamentally these projects were motivated by political factors and, as such, represented a move away from the rational decision-making model of the early Trudeau years.

This argument has been developed by Christopher Leo and Robert Fenton in describing why the federal government has used urban development corporations. One of the three major factors relates to the political attractiveness of these projects.[3]

> Urban development corporations have undertaken highly visible renewal or redevelopment projects with a readily identifiable "image" that it is easy for federal representatives to point out at election time and in which it is easy to trace the federal contribution to the satisfaction of even the most unsophisticated voter.
>
> . . . The fact that urban development corporations are individually tailored to the requirements of a particular city is important as well, for it gives the federal government the invaluable advantage—especially in such a regionally torn polity as Canada —of an unclear definition of its obligation for a repeat performance elsewhere (Leo and Fenton 1990, 193-95).

Highlighting this shift from a concern for rational policymaking to a context where political criteria dominate underlines the importance of situating the analysis of urban policy within the context of overall government policymaking. The general shifts in policymaking philosophy

---

[3]See Leo and Fenton 1988. The other two factors are the expenditure limits and the growing power of capital.

and structures influence the way in which one particular set of issues, in this case urban-related ones, will be dealt with. Peter Aucoin's description of organizational change in the machinery of Canadian government as being "from rational management to brokerage politics" captures the major shift over the 20-year period from 1968 to 1988 (1986, 17).

> Whereas Trudeau was most concerned with the role of knowledge and analysis in the pursuit of comprehensive planning in rational decision-making, Mulroney has a much more political conception of ideal government, namely the pursuit of compromise among competing interests.

What this implies is that there is much less likely to be a move on the part of the federal government to establish an explicit urban policy. First of all, comprehensive rational decision making is not a goal. Second, as Aucoin argues, the brokerage model does not imply general cabinet policies on specific areas but rather individual contacts between ministers and the prime minister leading to specific actions. And third, if the goal is compromise among competing interests, it is unlikely that explicit policies will be introduced in areas where important interests, such as the provinces, are likely to be opposed. Therefore, urban policy, if it exists, will more likely consist of activities having an urban focus or that particularly apply to urban areas than of explicit or coherent urban policy.

There are other trends that illustrate the shifts in federal government policymaking since the creation of MSUA: "the rise of conservatism, increased skepticism about the efficiency of planning by government for state intervention, and the recognition of the limits of the state to eradicate the conflicts of interests inherent in the political condition" (Aucoin 1986, 18). These have been spelled out in a number of studies, including the *How Ottawa Spends* series.[4] As Katharine Graham argues in the 1990-91 edition, "The government's agenda has become increasingly focussed on expenditure control and reducing the role of the federal state in both the social and economic fabric of Canada" (Graham 1991, 2).

The policy agenda has therefore shifted to concern for cutting costs, increasing efficiency, reducing the role of government, and increasing the role of the private sector. All these trends have impacted on the way in which issues get dealt with or do not get dealt with. At the same time, there are other political/institutional factors that come into play, such as

---

[4]See, among others, Wilson 1989; Maslove 1984; Graham 1985, 1991.

the desire for consensus and the seeking of federal-provincial harmony. These too act on the kind of consideration that will be given to urban-related issues.

There are also political factors that should be included in the analysis. The federal cabinet of the early Trudeau years was clearly dominated by people representing urban ridings—Montreal, Toronto, and Vancouver. This is much less true of the Mulroney government in which a majority of the central figures do not come from ridings in major urban areas. Mulroney may have worked in Montreal, but he is an M.P. from the north coast of the St. Lawrence.

And, to complete our comparison of the two periods, the demographic changes were less dramatic in the 1980s than in the 1960s. The 1960s were a period of rapid urbanization and led to major social debates about the maximum size of cities and the ability of political systems to manage and control urban growth. The 1970s were very different and indeed led to worldwide questions about counterurbanization (Champion 1989; Simmons and Bourne 1989). Urban growth was more pronounced in the 1980s than in the 1970s but it still remained far more moderate than in the earlier period of rapid growth. The demographic pressures are therefore less dramatic at the present time, and this is certainly one of the factors that explains the differences between the policy context of the late 1960s and that of the present day.

With this general background in mind as a context for the evaluation of federal policy, we turn now to a description of current federal government "urban" activities. The intention is to include those programs that bear in some significant way on the development of urban areas. There will not necessarily be agreement on the list of programs as the distinction between urban-related issues and those that merely take place in cities[5] is subject to interpretation, as is the appreciation of which programs are indeed significant.[6] The classification is in terms of the factor being influenced. Brief descriptions are given of federal activities influencing land, infrastructure, housing, social development, and those aimed at the international field.

---

[5]This distinction picks up on Harvey Lithwick's distinction between problems of cities and problems in cities (Lithwick 1970).

[6]Clearly the list is not intended to be definitive. I would very much like to receive comments or suggestions of other programs or activities that should be included.

URBAN LAND

In looking at federal government activities that influence urban land, it is useful to begin with the Bureau of Real Property Management.[7] Created in 1986, the bureau was one of the results of the Nielson Task Force on Program Review. It was set up as part of the reorganization of federal activities relating to the management of real property. Treasury Board consolidated responsibility for policy relating to the central management of real property, leaving the Ministry of Public Works with responsibility for managing certain properties and for providing services (architectural and engineering, property management) to government departments. Individual departments and agencies, including public works, are custodians of specific federal properties, but the bureau has the responsibility to look at the whole portfolio in terms of general policies. Two thrusts are currently central: creating a directory of all federal real property and identifying problem properties. In conformity with the recommendation of the Nielson Task Force that the government only keep the property it needed for its current programs, this change led to the identification of properties to be disposed of. As well, the government's policy is to manage more effectively the property it wishes to keep.

> Given the current climate of fiscal restraint, real property managers are exploring a wider range of options and taking creative, innovative approaches that will enable the government to make the most productive use of its assets, and that will offer the best economic return to the Crown in the long term, consistent with meeting policy and program objectives (Treasury Board 1989, 1).

The bureau is not explicitly concerned with urban policy, but because of the importance of federal government holdings in the major urban centers and the potential impact of development on these lands, the bureau's policies have a clear potential influence on urban development. In fact, the bureau began by looking at the Toronto area to identify opportunities for better management. The sites identified are then developed by other agencies, as the bureau has no role in implementation. Examples mentioned from the Toronto area were the Downsview military

---

[7]Information for this section comes largely from an interview with W. Roberts, director, Portfolio Management, Bureau of Real Property Management and from the following documents: Treasury Board 1988, 1989.

base and Environmental Services land in Vaughan, now both being developed by Canada Mortgage and Housing Corporation (CMHC), and the Toronto Harbourfront, now being studied by the Royal Commission on the future of the Toronto Waterfront.

The Bureau of Real Property Management gives the federal government a tool for addressing questions of real property development. It is too soon to judge the impact of this tool but, given the federal interest in more aggressive management, it may lead to increased federal involvement in urban development.

A word more on the Royal Commission on the Future of the Toronto Waterfront.[8] Set up as a one-person Royal Commission with the nomination of David Crombie on March 30, 1988, the commission has developed a very active research and information function. Having been created to deal with the political controversy generated by the Harbourfront development, the Interim Report indicates that the commission sees itself as trying to create a new consensus about the direction of development.

> The people of Toronto instinctively understand this. They understand the importance of what is being done on their waterfront today. . . . And the care, indeed the passion, with which they have presented their views and ideas to this Commission says that they will accept nothing but the best we can do—that they want it done right. . . .
>
> They offered words to describe their instincts about Toronto. Words like opportunity, tolerance, and orderliness. Words that speak of the virtues that reach back to our roots, explain our sense of civic stewardship, and underpin the City's ongoing success. . . .
>
> Forging consensus rooted in these core values is the dull, hard work of democracy—an unrelenting, never-ending task that requires the energies, interests, and imaginations of many people over long periods of time (Royal Commission on the Future of the Toronto Waterfront 1989c, 9-11).

---

[8]Information for this section comes from the following Royal Commission documents: 1989c and 1990b, reports of various working groups, including 1989a, 1989b, 1989d, 1989e, and 1990a, as well as the newsletter and bibliography of the Canadian Waterfront Resource Centre established by the Royal Commission.

The attempt to build a consensus around the combination of opportunity and orderliness within a climate of tolerance is perhaps easier to do on paper than on the waterfront, but the Royal Commission does seem to have established a strategy to achieve this goal. Two aspects of the Royal Commission are particularly interesting in terms of its policymaking role: the federal-provincial aspect and the importance given to research and information. The commission began as a federal body but added a provincial mandate in October 1989. This may well be the first instance of a commission with mandates from both federal and provincial levels of government and therefore represents an innovation in the machinery of federalism.

The Royal Commission has been particularly concerned to make information available on issues relating to waterfront development. In addition to setting up the Canadian Waterfront Resource Centre, "the research and education arm of the Royal Commission" (Royal Commission 1989c, 206), the commission has been active in publishing and in distributing reports. In this era of cost-recovery, the fact that commission reports are available free of charge indicates a deliberate strategy to stimulate wide public debate and shape the terms of that debate. The commission will continue to make recommendations to both the federal and the Ontario government on the development of the Toronto Waterfront. Clearly these recommendations will be wide-ranging and broadly based and their potential impact on the development of the Toronto region considerable, but the evaluation of the commission's success is still a long way in the future. It is interesting to note that in its second interim report of August 1990, the commission talks of the Greater Toronto Bioregion and agrees that "it is imperative to develop administrative mechanisms that bring jurisdictions together to solve problems cooperatively" (Royal Commission 1990b, 46-47).

CMHC is also involved in land development.[9] The most interesting projects, in terms of urban impact, are in the Toronto area (Downsview and Vaughan) and in the Vancouver area (a site in Burnaby and a second project in Kitsilano that, in itself, involves about 15 small sites of veterans' housing). The two Toronto area projects demonstrate "the continued commitment of the federal government to assist in addressing

---

[9]Information for this section comes from an interview with Mr. Lorne Finley and from CMHC annual reports. Information on the written documentation that was consulted for CMHC generally can be found in the section on the housing activities of CMHC.

affordability problems in high demand-driven areas" (CMHC 1989, 14). Despite the current federal government's preference for using the private sector, CMHC is directly developing both the Downsview and the Vaughan site. Clearly political concerns that these projects result in some reasonably affordable housing have prevailed over an ideological preference for the private sector. In Vaughan, a community concept plan exists, and the vision of an integrated community of medium-density housing will clearly be opposed by the municipal authorities, representing the political will of neighbours housed in much more expensive, low-density housing. Public development by CMHC is at least in theory better able to resist those local political pressures, although the final outcome is not at all clear.

The federal government also influences land development through the work of the National Capital Commission.[10] The recently published Federal Land Use Plan established guidelines for federal land within the national capital region. Despite the importance of the National Capital Commission's role in the development of federal land, the fact that the commission is primarily involved in the urban area of Ottawa-Hull makes it less central to the more general purposes of this chapter. Certain activities of the commission, such as the conference on waterfront development, have had a national impact but these are limited in number.

URBAN INFRASTRUCTURE

Turning now to programs relating to infrastructure, we will look first at federal water policy and then at questions relating to transportation. Later on in the chapter when we look at the way urban issues do, or do not, get on the policy agenda, we will look at the way the general question of urban infrastructure has evolved politically but here we will concentrate on specific programs.

Federal water policy is important to examine because of its influence on the outcome of discussions about federal responsibility for the state of urban infrastructure.[11] As we will see later the federal government's

---

[10] Information for this section comes from the Federal Land Use Study and from my experience as a member of the National Capital Commission Planning Committee from 1985-1989.

[11] Information for this section comes from an interview with R. L. Pentland, Environment Canada, and from the following documents: Pearce, Bertrand, MacLaren 1985; Environment Canada 1987; Tate 1989; Portland 1985; and Jones

refusal to finance a program of assistance for urban infrastructure was motivated by concern for deficit reduction and by the feeling, based on water policy considerations, that user pay financing was the desired solution and that federal assistance would therefore be counterproductive from both an economic and environmental point of view.

Recent policy began with the creation of the three-person federal inquiry on water policy. Set up in the early 1980s when Charles Caccia was Minister of the Environment, the inquiry allowed the federal government to begin to deal with some of the large policy questions that were emerging: water export, climate change, and municipal infrastructure. It reported in 1985.

The federal inquiry on water policy did not come to a clear agreement on the question of municipal infrastructure. However, in the 1987 federal water policy document that followed on the report of inquiry, water pricing was the first strategy. More specifically, the document argued that "major government funding of water and sewers without such realistic pricing leaves consumers unaware of the true cost of the resource use, and the water tends to be wasted through excessive demand and inefficient use" (Environment Canada 1987, 21). The document went on to indicate certain areas where exceptions to a hands-off policy might be considered, such as promoting research and development and other federal and provincial "development priorities." One of the few exceptions has been the federal assistance to Halifax for municipal infrastructure. It can be explained in terms of the Nova Scotia government's regional development priorities, of the important R&D component involved in the project and, undoubtedly, of the fact that the then Minister of Public Works represented a Halifax riding. But with few exceptions the federal government has refused assistance to municipalities, arguing that realistic pricing policies will both provide money for maintaining and expanding facilities and be more environmentally sensitive.

In addition to refusing to finance urban infrastructure, the federal government has tried to influence provincial and municipal policy by publishing material, speaking at conferences, working through the newly formed Canadian Water and Wastewater Association (CWWA), and generally trying to build support for user-pay policies. The federal message is clear: user-pay financing is environmentally and economically

---

1990.

sound. Municipalities should be encouraged to move towards user-pay models (Tate 1989).

The fact that then Ontario Prime Minister, in the middle of the 1990 election campaign, raised the possibility of higher water rates is seen as an indication that the federal policy is gaining support.

Water policy considerations have tended to dominate debates about urban infrastructure even though they represent only one part of urban infrastructure policy.[12] In a broader sense, urban infrastructure is an issue that was developed, promoted, and lobbied for by the Federation of Canadian Municipalities.[13] An FCM Task Force created in 1983 published a study "Municipal Infrastructure in Canada: Physical Condition and Funding Adequacy" in 1985. This led to the launching of the Big Fix Campaign calling for a tripartite program of public investment in municipal infrastructure amounting to 15 billion dollars over five years, to be jointly shared by the three levels of government. The proposal was picked up by the then leader of the Liberal Party, John Turner, during the 1988 election campaign but shortly afterwards the campaign became focused on the free trade issue, and urban infrastructure was lost to sight. The federal government has refused to agree to this proposal, arguing that budget deficit reduction is a priority and that, as we have just discussed, user-pay programs are more appropriate ways of solving infrastructural problems. Urban infrastructure has not made it on to the federal policy agenda.

This should not be taken as an indication that the FCM is making no headway as a lobby for municipal interests. The 1980s were a period of considerable growth for the FCM. It more than tripled its membership from 1983 to 1990, going from some 200 members to some 600. In 1962 there were six employees and a budget of some $300,000 whereas by

---

[12]The Federation of Canadian Municipalities (FCM) report on urban infrastructure needs established the division as follows: roads 40 percent, sewage collection 16 percent, water distribution 13 percent, sewage treatment 11 percent, water treatment 10 percent, bridges 9 percent.

[13]Information for this section comes from an interview with Jim Knight, executive director of the FCM, and from the following FCM documents: *Towards Sustainable Communities* 1990; *Municipal Economic Development Program* n.d.; publications of the Municipal Race Relations Program; material on the International Program of the FCM, and copies of FCM press releases for the period June 1989-June 1990.

1990 there were 35-40 employees and a budget of several millions.[14] Fees almost tripled during this period, with the maximum limit for an individual fee going from $35,000 to $100,000. This funding is important as the FCM funds its core operations through its own fees, thereby ensuring their autonomy. The FCM has had some major successes, notably with relation to the federal Goods and Services Tax (GST)[15] and with the funding of a variety of activities. A number of federal departments have used the FCM as a way of encouraging community-based activities without involving direct links between federal departments and municipal officials.[16] In addition the FCM sees the political climate for its activities as more favourable, arguing that the provincial "deep suspicion" of the FCM that was true of the MSUA period has been replaced by "grudging acceptance."[17]

The FCM has readjusted its original urban infrastructure lobbying strategy (Federation of Canadian Municipalities 1990, 57), de-emphasizing the total dollar value and arguing for incremental federal involvement. The federation also decided to reassess its position on user- pay policies and to tie the issue to the environment. It concluded that, "FCM should continue to lobby all political parties in order to keep the issue of infrastructure alive should a recession occur. The launching of a major infrastructure program will be a counter-cyclical measure creating jobs for blue collar and other workers likely to be laid off" (pp. 51-52). Now that the recession is clearly here, it will be interesting to watch the fate of the urban infrastructure proposal. But for the moment urban interests have not succeeded in putting the question of urban infrastructure on the federal policy agenda.

The FCM has not been the only organization active in the field of urban infrastructure. Road construction has been the focus of The Road Information Program (TRIP) Committee of the Canadian Construction

---

[14]Interview with Jim Knight.

[15]An agreement was reached at the end of May 1990 between the Minister of Finance and the FCM on the level of rebate that municipalities will qualify for in relation to the federal Goods and Services Tax.

[16]The Municipal Economic Development program was financially supported by the Ministry of Regional Economic Expansion, the Race Relations program by the Secretary of State, the international program by the Canadian International Development Agency, the Urban Safety Conference and perhaps further crime prevention activities by the Department of Justice.

[17]Interview with Jim Knight.

Association. This committee has been arguing the need for a special program of financial assistance for road construction. Up until the present, the federal government has not agreed to this proposal.

One other minor reference in the area of transportation relates to the activities of the Royal Commission on National Passenger Transportation.[18] One of the very few urban references in the federal government's central document on environmental policy, the Green Plan, relates to urban transportation issues, in which the Royal Commission is alleged to be interested. The commission's Director of Research expressed surprise at this reference as he does not see the commission directly involved in urban transportation questions, considering that its mandate concerns "inter-city passenger transportation." The two areas of research interest he sees as having greatest potential urban impact are jurisdictional questions,[19] and intermodal connections.[20]

HOUSING

Turning to housing activities, a detailed analysis of the activities of Canada Mortgage and Housing Corporation (CMHC) is clearly not possible within the confines of this chapter.[21] Instead, the intent is to

---

[18]Information for this section comes from a telephone conversation with John Sargent, director of research for the commission, and from written documentation on the mandate of the commission and its proposed research areas (see Royal Commission on National Passenger Transportation n.d.).

[19]The description of proposed research relating to jurisdictional questions includes existing coordination mechanisms and problems of interpretation/ coordination. The description also includes the "issue of whether increase in importance of regional governments relative to national governments, in Canada and elsewhere, will pose new problems for achieving integrated transportation systems."

[20]The three specific areas of research interest relating to intermodal connections are aspects of current situation (jurisdictional divisions, etc.) that may impede intermodal connections, benefits/costs of such corrections, and policy response.

[21]Information for this section comes from interviews with Peter Spurr, Research Division, CMHC; Stephen Pomeroy, Manager, Centre for Future Studies in Housing and Living Environments, CMHC; and with Debra Darke, Head, Research Division, CMHC, and from the following documents: Anderson 1989; Canadian Housing and Research Association 1990; Canada Mortgage and Housing Corporation 1989, 1990a, 1990b, 1990c, 1990d, 1990e; Centre for

indicate new thrusts within CMHC and specifically to suggest that renewed interest in the community context, in the urban environment, and in using the production and dissemination of research and information gives CMHC activities greater potential to have an impact on urban development than has been true generally for the post-MSUA period. This expansionist interpretation of CHMC may be subject to revision, however, in the context of the constitutional debate—a point we will return to later. Any radical decentralization of federal-provincial roles in the area of housing would necessarily provide a less favourable environment for an expansionist CHMC.

CMHC's 1991-1995 Strategic Plan outlines the corporation's resources in devising new approaches to be its information base, its links to all the national players, and its international role. Given these factors, the corporation will increasingly play the role of "catalyst" and "facilitator" (CMHC 1990a, 3), joining with a wide variety of other federal and nonfederal actors. Three interrelated ways of looking at the broader context and the way in which housing concerns can relate to this context are discernible: quality of life, sustainable development, and the relations between social policy and housing policy. All of these formulations involve CMHC in partnerships or alliances with other groups and all involve consideration of a multifaceted community context.

CMHC activities that relate to the development of those foci have been the creation of the Centre for Future Studies in Housing and Living Environments, participation in informal meetings of a broad group of largely federal agencies interested in quality of life and community issues, the encouragement of the new research mandate of the Intergovernmental Committee on Urban and Regional Research (ICURR), the creation of tripartite committees "composed of federal, provincial and municipal representatives and set up over the past year in urban centres across Canada" (CMHC 1990a, 7), a document on CMHC activities that address environmental concerns, and a series of conferences on housing options for the elderly. By looking at the relations between housing and environmental concerns and between housing and social policy, CMHC is clearly positioning itself to have a place on major policy questions.

A brief look at the research priorities of the Centre for Future Studies in Housing and Living Environments illustrates CMHC's strategy to position itself as a central player in evolving federal policy debates. The

---

Future Studies n.d.; and Spurr 1988.

centre was created in the spring of 1989 to be a focal point for future-oriented research within the corporation. After an initial period spent consulting on its mandate within the corporation and following a number of staff movements, the centre is now beginning to move to a phase of more direct research activity. It has delimited four research areas: (1) the implication for housing of demographic, social, and economic change; (2) the future relationship between housing and social policy; (3) changing urban and rural living conditions; and (4) the impact of new technology on housing and living environments (CMHC 1990a, 24-27). The themes mentioned—an effective and equitable social safety net, sustainable development, healthy communities, urban safety and crime prevention, emerging technologies—clearly touch on a variety of areas that will be central to federal policy development in the 1990s. The corporation's aim is to develop greater awareness and expertise in these areas and to have this expertise recognized within the federal government and within the broader policymaking community.

This discussion of CMHC activities is clearly very limited. It does, however, indicate that there are signs of renewed interest in the broader community context of housing policy. Pursuing this theme of the broad community context leads to the description of federal activities relating to community social development. Two initiatives seem particularly significant: the Healthy Communities Project and the Ministry of Justice's interest in urban security.

HEALTHY COMMUNITIES

The Healthy Communities Project was funded by Health and Welfare Canada from 1988 to 1991 and sponsored by the Canadian Institute of Planning (CIP), the Federation of Canadian Municipalities (FCM), and the Canadian Public Health Association (CPHA).[22] It stems from Canadian and international thinking about health promotion and ways to emphasize preventive rather than curative methods of health care. Three interconnected ideas are at the base of the project: the impact of socio-economic conditions on health and life expectancy, the link between health and empowerment, in the sense that those people who have more control over their own lives are healthier and, finally, the importance of

---

[22]Information for this section comes from an interview with Susan Berlin, Coordinator for the Canadian Healthy Communities Project, and from the Project's Newsletters and Information Kit.

the community as a context for the establishment of health promotion policies. Thus the project assumes that broadly based community activities (both in the sense of the groups and the areas of policy involved) are likely to be the most productive in promoting good health.

The Canadian project developed over several years and through a series of events, including an International Conference on Health Promotion in 1986 cosponsored by the World Health Organization (WHO), Health and Welfare Canada and the Canadian Public Health Association and the publication of *Achieving Health for All* by federal Minister of Health and Welfare Jake Epp. The conference developed the Ottawa Charter for Health Promotion, which stated that "the fundamental conditions and resources for health are peace, shelter, education, food, income, a stable eco-system, sustainable resources, social justice, and equity. Improvement in health requires a secure foundation in these basic prerequisites" (Ottawa Charter for Health Promotion n.d.).

In June 1988 the federal government agreed to fund a national office to promote and coordinate healthy communities across Canada.[23] By mid-September the national office existed and, through publication of newsletters and direct contacts, it began to coordinate and support individual communities undertaking Healthy Communities projects. The criteria for local participation are as follows: a council resolution of political commitment to a broad public policy approach to health, a commitment to an interdepartmental and intersectoral strategy, a commitment to full community participation in the project, a commitment to sharing information derived from the project with other participating municipalities and a commitment to undertaking an evaluation process for local projects (Canadian Healthy Communities Project, Newsletter 1989, 2). The coordinator refers to the Healthy Communities project as being fundamentally a "municipal management" project.[24] Although it includes smaller communities, it has certainly involved the major Canadian urban

---

[23]Press release, June 2, 1988. The federal government contributed $650,345. In May 1991 it announced that its contribution was ending because of financial pressures. It is not clear what this will mean to ongoing activities, but certainly the federal presence will not continue.

[24]Interview with Susan Berlin.

centres.[25] At the time of the announcement of federal financing, the 16 municipalities already active included all the largest cities.[26]

Federal policy in this area is to finance activity and not to act directly. This is in keeping with the program's objective, which is to increase the capacity of communities to act through their municipal governments in a way that brings in a wide variety of actors and areas of activity. However, it does mean that the program does not directly involve the federal government in urban policymaking as such. It may increase the sensitivity of the federal government, particularly the Department of Health and Welfare, to the issues involved in urban policy, but it does not oblige the federal government to make policy. Indeed, federal cost-cutting measures brought an end to federal funding in 1991, and any continuation of a federal role in the Healthy Communities project seems unlikely.

URBAN SECURITY

The federal government's Urban Security initiatives are similar to the Healthy Communities initiatives in that they involve the recognition of the community context and therefore the recognition of municipalities as legitimate actors.[27] They are also similar in that they argue that only broadly based action touching a wide variety of socio-economic factors can solve the problem in question (in this case, crime, in the case of Healthy Communities, health). Indeed, the list of factors "conducive to

---

[25]The European counterpart is called the Healthy Cities project whereas "Healthy Communities" was chosen here to allow for the participation of smaller centres and also, undoubtedly, with an eye to provincial susceptibilities.

[26]The 16 were Dartmouth, Quebec City, Montreal, Sherbrooke, Rouyn-Noranda, North York, Windsor, Ottawa, Toronto, Winnipeg, Regina, Saskatoon, Calgary, Edmonton, Vancouver, and Victoria. The list undoubtedly reflects the importance of the municipal public service in developing these projects.

[27]Information for this section comes from an interview with Lorraine Touchette, Policy Analyst, Policy Development Section, Department of Justice, and from the following documents: Canadian Council on Social Development and Canadian Criminal Justice Association 1987; Canadian Council on Children and Youth 1989; the draft resolution to be presented to the 8th United Nations Congress on the Prevention of Crime and the Treatment of Offenders, and the Report from the European and North American Conference on Urban Safety and Crime Prevention.

crime" is as broad as is the Ottawa Charter for Health Promotion (Justice Canada n.d.).

(a) poverty, unemployment, the lack of decent housing at reasonable cost, and unsuitable education systems;

(b) the increasing number of citizens who have no prospect of social integration, coupled with a worsening of social inequalities;

(c) loosening of social and family ties, accompanied by parental upbringing that is frequently made more difficult by living conditions;

(d) the difficult conditions under which people emigrate to towns or other countries;

(e) the destruction of original cultural identities, together with racism and discrimination, which may lead to disadvantages in the social, health, and employment spheres;

(f) changes in the urban environment that promote crime by creating residential areas deprived of neighbourhood facilities;

(g) the difficulties for individuals in modern society to become properly integrated in their communities, families, or schools and to identify with a culture;

(h) drug addiction, whose spread is promoted by factors referred to above;

(i) the increase in organized criminal activities, particularly drug trafficking and the receiving of stolen goods, the success of which require assistance from within the community.

What is important to underline is not the length of the list but the fact that the solution is not seen to be the exclusive domain of the professional experts, the police, or health professionals, but rather the organized participation of the full range of community interests. "We must go beyond a response by our criminal justice system—police, courts, and corrections—if we are to prevent crime in our cities" (European and North American Conference on Urban Safety and Crime Prevention 1990, 4).

This activity began during Robert Kaplan's term as federal solicitor-general. Kaplan was a firm believer in a broad thrust to crime prevention, including but going beyond the police, and he encouraged officials to be active. Among other activities, the solicitor-general's department funded a workshop in 1987 on Crime Prevention through Social Development, cosponsored by the Canadian Council on Social Development and the Canadian Criminal Justice Association. The resulting publication made the argument for "a more comprehensive approach" to crime prevention.

Although not often recognized as "crime prevention" programs, current research suggests that targeted social programs addressing problems of poverty, unemployment, family dysfunction, alcohol abuse and inadequate housing have the potential to reduce crime (Canadian Council on Social Development and Canadian Criminal Justice Association 1987, 1).

Responsibility for this approach was transferred to the Department of Justice in a decision announced in March 1987 clarifying the areas of responsibility of justice and the solicitor general.[28] A number of recent and current activities illustrate the interest of the department of Justice in this area. The department gave substantial funding to an October 1989 European and North-American Conference on Urban Safety and Crime Prevention. It also negotiated the involvement of other federal departments in the conference, which was cosponsored by the Federation of Canadian Municipalities (FCM), the Forum of Local and Regional Authorities of Europe for Urban Security, and the United States Conference of Mayors. The conference led to the drawing up of the draft resolution for presentation to the U.N. Justice has also funded research on a number of municipal initiatives in crime prevention. It is currently examining a policy proposal for a crime prevention program and, together with eight other federal departments and agencies, is considering mechanisms for the coordination of federal policy in the area of crime prevention.[29] Different possibilities are being discussed, such as the establishment of a National Crime Prevention Council or a system of agreements between departments. Again it is too soon to talk of results or even of specific programs, but clearly the Department of Justice is

---

[28]Press release, March 1987. This transfer was also a result of the Nielson Task Force, which highlighted the fact that both departments were actively involved in criminal justice policy. The ensuing fight was won by the minister of justice.

[29]The units involved are Department of Justice; Department of the Solicitor-General; Department of the Secretary of State of Canada; Canada Mortgage and Housing Corporation; Department of National Health and Welfare; Office of the Coordinator, Status of Women; Department of Indian Affairs and Northern Development; Department of Employment and Immigration; Royal Canadian Mounted Police; Department of National Defence; Department of External Affairs.

increasingly interested in working with municipalities to establish community-based anticrime activities.

INTERNATIONAL LINKS

The last set of government programs to be looked at are those relating to the international level. This has been an area where the FCM has developed considerable activity. The FCM has been funded by CIDA to set up an international office to pursue a variety of programs: the municipal professional exchange program, the Chinese Open Cities project, Africa 2000: the Municipal Response, and the Latin American Training Project (Federation of Canadian Municipalities 1990, 31-32. See also Smith and Cohn, this volume). These projects operate within the framework of FCM interest and activity in municipal twinning and the encouragement of municipal trade missions. That interest relates to the federal government's recognition of the importance of cities in international development and of municipal expertise in areas relating to the provision of urban services and the establishment of urban growth and development strategies.

THE PLACE OF URBAN ISSUES ON THE
FEDERAL POLICY AGENDA

Rather than trying immediately to analyze the significance of federal activities, we will look at the question of urban influence from the top down. What major policy initiatives are currently highest on the agenda and to what extent are urban factors part of these initiatives? The two obvious examples in 1991 were, first, environmental policy as expressed in the federal Green Plan (Government of Canada 1990) and, second, the constitutional debate. What do we find?

In the case of environmental policy and the Green Plan proposals, urban influence is minimal. Urban interests or an urban focus were almost entirely lacking from both the first and the final versions of the Green Plan. There was little or no recognition of the importance of an urban context for environmental policies and programs. Despite active lobbying, those promoting urban interests do not appear to have been successful in getting the document modified to better reflect urban reality.[30] For the moment, therefore, taking the Green Plan document as a reflection of the federal policy agenda for the environment, urban concerns are nowhere. It is also clear that environmental concerns are very important issues on the policy agenda at the present time. Policy actors are all concerned to relate their interests to environmental considerations. To the extent that urban interests are not able to do this, their marginal status in terms of the federal policy agenda is confirmed.

The second area is that of the constitution, and here again urban influence is almost, if not completely, excluded. The constitutional debate is still underway, and it is not yet possible to foresee its outcome for urban questions. At the present time, proposals on the table would seem to indicate that greater decentralization to provincial governments in the area of social housing is likely. This would not mean the end of CHMC, which would continue its market housing programs and its research activities, but it would certainly not suggest an expanded role. Indeed, it seems possible at the present time that the outcome of the constitutional debate will lead to a reduced federal interest in urban questions. The few public calls for a role for Canadian municipalities in the constitutional debate tended to be ignored or, worse, treated as amusing. The FCM has begun to articulate a constitutional position for municipal government by setting up a task force on this question and by approving a resolution arguing for a municipal role in the constitutional debate.

> WHEREAS Canada's municipalities have become the centre stage of a modern and interdependent industrialized society with all the accompanying social, material, cultural and environmental challenges;
>
> WHEREAS federal, provincial and territorial orders of government are shifting an ever greater burden from their jurisdiction onto the shoulders of municipalities at a time when municipalities themselves are faced with the staggering problems of renewing urban infrastructure and meeting a host of environmental and social challenges;
>
> WHEREAS the ability of municipalities to deal with these challenges requires a federal, provincial, territorial and municipal agreement on a new distribution of powers and fiscal resources;

---

[30]It is clear from interviews that this point has been made by a number of sources to Department of the Environment officials responsible for drawing up the Green Plan. No indications were given as to the response of those officials.

WHEREAS the federal government, in its Speech from the Throne, committed itself to assessing the various proposals for constitutional reform and submitting to the people of Canada, constitutional proposals for the renewal of the federation;

BE IT RESOLVED that the Federation of Canadian Munici- palities, as the national voice of local government, be invited by the federal, provincial and territorial governments to participate in this process with a view to obtaining the recognition of municipal government in the constitutional framework of the country;

BE IT FURTHER RESOLVED that the Federation of Canadian Municipalities work with its provincial/territorial affiliates to arrive at a common position on the constitutional question (Federation of Canadian Municipalities 1990).

It is interesting to see this renewed FCM concern for the place of municipal government in the constitutional debate. Certainly, up to the present, urban and/or municipal interests have not been seen as having a role to play in constitutional negotiations. This certainly is the "top" political issue in Canada at the present time, and urban interests are very far from the central definition of the issue.

CONCLUSION

Looking at environmental and constitutional policy thus tempers our evaluation of the urban-related activities of the federal government. There are a number of relatively new activities, or new signs of potential activity, that indicate a renewed interest in urban centres as a focus of and as actors in federal policies. At the same time when we step beyond these activities and look at the overall federal policy agenda and its formulation, urban issues are invisible, if not totally nonexistent.

How do we reconcile the signs of federal activity with the lack of urban impact on the major political issues of the day? More specifically, to what extent do the perspectives outlined at the beginning of the chapter help us to understand the current situation in regard to urban-related activities of the federal government?

Gurr and King's (1987) analysis of the importance of the pursuit of programmatic goals on the part of officials is illuminating in this regard. Several of the activities we described can be understood in this light. Kaplan's interest in crime prevention, the Bureau of Real Property Management, the water pricing policy—all of these are at least in part related to officials, elected and appointed, pursuing program goals that were not directly urban but impacted indirectly on urban matters. Indeed, the programmatic goals of the Nielson Task Force operation were also important in this regard, because raising questions about the efficiency of government action tended to lead to efforts to focus activity. In some cases this led to an interest in urban areas.

In addition, the influence of demographic changes can also be used to understand the activity we observed. The 1980s saw urbanization once more on the increase, whereas in the 1970s urban growth was much less strong and, in some places, was clearly less than overall population growth (Simmons and Bourne 1989). We could understand from this that the federal reaction was clearly less vigourous than in the fast growth period of the 1960s but more active than in the 1970s. As Gelfand (1980) argues, this difference does not explain the precise way in which institutions and political forces channel or structure the demographic impact, but it does suggest a way of explaining patterns, or waves, of activity.

Finally, our material suggests the usefulness of looking at this question in terms of the debate over the role of the state. The present period has been one where the private sector has been in ascendancy and where all states are talking about fiscal constraints, budget cuts, etc. From the point of view of government it is a period neither of expansion nor of optimism. Society is not at all certain that government decision making can be comprehensive or rational. In part this is owing to a recognition of the importance of the role of many other social actors—interest groups, professional groups, the population, etc.—but also because the possibility of significant structural reform within government seems unlikely. The federal government's preoccupation with deficit reduction and its desire to limit its responsibilities make it more interested in formulating a discourse of partnership with other social actors. Cutting down on the size of the federal government is the other side of the recognition of the capacity of communities. But handing over responsibilities to other actors is always a difficult process, and the federal government is not at all convinced of the capacity of municipal governments. On the other hand the reasons for doing so are clear: the federal government's budget reduction priorities plus its ideological predisposition to reduce the size of government. For this reason decentralization is the order of the day, or at least less suspect than it was previously. It may well be that an increasing number of federal policies will be thinking of an urban context and, even more specifically, will be looking for participation from municipal authorities. It is not urban policy in the sense of a direct federal influence over the direction of urban development, but it is urban-related in the sense of recognizing the legitimacy of urban actors. Canadian intergovernmental relations in an age of restraint may offer certain opportunities for the large cities to become more important participants in federal policymaking.

REFERENCES

Anderson, George D. 1989. *Housing Policy in Canada.* Ottawa: Canada Mortgage and Housing Corporation, Lectures Series, No. 3.

Andrew, Caroline. 1988. "La politique urbaine: ruptures et constantes." In *L'Ere des libraux,* ed. Yves Bélanger and Dorval Brunelle, Sillery: Presses de l'Université de Québec, 343-56.

Artibise, Alan F. J., and Matthew J. Kiernan. 1989. *Canadian Regional Development: The Urban Dimension.* Ottawa: Economic Council of Canada, Local Development Paper No. 12.

Ashford, Douglas E. 1986. *The Emergence of the Welfare States.* Oxford: Basil Blackwell.

Aucoin, Peter. 1986. "Organizational Change in the Machinery of Canadian Government: From Rational Management to Brokerage Politics." *Canadian Journal of Political Science* 19 (March): 3-28.

Bennett, Robert J. 1990. *Decentralization, Local Governments, and Markets: Towards a Post-Welfare Agenda.* Oxford: Clarendon Press.

Canada Mortgage and Housing Corporation. 1989. *Annual Report.* Ottawa: CMHC.

_____. 1990a. *Annual Report.* Ottawa: CMHC.

_____. 1990b. *CMHC Activities Which Address Environmental Concerns.* Ottawa: CMHC.

_____. 1990c. *Initiatives Relating to Housing Choices for Older Canadians.* Ottawa: CMHC.

_____. 1990d. *Policy and Research Initiatives.* Ottawa: CMHC.

_____. 1990e. *Strategic Plan 1991-1995.* Ottawa: CMHC.

_____. n.d. *Centre for Future Studies in Housing and Living Environments.* Ottawa: CMHC.

Canadian Council on Children and Youth. 1989. *Safer Tomorrows Begin Today.* Ottawa: CCCY.

Canadian Council on Social Development and Canadian Criminal Justice Association. 1987. *Crime Prevention Through Social Development.* Ottawa: CCSD.

Canadian Housing and Research Association. 1990. *Access to Housing.* Ottawa: CMHC.

Canadian Healthy Communities Project. n.d. *Information Kit.* Ottawa: CHCP.

_____. Various. *Newsletters.* Ottawa: CHCP.

Canadian Waterfront Resource Centre. n.d. *Bibliography.* Toronto: The Royal Commission on the Future of the Toronto Waterfront

_____. Various. *Newsletter.* Toronto: The Royal Commission on the Future of the Toronto Waterfront.

Champion, A. G. 1989. *Counterurbanization: The Changing Pace and Nature of Population Deconcentration.* London: Edward Arnold.

Environment Canada. 1987. *Federal Water Policy.* Ottawa: Environment Canada.

European and North American Conference on Urban Safety and Crime Prevention. 1990. *Report.*

Federation of Canadian Municipalities. n.d. *International Program.* Ottawa: FCM.

_____. n.d. *Municipal Economic Development Program.* Ottawa: FCM.

_____. n.d. *Municipal Race Relations Program.* Ottawa: FCM.

_____. 1989-1990. *Press Releases.* Ottawa: FCM.

_____. 1990. *Towards Sustainable Communities.* Ottawa: FCM.

Feldman, Elliot J., and Jerome Milch. 1981. "Coordination or Control? The Life and Death of the Ministry of State for Urban Affairs." In *Politics and Government of Urban Canada, Selected Readings*, 4th ed., ed. Lionel D. Feldman, Toronto: Methuen, 246-64. .

Gelfand, Marc I. 1980. "How Cities arrived on the National Agenda in the United States." In *Financing Urban Government in the Welfare State*, ed. Douglas E. Ashford, London: Croom Helm, 28-49.

Gertler, Len. 1979. "The Challenge of Public Policy Research." *Canadian Journal of Regional Science* 2 (Spring): 77-89.

_____. 1982. "Introduction: Public Policy—Urban and Regional Issues." *Canadian Journal of Regional Science* 5 (Spring): 1-4.

Graham, Katherine. 1985. *How Ottawa Spends, 1989-90: The Buck Stops Where?* Ottawa: Carleton University Press.

_____. 1991. *How Ottawa Spends, 1990-91: Tracking the Second Agenda.* Ottawa: Carleton University Press.

Government of Canada. 1990. *Canada's Green Plan.* Ottawa, Supply and Services Canada.

Gurr, Ted Robert, and Desmond S. King. 1987. *The State and the City.* Chicago: The University of Chicago Press.

Health and Welfare Canada. 1990. n.d. *Achieving Health for All.* Ottawa: Health and Welfare Canada.

Jones, Allen. 1991. "Is There Light Down the Tunnel?" *Civic Public Work* 43 (November/December): 9.

Justice Canada. n.d. *Draft resolution to be presented to the 8th United Nations Congress on the Prevention of Crime and the Treatment of Offenders.*

Leo, Christopher, and Robert Fenton. 1990. "Mediated Enforcement and the Evolution of the State: Canadian City Centre Development." *International Journal of Urban and Regional Research* 14 (2): 185-206.

Lithwick, N. H. 1970. *Urban Canada: Problems and Prospects.* Ottawa: CMHC.

Maslove, Allan M. 1984. *How Ottawa Spends, 1984: The New Agenda.* Toronto: Methuen.

Oberlander, Peter H., and Arthur L. Fallick. 1987. *Ministry of State for Urban Affairs: A Courageous Experiment in Public Administration.* Vancouver: The Centre for Human Settlements, University of British Columbia.

Ottawa Charter for Health Promotion, n.d.

Pearce, P. H., E. Bertrand, and J. W. MacLaren. 1985. *Currents of Change: Final Report of the Inquiry on Federal Water Policy.* Ottawa: Environment Canada.

Portland, R. L. 1985. *Implications of Federal Water Policy in Ontario.* Speech.

Royal Commission on the Future of the Toronto Waterfront. 1989a. *Access and Movement.* Toronto: The Commission, Report of Working Group 3.

_____. 1989b. *Housing and Neighbourhoods.* Toronto: The Commission, Report of Working Group 2.

_____. 1989c. *Interim Report.* Toronto: The Commission.

_____. 1989d. *Jobs, Opportunities and Economic Growth.* Toronto: The Commission, Report of Working Group 5.

_____. 1989e. *Parks, Pleasures and Public Amenities.* Toronto: The Commission, Report of Working Group 4.

_____. 1990a. *A Green Strategy for the Greater Toronto Water-front.* Toronto: The Commission, Report of Working Group 8.

_____. 1990b. *Watershed: Second Interim Report.* Toronto: The Commission.

Royal Commission on National Passenger Transportation. n.d. *Mandate.* Ottawa: Commission.

Simmons, J. W., and L. S. Bourne. 1989. *Urban Growth Trends in Canada, 1981-86: A New Geography of Change.* Toronto: University of Toronto, Centre for Urban and Community Studies.

Spurr, Peter. 1988. "The Changing Role of Canada Mortgage and Housing Corporation in Urban Affairs." Conference presentation.

Tate, D. M. 1989. *Municipal Water Rates in Canada: Current Practices and Prices*. Ottawa: Environment Canada.

Treasury Board of Canada. 1988. *Challenge 88: The State of Federal Real Property Reforms*. Ottawa: Bureau of Real Property Management.

_____. 1989. *Meeting the Challenge: Innovative Practices of the Federal Real Property Community*. Ottawa: Bureau of Real Property Management.

Wilson, M. T. 1989. *Retreat from Governance*. Hull: Voyageur Publishing.

Chapter 14

Urban Sprawl in the Montreal Area— Policies and Trends

François Charbonneau
Pierre Hamel
Michel Barcelo
University of Montreal

Ever since the disappearance of the illusion of prosperity, nourished by the huge projects so dear to the administration of Mayor Jean Drapeau during the 1960s and 1970s, the Montreal urban area has been faced with a series of socio-economic difficulties stemming primarily from the shrinking of its economic space. In addition to calling into question the strategies of the principal local actors, these difficulties have raised some embarrassing questions about urban planning and development. Can the urban area continue to expand with impunity with the resulting increased social costs related to sprawl and with deteriorating or poorly performing infrastructures that the central city has fewer and fewer resources to maintain? What can be done by the Quebec government and the local authorities? Have the measures put forward by the provincial government since 1978, when it established a preferable or preferential "option" for the Montreal area, been adequate, and have they been effective in reversing a trend that went far beyond the *laissez-faire* attitude tradition-ally taken by Quebec municipalities in the matter of urban planning? What has, in fact, been the impact of these measures and of this policy?

In their work on New York, Michael N. Danielson and Jameson W. Doig (1982) clearly showed the complexity of the interaction between public authorities and private action groups in the development of an urban area and its territorial configuration. According to these writers, it is false to think that public policies have little effect on the form or structure of urban space. If private actors, particularly real estate promoters and investors in the industrial and service sectors, play a significant role in the form and evolution of the urban complex, they intervene within a context they do not fully control and of which public policies and investment often seem to be the determining factors. In the case of Montreal, housing policies along with investment in the transportation infrastructure have established conditions favourable to urban sprawl. Added to these have been certain local initiatives in land use and development as well as a conciliatory attitude on the part of the Quebec government.

Since 1978, by putting forward a constrictive policy aimed at defeating the process of sprawl, the Quebec government has been engaged in a process that breaks with its previous choices, at least to all outward appearances. The difficulty with making such a perspective operational depends on several factors, not the least of which is the resistance of local authorities to a decision imposed on them by the provincial level.

Ultimately, the absence of a regional government[1] could be considered here as a significant institutional factor. In fact, this absence is the reflection of an explosive situation clearly expressed by the imposition of local strategies whose future reconciliation will require a political choice at the provincial level.

The following text is made up of five sections. First, we outline schematically the principal structural tendencies that have marked the evolution of the Montreal urban area. Second, we deal with the contents of government policy aimed at countering urban sprawl by situating it in its context. Then, we consider both how this policy was implemented and what its real impact has been on the form of the urban area's development between 1981 and 1986. Finally, we define several possible interpretations in order to clarify public choices regarding the problem of urban sprawl for the entire Montreal urban area.

---

[1] The Communauté Urbaine de Montréal cannot be considered a true regional government. First, this structure does not include the entire urban region. Second, representatives who act at this level have not been elected at this level. They have been elected on a municipal basis. The CUM council is made up of suburban mayors and the mayor and councillors of the city of Montreal.

STRUCTURAL TENDENCIES AND THE FORM OF THE MONTREAL URBAN AREA: THE REGIONAL SETTING

Tourists strolling for the first time through the streets of downtown Montreal usually tell us they have the strange impression that a recent catastrophe has occurred. Within the city centre, empty lots and barricaded houses cut unpleasantly across the fabric of the built-up sector as if urban development here were destined to be a "mission impossible." This situation accounts for the malaise experienced by Montrealers with regard to their city for the last 15 years: a feeling of helplessness expressed as a fatalism that eludes those primarily responsible. Paired with the destructuration of its traditional industrial fabric and with the increased impoverishment of a good part of its population, this city, formerly the engine of the Quebec economy, has been passing through a very difficult period in its history, especially since the middle of the 1970s.

In several respects, what is happening to Montreal is not very different from what can be observed in several other large urban areas in North America where the effects of the aging of their industrial structures that has accompanied postwar expansion and the difficulties of reconversion have been made worse by the exchanges and competition now taking place on an international scale. In this context, the centres of large cities are coping with problems of social integration and economic revitalisation, as well as challenges related to urban infrastructure, which, from several points of view, closely resemble those that planners had to cope with at the beginning of the century.

The "Centre—Periphery" dichotomy, to borrow an expression from Pierre George (1989), no longer has quite the same meaning it had at the beginning of the 20th century, however, even if it can be said that our sense of centrality today is not so different from the one that existed in earlier years. In the North American tradition, the modern conception of urban centrality dates back to the beginning of the 19th century, when the phenomenon of the suburb made its appearance. Observers of the time described suburbanisation as a multidimensional process, taking place within American culture. The fact remains, however, that it was perceived pragmatically in relation to the travel generated by the new configuration of urban space: "a process involving the systematic growth of fringe areas at a pace more rapid than that of core cities, (and) as a lifestyle involving a daily commute to jobs in the center" (Jackson 1985, 13).

Recent tendencies—cultural, socio-economic, and socio-spatial—have managed to change the nature and intensity of the pressures exerted on the centre. First, the suburbs are no longer exclusively inhabited by the middle classes. Second, the configuration of the suburban landscape is completely different from what it was before: for example, at this time we can observe great heterogeneity of social composition and the economic functions attached to it. As underlined by Mark Baldassare (1986), if it is true that certain suburban cities continue to play a role as satellites of the central city, it is also true that an increasing number of suburban cities plays a multifunctional role as "all purpose communities with a mix of residential, commercial, and industrial functions" (Baldassare 1986, 44). Furthermore, the social meaning of the suburb has changed. As spaces capable of welcoming economic vitality, they have become true reflections of the city: "In thirty years, the suburb has changed meaning. From rejected space, waste space, it is acceding to a status of full-blown urbanity" (Burgel 1986, 9).

The urban space of the Montreal area has undergone transformations similar to those observed in the majority of large cities of the western world. In 1986, the Montreal metropolitan region had a population of 2.9 million inhabitants. A little over a million of them lived within the geographic perimeter of the city of Montreal. The others were found either in the 28 other municipalities located on the island of Montreal (700,000 inhabitants), which along with the city of Montreal participate in a metropolitan politico-administrative structure (the Montreal Urban Community) that is responsible for certain intermunicipal services, or in the 72 municipalities that make up the northern and southern suburban rings of the urban area (1.2 million inhabitants).

The present configuration of the metropolitan region can be explained as much by structural factors that spill over from the local scene as by the singular process of Montreal urbanisation, to which must be added the relationship of the centre to the periphery and the specific form taken by suburban expansion. Among the factors that explain this expansion, researchers usually speak first of the transportation system. Montreal's first residential suburbs date back to the end of the nineteenth century (1892). They were created through the existence of electric streetcars. Up to the end of the Second World War, suburban development conformed to a multifunctional model of urban land use. Suburban growth closely copied the central city by extending or reproducing the initial hub (Dansereau and Foggin 1982). Since the 1950s, however, the proliferation of the automobile has had a direct impact on urban sprawl, encouraging residential construction in a periphery farther and farther from the centre.

As soon as that process began, the urban form of the Montreal area would never be the same as it was. Its density would become lower, its economic activity would disperse over more and more territory, and land use would take on a more and more monofunctional form. As we are reminded by Jean-Pierre Collin (1986), the idea of a mixture of industrial, commercial, institutional, and residential activities inside each urban neighbourhood, which was the case previously, would no longer prevail. Of course, these transformations did not result from a simple redefinition of the urban landscape. A series of socio-economic changes must be emphasized, including rapid industrial expansion during the war, the development of mass consumption, and the implementation of Keynesian policies that facilitated access to personal credit.

Thus, after the war, Montreal suburbs grew and developed at an impressive rate.[2] In 1941, the population in the Montreal region lived within a radius of 6 kilometres. Twenty years later, the radius had more than doubled. A similar tendency is reflected in the proportion of the population in the central city in relation to the overall population of the metropolitan region: in 1941, 45 percent of the population still lived in the central city, while in 1961, only 22 percent still lived there (Collin 1986).

Several factors can be identified to explain these changes. Three in particular are worthy of attention.

First, improvements in the transportation system were crucial, even though national and urban highway construction programs encouraging sprawl were not implemented before the 1960s. During the 1960s and 1970s, public authorities planned and implemented a very extensive freeway system: between 1958 and 1976, 250 miles of freeway were constructed. Divay and Gaudreau speak of a "highway network boom" (1982, 186). Such interventions did not merely generate an increase in travelling time from place of residence to place of work, they also helped to increase the rate of relocation of manufacturing companies to the periphery.

The second factor is related to government intervention in the housing market. Central Mortgage and Housing Corporation (now Canada Mortgage and Housing Corporation) was created in 1946. "Its objective

---

[2]Nevertheless, the city population continued to increase over that period. In 1956, 1,109,439 people lived in the city of Montreal while 1,191,062 lived there in 1961. The population continued to grow until 1971, after which it decreased, falling to 1,080,540 by 1976.

was to support the provision by the private sector of sufficient and adequate housing to Canadians and to maintain the level of employment in the construction industry" (Linteau 1987, 263). It is important to remember that in its early years the corporation was more preoccupied with the demands of the construction industry than with the social needs of the populace in the matter of housing.[3] That is why it addressed a majority of its programs to the middle classes by facilitating access to mortgage loans. It was also the case that the maximum price allowing a household to be eligible for accession to ownership was clearly less than the average price of new houses on the island of Montreal. Consequently, upwardly mobile young couples were forced to choose the outlying areas. Also, the impact of CMHC programs was equally significant with regard to the shape of suburban cities, inasmuch as construction companies had to respect the standards of construction established by the corporation in order to qualify for government aid. In addition, both the federal and Quebec governments directly encouraged sprawl by absorbing a large part of the costs inherent in dispersed and sporadic urbanisation that took the form of new residential developments, often along freeways.

The last factor to explain urban sprawl involves the process of de-industrialisation. As in the case of many other North American metropolitan regions, from the beginning of the 1960s Montreal experienced a loss of jobs in the manufacturing sectors. Between 1971 and 1980, the volume of employment in this sector decreased by 25 percent. Two reasons are given by Lamonde and Polèse, one being increased international competition and the other the relocation of manufacturing activities to the suburbs (Lamonde and Polèse 1985). Similar trends, although in smaller proportions, were also observed in the service sector: while the rate of employment in the city proper was 69.1 percent in 1971, it was only 55.2 percent in 1981.

These various factors help to explain a complex process whose most visible aspects are manifested directly in the land-use pattern and the

---

[3]Even though CMHC enacted its public housing program in 1949, the province of Quebec did not get its first social housing (the Habitations Jeanne-Mance in Montreal) until the end of the 1950s. The 1964 NHA amendments supporting construction of low-cost housing and cooperatives did not become effective in Quebec before the 1970s, partly because there was only limited and occasional support for social housing within the Drapeau administration.

spatial form of the urban area. They all provide reasons for urban sprawl, even if they aren't all taken from the same source.

By the end of the 1970s, the process had become widely recognized. From then on, it can be described by noting the dispersion of new residential centres, principally due to a road system in which the regional freeways are scarcely distinguishable from the local highways (numerous points of contact) while the true urban arteries, deficient in nature, do not allow a sufficient flow of traffic. In this respect, we propose the hypothesis that municipal divisions have discouraged the creation of the true urban arteries needed to encourage more integrated urban development.

To put it briefly, between 1971 and 1981 the dynamics of urban sprawl in the Montreal region had the following characteristics:

• between 1971 and 1976, the South Shore alone monopolised 63 percent of the population growth of the southern ring, while its growth represented 48 percent between 1976 and 1981 (Fauteux 1983);

• between 1971 and 1981, the outlying suburban municipalities received nearly 62 percent of the new metropolitan population (Fauteux, 1983), increasing considerably travel time in both directions with, the resulting obstruction of bridges and freeways and increased pressure for the construction of new infrastructure;

• in a decade, the metropolitan area (as defined by Statistics Canada) enlarged extensively while urban density (population per urbanised hectare) and residential density (population per residential hectare) continued to decrease (Dansereau 1982);

• up to 1986, the relative weights of the city of Montreal and Montreal Island compared to the metropolitan region continued to decrease; this had the effect of increasing the demand for new facilities throughout the territory (dispersal), thereby increasing the costs of urbanisation and accentuating the pressures on white zones (land not subject to the Agricultural Land Preservation Act[4]) and on farmland;

---

[4]This law, approved by the Quebec government in December 1978, pursues the following objectives: to protect agricultural land from industrial, commercial, and housing developments, to improve the agricultural autonomy of Quebec province, to favour the development of agriculture by reducing external constraints on its activities. Additionally, this law implied the creation of a special commission (la Commission de protection du territoire agricole du Québec), which is in charge of law enforcement and decides on zoning amendments.

• judging by the rates of unemployment and the downward trend in the average household income throughout the central core, central households were becoming poorer all the time (Conseil des affaires sociales et de la famille 1989).

Although of variable intensity, sprawl continued to progress up to the beginning of the 1980s and even beyond.

THE DEVELOPMENT OPTION FOR THE METROPOLITAN MONTREAL REGION

In the 1960s the political class showed little unease about the negative effects of urban sprawl. However, as the Montreal region experienced the repercussions of the aging of its industrial structure, the difficulties of reconversion, and a *laissez-faire* attitude harmful to its growth, this question suddenly became a subject of attention and political concern. We do not propose to analyse the collective amnesia during the 1960s and 1970s about urban sprawl, even though some elements of the *laissez-faire* attitude are concealed therein. What we are more interested in for the moment is to grasp the effective impacts of this concern and the policy it produced on urban planning and development. Before that, however, it is necessary to introduce the contents of the proposal put forth by the Quebec government at the end of the 1970s by locating it very briefly in its political context.

Political attention to the urban planning of Montreal by the government of Quebec constitutes an innovation inasmuch as that level of government traditionally did not dare—both for technico-administrative reasons (insufficient knowledge of the problems of urban Montreal) and for political reasons (fear of alienating the local authorities)—to intervene in urban planning in Montreal, especially since urban planning had always been treated as a local responsibility. At the end of the 1970s, factors encouraging urban sprawl were relatively unchanged. However, the economic and political situation was very different from what it had been during the period of postwar expansion and the feverish years of the Quiet Revolution.[5] Prospects for growth seemed to be a thing of the past

---

[5]The Quiet Revolution coincides with social and institutional transformations that took place in Quebec province from the beginning of the 1960s until 1967. This period was characterized by the end of a traditionalist era dominated for two decades by Maurice Duplessis and his conservative "Union Nationale" party and the emergence of a modernizing process in all aspects of economic and social

while the "boosterism" characteristic of the administration of Mayor Drapeau's Civic Party, which had succeeded in hiding for a time the serious structural difficulties facing the Montreal urban area, could no longer be used as an expedient (Léveillée and Léonard 1988). In this context, not only were the local authorities forced to formulate some strategies that were likely to supplant traditional *laissez-faire*, but the Quebec and federal levels of government were also challenged.

The results of the economic and urban difficulties faced by the Montreal urban area increased in number (OPDQ 1977; MAM 1977), and the consensus with regard to the definition of the problem seemed relatively far advanced, even if the priorities were not of course the same for all action groups. Moreover, it had to be admitted that the Montreal Urban Community, created at the end of the 1960s, had not managed to provide a rationale for development of the island of Montreal. Finally, the government of Quebec found itself obliged to better coordinate its activities in the area, taking into account the budget cuts it had to make and also some of the priorities in its mandate, such as the protection of farmland threatened by land speculation and uncontrolled urbanisation and the implementation of planning and development reform for the territory as a whole.

In this context the Parti Québecois government decided to move forward with a project to coordinate government action throughout the territory of Montreal, in the form of a "Preferred development option for the region of Montreal." The Minister of State for Development presented this development option to the mayors of the Montreal region in April 1978. It was reiterated by the minister responsible for regional planning and development. Two aspects are at the heart of the "Option"; urban sprawl and the quality of life in urban surroundings. Criticising the negative repercussions of urban sprawl from the point of view of public investments, the authors of the Option were worried at the outset by the impact of "centrifugal urbanisation" on the "gradual depopulation of the centre of the urban area." In the same vein, they spoke of the threat

---

life. This process was conducted by the Liberal Party under the leadership of Jean Lesage, which succeeded in building a welfare state and defining guidelines for intervention in the economy, at the same time energizing the Quebec nationalist movement. The Quiet Revolution was also characterized by a strong consensus among political leaders, the business community, and the labour movement on the need to modernize Quebec institutions in order to cope with twentieth century challenges.

hanging over farmland from suburban expansion, in particular for farmland in the southern ring, but also for farmland on Île Jésus (Laval) and in the northern ring. Furthermore, they did not evaluate urban sprawl solely from the angle of wasted public resources but also from the point of view of social and regional equity.

The second aspect, improvement of the quality of life, goes hand in hand with consolidation of the urban fabric. Preventing urban sprawl by a moratorium on freeways and on the financing of municipal infrastructure in nonurbanised zones (steps that first accompanied the formulation of the government Option) seemed to be a negative approach that needed to be complemented by a more positive attitude. For that reason, it was proposed to pursue jointly the goals of consolidating the urban fabric and improving the quality of life in urban centres. However, the concept of quality of life is not clearly defined in the document containing the minister's notes for his meeting with the mayors. Mention is made of certain forms of spatial organisation that are more suitable than others for "bringing together individual aspirations and the satisfaction of collective needs" (Léonard 1978, 9). The quality of life is also associated with the possibility for households to choose among various types of housing and transportation. Finally, it is linked to a series of environmental problems.

Concretely speaking, the Option, was to engage the provincial government in several fields (housing, urban infrastructures, public transportation, greenbelt). Even though it is possible to identify a certain number of measures, regulations, or programs related to these fields and to the spirit of the Option, there has never been any overall coordination by the ministries concerned nor any very clear government strategy to this effect.

As already mentioned by other researchers (Divay and Gaudreau 1982), despite the will to provide the government and local groups with a rational framework for dialogue about their decisions and interventions in the Montreal region, the Option did not spontaneously receive support from all public actors, either within the government or within the municipal sphere. At the outset, municipalities outside the island of Montreal "saw a blow to their possibilities of expansion" (Divay and Gaudreau 1982, 193). Their reservations led the provincial government to provide some clarification. It stated that the consolidation sought by the Option, in addition to the Island, "included also the near suburbs such as the Ville de Laval and the riverside municipalities to the north and south" (Divay and Gaudreau 1982, 193). In other words, it was not a question of stopping the development of cities in the immediate suburbs but rather of concentrating development "inside the present urban perimeter" (Divay and Gaudreau 1982, 193).

The suburban towns were not alone in raising concerns and objections. Even within the government there was a clash of visions and viewpoints on sustaining the development of the Montreal region that did not match the project put forward by the Ministry of State for Development. This led the government, a few years later, to clarify the contents of its preferential Option for Montreal. Submitted by the minister responsible for regional planning and development, the new proposal repeated certain principles put forward in the 1978 planning process and provided some clarifications (Gendron 1984). First, it emphasized that even if a slowdown in growth had been apparent in the entire metropolis over the previous five years, the basic tendencies continued to exist: "The Island of Montréal has seen its relative weight decrease in the metropolitan area as a whole, especially in its demographic aspects. Metropolitan sprawl is continuing" (Gendron 1984, 20). This is what led the government to reconfirm the necessity of maintaining its options, which meant recalling the choices made previously. These choices have three basic sections that can be summarised as follows:

- Consolidate the urban fabric within the present built-up fully developed perimeter;
- Give priority to redeveloping the oldest built-up territories of Montreal's central area and the city centres of Longueuil and Laval.
- Pay special attention to improvement of the quality of life on the Island of Montreal (Gendron 1984, 80).

The document is a little more specific with regard to improving the quality of life than the government was in its first version of the Option. Recommended in particular is "the protection and development of green space," the struggle against various types of pollution, better accessibility to public services, housing that corresponds to social needs, etc. A certain number of specific projects are also associated with these larger objectives.

A more significant characteristic of the proposal, however, is the kind of problems within which the government tried to situate it. Two points of view indicate the problems and government strategy: on the one hand there was the crisis of legitimacy that the state was experiencing; on the other hand there was recourse to the local level as a means and strategy of social recomposition. For that reason, the second version of the Option insists that it was put forward first of all to streamline government expenditures in the Montreal region.

Ultimately, it must be understood that in renewing its Option, the government was less preoccupied from the outset with the reconversion, renewal and development of Montreal than with cleaning up and streamlining the management of its public funds. In this sense, it is clear that the Option is in no way a normative or coercive framework for other actors, especially for the municipalities. The Option is meant to be at most a guide whose primary goal is to better delimit the thrust of the government's actions:

if it responded to the challenges of planning (improvement of quality of life, better integration of economic activities with the urban fabric, etc.), this option did so especially to guide the actions of the ministries. There was never any question that the government would impose on the municipalities development plans or choices; it simply presented the orientation which, while contributing to the rationalisation of its own interventionist activities and giving grounds for its choices, allowed the munici- palities to reflect this orientation in their own ideas, adapting it as necessary according to their objectives (Gendron 1984, 10).

Basically, these clarifications did not contradict the tenor of the ideas put forth by Minister Leonard in 1978 when he defined the "Option" for the first time. They added a long range view and some details that were not present before. The whole question of the context of development and the stakes of economic reconversion of the Montreal metropolitan region must be considered, with the knowledge that these aspects are closely tied to the primary dimensions of development, including problems stemming from sprawl.

IMPLEMENTATION OF THE PREFERABLE OPTION

The Option, as described in the speeches of certain politicians or through ministerial guidelines issued to the municipalities, may be considered a preface to the design of a true urban development strategy for the Montreal region. In the space of a few years, however, public actors have learned to regard it only as a way of regulating government expenditure and as a statement of good intentions that was never going to result in coherent policies with regard to the objectives put forth.

Even worse, a few years after the government restated the Option, the new provincial Minister of Transport, in agreement with the mayors of the closest suburbs, was relentless, and the word is used advisedly, in trying to prove that the moratorium on bridges and freeways was no longer necessary. Quite the contrary; according to him, it was henceforth necessary to modernise the transportation structure in the region by providing several bypasses and a new bridge to open up the city centre of Montreal.

In this contentious context, we carried out a study for the city of Montreal (Barcelo, Charbonneau, and Hamel 1990) in which we evaluated the Option's significance for the direction of provincial intervention in the region. This work showed how the change of direction by the new minister had managed to hobble a strategy that had borne fruit.

Two dimensions must be considered in evaluating the outcome of a public policy. First is to ask if the government, in its budget priorities and the application of the laws and programs affecting the objectives of the policy in question, is respecting its commitments, and to what extent? Second, beyond looking for political and institutional coherence, is to try to determine the real impact of these interventions on the overall problems they are supposed to resolve.

In order to reply to these two questions, we chose to approach successively the positions adopted by the provincial government with regard to the municipalities and the Regional County Municipalities (RCMs), concerning their urban planning projects and their effective impact. Since the Option is, in the last analysis, less a policy in the real meaning of the term than the preamble to a strategy aimed at controlling the application of several laws and programs of intervention to urban development, we had to choose a field of intervention at the provincial level closely related to the goals pursued. Analysis of government guidelines regulating the development of urban planning in Montreal region municipalities appeared to us to be the best way to respond to the first level of questions. Second, we will formulate a summary assessment of the real impact of the Option on the direction taken by the development of the urban area as a whole.

THE PREFERABLE OPTION AND THE
REGIONAL COUNTY MUNICIPALITIES (RCMS)

In the Montreal census metropolitan area (CMA), there are 13 RCMs, including the Montreal Urban Community (MUC) and the Ville de Laval. The application of the act respecting land-use planning and development represented a major test for giving concrete form to the Option's objectives, since the RCMs were to prepare regional development plans reflecting the government's advice. The municipalities had to make government advice an integral part of the first phases of development of these plans. One thing was certain: the ministry responsible for applying the law could force the local authorities to respect the interpretation of its guidelines as they were formulated.

Documents transmitted to the RCMs by the government thus constitute an instrument for assessing the extent to which the government judged its Option as the basis of an urban development strategy for the whole region. A detailed comparison of the evolution of official directives received by the various RCMs in the Montreal region shows that government policy with regard to application of the Option's orientation had the following characteristics:

1. as a general rule, the regional municipalities that were more distant from Montreal received the least clear and least restrictive interpretations of the Option.

2. The most recent guidelines are less infused with the spirit of the Option. The truly coercive instruments of urban planning (we are thinking primarily of agricultural zoning and restrictions on provincial roads) have become, with the passage of time, less and less important to the government in its interpretations of the plans.

3. The MUC and Laval received the clearest and most specific government notices on the interpretation of the Option and its vision of urban sprawl. Policies having direct effects on the restriction of sprawl (agricultural zoning and the moratorium on bridges and freeways) are more detailed in the guidelines received by the MUC and by Laval than in the guidelines received by the distant municipalities. Nonetheless, it is in the territory of the latter that action to limit sprawl should have been most vigorous.

4. Guidelines relative to the Option's objectives for the consolidation and redevelopment of old urban zones are absent or minor. There is an acknowledgement that any redevelopment of these old urban zones must deal with increased problems, such as the scarcity of empty land and its high cost. Documents sent to the MUC do not, however, identify any new actions that could help local authorities attack this kind of problem. The same can be said for the objective of consolidating manufacturing activities in the centre, a project judged to be crucial, and one that the government had said it would support with specific action.

5. The objective of consolidating the existing road network did not give rise, in the case of the MUC, to network improvements to relieve the freeway system, while in the suburban RCMs the program plans of the

Ministry of Transport provide for large-scale intermunicipal road and freeway projects. And no specific action involving public transportation in the suburban RCMs is listed in these program plans.

6.   For the municipalities on the North Shore, all the freeway and road projects listed in the Ministry of Transport program plans contradict in full or in part the guidelines previously sent to the municipalities concerning urban sprawl.

7.   For the South Shore, the ministry's freeway projects would change the existing network into a system of bypasses.

8.   After 1983, the guidelines for applying and respecting agricultural zoning are less and less firm. While the first government interpretations defined zoning as a major instrument for containing urban development within already built-up zones, the municipalities were later advised that they were entitled to request a revision.

9.   Section 16 of the act respecting Land Use Planning and Development grants the government the privilege of objecting to any proposal for a development plan proposed by an RCM before its adoption. The government has transmitted no formal objection to the perimeters of urbanisation proposed by the RCMs.

THE EFFECTIVENESS OF CONTROLLING URBAN DEVELOPMENT BY MEANS OF THE OPTION.

If we return to the three basic sections of the Option, while considering the preceding findings, we must draw the following conclusions:

1.   Regarding the first section (consolidation of the urban fabric inside the present fully serviced perimeter), the government was more and more lax in its interpretation, especially after 1985. The use of agricultural zoning for this purpose was effective only in a limited number of cases, and the freeway projects contradicted outright the spirit and letter of this section of the Option. During this time, the Ministry of Industry and Commerce approved expansion projects for the industrial zones without referring to the Option.

2.   The second section (giving priority to the redevelopment of old built-up areas in the central part of Montreal and the city centres of Laval and Longueuil) did not inspire any major government projects. Of course, government investment in public transportation as well as in cultural and university facilities, should be credited indirectly to this section. But apart from Revi-Centre (a provincial program for commercial revitalisation) and a program for the revitalisation of derelict businesses in the industrial

sector, the government undertook no decisive action. Especially in the field of housing, it did not act to reduce the cost of land and to redistribute it in the central zones.

3. It had to be expected that the third section (improvement of the quality of life on the island of Montreal), already suffering from the vagueness of its formulation, did not seem to receive much attention from the government. Any project to improve the quality of life was considered valid, whether its location was central or not.

Overall, the ambition to regulate urban development through the Option has not been expressed validly or vigorously in the regulatory mechanism most directly linked to it: the regional implementation of development plans. In its essentials, the Option has remained an expression of intent, coherent no doubt, but not leading to a real strategy for government action. It remains for us to take into account the combination of circumstances contributing to the urban development of the Montreal area in order to grasp how what has arisen from the Option has managed to influence it.

A SLOWDOWN IN URBAN SPRAWL

The regulation of urban form by Option-related administrative measures showed some laxity. Nonetheless, the dynamics of urban development in Montreal were transformed between the beginning of the 1970s and the end of the 1980s. It may be an exaggeration to credit the Option with having been the driving force for a redirection of development. On the other hand, it is highly probable that it played a role in the consolidation of the dense central urban zones, if only through the effects of the moratorium on bridges and peripheral freeways that accompanied it. In effect, the bridges and peripheral freeways had been the primary sources of encouragement of centrifugal tendencies in the Montreal region.

Without claiming to circumscribe and isolate the effective impact of the Option on urban sprawl, it is possible to establish whether or not there was a real change in the logic of development subsequent to its promulgation. In order to do this, we identified two historical periods that for the purposes of this analysis, were delimited by three census years, 1976, 1981, and 1986. Systematic comparison of residential development trends during the two periods (1976-1981 and 1981-1986) will allow us to situate more concretely the effects of the Option on the urban fabric.

First, however, it is necessary to define the process of sprawl and identify empirically the principal mechanisms involved. Too often, descriptions of the pattern of urban development of the Montreal area rest on an impressionistic representation of sprawl, to wit the expansion of the periphery by residential development in the suburbs. We propose a much more unifocal and quantifiable definition of the process. More specifically, leaving aside value judgments on the suburbs, we do not consider that all peripheral expansion must be attributed to the process of urban sprawl. A more objective way to evaluate the phenomenon is required.

In this respect, it seemed possible to construct a valid tool of measurement by using an inventory drawn up by the Ministry of Municipal Affairs of serviced and serviceable land throughout the region (MAM 1977, Chart 7). In a cartographic document about urbanisation in the Montreal metropolitan area experts from the Ministry of Municipal Affairs estimated that the area already serviced in 1975-78 could support at least 350,000 additional inhabitants, which allowed the area to offer building lots at prices much below those of other large urban centres in Canada.[6] Let us remember that the population of the region in fact grew by only 80,000 inhabitants between 1976 and 1986.

In the following pages, we consider that urban sprawl corresponds to residential construction on unserviced land as designated in MAM's inventory. This method of evaluation will permit us to avoid making value judgments on the development of suburban cities, the emigration of jobs from the centre to the outside, etc. In any big city, there are in effect former urban centres (old villages etc.) whose expansion must not be automatically equated with sprawl and the waste of land resources.[7]

---

[6] Furthermore, Montreal's recently published Master Plan mentions that 20 percent of the downtown area is still available for urban development.

[7] To establish the data base at the source of the measurement of urban sprawl, we assigned the majority of census tracts for the 1976, 1981, and 1986 censuses to one or other of the two areas of urbanisation (serviced areas and unserviced areas). Because of having to adjust for differences between census tract boundaries and the chart of serviced land, the absolute figures differ slightly from data published on the CMA, but the results clearly reflect the reality of the pattern of urbanisation that dominates the landscape of Montreal.

SLOWDOWN OF DECLINE IN GROWTH
AND EXTENDED URBAN SPRAWL

At first sight, the figures compiled in the last census (Table 14.1) suggest a real slowdown in urban sprawl for the period from 1981 to 1986. Various data indicate what some analysts might regard as a change in the logic of Montreal urban development, i.e., a reversal of former tendencies in favour of a consolidation of central or peripheral zones that are already urbanised.

Various statistics confirm this positive vision of recent trends in the development of the Montreal region. Our data indicates that population loss in the serviced areas stopped after 1981 (from -3 percent to +0.5 percent throughout the CMA), while growth in the number of households and the number of housing units still remained low, but stable. As others have shown (OPDQ 1977) by comparing the present situation of the island of Montreal to the considerable share of growth in its urban ring, the strong decline in the island's growth observed between 1971 and 1981 henceforth is part of history. Or so we hope.

The much improved balance in the demographic exchanges between the central city and its urban ring (Table 14.2) cannot, however, close the discussion of the costs and inconveniences of Montreal urban sprawl, nor lead to the conclusion that spatial dispersion and wastage of land resources through low-density residential development have been interrupted. A number of facts warn us to be prudent:

1. The interior dynamics of development of the serviced areas (Table 14.1—inner growth) is still largely lower (by 6.8 percent between 1976 and 1981 for population and by 6.2 percent between 1981 and 1986 for number of households) than that of unserviced areas (from 39 percent between 1976 and 1981 for population and 15 percent between 1981 and 1986 for number of households) even if the absolute figures of the last census indicate a reestablishment of growth in favour of serviced areas (twice the number of housing units). This is because the decline in the number of households in the serviced areas corresponds to an illusory adjustment insofar as the creation of new households in these old central areas derives from the reduction in the ratio of persons per household. This can be seen in our data in the small increase in the number of families in the serviced areas (2.2 percent or 12,345) while the areas that were not serviced in 1976 are still growing strongly (13.1 percent or 17,880). Other studies have shown that the formation of new nonfamily households of single persons or of reduced size in the central core of

Table 14.1. Urban Growth According to Urbanised Areas

A. Raw Data

Areas	Years	Population	Households	Dwelling Units	Families
Unserviced	1976	405,819	16,113	N.A.	N.A.
	1981	509,975	161,365	161,270	136,545
	1986	556,190	186,140	186,200	154,425
Serviced	1976	2,435,353	819,059	N.A.	N.A.
	1981	2,351,475	874,645	874,570	615,025
	1986	2,364,110	929,185	929,165	627,370
Total	1976	2,841,172	935,172	N.A.	N.A.
	1981	2,861,450	1,036,010	1,035,840	751,570
	1986	2,920,300	1,115,325	1,115,365	781,795

B. Interior Growth of Unserviced Areas

Years	Population	Households	Dwelling Units	Families
1976-81	104,156	45,252	N.A.	N.A.
1981-86	46,215	24,775	24,960	17,880
1976-81	25.7%	39.0%	N.A.	N.A.
1981-86	9.1%	15.4%	15.5%	13.1%

C. Interior Growth of Serviced Areas

Years	Population	Households	Dwelling Units	Families
1976-81	-83,878	55,586	N.A.	N.A.
1981-86	46,215	24,775	24,930	17,880
1976-81	-3.4%	6.8%	N.A.	N.A.
1981-86	0.5%	6.2%	6.2%	2.0%

D. Distribution of CMA Growth among Serviced and Unserviced Areas

Areas	Years		Population	Households	Dwelling Units	Families
CMA	1976-81	N +	20,278	100,838	N.A.	N.A.
	1981-86		58,850	79,315	79,525	30,225
Unserviced	1976-81	N +	104,156	45,252	N.A.	N.A.
	1981-86		46,215	24,775	24,930	17,880
	1976-81	as % of region	514	45	N.A.	N.A.
	1981-86		79	31	31	59
Serviced	1976-81	N +	-83,878	55,586	N.A.	N.A.
	1981-86		12,635	54,540	54,595	12,345
	1976-81	as % of region	-414	55	N.A.	N.A.
	1981-86		21	69	69	41

E. Unserviced Land as Percentage of CMA Total

Years	Population	Households	Dwelling Units	Families
1976	16.7	14.2	N.A.	N.A.
1981	21.7	18.4	18.4	22.2
1986	23.5	20.0	20.0	24.6

Table 14.2.   *Urban Growth According to Proximity of the Center and the Areas of Urbanisation*

	Years	Population	Households	Dwelling Units	Families
			Raw data		
Noncentral Unserviced	1976	405,819	116,113	N.A.	N.A.
	1981	509,975	161,365	161,270	136,545
	1986	556,190	186,140	186,200	154,425
Noncentral Serviced	1976	1,387,139	420,886	N.A.	N.A.
	1981	1,411,300	475,630	475,790	382,375
	1986	1,455,420	520,985	520,985	403,965
Central city Serviced[1]	1976	1,048,214	398,173	N.A.	N.A.
	1981	940,175	399,015	398,780	232,650
	1986	908,690	408,200	408,180	223,405
Total	1976	2,841,172	935,172	N.A.	N.A.
	1981	2,861,450	1,036,010	1,035,840	751,570
	1986	2,920,300	1,115,325	1,115,365	781,795

% of CMA Growth

Noncentral	1976	63%	57%	N.A.	N.A.
Central city		37%	43%	N.A.	N.A.
Noncentral	1981	67%	61%	62%	69%
Central city		33%	39%	38%	31%
Noncentral	1986	69%	63%	63%	71%
Central city		31%	37%	37%	29%

Total CMA Growth

Noncentral	1976-81	7%	19%	N.A.	N.A.
	1981-86	5%	11%	11%	8%
Central city	1976-81	-10%	0.00%	N.A.	N.A.
	1981-86	-3%	2%	2%	-4%

Interior Growth - Unserviced Areas

Noncentral				
1976-81	26%	39%	N.A.	N.A.
1981-86	9%	15%	15%	13%
Central city				
1976-81	nil	nil	nil	nil
1981-86	nil	nil	nil	nil

Interior Growth - Serviced Areas

Noncentral				
1976-81	2%	13%	N.A.	N.A.
1981-86	3%	10%	9%	6%
Central city				
1976-81	-10%	0.00%	N.A.	N.A.
1981-86	-3%	2%	2%	-4%

[1]Central city areas are all serviced.

Montreal is associated with impoverishment (Conseil des affaires sociales 1989).

2.   The proportion of the population living on unserviced land in the whole Montreal region (CMA) remains to be examined. From 17 percent of the population and 14 percent of the households in 1976, this proportion rose to nearly 25 percent of the number of families and 24 percent of the population in 1986 (cf. Figures 14.1 and 14.2).

3.   The number of households and the number of housing units increased more rapidly than the number of families. At the same time, the increase in family households is not distributed equitably among the serviced and unserviced areas, but works to the advantage of the latter. That is the evidence. Nearly 70 percent of the growth in housing units and in households for the whole of the Montreal region has gone into the serviced areas in response to pressing needs. On the other hand, the growth of families and of the population reverses this profile. Total demographic growth in the Montreal region always occurs to the advantage of the unserviced areas: respectively 79 percent and 59 percent of total growth in population and in families took place in unserviced areas. These proportions are considerable (cf. Figures 14.3-14.6).

Sprawl, in the very restricted sense in which we use it here—i.e., residential development within unserviced zones when the region's low rate of population growth should in fact encourage the in-filling of older urban centres—thus continues to flourish unabated.

DISPERSED DEVELOPMENT IN A
ZERO GROWTH CONTEXT

In what way has urban sprawl, as we have just described it, been accompanied by spatial dispersion in distant low-density housing groups? To obtain a clearer image, it is necessary to refine the analysis of the serviced and unserviced areas according to the distance of these zones from the urban centre.

In the following paragraphs, the centre of Montreal is delimited by grouping certain former urban nuclei with the centre of the city of Montreal and its bordering districts.[8] The centre coincides, in this case, with the perimeter of the central city.

---

[8]We are going back to the delimitation proposed by the MUC.

Figure 14.1.   *Evolution of Unserviced Areas (1976-1986)*

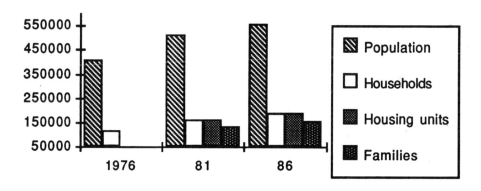

N.B.   Population and households only for 1976.

Figure 14.2.   *Evolution of the Proportion of Unserviced Areas in the Montreal CMA*

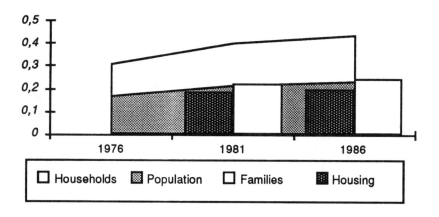

Figure 14.3.   *Share of the Growth in the Montreal Region Monopolised by Service Areas*

Figure 14.4.   *Share of the Growth in the Montreal CMA Monopolised by Unserviced Areas*

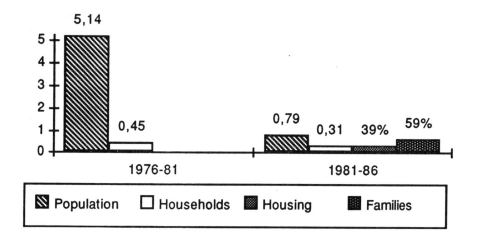

Figure 14.5.   *Comparison of the Evolution of Population and Households in Unserviced Areas*

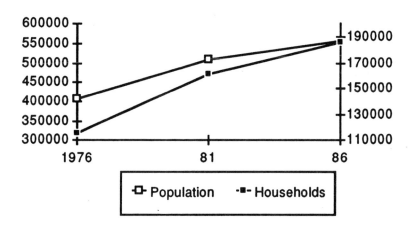

Figure 14.6.   *Comparison on the Evolution of Population and Households in the Serviced Areas*

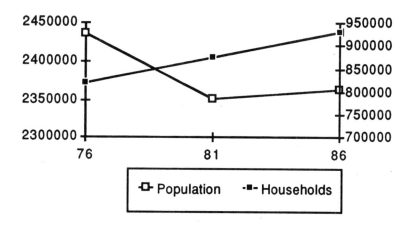

In 1986, after a decrease in population growth of relatively pronounced proportions, particularly between 1976 and 1981, the central city
still contained 31 percent of the population and 37 percent of the
households and housing units (Table 14.2). Between 1981 and 1986,
however, the centre of the region again lost about 9,000 families and
30,000 inhabitants, to the advantage of the peripheral zones. In other
words, taking into account the distribution of total growth of the
metropolitan region (Table 14.3), a good part of the population gains of
the periphery were at the expense of the centre, since the centre posts a
negative balance of -54 percent.[9]

This process of demographic withdrawal from the central city, or
more precisely the exchange of populations between the central city and
the rest of the urban area, occurred because of the decrease in the number
of families living in the centre. While the centre accounted for 12 percent
of the increase in population and households between 1981 and 1986, it
was in clear retreat with regard to the number of families (internal growth
of -4 percent), as we have just seen. This implies for the centre a
negative score of -31 percent for the total growth of families within the
Montreal region (Figure 14.7).

Many will say there is nothing dramatic in this rebalancing of
population and in such a distribution or segregation of classes of
households between the centre and the periphery. Such an interpretation
can be true insofar as demography justifies it, and insofar as such a
movement does not directly generate a waste of land and financial
resources through the encouragement of sporadic, dispersed development,
nearly always in undeveloped zones. And of course it must not be
forgotten that this all occurs in a context in which the central or already
developed areas could support more growth than they are supporting at
present.

It must therefore be concluded that in the metropolitan region, the
dynamics of peripheral development have been achieved to the detriment
of the centre and primarily to the benefit of unserviced areas. In effect,
although the growth of noncentral areas seems to be slowing down in
comparison to the growth of the overall region (Table 14.2), it still
constitutes 88 percent of the growth in households and housing and 154

---

[9]The 1986 census data on spatial mobility of households by enumeration
sector were not yet available at the time this study was carried out. They would
allow us to follow the displacement of classes of households from the centre to
the periphery and inversely.

Table 14.3.   *Distribution of the Total Growth of the Proximity of the Centre and the Areas of Urbanisation*

Year		Population	Households	Dwelling Units	Families
Montreal Region					
1976-81	Growth	20,278	100,838	N.A.	N.A.
	as % of region	100%	100%	N.A.	N.A.
1981-86	Growth	58,850	79,315	79,525	30,225
	as % of region	100%	100%	100%	100%
Central City					
Serviced					
1976-81	Growth	-108,039	842	N.A.	N.A.
	as % of region	-533%	0.80%	N.A.	N.A.
1981-86	Growth	-31,485	9,185	9,400	-9,245
	as % of region	-54%	12%	12%	-31%

			Others Zones			
Serviced	1976-81	Growth	24,161	54,744	N.A.	N.A.
		as % of region	119%	54%	N.A.	N.A.
	1981-86	Growth	44,120	45,355	45,195	21,590
		as % of region	75%	57%	57%	71%
Unserviced	1976-81	Growth	104,156	45,252	N.A.	N.A.
		as % of region	514%	45%	N.A.	N.A.
	1981-86	Growth	46,215	24775	24,930	17,880
		as % of region	79%	31%	31%	59%
Total	1976-81	Growth	128,317	99,996	N.A.	N.A.
		as % of region	633%	99%	N.A.	N.A.
	1981-86	Growth	90,335	70,130	70,125	39,470
		as % of region	154%	88%	88%	131%

Important notes:
•The central areas are serviced.
•The results of this table should not lead to confusion. The zones obtain either a positive or negative share of total CMA growth. Thus, a percentge of + or - 100% means that the given zone gained or lost, by itself, more than the percentage gained or lost by the CMA.

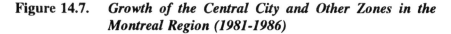

Figure 14.7.   *Growth of the Central City and Other Zones in the Montreal Region (1981-1986)*

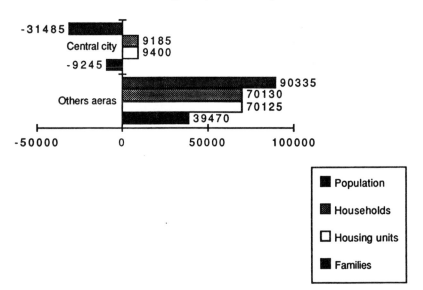

percent of the growth in population (Table 14.3). For each of these last three variables respectively, the unserviced part of the noncentral zones monopolizes 31, 31, and 79 percent of the rates of growth. This balance in favour of the undeveloped areas is still related to having the absolute growth of the population attributed to them and to taking advantage of the spatial mobility of families in the Montreal area.

A LACK OF REGIONAL CONSCIOUSNESS

In summary, through its Option the government of Quebec showed its intention of putting a brake on urban sprawl in the Montreal region. This occurred within a special political context in which social and political awareness of the economic difficulties faced by the Montreal area was stronger than it had been previously. As we have seen, however, resistance to the project by some suburban municipalities and by some elements within the government itself succeeded in blocking the development of a truly interventionist strategy agreed on by all the groups concerned.

In this sense, despite the fact that the progression of urban sprawl, in the strict sense, definitely decreased during the 1981 to 1986 period, the phenomenon certainly continued to exist. In other words, urban sprawl on the periphery of the central city constitutes a significant phenomenon accompanying the decline of the centre, reflecting the small rate of population increase on the central island. From this point of view, sprawl is a process that wastes resources despite virtually no demographic growth.

At the outset, the list of measures aimed at reducing overconsumption of space, limiting the practice of wasting land resources, making public services profitable, and improving the quality of life, was a long list. However, not all the measures were put into effect. The ones that were finally retained were both insufficient and inconsistent. Primarily, demographic and socio-economic changes succeeded in slowing down sprawl, as we have observed. This means that the adjustments proposed by the government of Quebec did not succeed in redirecting the logic of urban development, as had been planned in the political descriptions of the Option.

To explain the gap between government speech and government practice, and the reasons why the government of Quebec in the end was hesitant to impose on the RCMs coercive measures with regard to the development factors at stake for the Montreal region as a whole, two explanatory hypotheses are worth considering.

The first hypothesis deals with the "ruralist" vision of development that has always prevailed within the principal Quebec ministries responsible for this question. For example, while two thirds of the population of the Montreal area lives within a single regional entity, the Montreal Urban Community, the other third is dispersed within the 12 RCMs. Now the RCMs seem to have more significant political and electoral weight than the heart of the urban area. Bill 125, which created these entities, aimed first to resolve the problems of the regional subcentres rather than those of the central city. This can be explained by the fact that the interests of the political class in the suburban regional municipalities are very closely linked with real estate promoters (which is not the case inside the central city, or else it exists to a much smaller degree.) And as the government still seems to have a tendency to perceive urban development primarily as a matter of suburban expansion, it has committed itself more readily to alliances with regional municipalities in the suburban ring.

The second hypothesis invokes the ensemble of relationships that exists between the municipalities and the government of Quebec in the wider context of restructuring the state. These relationships became more apparent after the end of the 1970s (Hamel and Jalbert 1991). From that time, the government of Quebec chose to commit itself to decentralisation measures that were expressed, among other things, by the creation of a new system of municipalities (the RCMs) and by the reform of municipal taxation.

Despite the success of these reforms, it is important to emphasize that the government did not recognize them as an opportunity to review in depth the system of relationships between the government and the municipalities. In the spirit of these reforms directed toward an improvement in the administrative performance of local collectivities, the expression of decentralisation was at most an element of political strategy whose objective was to reaffirm the hegemony of the provincial government over the entire municipal system. In this context, the centre of the Montreal urban area was not in any way an exception. Its treatment was similar to that of all the other municipalities in Quebec.

The consequences of the bankruptcy or the abandonment of the government Option for Montreal and for Quebec are variable, according to our interpretation of the development and planning stakes at risk in the Montreal urban area. Formerly, the fate of Quebec seemed linked to that of Montreal. As the primary centre of innovation and vitality, both culturally and socio-economically, Montreal fulfilled the functions of leadership—the centre of decision-making, service, and communication—that no other region in Quebec was able to assume. Even if this reality remains true in part, changes on the international level and the dynamics of various other regions have to some extent modified the strategic role played by Montreal in the economy of Quebec. But Montreal still remains an important lynch-pin in that economy. That is why, on the provincial level, it is a question of some importance whether or not the region will return to the leadership position it held in the past.

When we consider that we are living inside a highly advanced tertiary economy in which the quality of life and of development have become decisive factors for the thrust of economic activity, we arrive at a very negative interpretation of the abandonment of the Option. This stems primarily from the fact that such a choice involves extra costs that have direct repercussions on the capacity of local authorities to act to improve the quality of life, the maintenance of public services and facilities, and their modernisation.

The crisis experienced at the present moment by the administration of the central city with regard to the cost of urban services is directly related to this fact. The Option that the government of Quebec, with the suburban municipalities, has in fact refused to validate since the 1970s remains on the agenda. The crisis in public finances forces us to reconsider it seriously today.

Our analysis of urban sprawl and its impact on the urban development of the Montreal region has highlighted, above all, the role of a major actor therein, and that actor is the provincial government. It should not be forgotten that the choices made at this level would not have been possible without the agreement or the connivance of all local groups in the region. What is in question, then, is probably the lack of regional consciousness shown by local action groups. Containment of urban sprawl, improvement of the quality of life, the rebirth of Montreal: those are the stakes. They cannot be treated separately and they demand, in the short term, the emergence of a true regional awareness. Otherwise, the provincial government will always have the choice of invoking contradictory pressures by local interests as an excuse for not acting.

REFERENCES

Baldassare, Mark. 1986. *Trouble in Paradise: The Suburban Transformation in America*. New York: Columbia University Press.

Barcelo, Michel, François Charbonneau, and Pierre Hamel. 1990. "Option préférable d'aménagement et étalement urbain, 1978-1988, dans la région de Montréal." Notes de récherches, Faculté de l'aménagement, Université de Montréal.

Burgel, Guy. 1986. "La banlieue, mode ou miroir?" *Villes en parallèl*, no. 10 (juin): 9-12.

Collin, Jean-Pierre. 1986. "L'espace urbain de Montréal après la deuxième guerre mondiale: mutations et continuités." Montréal: INRS-Urbanisation.

Conseil des affaires sociales. 1989. "Deux Québec dans un." Rapport sur le développement local et démographique, Gaétan Mortin.

Danielson, Michael N., and Jameson W. Doig. 1982. *The Politics of Urban Regional Development: New York*. Berkeley, Calif.: University of California Press.

Dansereau, Francine, ed. 1982. *Au-delà de la crise: les tendances dans le domaine de l'habitation*. Document de travail pour le Colloque Habitation 1982 organisé par la Revue Actualité Immobilière et l'INRS-Urbanisation.

_____, and Peter Foggin. 1982. *Quelques aspects du développement spatial de l'agglomération montréalaise* (Etudes et documents 3). Montreal: INRS-Urbanisation.

Divay, Gérard, and Marcel Gaudreau. 1982. "L'agglomération de Montréal: velléités de concentration et tendances centrifuges." *La Revue Canadienne des Sciences Régionales* 5: 183-98.

Fauteux, Martial. 1983. "La croissance de la population dans la région de Montréal, 1971-1981." *Cahiers de Géographie du Québec* 27: 165-83.

Gendron, François. 1984. *Option d'Aménagement de la région métropolitaine de Montréal*. Québec, Secrétariat à l'aménagement et à la décentralisation.

George, Pierre. 1989. "Les Franges urbaines: Les effets marginaux de l'urbanisation" *Espace, Populations, Sociétés*, no. 20: 357-64.

Hamel, Pierre, and Lizette Jalbert. 1991. "Local power in Canada: Stakes and Challenges in the Restructuring of the State." In *State Restructuring and Local Power*, ed. C. Pickvance and E. Préteceille, London: Pinter Publishers, 170-96.

Jackson, Kenneth T. 1985. *Crabgrass Frontier: The Suburbanization of the United States.* New York: Oxford University Press.

Lamonde, Pierre, and Mario Polèse. 1985. *Le déplacement des activités économiques dans la région métropolitaine de Montréal* (Etudes et documents 45). Montréal: INRS-Urbanisation.

Leonard, Jacques (ministre d'Etat à l'Aménagement). 1978. "Rencontre avec les maires de la région de Montréal" ("Option préférable d'aménagement pour la région de Montréal"). Quebec, Ministère du Conseil Exécutif.

Leveillée, Jacques, and Jean-François Leonard. 1988. "The Montreal Citizens' Movement Comes to Power." *International Journal of Urban and Regional Research* 12: 567-80.

Linteau, Paul-André. 1987. "Canadian suburbanization in a North American Context. Does the Border Make a Difference?" *Journal of Urban History* 13: 252-74.

Ministère des affaires municipales. 1977. *L'urbanisation dans la connurbation montréalaise: tendances actuelles et propositions d'orientation.* Québec, MAM, direction générale de l'urbanisme et de l'aménagement du territoire.

Office de Planification et de Développement du Québec (O.P.D.Q.). 1977. *Esquisse de la région de Montréal. Evolution et orientation du développement et de l'aménagement.* Montréal, O.P.D.Q.

Chapter 15

Provincial Transit Policymaking for the Toronto, Montreal, and Vancouver Regions

Frances Frisken
York University

A frequently noted characteristic of Canadian cities and metropolitan areas is the prominent role played by provincial governments in virtually all aspects of their administration. Canadian local officials and many Canadian political analysts have tended to view that role critically, seeing it as a clear violation of the principle of local autonomy. Studies comparing Canadian urban policymaking with that of other countries, particularly the United States, have tended to take a more benign view. They suggest that provincial hegemony in local affairs means that Canadian metropolitan areas are developing under the close supervision of governments able to act comprehensively on problems associated with population growth and territorial expansion, and in ways that balance the interests of the larger community against narrow expressions of individual, corporate, and municipal self-interest.

Differences between Canadian and U.S. urban transportation systems lend support to this view. In their provocative challenge to "the myth

I thank the University of Toronto-York University Joint Program in Transportation for financial support, Marc McAree for valuable research assistance, and Ken Cameron, André Cardinal, Pierre Lamonde, Andrée Lehman, Jacques Léveillée, Christopher Leo, Louise Roy, Andrew Sancton, and Peter Spurr for helpful comments on earlier drafts of this chapter. I also thank the many people who agreed to be interviewed for this study.

of the North American city," Michael Goldberg and John Mercer (1986, 142-45) linked Canadians' greater tolerance of government intervention in economic affairs in general, and the greater involvement of provincial (as compared to federal or local) governments in urban policy in particular, to such characteristics of urban Canada as a greater use of planning and development controls; more compact, more densely populated central cities; and transportation systems that are more oriented to public transit, less to automobiles, than those of the United States. Several international comparisons focusing specifically on transit have also pointed to public policy differences as helping to explain why Canadian transit systems tend to outperform those in the United States, at least in the sense of serving more riders per capita and requiring lower levels of subsidy (Cervero 1986; Colcord 1976, 15; Delcan Corp. 1988, Sect. 2, p. 9; Pucher 1988; Urban Land Institute and Gladstone Associates 1979, 181-93).

Support for such arguments is drawn mainly from what has happened within the boundaries of units of metropolitan administration (Metropolitan Toronto, the Montreal Urban Community, and the Greater Vancouver Regional District) established in Canada's three largest metropolitan areas between 1953 and 1969. The creation of those units was itself suggestive of provincial government interest in promoting areawide solutions to areawide problems. Of the three units, however, only the Greater Vancouver Regional District (GVRD) still accounted in 1991 for the vast majority of the Census Metropolitan Area (CMA) population and most of its current population growth. In the other two areas, the formally constituted metropolitan jurisdictions, Metropolitan Toronto and the Montreal Urban Community (MUC), contained much smaller and declining proportions of their CMA populations (Table 15.1).

Because provincial governments have shown no interest in increasing the size of metropolitan jurisdictions, they are now the only governments able to plan and provide services on an areawide basis. An examination of their policies has thus become an essential part of any effort to understand the way the Canadian state is dealing with the challenges of urban expansion. Urban transit policy has much to offer such an examination because it involves four types of decisions that help define the thrust of metropolitan policymaking. The first is to justify becoming involved in an activity that governments have traditionally treated as a local responsibility, theoretically capable of supporting itself out of revenues collected from users. This view has always coexisted with a tendency to look on public spending on roads and highways as necessary

Table 15.1. *Population Change in the Montreal, Toronto, and Vancouver Areas, 1971-1991*

	Pop. 1971	% CMA	Pop. 1991	% CMA	% Increase (Decrease) 1971-1991
Montreal					
CMA	2,743,208		3,127,242		14.0
Montreal Urb. Comm.	1,955,375	71.0	1,775,941	57.0	(-9.2)
City of Montreal	1,214,352	44.0	1,017,666	33.0	(-16.2)
Outside MUC	787,833	29.0	1,351,301	43.0	71.5
Toronto					
CMA	2,628,043		3,893,046		48.1
Metropolitan Toronto	2,086,017	79.0	2,275,771	58.0	9.1
City of Toronto	712,786	27.0	635,395	16.0	(-10.9)
Outside Met. Tor.	542,026	21.0	1,617,275	42.0	198.4
Vancouver					
CMA	1,082,352		1,602,502		48.1
Grtr. Vanc. Reg. Dis.	1,028,334	95.0	1,542,744	96.0	50.1
City of Vancouver	426,256	39.0	471,844	29.0	10.7
Outside GVRD	54,018	5.0	71,772	4.0	32.9

Source: Statistics Canada, *Census of Canada 1971, 1991.*

to sustain economic investment. Nonetheless, there is a variety of reasons—economic, political, social, and, increasingly, environmental—why a government may decide to assist public transit. Those it actually invokes thus constitute important statements about the way it perceives its responsibilities to the metropolis and its diverse constituencies.

Closely related to the need for a rationale for becoming involved in urban transit is the need to decide how transit funds will be distributed among different transit modes and purposes. Such decisions determine how the benefits of government support are distributed among different categories of transit users (suburban commuters as compared to local bus riders, for example). They will also largely determine the amount local governments have to pay out of their own funds to have this type of service, and thus the amount of attention they are likely to give to transit in their own policies.

Governments must also decide how a metropolitan transit system will be organized and administered, taking into account its traditional status as a locally operated or regulated service and the likelihood that local governments will want to have a say in how it is provided. The task of accommodating local preferences and aspirations becomes increasingly difficult as metropolitan areas expand to take in more municipalities. Furthermore, the greater the number of transit operators and local governments involved in transit delivery, the more difficult it is to coordinate or integrate services throughout a metropolitan area.

Local concerns and aspirations are also important to the fourth type of decision involved in urban transportation policymaking: to determine whether a financial commitment to transit justifies intervention in local land-use practices to encourage a pattern of settlement that facilitates transit use and minimizes obstacles to efficient transit operation. In some ways this is the most fundamental and sensitive of all decisions, given the incompatible facts that (1) land-use characteristics (particularly density and street layouts) are of critical importance to transit system performance and (2) local governments tend to be more determined to defend their rights to control the use of land than they are to perform virtually any other function assigned to them.

A central government faced with these decisions is under two types of pressure. One is the pressure to manage both the economy and its own fiscal well-being, whether by trying to attract or support new investment or by resisting pressures to spend money on services promising few economic returns. There are also pressures from a multitude of constituent interests, often represented by their local governments, advocating various and often conflicting solutions to growth-related problems. Because the tendency in metropolitan areas is for population and economic activity to decentralize and disperse, provincial governments, like all central governments, are likely to experience growing economic and political pressures to give higher priority to service demands emanating from outer than from inner parts of such areas (Kantor with David 1988, 279).

The next section of this chapter looks at the way provincial transit policies for Canada's three largest metropolitan areas have evolved. It is followed by an overview section comparing the main features of those policies and identifying similarities and differences among them. These accounts demonstrate that provincial government policies have contributed significantly to the expansion and improvement of public transit systems in all three regions. Even while making those policies, however, all three governments have tended to acquiesce, though to differing degrees, to those forces (like population and employment decentralization and the local land-use practices that support it) associated with the decline of public transit systems in metropolitan regions in the United States.

HOW PROVINCIAL POLICIES HAVE EVOLVED

The governments of Ontario, Quebec, and British Columbia did not become involved in public transit policymaking in a major way until the 1970s, although the Ontario government has assisted the development of rail rapid transit in the Toronto region since 1964. As can be seen from Table 15.1, transit policies evolved during a period when Canada's two largest urban regions were experiencing a falling off or even decline of population growth at the centre and an acceleration of growth at the fringe. Only in the Vancouver region was most new growth absorbed within the boundaries of the provincially designated metropolitan area, although only a small amount of the increase went into the city of Vancouver.

These development trends were not auspicious for transit, for they meant both a decrease in population densities and a decline in the proportion of regional jobs at or near the centre, tendencies associated historically with declines in transit use. Only in the Vancouver area did central densities increase, although not to levels already achieved in the

Table 15.2. *Changes in Population Density in the Montreal, Toronto, and Vancouver Areas, 1971 to 1991*

	Land Area sq. km. 1971	Land Area sq. km. 1991	% Incr. (Decr.) 1971-91	Pop./ sq. km. 1971	Pop./ sq. km. 1991
Montreal					
CMA	2,674	3,509	31.2	1,026	891
Montreal ,					
Urb. Comm.	492	494	0.4	3,974	3,598
Outside					
MUC	2,182	3,015	38.2	361	448
City of					
Montreal	158	177	12.0	7,690	5,742
Toronto					
CMA	3,628	5,584	53.9	724	697
Metropolitan					
Toronto	626	630	0.6	3,332	3,612
Outside					
Met. Tor.	3,002	4,953	65.0	181	327
City of					
Toronto	97	97	0.0	7,337	6,540
Vancouver					
CMA	2,785	2,786	0.0	389	575
Grtr. Vanc.					
Reg. Dis.	2,158	2,613	0.4	477	590
Outside					
GVRD	628	173	(-72.5)	86	346
City of					
Vancouver	113	113	0.0	3,771	4,172

Sources: Statistics Canada, *Census of Canada 1971, 1991.*

other two areas (Table 15.2). As a result, involvement in regional transit prompted the governments of Ontario and Quebec to consider the implications of regional development trends for the long-run success of their transit policies.

Toronto

For transportation planning purposes, the provincial Ministry of Transportation has defined the Toronto metropolis to comprise an area 50 percent larger than the CMA, taking in parts of the neighbouring Hamilton and Oshawa CMAs, and containing 36 municipalities. This Greater Toronto Area (GTA) is served by one interregional, two regional, and 14 local transit systems. The largest of these 17 systems is Metropolitan Toronto's Toronto Transit Commission (TTC). The TTC's service area accounted for 83 percent of the GTA's transit riders in 1986 but contained only 52 percent of its population (Transit Advisory Group 1987, 23, 146).

The Ontario government's first attempt to give the Toronto area a metropolitan transit system occurred when it created Metropolitan Toronto in 1953 and established the TTC as a public corporation with sole authority for providing transit service within Metro's boundaries. The move entailed transferring ownership of the Toronto Transportation Commission from the city of Toronto to the Metropolitan Toronto Council, changing its name, increasing its board membership from three to five, and expanding its jurisdiction from 91 to 622 square kilometres. Despite substantially increasing the TTC's responsibilities, the Metropolitan Toronto Act required the new agency, like the one it replaced, to be self-sustaining.

The beginning of Metropolitan Toronto coincided with the opening of the Yonge Street subway, a project undertaken by the TTC in 1946 with surplus revenues accumulated during the war.[1] The subway's success in sustaining transit ridership in its service corridor at a time of declining ridership elsewhere convinced Metro Council not only to approve two additional subway lines and contribute to their capital costs but also to adopt a 1964 transportation plan calling for a "balanced transportation system" consisting of both highways and subway lines. The

---

[1]This discussion of the TTC's origins and history summarizes material in Frisken, 1985.

process of building political support for transit was often marred by conflict, however, much of it related to the TTC's inability to satisfy suburban expectations for better service while covering its expenses out of the fare box. To keep costs down, the TTC refused to extend services to suburban districts with low residential and employment densities. It also maintained a zone fare system that worked to the disadvantage of suburban commuters to downtown Toronto. Nonetheless it soon found itself in financial difficulties because of declining ridership, substantial postwar inflation, and an obligation to pay off debts incurred by the city for subway construction and by Metro for the purchase of suburban bus lines. Suburban representatives on Metro Council refused to support an operating subsidy, however, as long as the zone fare system remained in place. The city maintained for its part that a change in the fare structure would force passengers on heavily used city routes to subsidize suburban riders.

Growing Provincial Involvement

While it was difficult to convince a majority of Metro Council members to support operating subsidies, it was easier to win majority support for subway construction, especially if the suburbs would benefit. Thus in 1964 Metro Council voted to extend the east-west Bloor subway into the outer Boroughs of Etobicoke and Scarborough and to pay 70 percent of its capital costs and of the TTC's accumulated capital debt. This decision coincided with a period of growing provincial concern about the high costs of building urban roads. At Metro's request, therefore, the government agreed to pay 33.3 percent of subway roadbed costs, a contribution that had risen to 50 percent by 1970.

The high cost of building roads was also the reason given by the government in 1967 for inaugurating an experimental commuter rail service (Government of Ontario, or GO, Transit) on 145 kilometres of railroad track linking downtown Toronto with towns to the east and west of Metro Toronto.[2] Over the next 20 years it would expand that service into a 1,500 kilometre network of rail and bus lines covering most of the Toronto CMA and some districts outside it.

---

[2]Decreasing use of this track by the federally owned Canadian National Railways and the privately owned Canadian Pacific Railways made it possible both to launch and to expand this system. Employees of the two railway companies operate the trains, which are purchased by the Ontario government.

The next phase in provincial transit policy began in June 1971, when recently installed provincial premier William Davis announced that his government would not support continued construction of the north-south Spadina Expressway, the focus of a prolonged dispute between local residents and those metropolitan interests who considered it an essential part of the area's transportation network. Instead, the premier said, the government would divert a substantial share of its urban transportation assistance from roads to transit. Over the next two years, the government increased its subsidies for subway construction and capital equipment to 75 percent. (Municipalities were expected to pay the other 25 percent, thereby relieving transit operators of all capital costs.) It made money available for capital improvements to surface transit and agreed to share transit operating deficits with municipalities on a 50-50 basis. It also agreed to pay the full costs of two experimental initiatives: an intermediate capacity rapid transit system (ICTS) based on advanced technology and demand-responsive dial-a-bus services to several northern suburban districts poorly served by conventional transit.

The government initially placed a ceiling on its operating subsidies, raised it in 1973, and removed it altogether in 1974 after the TTC agreed not to raise its fares. The easy availability of provincial funds resulted in rapid expansion of transit services both inside and outside Metro. The TTC, its board now dominated by present and former Metro politicians, did away with the zone fare system and added new services that TTC staff had opposed as financially unwise. Per capita ridership increased but operating subsidies increased even faster, from $6.75 million in 1972 to $45.4 million in 1975, with the bulk of them going to Metro Toronto.

Retrenchment began in 1974 with cancellation of two of the three dial-a-bus experiments because of high operating costs. (The third ended two years later.) In 1975 the government allowed the TTC to increase its fares; in 1976 it restored the ceiling on subsidies and in 1977 adopted formulae under which it would pay a fixed percentage of operating costs, the percentage to vary with municipal population size. Smaller municipalities would receive larger subsidies, with the ratio varying from 13.75 percent for Metro Toronto to 25 percent for municipalities having fewer than 100,000 people. The province would continue to pay 100 percent of GO Transit's operating deficit. With additional subsidies for specific purposes, these financial arrangements have remained in place ever since.

The most contentious element of provincial-local transit policymaking was the elevated intermediate capacity transit technology. The government launched development of this system by choosing a West German firm from among a number of contenders to build a prototype version on the grounds of the Canadian National Exhibition in downtown Toronto. It also created a public corporation, the Ontario Transportation Development Corporation, to participate in its development after noting that the private sector was reluctant to invest in such a venture (Maule 1985, 4). It soon changed the agency's name to the Urban Transportation Development Corporation (UTDC) in hope of getting federal government support.

Work on the prototype line on the exhibition grounds ended abruptly in 1974 when the German government withdrew from the project, citing mounting costs and technical difficulties. In the settlement that ended its agreement with the German firm, the Ontario government recovered most of its investment in the system and exclusive rights to the technology, which it turned over to UTDC. With continuing financial support from the province, UTDC went on to develop a slightly less sophisticated but still technically advanced elevated intermediate capacity transit technology for which it was actively seeking customers by the early 1980s. Part of this strategy was a proposal to build an elevated ICTS line between the eastern terminus of the Bloor Street subway and a Town Centre being developed in the eastern suburb of Scarborough. Metro and the TTC went along with this proposal after the province agreed to pay the full difference in cost between building the elevated line and building a conventional surface rail line of the type originally recommended by the TTC. The province also agreed to pay a special operating subsidy for the line once it opened.

The early 1980s were not auspicious years for transit. A 1982 provincial proposal to upgrade and expand the GO Transit network using light rail technology was abandoned because of budgetary constraints. A 1984 Metro-TTC rapid transit plan (Network 2011) seemed in danger of meeting the same fate. It was premised on the expectation that provincial support for transit expansion within Metro would remain at the level achieved with construction of the Scarborough line. In 1985, however, the Minister of Transportation for the recently elected Liberal government announced that his government planned to limit new capital spending on transit systems (*The Globe and Mail* 1985).

Addressing the Organizational Issue

Transit-related activities intensified under the Liberals nonetheless, for two reasons. One was the implicit competition for provincial transportation funds between Metro interests anxious to proceed with Network 2011 and interests outside Metro demanding better roads and transit service. A second and related reason was a dramatic increase in travel between Metro and the outlying municipalities, most of it by automobile, as a result of the rapid growth of the suburban population. By 1987, therefore, both the Ministry of Transportation and Metropolitan Toronto had begun to prepare and issue comprehensive studies of transportation needs for a Greater Toronto Area 25 percent larger than the CMA (The Municipality of Metropolitan Toronto and Toronto Transit Commission 1987; Ontario Ministry of Transportation 1988; Transit Advisory group to the Minister of Transportation for Ontario 1987). In this process the government ended a prolonged search for an organizational mechanism for regional transit planning and coordination by deciding to leave those responsibilities in the hands of its own Ministry of Transportation. In making that decision, it implicitly rejected alternatives that would have involved elected or appointed local officials on the board of a regional agency.

Government policy and practice were nonetheless subject to several types of municipal influence. A regional Transportation Planning Forum established in 1986 brought together provincial and local officials to conduct a comprehensive review of transportation needs and alternatives. It continued to meet on a regular basis after this work was complete. Local transit operators, who report to municipal councils, retained the right to decide where transit services would go within the constraints imposed by municipal councils and provincial subsidy formulae. Municipal councils could allow their transit systems to incur operating deficits that were more than twice the provincial allocation as long as they made up the difference themselves, but none was inclined to do this. Thus the development and expansion of local transit throughout the region was based largely on determinations by municipal councils that the difference between route costs and returns could be met by subsidy allocations. Special subsidies were the principal device used by the government to persuade municipalities to coordinate their services with those of GO Transit or neighboring transit operators.

A Fluctuating Interest in Regional Planning

Municipalities also made most of the land-use decisions affecting levels of ridership and ease of providing local transit service to suburban districts. They carried out that function within a well-established planning tradition that incorporated a recognition of the transit/land-use relationship but provided few incentives for taking it into account in local plans. That tradition dated back at least as far as 1959, when the authors of Metro's "draft official plan" (which encompassed twice as much territory outside as inside Metro's boundaries) advocated a mix of residential densities in the suburbs as a way of enhancing transit use and viability. Political resistance to the idea of subordinating local to metropolitan planning goals prevented Metro from adopting an official plan until 1980. Nonetheless, several land-use and service policies adopted by Metro or its member municipalities in the 1950s and 1960s have been linked to the TTC's ability both to increase its ridership and to require a level of subsidy that is low by North American standards (Bower 1979; Frisken 1991). The provincial government indirectly supported these policies by imposing strict controls on septic tank development in the suburbs at a time when few municipalities had piped sewage disposal facilities. Because of those controls, Metro absorbed most of the area's rapid population growth in its early years, undoubtedly at higher densities than would have occurred in a less controlled environment.

In 1970 the government seemed ready to exercise even greater planning control in the area when it outlined a long-term development concept for the Toronto Centred Region (TCR). Among other things, the TCR concept called for the containment of future growth within an urbanized zone along the shore of Lake Ontario, where it would be channelled into well-defined municipalities linked by a "highly sophisticated transit system" (Government of Ontario 1970, 18). The concept had only limited influence on the way the area developed, however. Of greater importance were the initiation and expansion of GO Transit, the construction of major highways to the north and to the west of Metro, and provincial financial and technical assistance to the construction of major trunk sewer and water lines to the east, north, and west of Metro. Their effect was to facilitate the dispersal of low-density residential and industrial districts throughout much of the CMA.

The creation of five two-tier regional governments outside Metropolitan Toronto between 1971 and 1974 entailed a consolidation of existing municipalities into larger units, thereby producing a more complex but less fragmented political system. The government abandoned its intention to make transit a responsibility of the regional councils, however, in the face of objections from municipal governments and local transit operators.

The government's surrender to private development interests and municipal governments was so complete by the late 1970s that it made little effort to persuade regional governments to produce the plans mandated in their founding legislation. The one exception was Metro Toronto, which the government insisted had to have an official plan. Work on that plan had begun at a time when strong citizen opposition to intensive redevelopment in downtown Toronto was producing demands for the decentralization of high-density office and residential development away from the core city. Thus the plan that Metro Council approved in 1980 called for high-density, multi-use suburban subcentres to be linked by rapid transit with each other and with downtown Toronto. It also emphasized the need to increase residential densities within Metropolitan Toronto (The Municipality of Metropolitan Toronto 1980, 15).

The provincial government had full authority to approve or require changes in local plans until 1982, when it issued a revised planning act that allowed it to delegate many of its approval powers to regional governments if they requested them. Regional governments tended to base their own plans or planning philosophies on the plans and preferences of their member municipalities, however, rather than on clearly articulated regional planning goals. Because local transit remained a local responsibility, planners in the regions also lacked an incentive to try to persuade local planners and politicians to consider transit in their planning decisions, as Metro planners had tried to do. In general, suburban planning practices paid little attention to the operational requirements for effective local transit operation (Frisken with McAree 1989). Nor did they pay much attention to the potential of GO Transit to serve either suburban development or transportation goals. Despite its well-established local planning system and its regional planning tradition, therefore, Ontario's transit policy evolved in virtual isolation from the land-use decisions that were shaping the region.

Renewed Commitment to Transit

In 1988, the provincial government decided to proceed with construction of an east-west expressway to the north of Metro and postpone indefinitely a decision on whether to fund the facility given highest priority in the Metro/TTC Network 2011 plan. These decisions seemed to attest to the growing political strength of interests pressing for better suburban roads and a decline in the influence of those arguing for more transit. Soon afterward, however, the Ministry of Transportation issued three separate policy statements expressing a growing provincial commitment to enhance the role of transit throughout the area. The most comprehensive of these projected a $5 billion provincial outlay on transportation infrastructure over a 20-year period (Ontario Ministry of Transportation 1990). It assigned only $690 million to new roads or road improvements and committed the rest to transit. The transit proposals combined Network 2011 additions to Metro's rapid transit system with proposals to increase train service on seven existing GO Transit routes linking downtown Toronto with municipalities to the east, the north, and the west of Metro. Funds to build the new lines were expected to come both from the province and municipalities and from the private sector.

The NDP government that replaced the Liberals in 1990 largely endorsed these proposals while adding funds to upgrade maintenance on the TTC system, neglect of which had been blamed for a fall in TTC ridership. The introduction of new transit lines has been stalled, however, both by the many delays inherent in the province's lengthy and complex environmental review process and by fiscal constraints.

The government activities with greatest potential for affecting the quality and role of transit in the Toronto area are those aimed at influencing the area's future development. The most far-reaching of these is an attempt by a provincial Office for the Greater Toronto Area (OGTA) to get local governments, private developers, and other interested groups and individuals to agree on growth-management policies that will help control government infrastructure costs, limit "sprawl," protect the environment, and enhance "quality of life" but without detracting from the region's ability to attract and sustain economic investment. The structural alternative that seems to command greatest support calls for a channeling of future growth into well-defined urban communities or "development nodes" at densities high enough to encourage increased use of transit both between and within communities.

The second initiative has been the preparation of a set of guidelines to encourage local planners and politicians to take account of transit operator and user requirements in their land-use decisions (Ontario Ministry of Transportation and Ministry of Municipal Affairs 1992). The third is a comprehensive review of the provincial-local planning system carried out by a special commission appointed by the NDP government late in 1990. Its purpose is to make the objectives of Ontario's land-use planning system more explicit and to try to integrate environmental, energy, agricultural, and heritage concerns into land-use planning (Commission on Planning and Development Reform in Ontario 1993). These initiatives attest to an unusually high degree (for North America) of government awareness of the need to integrate transit with other aspects of urban development. Nonetheless, they have to be reconciled not only with traditional suburban planning practices and preferences that have not been supportive of transit, but also with strong pressures on both the provincial and local governments to support any type of activity that will help pull the province out of a serious recession.

Montreal

With 104 lower-tier and 13 upper-tier municipalities in 1991, the Montreal CMA is the most politically fragmented of the three regions looked at in this study. At its core is the Island of Montreal, whose 29 municipalities make up the Montreal Urban Community (MUC), a two-tier metropolitan government created by the province in 1969 to provide selected areawide services. Transit services on the Island are provided by the Montreal Urban Community Transport Society (MUCTS), which in 1986 contained 60 percent of the area's population but accounted for 86 percent of its transit ridership. There were 24 other transit agencies operating in the region.

Direct provincial involvement in the financial and physical development of the Montreal region's public transit system began in the 1970s, although it was preceded by a long history of provincial intervention in local transit matters. Before 1951 the government's role was to arbitrate recurring disputes between the city of Montreal and the privately owned Montreal Tramways Company (Dagenais 1982, 102-09). Then in 1951 it passed legislation requiring the city of Montreal to buy out the company for $4.2 million and assume responsibility for its nearly $40 million debt. At the same time it put the system (which provided service to the city of Montreal and to 15 of its Montreal Island suburbs) under the control of a five-member Montreal Transportation Commission (MTC), two members appointed by the province, two by the city of Montreal, and one by Montreal suburbs. This mode of transfer was characteristic of the way the rural-dominated provincial legislature tended to deal with city and regional problems. It periodically intervened in the city's affairs in response to charges that local officials were guilty of corruption or financial mismanagement. It often added to the city's financial difficulties, however, by making it bear the brunt of the costs of regional expansion, as when it forced the city to annex hastily developed, bankrupt municipalities while refusing it the right to annex wealthier ones (Sancton 1985, 26-27). Undoubtedly this approach to regional issues contributed to a long-standing feature of the area's regional politics: the city of Montreal's determination to remain the dominant force in any regional organization and its suspicion of the motives underlying any provincial attempt to promote city-suburban cooperation.

Relations between the provincial government and the city began to improve after 1960, when the Liberal party headed by Jean Lesage (with strong support from the city of Montreal) defeated the rural-based Union Nationale regime headed by Maurice Duplessis. The Liberals ushered in that period in Quebec history known as "The Quiet Revolution"—a period characterized by rapid expansion of government spending on public services and the growth of a professional civil service. The government's aim to strengthen Quebec's industrial capacity led it to pay more attention to urban needs and urban development processes. Its main contribution to transportation in the Montreal area, however, was to construct new highways throughout the region, a policy begun by the previous regime.

Road construction was also a priority of the city government headed by Mayor Jean Drapeau, which between 1961 and 1967 not only spent half the city budget on road improvements but also persuaded the provincial and federal governments to build high speed expressways linking city with suburbs (Kaplan 1982, 425-27). Neighborhood opposition to urban highway construction neither gained much sympathy from the city administration nor prompted a reevaluation of urban transportation policy, as happened in Toronto, Vancouver, and other metropolitan areas throughout North America (Kaplan, 1982, 427; Colcord and Polan n.d., 55). Most of the road projects were thus completed with only minor changes. During this same period, the Drapeau administration decided to develop a subway system within the city. The provincial government agreed that the city could do so but specified that any capital and operating losses would have to be borne entirely by municipalities served by the MTC (Quebec, Statutes 1965, s. 57b).

The decision to build a subway, like the decision to push ahead with expressway construction, was part of the Drapeau administration's emphasis on massive projects that would elevate the city's status among world cities and attract outside investment (Trépanier 1993). One of these projects, the 1967 World's Fair, provided an impetus to both subway construction and road building in the early 1960s. The desire to have the suburbs share the costs of these ventures was a major reason for an aggressive strategy, carried out under the slogan "Une île, une ville," to annex all suburban municipalities on Montreal Island (Sancton 1985,

95-27). As part of this strategy, the city added suburban extensions to its long-range plan for subway expansion and promised to integrate failing suburban rail commuter lines into the MTC's bus and subway system (Kaplan 1982, 437). It was the province that finally decided the terms of suburban participation, however, by passing legislation in 1965 that required island municipalities to contribute to the annual transit operating subsidy on the basis of their share of total assessed property value. As a way of mollifying the suburbs, the city subsequently authorized MTC to abolish zone fares and make substantial improvements to suburban bus services (Kaplan 1982, 438). The only municipalities left out of these arrangements were 12 West Island suburbs, which continued to be served by private operators until the province made them part of the island system in 1980 as a way of making them help pay its operating deficit (Sancton 1985, 117, 128).

The Province Agrees to Help

In 1970 the MTC was absorbed into the newly created Montreal Urban Community, its membership reduced to three and its name changed to the Montreal Urban Community Transport Commission (MUCTC). The MUC became responsible for the system's capital debt and for financing future subway extensions. Municipalities were not called on to contribute to transit operations until 1971, however, by which time a decline in ridership, rising debt servicing costs and a policy of keeping fares low to maintain ridership had put the MUCTC in a deficit position (Lamonde 1990, 27). In 1972 the provincial government merged two departments, the Ministry of Transport and the Ministry of Roads, into a single Ministry of Transport that began to take more interest in urban transit. By 1973 it was contributing almost half the capital costs of a Metro extension (Colcord and Polan n.d., 48-49). The operating deficit continued to rise, however, and the province began to supplement municipal contributions on an ad hoc basis. By 1976 it had not only committed itself to a program of regular operating subsidies but also had assumed 60 percent of the costs of servicing the subway system's capital debt (Canadian Urban Transit Association 1984, 26).

The success of the Parti Québecois in the 1976 provincial election gave Quebec a government committed to the large-scale expansion of social and urban services. In a transportation plan issued in 1979, the government not only agreed to support several extensions to the Metro system (with 100 percent provincial funding of capital costs), but also proposed a system of three electrified suburban commuter lines on existing railway rights-of-way linking downtown Montreal to suburban communities both on and beyond Montreal Island. The railways had already announced their intention to abandon service on these lines, and the province had instituted ad hoc subsidies to keep them in operation. It tried to turn over their management to the MUCTC and the Société de transport de la rive sud de Montréal (STRSM), which provided transit service within seven communities immediately south of Montreal (Gouvernement du Québec 1987). Montreal Island municipalities opposed the idea, with some objecting to its implicitly high costs to island taxpayers; others claiming that transit improvements to municipalities off the island of Montreal would exacerbate decentralization. The province nonetheless proceeded to modernize one of the badly deteriorated lines with federal assistance, and the MUCTS[3] agreed to manage two of the lines (with provincial subsidies) until 1992. Service on the third line was abandoned.

The rapid increase in operating subsidies, which rose from $87.3 million to $578.4 million in the Montreal area between 1972 and 1986 (Gouvernement de Québec 1988, 87), became a contentious issue after the provincial Liberals replaced the Parti Québecois in 1985. A search for ways to limit expenditures culminated in a 1987 decision to freeze operating subsidies at their current levels, with built-in adjustments for inflation, as a way to induce municipal transit operators to control costs. (Only municipal governments that also contributed to operating costs would qualify for subsidies.)

Adding to Institutional Complexity

Throughout this period, the government was both looking for ways to coordinate transit services in the region and adopting measures that would make coordination more difficult. The creation of the MUC in 1970 had meant the eventual takeover of all transit services on Montreal Island by a single operator but had excluded the fast growing areas on the north and south shores of the St. Lawrence. Even before the MUC was formed, the 14 municipalities on Ile-Jésus, north of Montreal, had come together to form the city of Laval, which created its own transit operating

---

[3]The Montreal Urban Community Transport Society (MUCTS) replaced the MUCTC in a 1985 reorganization intended to give greater representation to MUC municipalities and urban transit users.

agency, the Société de transport de Laval (STL). South shore municipalities successfully resisted consolidation (which the government was promoting at the time), but seven of them agreed in 1973 to participate in a single transit agency, the STRSM. In 1979 a provincial Land Use Planning and Development Act established a system of regional county municipalities (RCMs) throughout the province. These were intended primarily to prepare regional plans and stimulate local planning, not to provide regional services. Eleven of these RCMs, in addition to the MUC and the city of Laval, were wholly or partly within the boundaries of the Montreal CMA.

The government added to this institutional complexity by enabling individual municipalities to operate their own transit systems or, after 1984, to participate in intermunicipal transit councils to which they contributed a share of local subsidies. The move was part of a government program to delegate more authority to local governments in the interest of reducing provincial contributions to local services. By 1986 there were 22 municipal or intermunicipal transit operators in the region, in addition to the three transport societies.

Promotion of Land-Use Planning

The 1979 Land Use Planning and Development Act culminated 10 years of government efforts to establish a basis for both regional and local planning in Quebec, where a local planning tradition had never become well established. Before the 1970s the principal form of planning done in the Montreal region was of the type (principally zoning) performed by local municipalities on a voluntary basis or carried out by specialized government agencies. Municipalities had tended to use their planning and servicing powers to entice or hasten new private development; provincial agencies to promote narrowly defined functional objectives. The two agencies credited with having greatest influence on the development and character of the Montreal area during the 1950s and 1960s were the federal government's Central Mortgage and Housing Corporation,[4] whose backing for low interest mortgages encouraged rapid residential development on the urban fringe, and the provincial Ministry of Roads, which built 250 miles of expressway within and around

---

[4]The name was changed to Canada Mortgage and Housing Corporation in 1979.

Montreal Island between 1958 and 1976.   These roads and the bridges that linked them to the island opened up large tracts of fringe land to low-density suburban development (Divay et Gaudreau 1982, 185-86). Ridership on the Montreal transit system remained high by North American standards nonetheless, despite the loss of central population that accompanied decentralization, because of the city's relatively high residential densities (the majority of the population lived in apartments), relatively low household incomes, and the fact that a large proportion of metropolitan area jobs remained in or near the centre (Colcord and Polan n.d., 14-16).

    An interest in promoting both local and regional planning became an aspect of Quebec's Quiet Revolution of the 1960s but generated little response on the island of Montreal. Mayor Jean Drapeau was antagonistic to comprehensive planning, preferring to plan individual projects (including roads and transit) in isolation from each other. He promoted the annexation of suburban municipalities as the only way to manage metropolitan expansion.   His administration's enthusiasm for large and expensive projects also made it unwilling to devote city resources to renovating older sections of the downtown business district or renewing the city's aging housing stock and deteriorating neighborhoods (Kaplan 1982, 450-59). Thus the city administration helped to foster decentralization both by building roads and by raising taxes to pay for major projects while doing little to attract new business and residents to the central part of the city.

    The Quebec government first manifested its growing interest in urban planning by mandating the MUC and the two other urban communities (in the Quebec City and Ottawa regions) to produce regional plans within three years of their creation in 1969.   In 1973 MUC planners issued *Proposals for Urban Development*, which included proposals for two suburban subcentres, one in the western section and one in the eastern section of Montreal Island, as a way to ease development pressure in the CBD, bring order to suburban development, and facilitate the creation of new public transit networks (Sancton 1985, 129). The proposals gained no support from the city of Montreal, which unlike Toronto had no interest in discouraging private development in the core.   They also encountered strong opposition from many suburban governments, which saw them as a threat to their own development aspirations. The plan never received MUC approval.   The proposed subcentres developed nonetheless in response to market pressures, but without connections to the region's rapid transit system.

The 1970s brought growing awareness among Montreal area and Quebec politicians that both the city and the island of Montreal were suffering substantial losses of both population and industry. The city reacted by setting up an economic development department to attract new industry to designated industrial parks, promote the construction of new housing, and help improve run-down commercial areas (Whelan 1989; Martin 1989). The MUC, still immobilized by the conviction of both city and suburban politicians that anything that benefited the one would harm the other, was unable to develop a strategy to address the problem. In 1982 the government stepped in, specifying that MUC, like the Regional County Municipalities, would have to approve a regional plan.

The plan the MUC finally approved in 1987 added one new subcentre to the two already identified in the 1973 *Proposals.* It was criticized as little more than a recognition of existing land-use patterns, lacking in vision and providing no clear alternative responses to current socio-economic trends (Trépanier 1993). Nonetheless, the fact that city and suburban representatives could agree on a document calling both for intensified development in the outlying sectors of the island and for "revitalization and revalorization" of the central zone represented a step forward in the ability of MUC members to agree on common objectives. It signified a growing awareness that they faced a common threat from expansion occurring on the north and south shores while the island was losing population, despite the fact that 15 percent of its land was still undeveloped and could accommodate 50,000 new homes and 25,000 new manufacturing jobs. That awareness was not strong enough between 1982 and 1986, however, to overcome the city's opposition to construction of proposed subway lines that would improve service to island suburbs. As a result of that opposition, those lines did not get built (Léonard and Léveillée 1986, 99-100).

The Province and the Region

The province was also responding to development trends in the Montreal region in conflicting ways. Its first initiative was to create a Montreal Region branch of the *Office de planification et de développement du Québec (OPDQ),* a provincial agency established in 1967 to prepare development plans for 10 provincial development regions. While the OPDQ had no implementing authority, its studies helped to make provincial and local officials more aware of what was happening in the region (Trépanier 1993). Growing criticism of the negative consequences of urban sprawl, together with concern about the rising costs of servicing an increasingly scattered population, prompted the Parti Québecois government to initiate a series of policies aimed at controlling the region's rate and pattern of growth. Chief among these was *l'Option préférable d'aménagement pour la région métropolitaine de Montréal* (the *Preferable Option for the Montreal Region)*, which called for containment of future growth within the already-urbanized parts of the region, and an agricultural zone law, which clearly specified those areas on the perimeter that were to remain in agriculture (Charbonneau, et. al., this volume; Trépanier 1993).

In support of *l'Option préférable* the government announced a moratorium on highway-building in the Montreal region and promised to increase its investment in public transit. It was in this context that it issued its 1979 transit-oriented transportation plan and enacted legislation to promote regional and municipal planning. The provincial cabinet approved *l'Option préférable* without making provision for its implementation, however, although it did create a Commission for the Protection of Agricultural Land to administer the Agricultural Zone Law. Moreover, it linked its planning legislation not only to the objective of stopping urban sprawl but also to the objective of promoting the values of local democracy and administrative decentralization (Quesnel 1990, 31). Given that these objectives often come into conflict when regional issues are being decided (see Smith and Bayne, this volume), its commitment to managing the region's development was at best uncertain.

Uncertainty became even more pronounced after the Liberals were returned to office in 1985. In 1988 the government responded to growing automobile congestion in the Montreal region with a transportation plan calling for the expenditure of $1.6 billion on regional transportation improvements over a 10-year period, with slightly more than half to go to highways (Gouvernement du Québec, Ministère des transports 1988). It assigned a large proportion of proposed expenditures to the maintenance and repair of facilities that had been neglected over the previous decade. In addition, however, its plan proposed construction of new highways in the outer part of the region and gave priority to construction of a subway extension to Montreal North (with the potential of serving riders from Laval) over an extension advocated by MUC planners to serve east-island commuters and the eastern subcentre of Anjou. This latter extension was one that had earlier been stalled by city-suburban infighting. Nonetheless, critics charged that it was not only contrary to objectives contained in the MUC plan that the government had approved only two years earlier but that it violated principles contained in *l'Option préférable* (Charbonneau, et al., this volume; Communauté urbaine de Montréal 1989; Lamonde 1989, 97-107). The proposed additions to the area's transportation system, they said, would only enhance tendencies to decentralization and sprawl, with the result that transit ridership would decline and automobile use increase.

A Partial Solution to Organizational Complexity

The government's immediate concern, however, was to find ways to curb deficits incurred by the Montreal Urban Community Transport Society (MUCTS). These had continued to rise despite the funding formula adopted in 1986, a tendency provincial officials blamed on the refusal of MUC to allow the MUCTS to raise its fares. The MUC insisted for its part that the deficit resulted from the refusal of Laval and south shore municipalities to contribute to the MUCTS's operating costs, even though their residents were heavy users of MUCTS services. It began to send those communities an annual bill, which they refused to pay. This highly divisive issue prompted the government to step up its efforts to promote an organization to coordinate services and integrate fares among the three transport societies. A major stumbling block was the city of Montreal's insistence that it should have a veto over the decisions of any regional organization, a position based on the belief that any organization dominated by suburban interests would act against the interests of the city's large low-income, unemployed, and ethnic minority populations (Interview with Roy and Ceccaldi, 1989).

The province achieved a partial resolution of the organizational problem in 1989 when representatives of the three transport societies agreed to participate in a 13-member regional transit coordinating agency (Conseil métropolitain de transport en commun) on which Montreal would have a plurality of members. With the agreement came an additional provincial subsidy of $26.5 million on the understanding that "this . . . will eliminate the need for any additional funding to balance annual budgets" (Gouvernement de Québec Press Release, November 6, 1989). The government also agreed to pay the full capital costs of major subway and commuter lines. While the agreement redistributed the existing operating and subway construction deficit among municipalities in the three service areas according to their assessment, it incorporated mechanisms to compel each commission to assume the financial consequences of its own decisions, especially as these affected the cost of monthly passes and the annual rate of deficit increase. If MUC politicians wished to use lower transit fares to assist low-income residents, in other words, they could not pass the additional costs on to the suburbs.

Scarcely had this agreement been worked out than the government announced its intention to reduce spending on municipal services by shifting more responsibilities to municipal governments and the municipal tax base (Ryan 1990). The move represented a partial retreat from programs put in place during the "Quiet Revolution," which the government said had added substantially to provincial expenditures without generating a corresponding increase in local taxes. The aim was to save $463.5 million by 1993-94, almost half of it by eliminating most operating subsidies to public transportation agencies. The government promised to retain the special subsidy to the recently created regional coordinating agency, at least for the short term. Other operating costs, it said, should be covered by fare increases (users' contributions to operating costs having fallen from 48.8 percent in 1986 to 29.5 percent in 1990) and by higher municipal subsidies. Municipalities would have the right to raise extra revenues for this purpose by imposing a tax on parking and a special tax on nonresidential properties, but only up to a ceiling the government would set for each municipal or intermunicipal organization.

Cancellation of provincial operating subsidies for public transit came amid signs that the Liberal government had little interest in constraining outward growth in the Montreal region; that it preferred instead to entrust the region's future to the combined activities of private investors and municipal governments, aided where necessary by provincial contributions to major infrastructural improvements (Charbonneau et al., this volume; Trépanier 1993). It had withdrawn support from projects to enhance the attractiveness of downtown Montreal and was failing to exercise meaningful oversight of municipal and RCM plans, particularly in the outer parts of the region. The Commission on Agricultural Land Preservation had also relaxed restrictions on the conversion of land from agricultural to urban use. Furthermore the government had weakened rather than strengthened its ability to develop or adopt a coherent perspective on areawide growth by dismantling the Montreal regional branch of the provincial OPDQ and breaking the Montreal Region into five separate administrative regions for study purposes. Thus it was compelling municipalities to assume financial responsibility for public transit at a time when its policies seemed to be supporting the spatial deconcentration and political fragmentation associated with transit decline in metropolitan areas in the United States.

Vancouver

Despite barriers to urban expansion posed by mountain ranges to the north, the Georgia Strait to the west and the American border to the south, Metropolitan Vancouver is the least densely populated of the three metropolitan areas under investigation. Several factors account for this characteristic. The Greater Vancouver Regional District (GVRD), which contains most of the area's population, is less fully developed than the other two areas; most new suburban growth is still occurring within its boundaries. Furthermore, the inclusion of large tracts of suburban land within agricultural land reserves helps to lower average residential density figures in affected municipalities. Finally, as figures in Table 15.2 indicate, there has been a long-standing tendency for Vancouver-based development to occur at lower densities than development in the other two areas. Lower population density and a more spread out population undoubtedly help to explain why public transit use in the GVRD is much lower than it is on the other two metropolitan systems; about 80 rides per capita in 1989 as compared to 212 for Metropolitan Toronto and 180 for Metropolitan Montreal. In 1985, 32 percent of the region's population served by transit lived in the city of Vancouver and accounted for 60 percent of daily transit ridership (GVRD Development Services 1987, 2-5).

Transit in the Vancouver area has never been a local responsibility, a characteristic of some importance to an understanding of the dynamics of transit decision making in that region. Before 1961 it was operated by the privately owned B.C. Electric Company; after that date it was the responsibility of a provincially appointed public corporation, B.C. Hydro, which the province created after buying out B.C. Electric as a way of gaining control over provincially financed power projects (Munro 1983). B.C. Hydro had little enthusiasm for its role as transit operator. Neither did the province's rural legislators and voters, who complained that they were helping to subsidize urban transit through their hydro bills. Consequently the Vancouver system was allowed to decline throughout the 1960s while local and provincial officials developed plans for an ambitious freeway network to link the city with its suburbs.

In 1965 the provincial government created the Greater Vancouver Regional District (GVRD) and other regional districts throughout the province both to assume responsibility for a number of regional services previously administered by special purpose authorities and to conduct regional planning. Soon afterward a vigorous citizen campaign against a freeway through Vancouver's historic Chinatown led the GVRD and other agencies to reexamine the area's transportation options. This process resulted in a succession of studies calling for reduced emphasis on the automobile and more attention to transit (Kopystynski and Powlowski 1980, 35-36; Oberlander and Smith 1993). Freeway opponents also gained control of the Vancouver city council, which rescinded its support for the freeway.

GVRD planners then began work on a plan that would give priority to transit. The GVRD Board also began to negotiate with the province for the right to take over transit from B.C. Hydro. These negotiations foundered, as have similar negotiations since that time, on the question of how transit deficits would be allocated and paid for. The provincial government wanted to place a limit on its total financial involvement during a period of rising transit costs, thereby implying a steady increase in the local share; local politicians on the GVRD Board refused to contribute toward transit operating costs out of property taxes. Property taxes already covered a larger share of municipal expenditures in British Columbia than in most other provinces, and local politicians were loathe to take the political risk of increasing them.

Direct Provincial Involvement Begins

A left-leaning New Democratic Party (NDP) government elected in 1972 was more ready to respond to pressures for transit improvements than was the conservative, business-oriented Social Credit (Socred) government it replaced. It was no more willing to hand over responsibility for transit to the GVRD, however. Instead it assigned that responsibility to a newly created Bureau of Transit Services. During the NDP's brief time in office (1972-1975), the bureau upgraded service in both the city and suburbs, introduced express buses from suburban centres into downtown Vancouver, and provided financial support to maintain a basic transit fare of 25 cents to encourage ridership. These policies, combined with the costs of inflation, resulted in an increase in the provincial subsidy per passenger from 6¢ to 30¢ a ride between 1972 and 1976, some of it paid by B.C. Hydro, the rest by provincial grants (Adams 1976). The government justified the costs as savings in outlays on provincial highways.

The return of the Socreds to power in 1975 brought an immediate resumption of negotiations concerning the GVRD's role in regional transit planning and operations. The GVRD continued to oppose using property tax revenues to cover the local share of the operating deficit, although some members apparently expected the province to impose this requirement, thereby relieving local elected officials of the blame (Tennant n.d., 61). Instead of creating a regional transit agency, however, the government in 1978 created a provincewide Urban Transit Authority to take over transit services administered by B.C. Hydro in the Vancouver and Victoria regions and by the Department of Municipal Affairs in other parts of the province. Under legislation setting up this authority, municipalities could establish a special property tax to raise funds for the municipal portion of the operating deficit. Alternatively, they could ask the cabinet to impose a special levy on electricity or a special tax on gasoline within the transit service area. After heated debate, the GVRD Board decided to ask the province for both special levies rather than make transit a charge on the property tax. Its only departure from that position was to accede in 1982 to a request from the business community for a nonresidential property tax to replace the local power levy on commercial accounts.

Organizational Disputes Persist

The organizational changes initiated in 1978 resulted in a short-lived division of responsibility for funding, operating, and planning the transit system among three organizations: the Urban Transit Authority, a Metro Transit Operating Company, and the GVRD (GVRD 1982, 1). Difficulties soon arose in coordinating the activities and maintaining harmony among the three organizations, labelled the "three-headed monster" by its critics (Oberlander and Smith 1993). A special GVRD committee prepared a case for a single regional transit authority consisting of provincial and local representatives, citing "the principle of local determination" as its rationale, but did not suggest any changes in the source of local funds (GVRD 1982, 35). The government instead relieved the Regional District of transit responsibilities altogether and assigned them to the provincial transit authority, now renamed British Columbia (BC) Transit. It took this step not only because of the GVRD's stand on local financing but also because of the GVRD's public opposition to the government's preferred technology for a light rapid transit line running from downtown Vancouver to the nearby town of New Westminster.

The GVRD had first proposed rapid transit in this corridor in the early 1970s and had subsequently prepared studies recommending a conventional light rail system, with cars running on rails at grade. The government instead decided in 1979 to build an elevated system (SkyTrain) using technology being developed by Ontario's Urban Transportation Development Corporation (UTDC). The decision was apparently influenced by a $300 million performance bond posted by the Ontario government, a UTDC promise that 60 to 70 percent of the system's components would be manufactured by B.C. industry, and the prospect of federal government assistance. The goverment's assurances that it would pay the entire difference between the cost of the conventional and the advanced technologies failed to mollify local officials, who expected that the line's higher operating costs would result in demands for larger local contributions.

Lack of Consensus on Regional Planning

The development of the SkyTrain and subsequent debates about future light rapid transit lines were closely linked not only to organizational and financial issues but also to debates about planning and development in the region. Like the Toronto area, the Vancouver area has a planning tradition dating back to the period right after World War II. The complete divorce of transit delivery from municipal administration meant, however, that an interest in transit/land-use linkages was slow to develop. The first official regional plan, produced by the municipally appointed Lower Mainland Regional Planning Board (LMRPB) in 1966, proposed that future residential development be confined within compact centres ("cities in a sea of green") as a way of protecting farmland, with highways as the principal linkages among them (Kellas 1983, 3). The LMRPB was dissolved in 1968 after some of its members publicly criticized provincial decisions affecting land use in the region (Tennant n.d., 12). Its plans and planning responsibilities were handed over to the GVRD and three other regional districts established in its territory of jurisdiction.

The GVRD began to revise the regional plan at a time of growing citizen concern with rapid population growth, increasing development pressures on the central city, and rising housing costs. While maintaining LMRPB policies, therefore, it placed greater emphasis on managing growth and on developing proposals for improvements to the region's public transportation system (Kellas 1983, 3-4). Its principal contribution to regional policy was the Livable Region Program approved by the GVRD Board in 1975. This was essentially a set of five general principles with virtually no agreed-upon method of implementation (Kellas 1983, 12). Nonetheless the principles have continued to influence public debate about the way the region should develop. They called for the setting of residential growth targets; promotion of a balance of population to jobs in each part of the region (an objective that implied more jobs in the suburbs and more housing in the city of Vancouver) as a way of reducing long-distance commuting; the development of "regional town centres" to relieve development pressures on the city of Vancouver; the protection of the area's natural environment; and a transit-oriented transportation system.

In keeping with the Livable Region strategy, proposals for the development of the LRT system have been closely linked to proposals for the development of Regional Town Centres. The provincial government supported the regional town centre strategy by establishing public corporations to promote redevelopment of downtown New Westminster and new development at Lonsdale Quay, in the vicinity of the SeaBus terminus on the north shore of Burrard Inlet, directly across from the city of Vancouver. A more contentious policy was the system of Agricultural Land Reserves initiated by the NDP government. Not only did it conflict with the growth aspirations of development-minded municipalities but it also commanded less support from the Socreds than it had from the NDP. Consequently there were major conflicts between the GVRD and local municipalities and between the GVRD and the government over proposals to allow land to be removed from the reserves and converted to urban use. One of these conflicts contributed to a 1983 provincial decision to relieve regional districts of their planning responsibilities (Oberlander and Smith 1993). Nonetheless, according to one GVRD official, the Agricultural Land Commission (which administers the land reserves) had "tremendous influence" on containing growth in the Greater Vancouver Area by forcing municipalities to decide which areas were going to develop and which were not (Cameron interview, 1989).

Apart from controls exercised by the Agricultural Land Commission, the B.C. government's role in local planning mainly takes the form of a variety of uncoordinated land-use regulations that have been criticized as unnecessarily complex and cumbersome (Bish 1990, 117-18). The government seemed to be moving toward a provincewide planning system in 1980 when it proposed a new Land Use Act to provide a basis both for coordinating the activities of various provincial ministries and for making provincial scrutiny of local land-use decisions more consistent and understandable. The government withdrew provisions for interministerial coordination, however, in the face of opposition from cabinet members. It then allowed the legislation to lapse altogether at the end of a legislative session (Oberlander and Smith 1993). In 1983 it passed a *Municipal Amendment Act* that stripped regional districts of their planning and zoning powers. There was no longer a need for regional plans, it said, because municipalities all had plans in place.

Regional Transportation Issues Resurface

The B.C. government responded to increasing automobile congestion in the Vancouver area and other parts of the province by calling in 1988 for in-depth transportation studies in each of the province's eight Economic Development Regions. Within the Mainland Southwest region (consisting of the GVRD and three other regional districts in the Fraser River Valley, as well as the Sunshine Coast north of Vancouver) a special task force was set up to prepare a comprehensive transportation plan in less than six months. The Task Force study was a highly traditional approach to the area's transportation needs. While it advocated "land-use policies to slow the growth in transportation demand by promoting employment closer to where people live," it left an investigation of the relationship between alternative land-use scenarios and transportation networks for a later date (Greater Vancouver Transportation Task Force 1989, vii, 39-40). Its recommended "balanced approach" to transportation funding implied an $855 million expenditure on roads and a $640 million expenditure on transit by 1996—a division of resources that critics found too favourable to roads. Furthermore, its ordering of priority for construction of new rapid transit reversed that proposed in earlier GVRD studies (GVRD 1979).

The government added to dissatisfaction within the GVRD shortly after release of the Task Force report by announcing its intention to support two extensions to the SkyTrain system, the first across the Fraser River into Surrey and the second between downtown Vancouver and the suburban town of Richmond, as well as a new marine rapid transit service across Burrard Inlet to serve north shore communities. The marine service had never been considered by the GVRD; the proposed SkyTrain links were included in GVRD long-range plans but had been assigned lower priority than an extension to Coquitlam, which the province was not proposing to fund. Opponents claimed the provincial decisions had been motivated entirely by political considerations; provincial transportation officials insisted they would provide better transit service to some of the more rapidly growing parts of the region.

Provincial activities and the disputes to which they gave rise helped to bring about a more consultative provincial-local transportation planning process. After hearing GVRD criticisms of the task force report, the government issued a transportation plan in May 1990 that satisfied GVRD requests that the province assign priority to transit, or to road projects that benefited transit, and that it give regional officials an ongoing role in plan review and revision (Peterson 1990). It also established a special account to allow multiple-year transportation budgeting as an aid to long-range planning. It continued to insist that it would not give up its powers to determine transit priorities as long as it paid nearly 50 percent of transit costs and local municipalities continued to derive their share from traditional provincial tax bases (Johnson 1989). It did agree, however, that any of the three parties (the province, B.C. Transit, and the GVRD) involved in capital finance would have to seek the agreement of the other two parties if it wanted to build an extension. If one party decided to go ahead with an extension without such an agreement, it would have to pay its entire costs.

A second outcome of the government's transportation planning initiatives was renewed interest in and qualified support for regional planning. When the Transportation Task Force was formed, the GVRD's municipal members not only agreed that the GVRD should be represented on it but also decided that the GVRD should assume a nonregulatory planning role. The government then amended the Municipal Act to give all regional-districts the right to conduct regional planning on a cooperative (not mandatory) basis. A comprehensive program to update the Livable Region Strategy has resulted in restatements of its two transportation-related objectives: a transit-oriented transportation system and a more balanced interregional distribution of jobs and residences (GVRD 1990, 1991).

Apart from support given to town centre development, however, there are as yet few indications that either the provincial or local governments are willing to tackle the challenge of developing a more transit-oriented urban structure. Local politicians, especially in the suburbs, have been little inclined to depart from development patterns that assume or require heavy dependence on automobiles. A city of Vancouver policy of supporting or promoting medium- and high-density development on underused port and industrial lands accounted for most of the increase in the city population between 1971 and 1986. This policy coexists with one dedicated to the protection and preservation of existing low-density neighborhoods, however. Despite the area's relatively low population density, any proposal to alter existing land use, including a proposal to build a new rapid transit line, is likely to generate intense opposition from coalitions of community groups (Seelig and Artibise 1991, 34-35; *The Vancouver Sun* 1991). While opposition of this type is a feature of city politics everywhere, it is reinforced in the Vancouver area by citizen determination to preserve the advantages derived from the region's superb natural setting. Any structure that rises above its surroundings is likely to obstruct somebody's view.

COMPARATIVE OVERVIEW

Provincial governments played a crucial role in the development of urban mass transit systems in the Toronto, Montreal, and Vancouver areas in the 1970s and 1980s. There seems little doubt that if this formerly "local" service had remained in the hands of agencies owned or regulated by municipal governments, it would have undergone serious decline rather than expansion. Reasons for provincial decisions to become involved varied from province to province and from time to time. One that recurred several times in all three regions was political pressure to extend transit service to suburban municipalities in the face of reluctance or refusal on the part of both central city and suburban governments to finance such extensions. Such local attitudes derived not only from an unwillingness to pay for regional services out of local taxes but also from a belief that intermunicipal transit links would benefit rival municipalities in the ongoing competition for growth-related advantages.

The governments of Ontario and British Columbia have justified their contributions to transit, particularly high speed rail transit between city and suburbs, as a way to relieve road congestion and reduce demand for provincial outlays on costly and politically unpopular urban highways. This rationale was less influential in Quebec, where both local and provincial governments tended to treat transit as a supplement rather than an alternative to highway building. There the province's decision to contribute to transit was part of an awakened interest in urban issues and in improving social services.

Political and economic boosterism have also been important motives for decisions to invest in rapid transit. Ontario Premier William Davis announced the Intermediate Capacity Transit technology in an audiovisual presentation to a well-publicized gathering of municipal officials and members of the legislature. His government justified the creation of the Ontario (later Urban) Transportation Development Corporation as taking advantage of an opportunity to fill a gap in the transit equipment manufacturing industry. The B.C. government's decision to purchase UTDC technology was based not only on that company's promise to have a majority of the components manufactured in British Columbia but also on a desire to have a modern and innovative transportation showcase in place for the 1986 World's Fair (Oberlander and Smith 1993). Once again, the situation in Quebec was somewhat different. There it was the city of Montreal, not the province, that sought political and economic advantage from investing in a subway to enhance the 1967 World's Fair. The provincial government did not begin to contribute to capital costs until 1973, well after the World's Fair was over.

The fact that investment in rapid transit can serve a variety of provincial purposes, some of which have little to do either with local plans or priorities or with demonstrated demand for transit, helps to explain why the share of capital costs paid by the governments of all three provinces by the end of the 1980s was higher than their share of operating subsidies. Nonetheless, the first operating assistance provided by all three provincial governments was open-ended and allowed transit agencies to keep fares low while adding new services, particularly in the suburbs. As a result, it led to better service and more riders, but also to rapid increases in operating deficits. Cost increases prompted governments to develop subsidy policies that limited the growth of their own contributions and made local governments responsible for meeting costs that exceeded expenditure limits specified in provincial formulae. Thus, an interest in encouraging municipalities and transit operators to control costs and pursue efficiency soon gained ascendancy in provincial subsidy policies over the objective of enhancing transit accessibility to potential users. The only urban residents whose transportation needs have received special attention from provincial policymakers are (1) suburban commuters travelling to the city core and (2) physically disabled persons who qualify for the demand-responsive services provided in all three regions by specially equipped small vehicles.

A criticism sometimes directed at government investment in urban rapid transit is that it discriminates against surface transit systems and works to the disadvantage of those who use them. What these case studies show, however, is that aid to rapid transit can act as a catalyst for more generalized transit assistance. At least in Ontario and Quebec, government decisions to invest in rapid transit helped to highlight inadequacies in local bus operations (which not only provide service within local communities but also bring commuters to rapid transit terminals), thereby providing a justification for operating subsidies. Because these subsidies allowed transit systems to expand the scope of their surface operations, they likely made transit available to a larger proportion of city and suburban residents than would have received it otherwise. They also contributed indirectly to increases in per capita transit ridership.

It is difficult, therefore, to separate the benefits of capital from operating subsidies in trying to assess what provincial involvement has meant for the scope of transit service provided in the three regions. What is clear, however, is that by the late 1980s the evolution of transit policymaking had put provincial governments in a position to decide how both regional and local transit systems would develop in future. This was so both because they paid most or (in the case of Montreal) all the costs of new rapid transit lines and because they could use operating subsidies to influence the transit policies of local governments. By that time, provincial governments were also under growing pressure to take action to relieve a build-up of automobile congestion caused by a rapid growth of suburban populations.

In undertaking comprehensive examinations of regional transit trends and options, these governments also looked at alternative ways to organize transit delivery on a regional basis. There were two aspects to this undertaking. One was to find ways to coordinate the plans and services and integrate the fare structures of the various agencies involved in transit delivery. (The nature of the organizational challenge they faced is summarized in Table 15.3). The second was to find ways to involve local governments (or their transit operators) in regional transit planning and operation. To satisfy both objectives, provincial governments had to find ways to secure cooperation from local councils and local agencies that were often suspicious of each other's motives and fearful that participation in a regional organization implied higher costs to local taxpayers. The compromises made to overcome or circumvent such attitudes resulted in administrative arrangements that cannot be categorized in terms of a simple central-local dichotomy.

The organizational outcomes were different in each metropolitan area. In the Vancouver area, transit planning and service coordination were a problem for only a brief period in the early 1980s, when the government departed from a tradition of having transit provided by a provincial crown

Table 15.3. *Local Governments and Transit Operators in the Three Metropolitan Areas: Late 1980s*

Metro Area	# Municipalities	Transit Operators
Toronto	6 regional municipalities 30 local municipalities	1 interregional (GO) 2 regional 14 local
Montreal	13 regional municipalities 104 local municipalities	1 interregional (MUCTS) 1 regional Society 1 intermunic. Society 22 municipal or inter- municipal boards
Vancouver	1 regional district 18 municipalities 3 electoral districts	1 (B.C. Transit) 1 regional advisory board

corporation and divided operational and planning responsibility among a provincial authority, a metropolitan operating company, and the GVRD. That situation ended in 1983, when the creation of B.C. Transit gave the area a single transit operator directly accountable to the provincial Ministry of Municipal Affairs. B.C. Transit operates an integrated regional system with a three-zone fare system (a source of dissatisfaction in the outer parts of the region), which it can extend to take in additional territory as the region expands.

In Ontario, the government concluded many years of study by deciding not to act on successive recommendations for a regional agency. Instead, it allowed its Ministry of Transportation to make informal arrangements to work with local governments and local transit operators to develop a more integrated system for the Greater Toronto Area, which it defined to include all the territory likely to experience development in the foreseeable future. It also used special subsidies to help reduce fares on local bus services to GO Transit stations and on bus services that cross municipal boundaries.

The Quebec government set out to convince the region's three largest transit operators to coordinate their fare and service policies. It helped establish a regional transit organization and made it responsible for transit coordination, fare integration, and system planning. Because that organization's jurisdiction is limited to the territory served by the three largest operators, however, it lacks both the authority and the membership to influence transit decisions in the rapidly developing outer municipalities or to integrate them into an effective regional system.

Local officials were involved in these arrangements in different ways. In the Vancouver area, a Greater Vancouver Transit Commission consisting of local elected officials was established to advise on fares, routes, and service levels. B.C. transit retained full authority to make such decisions, however. In Ontario, local governments and their transit operators continue to decide on local fares and services. While the government maintained sole right to decide how, where, and when the GO commuter system will expand, it developed elaborate mechanisms for consulting local officials about regional transit issues. In Quebec, the government withdrew from regional transit matters as soon as it had set up the regional agency. The agency's board is made up entirely of municipal members; it has no provincial representation.

The degree to which local governments are involved in transit planning and operations is closely linked to the nature of their contributions to transit operating deficits. Municipal officials in the GVRD were granted only limited opportunity to participate in transit decision making at least in part because of their refusal to authorize the use of property tax funds to cover the local share of operating deficits. In Ontario, where operating deficits on local transit are shared equally by the provincial and local governments, there has been a greater tendency to treat local governments as partners in transit policymaking. The Quebec government's willingness to grant municipalities full autonomy in transit operation coincided with its desire to make municipal governments fully responsible for transit operating deficits.

Despite differences in the degree and type of their formal involvement in transit administration, municipalities in all three regions are similarly able to influence the evolution of regional transit systems through their land-use planning practices and their control of local streets. Such influences have tended to be largely negative from a transit perspective. The types of development favored by most suburban governments have typically supported patterns of outward growth that are difficult and costly to serve by transit. The transportation studies conducted in the late 1980s made it abundantly clear that automobile ownership and use in the three regions had continued to increase faster than population despite government support for transit. They also demonstrated that increasing proportions of regional populations and regional jobs were locating in the outer suburbs, where both densities and transit use were substantially lower than in the more central parts of the regions. Thus provincial governments had to decide whether to adapt their transportation policies to these development tendencies or whether to intervene in local land-use practices and otherwise try to alter them in ways likely to support transit.

Once again the three provincial governments reacted differently. Ontario not only made the strongest financial commitment to transit but also promoted areawide discussion of changes that would have to occur in local, regional, and provincial land-use practices to effect a significant shift in ridership away from automobiles and toward transit. Quebec seemed ready to acquiesce to prevailing land-use trends by curtailing its involvement in both public transit and regional planning while making improvements to roads and bridges to enhance automobile travel to, from, and among the region's outer districts. The British Columbia government adopted a stance somewhere between these two positions. While it seemed little inclined to take the initiative in addressing issues associated with regional growth, it agreed to allow the GVRD to try to build a consensus among member municipalities about how the region might achieve a more transit-oriented urban structure.

CONCLUSION

Despite differences in the way provincial governments have defined and addressed metropolitan transportation issues, mass transit systems in all three regions are at a critical point in their development, their future in the hands of governments experiencing growing pressures to focus their urban policies on areas outside the more densely built-up, transit-oriented central municipalities. Those pressures come from suburban landowners anxious to proceed with new development for residential or business purposes, from the growing number of municipalities being overtaken by urban expansion at the fringe, and by private automobile owners and their lobby organizations. They also face pressure not to take actions that may discourage investment or add to government costs during a prolonged period of economic restructuring and fiscal constraint. In addition, they are likely to encounter ambivalence or outright resistance from both inner and outer districts to the idea of more concentrated, higher density forms of residential development.

Thus far, only the government of Ontario has been willing to confront these pressures in a comprehensive way. Its willingness to do so can be traced to a somewhat more cooperative tradition of provincial-municipal and intermunicipal relations in transit-policymaking in this area than in the other two, as well as to a better-established and more widely accepted provincial framework for local and regional planning. Even the Ontario government has proceeded with caution, however, trying to build consensus among the many parties interested in the way the area develops rather than using its authority over municipalities to make them conform to a prescribed vision of the area's future. As in the other two areas, therefore, the future of transit in the Toronto area will depend as much or more on the policies and actions of local governments as it does on those of the province.

REFERENCES

Adams, Neale. 1976. "Transit or Roads for British Columbia." *Transit Canada* 12 (July-August): 19-21.

Bish, Robert L. 1990. *Local Government in British Columbia,* 2d ed. Richmond, B.C.: Union of British Columbia Municipalities.

Bower, R. J. 1979. "The Influence of the Subway System on the Growth of Metropolitan Toronto." In *New Urban Rail Transit: How Can Its Development and Growth-Shaping Potential be Realized?* Report prepared for the Subcommittee on the City of the Committee on Banking, Finance, and Urban Affairs, U.S. House of Representatives, 96th Cong., 1st. sess. Washington: Government Printing Office, 17-28.

Canadian Urban Transit Association. 1984. *Government Funding Policies for Urban Transit in Canada, 1983-1984.* Toronto: CUTA.

Cervero, Robert. 1986. "Urban Transit in Canada: Integration and Innovation at Its Best." *Transportation Quarterly* 40 (July): 293-316.

Colcord, Frank C. 1976. *Urban Transportation Decision Making. Final Report.* Washington, D.C.: U.S. Department of Transportation, Office of Transportation Economic Analysis.

_____, and Steven M. Polan. n.d. "Urban Transportation Decision Making: 8. Montreal: A Case Study." Draft Final Report, prepared for U.S. Department of Transportation, Office of Transportation Economic Analysis, Washington, D.C. Manuscript, n.d.

Commission on Planning and Development Reform in Ontario. 1993. *Final Report.* Toronto: The Commission. June.

Communauté urbaine de Montréal. 1989. *Un Plan de Transport en fonction des besoins réels de la population.* Mémoire présenté à la Commission de l'aménagement et des équipements. Montréal: Janvier.

Dagénais, Jean-Pierre. 1982. *Ironie du Char: Un essai sur l'automobile et la crise des transports à Montréal.* Montréal: Author.

Delcan Corp. 1988. A Transportation Planning Overview for the Province of British Columbia. Victoria, B.C.

Divay, Gérard, et Marcel Gaudreau. 1982. "L'agglomeration de Montréal: Velleites de concentration et tendances centrifuges." *The Canadian Journal of Regional Science* 5: 183-98.

Frisken, Frances. 1985. *Public Transit and the Public Interest: An Empirical Analysis of Two Administrative Models.* Report No. 15. Winnipeg: Institute of Urban Studies.

_____. 1991. "The Contributions of Metropolitan Government to the Success of Toronto's Public Transit System." *Urban Affairs Quarterly* 27 (December): 268-92.

_____, with Marc McAree. 1989. *Relating Municipal Land Use Practices to Public Transit Operations in the Greater Toronto Area: Constraints and Opportunities.* A report prepared for the Municipal Transportation Policy Office, Ontario Ministry of Transportation. June.

The Globe Mail. 1985. July 17.

Goldberg, Michael A., and John Mercer. 1986. *The Myth of the North American City.* Vancouver: University of British Columbia Press.

Gouvernement du Québec. 1987. Comité ministériel des conseils intermunicipaux de transport sur les services de trains de banlieue dans la région de Montréal, *Rapport.* Québec, Que.

_____, Ministère des transports. 1988. *Le Transport dans la région de Montréal. Plan d'Action: 1988-1998.* Québec, Que.

Government of Ontario, The. 1970. *Design for Development: The Toronto-Centred Region.* Toronto: The Queen's Printer, May.

Greater Vancouver Regional District (GVRD). 1979. *The Rapid Transit Project: Final Report Summaries and Staff Committee Recommendations,* #2. Burnaby, B.C.: December.

_____. 1982. "A Review of Organizational Requirements for Transit in the Lower Mainland." Draft Report of the Organizational Review Committee to the Transit Committee of the Board of Directors. Burnaby, B.C.

_____. 1990. "Completion of the Review of the Report of the Greater Vancouver Transportation Task Force." Burnaby, B.C.: February 28.

_____. 1991. "The Regional Role in Transportation and Land Use Planning in the Lower Mainland." Discussion Paper. Burnaby, B.C.: October.

GVRD Development Services. 1987. *1985 Metropolitan Vancouver Origin-Destination Survey. Summary of Household and Travel Demand Statistics.* May.

Greater Vancouver Transportation Task Force. 1989. *Freedom to Move.* Burnaby, B.C., July.

Johnston, Rita M. 1989. Letter to Mayor Donald A. S. Lanskail, Chairman, Vancouver Regional Transit Commission, re "Local Share of Transit Expenditures for 1989/90." February 27.

Kantor, Paul, with Stephen David. 1988. *The Dependent City: The Changing Political Economy of Urban America.* Glenview, Ill.: Scott, Foresman.

Kaplan, Harold. 1982. *Reform, Planning, and City Politics: Montreal, Winnipeg, Toronto.* Toronto: University of Toronto Press.

Kellas, Hugh. 1983. "Implementing Greater Vancouver's Transit and Land Use Strategy." Presented to 1983 American Planning Association Conference, April 17.

Kopystynski, Adrian, and Syd Powlowski. 1980. "The Genesis of L.R.T. in Vancouver." In *Light Rail Transit in Vancouver—Costs, Potentials and Alternatives*, ed. M. C. Poulton, Vancouver: U.B.C. Centre for Transportation Studies, 16-53.

Lamonde, Pierre. 1989. *Développement urbain et stratégie de transport pour Montréal, horizon 2001.* Montréal: INRS-Urbanisation.

_____. 1990. *Le financement du transport en commun métropolitain: de Montréal à Rabat.* Montréal: Institut national de la recherche scientifique.

Léonard, Jean François, and Jacques Léveillée. 1986. *Montréal After Drapeau.* Montreal: Black Rose Books.

Martin, Madame Diane. 1989. "Exposé." Congres de l'Association Canadienne des Sciences Régionales. Montréal, June 2.

Maule, Christopher J. 1985. *The Urban Transportation Development Corporation: A Case Study of Government Enterprise.* Ottawa: Economic Council of Canada.

The Municipality of Metropolitan Toronto. 1980. *Official Plan for the Urban Structure: The Metropolitan Toronto Planning Area.* Toronto: Municipality of Metropolitan Toronto.

_____, Toronto Transit Commission. 1987. *Future Transportation Needs in the Greater Toronto Area.* Toronto, March.

Munro, Gary. 1983. "Urban Transit in Vancouver." Paper presented at the Canadian Political Science Association meeting, Vancouver, B.C., June 8.

Oberlander, H. Peter, and Patrick J. Smith. 1993. "Governing Metropolitan Vancouver: Regional Governance, Public Policymaking and Intergovernmental Relations in British Columbia." In *Metropolitan Governance: American and Canadian Intergovernmental Perspectives*, ed. Donald N. Rothblatt and Andrew Sancton, Berkeley: Institute of Governmental Studies Press, University of California, 329-73.

Ontario Ministry of Transportation. 1988. *Transportation Directions for the Greater Toronto Area.* Toronto, May 24.

_____. 1990. *Let's Move: Transportation Solutions for the '90s.* Toronto, April 5.

Ontario Ministry of Transportation and Ministry of Municipal Affairs. 1992. *Transit-Supportive Land Use Planning Guidelines.* Toronto: The Ministries, April.

Peterson, Doug. 1990. "Memorandum to Chairperson, Regional Administrative Advisory Committee, Greater Vancouver Regional District, re Provincial Transportation Plan. May 29.

Pucher, John. 1988. "Urban Travel Behavior as the Outcome of Public Policy: The Example of Modal-Split in Western Europe and North America." *American Planning Association Journal* 54 (Winter): 509-20.

Quebec *Statutes.* 1965. An Act to amend the charter of the Montreal Transportation Commission, c.86.

Quesnel, Louise. 1990. "Political Control over Planning in Quebec." *International Journal of Urban and Regional Research* 14 (March): 25-48.

Ryan, Claude, Minister of Municipal Affairs. 1990. "The Sharing of Responsibilities Between the Government and Municipalities: Some Needed Adjustments." Statement to the Table Quebec-Municipalites. Quebec, December 14.

Sancton, Andrew. 1985. *Governing the Island of Montreal: Language Differences and Metropolitan Politics.* Berkeley: University of California Press.

Seelig, Michael Y., and Alan F. J. Artibise. 1991. *From Desolation to Hope: The Pacific Fraser Region in 2010.* Vancouver: University of British Columbia, School of Community and Regional Planning.

Tennant, Paul. n.d. "The Evolution of Regional Government in Greater Vancouver: 1914-1979." Unpublished draft. Vancouver: Department of Political Science, University of British Columbia.

Transit Advisory Group to the Minister of Transportation for Ontario. 1987. *Crossing the Boundaries: Coordinating Transit in the Greater Toronto Area.* Toronto, December.

Trépanier, Marie-Odile. 1993. "Metropolitan Governance in the Montreal Area." In *Metropolitan Governance: American and Canadian Intergovernmental Perspectives,* ed. Donald N. Rothblatt and Andrew Sancton, Berkeley: Institute of Governmental Studies Press, University of California, 53-110.

Urban Land Institute and Gladstone Associates. 1979. *Joint Development: Making the Real Estate—Transit Connection.* Washington: The Urban Land Institute.

The Vancouver Sun. 1991, June 1.

Whelan, Robert K. 1989. "Urban Development in Montreal: A Comparative, North American Perspective." Paper presented to the annual meeting of the Urban Affairs Association. Baltimore, Maryland, March 15-18.

INTERVIEWS

Cameron, Ken, Greater Vancouver Regional District, June 16, 1989.

Cardinal, André, Acting Director of Planning, Communauté urbaine de Montréal, May 17, 1989.

Ceccaldi, M. Xavier, Interim Manager, General Planning, Société de transport de la Communauté urbaine de Montréal, May 15, 1989.

Hargreaves, Daniel, Gouvernement du Québec, June 1, 1989

Lehman, Andrée, Chief of Policy Department, Quebec Ministry of Transport, May 19, 1989.

Leicester, Glen, B.C. Transit, June 16, 1989.

Lewarne, Bill, former Chair of GVRD Transportation Committee, June 17, 1989.

McLean, Jim, Greater Vancouver Regional District, June 16, 1989.

Puccinni, Richard, Executive Director, Municipal Transportation Division, Ontario Ministry of Transportation, August 14, 1989.

Roy, Louise, President and General Manager, Société de transport de la Communauté urbaine de Montréal, May 15, 1989.

Simard, Hubert, Montreal City Councillor and Chair of Planning Commission, Communauté urbaine de Montréal, May 17, 1990.

Théberge, Yvon, Engineer, Quebec Ministry of Transport, May 19, 1989.

Ward, Larry, SkyTrain General Manager, British Columbia Rapid Transit Company, June 15, 1989.

Chapter 16

Metropolitan Change and Political Disruption:
The New Left, the New Right, and the Postwar Orthodoxy

Warren Magnusson
The University of Victoria

The metropolis is certainly no respecter of boundaries. Wherever we set boundaries—in our imagination, our maps of urban life, or our political institutions—it soon overcomes them. This is partly a matter of expansion: the ceaseless spillage of new suburbs, the spin-off of satellite towns, and the transformation of independent communities into appendages of the great city. However, it also involves the constant reorganization of metropolitan life, which disrupts communities, throws up new ones, changes the relation between city and suburbs, spins off new centres within the built-up area, and almost immediately decentres the nodes it establishes. The very concept of the metropolis is a sign of this, for it was invented to designate an urban reality that could no longer be understood as a self-contained city with a fixed structure. The metropolis may have principles of organization, but it lacks genuine boundaries.

This boundlessness is at odds with the political principles of our age. Those principles demand the containment of "societies" within states, and subsocieties within provinces, districts, cities, or other units with definite geographic limits (Walker and Mendlovitz 1990). The ideas and practices of sovereignty lead us to believe that societies or subsocieties must be properly contained if they are to be effectively governed. Thus, the metropolis appears to be ungovernable, because it is uncontainable. Unfortunately, this uncontainable urban form is overwhelmingly predominant: what is not metropolitan is marginal. Although some regions seem to be permanently excluded from the metropolis, this is rarely so: logging and mining camps, wilderness reserves, agribusiness centres, and market towns for the tourists and cottagers are outliers of the metropolitan system, no more marginal than industrial sites and shopping strips in "the city." The metropolitan system links cities with one another, and with the territories they exploit, in ways that make nonsense of political and administrative divisions. The metropolis we would govern is everywhere and nowhere.

To look at the metropolis in this way is to call attention to the processes that have recently been disrupting established political spaces. The most prominent of the threatened spaces are the ones formed by the state system (Magnusson and Walker 1988). If anything has changed in the past 20 years, it is not so much that the municipality has lost its purchase on the metropolis—that happened a long time ago—but that the state has lost control of society.[1] Perhaps the idea that the state could control society was always an illusion: the dynamics of capitalism and the scientific and technological revolutions may never have been susceptible to effective state control. Nevertheless, the idea that the world was divided into distinct societies, with their own economies and governments, seemed quite plausible until the early 1970s. Now, the presence of a global economy, to which every individual, business, community, and state must relate, seems undeniable. Moreover, the global village, which Marshall McLuhan imagined a generation ago (McLuhan 1964), actually does watch CNN together—although perhaps with less energetic involvement than he expected. Political passivity in this situation is hardly surprising, since it is no longer clear how ordinary people can be effective politically, let alone govern themselves, in this new world order.

In a sense, the dilemma of the metropolis, which has vexed the architects of local government for a century and a half (Magnusson 1981), is now the dilemma of government in general. Some—like Jane Jacobs (1980, 1984) or Murray Bookchin (1986)—believe that the new world order is one in which metropolitan cities can regain their position as autonomous centres for the organization of economic, social, and

---

[1] I here invoke the conventional idea that "the state" stands over and apart from society. For more complex views, see Magnusson and Walker 1988, and the ensuing controversy: Jane Jenson and Fuat Keyman, "Must we all be 'postmodern'?" *Studies in Political Economy* 31 (Spring 1990), 141-57; Magnusson and Walker, "Socialism and Monetheism: A Response to Jenson and Keyman," *Studies in Political Economy* 34 (Spring 1991): 235-39.

cultural life, and hence for independent politics and government. Others are not so optimistic (Harvey 1989). In any case, it seems clear that postwar attempts to "fix" the metropolis in neat containers, suitable for the Keynesian welfare state, have not succeeded. To many, this has been a grave disappointment, since they believe it is impossible for us to have a better society unless the state gets control of it and regulates it for the public benefit. To others, on both the left and the right, the disruption of the postwar project still appears, in retrospect, to have been essential for human liberation. The facts, of course, are more complex: we have to look at them historically to understand them.

THE POSTWAR ORTHODOXY

If the postwar era did not end in 1973, it was certainly over by 1989. The earlier date, associated with the Arab oil embargo, is conventionally taken as the point at which the Keynesian welfare state began to unravel. From then on, it is difficult to point to any serious advances in the welfare state in Europe or North America. The fiscal and, increasingly, ideological pressures have been in the opposite direction: toward privatizing responsibility, targeting state aid for the most needy, and generally limiting demands on the public treasury. At the same time, the rudimentary systems of national economic management, associated with Keynesianism and French indicative planning, have been under attack as obstacles to economic restructuring and impediments to capitalist efficiency. The political successes of Reagan and Thatcher and the failure of the first socialist government under Mitterand brought this attack to a head.

In Canada, 1975 is perhaps the most significant marker year (Calvert 1984). This was the year of the first restraint budget at the federal level, the defeat of the New Democrats in British Columbia, and the collapse of Ontario's programme of regional government. The last of these is of considerable interest here, for it marks an important turning point in the drive to rationalize local government on the principles of the Keynesian welfare state. For over 20 years, Ontario had been a leader in the development of modern institutions of local government (Higgins 1986, Ch. 5); its pulling back was symbolic of a change in conditions and a shift in sensibilities.

On the surface, the Ontario government was defeated by traditionalist resistance of a sort it had always faced. Traditional municipal government had developed in a pre-Keynesian, prewelfarist era. It allowed communities to provide for a few public amenities, but more importantly to promote local business and provide the minimal services and regulations necessary for it to flourish. The market economy itself was expected to provide the framework for community and individual activity. State interventions were supposed to be at the margins. Local authorities were expected to operate within the market economy, responding to its pressures and opportunities. Although they might gain by concerting their actions—as private companies did when merging—this was a matter to be judged from below. To talk of a rational plan of local government organization, with boundaries and functions specified in accordance with some conception of what local authorities ought to be doing, was both utopian and authoritarian. Municipalities, like the private businesses and private individuals they served, had to be free to respond to the changing conditions of a market economy—conditions that certainly were not governed by anyone's central plan.

Laissez faire implied that municipalities could be big or small, active or passive, multipurposed or single-minded: it precluded the sort of strict preconceptions that informed plans of general reorganization. However, such plans were articulated with increasing fervour in Ontario and elsewhere after the Second World War. They presupposed a new relation between the state and civil society—one in which the state would contain and rationalize the market but not displace it. The unexpressed premise was that, thanks to the new tools of monetary and fiscal policy, it would be possible to manage a national economy to secure steady growth, full employment, and stable prices. The economy would generate a surplus that could be used for public as well as private purposes: indeed, a shift of expenditures in favour of public services was necessary to make up for deficiencies in privately generated demand, and so to keep the economy expanding. However, economic efficiency demanded that these funds be spent more rationally than in the past, to improve public welfare and increase economic productivity.

As various commentators pointed out, the old rural society, in which cities were isolated centres, seemed to be disappearing in favour of an urban or metropolitan society with a rural fringe. This urban society was spreading and solidifying its internal linkages. As it did, it erased the original communities. Much more intensive, multidimensional planning seemed to be required to regulate urban spread and govern its internal development, as well as provide for expensive new public services and facilities. Levels of education and health care or means of transportation that seemed perfectly adequate for an essentially rural society now seemed woefully deficient. Moreover, a relatively unregulated rural life had to give way to a highly regulated urban life. To meet these demands, more professional governments with wider vision and larger resources were required, not the traditionalist municipal authorities.

Up to a point, fiscal equalization solved the problem of inadequately constructed local authorities. Such equalization occurred at both the federal and provincial levels. However, to dump money on authorities that could not use it effectively seemed a waste. To meet the new requirements, authorities had to acquire professional staffs capable of planning and administration in accordance with the new standards. To be maximally efficient, they had to be organized on a certain scale, have geographic boundaries that made sense in terms of their functions, and have jurisdiction over complementary activities. This pointed towards the creation of "metropolitan" or regional authorities to replace the old municipal bodies. Failing that, functions had to be provincialized.

The provincialization of public administration was arguably the predominant feature of the reorganization of government after World War II. Its effects were most apparent with respect to health, education, and welfare services, transportation, and certain forms of environmental regulation. Although some discretion was left to local authorities, the trend was towards a provincial administrative system that could deliver standard public services and provide uniform regulations for the whole province. The federal government in turn encouraged more uniformity among the provinces. In this system, traditional municipalities were an expensive nuisance, but they could be more easily tolerated where something like the old rural society retained its vigour. The great pressures for municipal reorganization were in the areas where rural society had been swamped by urbanization or where it had been transformed into a welfare dependency.

Municipalities generally were at one remove from the development of the new provincial welfare states. On the other hand, they played—or were supposed to play—key roles in developing the physical infrastructure of the new urban society and allocating land use within it (Magnusson and Sancton 1983). The pressure upon them was to assume responsibility for physical planning. Most of them did this in form but not in substance. Land-use allocation continued to be market-driven, and this allowed for an entrepreneurial politics within and between municipalities that fit better with traditional patterns than with the ambition for a planned economy. Although the trend was towards more effective planning, there were strong resistances to this at every level of government, and Canadian planning never reached European standards of efficacy (Bourne 1975).

This failure was matched by another: the inability of the modernizers to create a new space for urban and local politics that matched the needs of people in the emergent society. If there was a model of such a space, it was to be found in the provinces themselves. They had emerged by the 1970s as more or less autonomous political units, with their own party systems, modern bureaucracies, and responsibilities that extended across the whole range of public concerns. Provincial politics was worth the interest of people who lived in an urban society. It dealt with the governance of significant regions, and there was a sufficient accumulation of power in the provincial capitals to make credible the claim that these were centres from which effective action could be taken on a wide range of problems. Many reformers hoped that metropolitan or regional governments with a similar political significance could be established. But no province was anxious to devolve much authority on such bodies, and nowhere was there strong political pressure to do so. In retrospect, this absence of pressure is hardly surprising since the provinces themselves afforded more meaningful spaces for regional politics.

In a sense, traditional municipal politics had been located in civil society rather than in the state. It was in a domain where people were free to pursue their interests, as individuals or members of local communities, without much regard for the wider society. Responsibility for regulating this activity rested with a legislature over and above the municipalities. Here, great principles were supposed to be considered, but in municipal affairs there was more latitude—more freedom to be self-interested. The effect of the modernizing reforms was to integrate municipal councils into the state—to make them responsible to the wider society for implementing policies and providing services that the legislature had decided upon. The modernizers thought that regional, metropolitan, or even local authorities could still have considerable latitude as intermediary agencies. This would be especially true if they pressed their powers to the limit and took control of the physical, social, and economic development of their own areas. State planning could provide the framework for a principled politics, responding to different conceptions of the future.

The trouble with this modernizing vision is that it squeezed local politics between the state and the market. Local councils were to be administrative agencies in a planning system that reserved the most important decisions for higher authorities. The system itself was designed to respect and protect the market. The crucial politics of the day related to the boundaries of state action, and the defenders of *laissez faire* were largely successful in confining state planning to the public sector itself. This meant that economic development, and hence land allocation, continued to be market-driven, and public planning was largely adaptive. Local authorities thus found that their freedom of action was severely constrained by the autonomous logic of the market on the one hand and the requirements of government policy on the other. Really serious differences could hardly be expressed in local politics because the range of choice for the local authorities was so narrow.

These constraints were only effective, however, insofar as people accepted the logic of the Keynesian welfare state. By the 1960s, that logic was under serious challenge from the left and the right.

NEW LEFT INSURGENCY

The new left that emerged in the 1960s was not an organization, but a movement—a change in sensibilities by no means confined to the left itself (Gitlin 1987). It was marked not only by a suspicion of capitalism but also by a profound antistatism that found expression in demands for participatory democracy, community control, and the empowerment of the disadvantaged. The disadvantaged were variously defined to include students and young people, racial minorities, counter-cultural communities, women, gays, and others. Old notions of the left, that privileged the working class as the agent of social change, were put into question. So too were the statist assumptions of communism in the East, social democracy in western Europe, and liberal reformism in North America. The new left pointed toward a cultural revolution from below that would transform civil society. A new society, without constrictive boundaries, would retake the powers given over to the state, the corporations, the universities, and all the other bureaucratic institutions that dominated people's lives.

The rise of the new left was bound up with the emergence of a globalized urban society—an unbounded metropolis—in the capitalist West. This was a society linked by the new media of instantaneous communication and rapid interurban and intercontinental transportation. It was a society of relative affluence, with a large, mobile population of students and young people, who shared increasingly in a distinctive transnational culture. It was also a society in which the urban environment was changing dramatically. Concentrated cities were being opened out into sprawling suburbs, linked by highways and airports. Downtowns were being redeveloped as financial control centres and cultural meccas. And, in the shadows between the glittering office towers and the plush suburbs, appeared the new immigrants from the South: black Americans, Caribbeans, Asians, Africans, and Latinos. Although these processes were more advanced in the United States than elsewhere in the 1960s, they were also apparent in Canada, Australia, and western Europe, and helped to generate similar unrest. Among the issues identified were ones like housing and transportation that fell within the ambit of municipal government.[2]

The new left sensibility found its most significant expression in a series of critiques of the conditions of life in a globalized urban society: a critique of racism that pointed toward the manifold exclusions of people of colour in a white society; a complementary critique of imperialism that raised issues about western exploitation and manipulation of the rest of the world; a critique of militarism, as it manifested itself in the Cold War, in imperialist domination, and in the organization of a military-industrial complex; a critique of capitalism, not only as a system for the exploitation of labour but also as a materialist ideology, blind to spiritual values; a critique of mindless consumption that wasted people's lives and devoured and despoiled the environment; a critique of patriarchy, as a system that condemned half the species to subordination; and a critique of the various exclusions, of the homosexual, the disabled, and others who could not live up to the models of middle-class suburbanism. These critiques pointed towards forms of politics that challenged existing political, social, and cultural boundaries—including the ones that constituted the Keynesian welfare state, and put the municipalities in their peculiar position at the juncture between the state, the market, and everyday life.

It is tempting to distinguish between the urban social movements identified with the new left, and the ones—like feminism, for instance—that focused on something other than the city. However, this would be to impose an academic boundary alien to the politics of the new left. In an important sense, that politics reflected the realities of the unbounded metropolis, or global village. For the insurgents, the refusal to recognize established boundaries—cultural, social, and political—was fundamental

---

[2]In Canada, the municipalization of many other "urban issues" has been inhibited by the structure of the local state, which confines councils to a relatively narrow range of responsibilities.

to effective politics. This was true in both the early ferment of the 1960s and the subsequent movements and organizations of the 1970s and '80s. Characteristic of the "new social movements" was the recognition of some global phenomenon as problematic and the claim that this problem had to be met by immediate local action. The supposition was that the existing institutions of the state, and the political organizations that focused on it, were not to be trusted. New communities for change had to be created and new forms of action developed, in autonomous political spaces (Breines 1989). Movements or "communities" that developed within these spaces then could intervene in the state or in other social institutions. In the process, they could break through the established boundaries and open the space for global change.

In so far as the municipality appeared simply as a "local apparatus of the state," it seemed an unlikely locus for effective politics. On the other hand, it represented, if only in a distorted way, the possibility of an authentically democratic politics rooted in the communities of daily life and marked by intense popular participation (Breines 1989). Many of the new left critiques were marked by a radical consciousness of the value of locality—a sense that economically or culturally disadvantaged communities were being threatened, that democratization entailed "community control" over the territories concerned, that people had to come together in their own neighbourhoods to resist the interventions that were disrupting their lives, and that people had to create for themselves the institutions, services, and facilities they needed to live better as individuals, families, and communities. The desire to nurture if not to form new local communities was expressed by movements of hippies and students, "back-to-the land" and later "urban gardening" movements, gays, feminists, and environmentalists of all stripes. Ethnic minorities and even occupational groups (like artists and theatre people) also made claims to community. These claims and aspirations did not neatly coincide and involved a variety of territories that were "in and against" existing metropolitan forms and the "local apparatuses" of the state.

It was in the context of a more general insurgency of the new left that a new progressivism focused on municipal politics began to take shape in the early 1970s (Harris 1987; Caulfield 1988; Magnusson 1990b). The movement was strongest in large metropolitan centres, where the disruptive effects of urban development were most apparent and the counter-cultural communities of the new left tended to collect. Many of the original issues raised were matters of democratic process. It was claimed that the municipal councils had really become the servants of the developers and their allies, that the procedures for decision making in the municipalities were so secretive that ordinary people could not know what was happening until it was too late, and that little serious effort was made to enable people to work out what they wanted for their own neighbourhoods (Lorimer 1972). These procedural complaints were connected to more substantive issues. It was said that a suburban form of urban life was being imposed—one that destroyed the diversity of the inner cities, disrupted viable low-income and middle-class neighbourhoods, forced people into automobiles and out of public transit, polluted the air, congested the streets, and made life in the central area more dangerous and less convenient. The new progressives believed that a more authentic urbanism, sensitive to the quality of life in the central cities, would emerge from a more democratic politics at the municipal level. This involved the mobilization of the silent majority, who had heretofore been little interested in municipal politics.

In almost every major city, new progressive political organizations emerged in the 1970s (Lorimer and MacGregor 1981). Some—like the Montreal Citizens' Movement and the Committee of Progressive Electors in Vancouver—were organized as disciplined political parties. Others—like The Electors' Action Movement in Vancouver—were much looser and practically undisciplined coalitions. In some places, like Toronto, citywide organizations were weak and ephemeral, and the residents' associations in particular neighbourhoods provided the strongest basis for electoral organization. People from all parties became involved. The Liberals briefly, and the NDP more consistently, tried to make themselves the vehicle for the new progressivism, but there were strong resistances to this. Although the NDP has made some advances, especially in Toronto, Ottawa, and the Vancouver area, these have not been spectacular. The traditional forms of nonpartisanship remain strong.

It would be wrong, however, to equate the impact of the new progressivism with the fortunes of the organizations associated with it. Much more significant has been the change in sensibility and in the practices of politics and government, most apparent in the central cities. Almost everywhere, municipalities have opened themselves up to greater citizen participation and become more sensitive to neighbourhood concerns about the disruptive effects of development. There is greater concern about the quality of the urban environment and the necessity of maintaining "livable" city centres. The preservation of historical buildings and old neighbourhoods, the recycling of old industrial sites, the transformation of waterfronts into park-like settings for various uses, and the development of new systems of public transportation all get wide support. The change in sensibilities is reflected not only in public policy, but also in the styles of development favoured by promoters. The idea that old cities should be recycled, rather than levelled in the process of redevelopment, is widely accepted.

It is also the case that the wider concerns of the social movements associated with the new left have entered into public policy. Environmentalism in municipal politics today is not simply a matter of protecting neighbourhoods and urban amenities. It is also a matter of controlling air and water pollution, regulating the production and disposal of toxic chemicals, recycling garbage, controlling smoking, eliminating CFCs, and so on. Many of these measures—like the control of CFCs—are understood as contributions to the solution of global, rather than purely local problems. They command support from "conservative" as well as "progressive" politicians.[3] Similarly, we can trace the impact of demands from women and minorities: equal opportunities programmes in public employment; pay equity measures; human rights codes and anti-discrimination ordinances; access programmes for the disabled; the redesign of public spaces to make them safer for women and more accessible to the disabled and to people with children. We can even find effects of the peace and international solidarity movements in declarations of nuclear-free zones, civic peace marches, "sister-city" and foreign aid programmes. Although measures of this sort by no means command universal support, they have become surprisingly common.

In its formative years, the new progressivism was rooted in concerns about consumption rather than production. Homes, neighbourhoods, amenities, and services were at issue, rather than jobs and business opportunities. The fact that both working-class and middle-class neighbourhoods were often threatened by urban development facilitated some unusual political alliances (Caulfield 1974). These alliances were fragile, however, for reasons implicit in the process of urban development. Middle-class neighbourhoods only needed to be protected against adverse change for them to thrive. From their perspective, "half-way" houses and public housing developments often appeared as adverse—as did tax rises to support public services. On the other hand, most working-class neighbourhoods needed considerable investment to upgrade

---

[3]The lead taken on the issue of styrofoam containers by conservative Toronto Councillor Tony O'Donohue, a frequent *bête noir* of the reformers, is indicative of this.

housing, add to the stock, and improve neighbourhood amenities and services. In the absence of controls, neighbourhood improvement often took the form of rehabilitation and in-fill construction by speculators oriented toward the profitable middle-class market. Thus, neighbourhoods were gentrified and the poor displaced onto an inflated housing market. Ironically, the more success the new progressives had in preserving the quality of life in the inner cities, the more difficult it was for the poor, the ethnic minorities, the single parents, and the cultural and counter-cultural communities to remain where they were.

These experiences have helped to sharpen the division between middle-class preservationists and the new progressives in municipal politics. They also have closed much of the gap between the old left and the new. The consolidation of the MCM in Montreal, the rise of COPE and collapse of TEAM in Vancouver, and the emergence of a strong municipal NDP (or surrogate organizations)[4] in many cities are all signs of this political realignment. The recomposed progressive organizations bring people from the new social movements together with labour activists, ethnic and minority leaders, neighbourhood workers, social service professionals, academics, and others to create a political milieu reminiscent of (if not identical with) the contemporary NDP. Out of this milieu have come strong demands for new programmes of public housing and social services, attuned to the needs of a socially diverse urban constituency. At the same time, there has been increasing emphasis on programmes to improve and diversify employment opportunities. This has put the new progressives "in and against" the agenda of the new right.

THE NEW RIGHT REACTION

Throughout the western world we can see what looks to be the final stage in the reconstruction of old industrial cities as nuclei in the postindustrial economy. This stage consists of the conversion of harbour and railway lands to other uses—offices and boutiques, up-scale housing, galleries and museums, waterside parks, convention centres, and sports stadia. American urbanists talk of Rouse-ification, after the firm that redeveloped Faneuil Hall in Boston and replicated its success in city after American city (Levine et al. 1988, 123). Canadians might prefer to give

---

[4]The Victoria Civic Electors, in my home city, is one example. Although in effect an NDP organization, it is constituted separately. There are similar organizations in some of the Vancouver suburbs.

more credit to the federal Liberals, who poured so much money into these lands in search of votes. Perhaps we should call the process Axworthing;[5] in any case, it is clear that the recycling of inner cities, in which many Canadians took particular pride in the 1970s, is part of a general process that is as evident in New Orleans or Baltimore (or indeed Liverpool or Glasgow) as in Vancouver or Toronto. In its characteristic forms, this process seems to represent the triumph of neo-conservatism over the Keynesian welfare state and the insurgency of the new left.

The new right, like the new left, represented a change in sensibility: a reassertion of both the values and the legitimizing claims of the old civil society in face of criticisms from the new social movements and pressures of Keynesian welfarism. Although the new left had been critical of the emergent regime of Keynesian welfarism, it tended to take the triumph over *laissez faire* for granted, and hence to assume a trend toward ever tighter regulation of the economy, more extensive public services, and at least a modest redistribution of resources in favour of the poor. Demands for more radical action presupposed this social base. Thus, the resurgence of conservatism caught the new left as well as the old off guard. Indeed, the new left was implicated in the rise of neo-conservatism insofar as its own critiques of welfare statism prepared the ground for a reassertion of the virtues of existing society. For conservatives, these were embodied in the nexus of family, religion, and private property, and were protected above all by the self-organizing relations of the market, which enabled individuals and families to secure themselves by their own efforts. From this perspective, the power of the state was to be invoked only to secure this nexus or to extend the values implicit in it; that power was not to be used for social reconstruction.

The resurgence of conservatism in the 1970s occurred in the context of the fiscal crisis of the welfare state. It seemed that a further extension or even the mere preservation of existing welfare services could not be achieved without unacceptable levels of taxation or public borrowing. What made these levels unacceptable was capitalist resistance, which became increasingly effective as the development of international capital markets enabled international investors to play one state off against another in demanding concessions. (The familiarity of this pattern to students of municipal politics is evident.) The crisis was such that capital

---

[5]In honour of Prime Minister Pierre Trudeau's Cabinet Minister Lloyd Axworthy, former director of the University of Winnipeg's Institute of Urban Studies and godfather of Winnipeg's much-touted Core Area Initiative.

had either to be appeased or to be confronted with a major extension of state control over investment. The apparent failure of the French socialists to make the latter strategy work seemed to confirm the wisdom of the appeasement strategy adopted by all the other capitalist states. However, this strategy had already been legitimized by a massive propaganda campaign that convinced most people that Keynesian welfarism would no longer work.

After the federal government adopted its restraint programme in 1975, the provinces sooner or later followed suit, forcing welfare agencies, hospitals, school boards, and municipalities to constrain their activities. One obvious effect was to destroy the promise of new inner-city housing for the poor. That promise had been contained not only in the new progressivism of municipal politics but also in the provisions of the National Housing Act of 1973, which had been influenced by the progressive critiques of the preceding years (Rose 1980). The supposition was that federally and provincially supported nonprofit housing, developed by a variety of municipal, charitable, and cooperative agencies, would provide working-class housing on a significant scale. This would make up for the demise of the old public housing programmes, which had been insufficiently sensitive to the urban fabric and to the social requirements of the people being housed. Despite some promising initiatives, however, the new forms of housing had little impact on conditions of life for the inner-city poor. There was simply not enough of it because the federal and provincial governments refused anything more than token funding.

In a similar way, fiscal restraint took the initiative away from a variety of other agencies at the local level. Ironically, this was especially true of the voluntary sector, which the conservatives have touted as the proper locus for most social services. In the context of Keynesian welfarism, the voluntary sector had come to depend on public funding and on the provision of certain core services by government agencies. In a sense, the voluntary sector was supplemental to the state sector. It had more freedom of action not only to develop innovative services but also to engage in a politics of social welfare—mobilizing constituents, agitating among the public at large, and pressuring governments. As such, it was a site for new left insurgency. The effect of fiscal restraint was to force voluntary agencies to pick up services abandoned by governments and to find alternative funding for their own activities. As a result, much of the energy that had gone into innovative programming and politicking had to be diverted into fund raising and bureaucratic management.

One way of understanding the neo-conservative thrust is as an effort as much to foreclose political spaces as to restrain public spending. Keynesian welfarism had opened up new political spaces, partly within the administrative apparatuses of the state but more importantly on their periphery. It enlarged the class of social service professionals and legitimized claims for public action to remedy social ills. Directly or indirectly, it supported an array of groups and organizations that developed new demands, organized new constituencies, and created new political spaces for themselves. Without confronting these groups directly, neo-conservative governments were able to constrain them by reducing financial support, off-loading activities, and attacking expectations for new public programmes. Thus, political spaces for the new left, which had emerged in the penumbra of the Keynesian welfare state, were disrupted or constricted.

The conservative revival has not found much expression in 'tax-re-volts' or other grass-roots movements at the local level. There has instead been a drift back to traditional municipal politics, legitimized by the rhetoric of neo-conservatism. Traditional boosterism is thus represented as entrepreneurialism. Deals with developers become 'public-private partnerships.' And civic trade junkets become responses to globalization. For the most part, this is a repackaging of old activities, but there is no doubt that the competition for business has forced municipalities to become more innovative. Whether this justifies grand claims about economic development strategies is questionable. The most obvious effect has been to intensify the pressures for downtown redevelopment, as exemplified in the post-modern monuments arising on the old railway and harbourlands.

Grass-roots conservatism finds expression in resistance to develop-ments, which—though they might have wider social benefits—do have adverse local effects. These include incinerators, dump sites, half-way houses, and public housing projects. Such NIMBYism can be partly explained in terms of market rationality—who wants a project that will reduce property values?—and it is fairly easily expressed within the conventional forms of municipal politics, which "centre" questions of land-use. People often say, however, that they are trying to protect the environment and preserve the quality of human life. Thus, their rhetoric points to values that transcend the market—values that are much more boldly advanced by the new left. An even more dramatic break from market rationality and the codes of conventional politics is apparent in the anti-abortion movement. To defend traditional religious and social ideas, the movement invokes a language of universal human rights ("the right to life") and uses political tactics developed by the new left. Anti-abortionists have defied the police and the courts, attacked private and public property, and disrupted the "normal" political process. Thus, they have pointed, like new left insurgents before them, to a form of "local politics" that bursts the bounds of established political spaces.

TOWARD A NEW POLITICS?

In the nineteenth century, theorists like Mill and de Tocqueville hoped that municipalities would be the main sources of vitality in the emergent liberal democracies. This hope has never been realized. Instead, municipalities have been trapped between the state and the market—at times expected to serve the purposes of the state (be they for economic planning, welfare administration, or whatever), at times simply to function in the market (promoting the economic interests of their communities), and often to do both simultaneously. These activities always have attracted some people's attention and have aroused the passions of the majority from time to time, but they have not engaged the popular imagination in the way Mill and de Tocqueville hoped. Such engagement depends on a coincidence between the spaces of municipal politics and the spaces of popular mobilization. Needless to say, such a coincidence has been the exception rather than the rule.

The new progressivism, which has produced local parties detached from federal and provincial organizations, provides a means for focusing a variety of new concerns on the municipal councils. However, the neo-conservative reaction has made it increasingly difficult to deal with these concerns within a municipal framework. One can see the effect on ostensibly social democratic politicians, like Jean Doré and Michael Harcourt, who have adapted themselves to the new entrepreneurialism (Judd and Parkinson 1990). To the extent that municipal councils break out of the boundaries imposed by the state and the market, it is as a result of their relation to social movements. This creates serious contradictions, for movement politics involves a restless questioning of identities and communities, inconsistent with fixed political spaces (Walker 1988).

The disruption of established political spaces is a fearful matter for anyone who assumes that the familiar boundaries are essential for order. For many, the confrontation at Oka in the summer of 1990 illustrated the dire consequences of a political practice that defied the norms and limits of the liberal-democratic nation-state. On the other hand, it also illustrated the realities concealed by our normal conceptions of "urban and local politics." It was, arguably, the most dramatic incident in municipal politics in recent years—provoked as it was by the municipal council's decision to extend a golf course onto land claimed by the Mohawks. Yet what ultimately happened could not be dealt with or comprehended in terms of municipal politics: an armed band, claiming to represent the Mohawk nation, confronted the armed forces of Canada, Quebec, and Oka; sovereignty was claimed and denied; different nations and communities were defended; a variety of modern and premodern political traditions were invoked. Despite the overwhelming military superiority of the Canadian state, there was no simple way of crushing this challenge to Canadian sovereignty, for the Mohawk Warriors had claimed a space not only in a Montreal suburb, but also in the global media. Clothed in a rhetoric of aboriginal rights, asserting a difference legitimized by the norms of the global village, the warriors achieved their victory in the media even as they were dispersed by the Canadian army.

Whatever one thinks of the Mohawk Warriors or the Right-to-Life campaigners—or the Greenpeace activists who challenged the French government in the South Pacific and disrupted Premier Peterson's election campaign in Ontario—they represent forms of politics that will not go away. Current social movements reflect conditions of life in a globalized urban society, where problems of personal security, economic opportunity, human rights, or environmental health cannot be contained within national, let alone municipal borders. Neo-conservatives have thought that "the market" would provide the discipline to contain popular insurgency but in every country they have had to rely on the powers of the state to keep people within bounds. The explosions of popular discontent have not only been "critical" and progressive—as in the movements associated with the new left—but reactionary and conservative—as in the present attacks on biculturalism, multiculturalism, gay rights, and feminism. Modes of social and political organization that "fix" people, either as buyers and sellers or as subjects of administration, cannot be very stable in a global village that promises everyone freedom and self-fulfillment.

Neo-conservative attempts to re-inscribe the old limits of politics, and prevent people from taking effective action on the matters of most concern to them, are liable to add to popular frustrations and encourage the nastier forms of fundamentalism. To avoid this, we need to keep open the spaces created by the social movements that came out of the new left insurgency. We should not expect these movements to respect the neat boundaries of the Keynesian welfare state (or the new entrepreneurial state that seems to have succeeded it). Instead, we should expect them to keep disrupting the forms and practices of politics as usual, refusing the existing political agendas, inventing new repertoires of action, and identifying communities for change that we had never anticipated.

In this, we shall find a continuing revaluation of the "local" as a space for politics. This may or may not lead to a new focus on the municipality as a venue for creative politics. If it does not, we need not weep, for what is the municipality but a temporary holding place for the vibrant politics of the metropolis?

REFERENCES

Bookchin, Murray. 1986. *The Limits of the City.* Montreal: Black Rose Books.

Bourne, Larry S. 1975. *Urban Systems, Strategies for Regulation: A Comparison of Policies in Britain, Sweden, Australia and Canada.* Oxford: Oxford University Press.

Breines, Wini. 1989. *Community and Organization in the New Left, 1962-1968: The Great Refusal.* New Brunswick, N.J.: Rutgers University Press.

Calvert, John. 1984. *Government Limited: The Corporate Takeover of the Public Sector in Canada.* Ottawa: Canadian Centre for Policy Alternatives.

Caulfield, Jon. 1974. *The Tiny Perfect Mayor: David Crombie and Toronto's Reform Aldermen.* Toronto: James Lorimer.

_____. 1988. "Canadian Urban 'Reform' and Local Conditions: An Alternative to Harris's 'Reinterpretation.'" *International Journal of Urban and Regional Research* 12: 477-84.

Gitlin, Todd. 1987. *The Sixties: Years of Hope, Days of Rage.* New York: Bantam Books.

Harris, Richard. 1987. "A Social Movement in Urban Politics: A Reinterpretation of Urban Reform in Canada." *International Journal of Urban and Regional Research* 11: 363-79.

Harvey, David. 1989. "From Managerialism to Entrepreneurialism: The Transformation in Urban Governance in Late Capitalism" *Geografiska Annaler* 71B: 3-17.

Higgins, Donald. 1986. *Local and Urban Politics in Canada.* Toronto: Gage.

Hodge, Gerald. 1986. *Planning Canadian Communities.* Toronto: Methuen.

Jacobs, Jane. 1980. *Canadian Cities and Sovereignty Association.* Toronto: Canadian Broadcasting Corporation.

_____. 1984. *Cities and the Wealth of Nations.* New York: Random House.

Judd, Dennis, and Michael Parkinson, eds. 1990. *Leadership and Urban Regeneration: Cities in North America and Europe.* Urban Affairs Annual Reviews, 37. Newbury Park, Calif.: Sage.

Levine, Marc V., et al. 1988. *The State and Democracy: Revitalizing America's Government.* New York: Routledge.

Lorimer, James. 1972. *A Citizens' Guide to City Politics*. Toronto: James Lewis and Samuel.

_____, and Carolyn MacGregor, eds. 1981. *After the Developers*. Toronto: James Lorimer.

Magnusson, Warren. 1981. "Metropolitan Reform in the Capitalist City." *Canadian Journal of Political Science* 14 (September): 557-58.

_____. 1990. "Progressive Politics and Canadian Cities." In *Challenges to Local Government*, ed. Desmond S. King and Jon Pierre. London: SAGE.

_____, and Andrew Sancton, eds. 1983. *City Politics in Canada*. Toronto: University of Toronto Press.

Magnusson, Warren and Rob Walker. 1988. "De-Centring the State: Political Theory and Canadian Political Economy." *Studies in Political Economy: A Socialist Review* 26 (Summer): 37-71.

McLuhan, Marshall. 1964. *Understanding Media: The Extensions of Man*. New York: Signet.

Rose, Albert. 1980. *Canadian Housing Policies, 1935-1980*. Toronto: Butterworth.

Walker, R. B. J. 1988. *One World, Many Worlds: Struggles for a Just World Peace*. Boulder, Colo.: Lynne Rienner.

_____, and Saul Mendlovitz, eds. 1990. *Contending Sovereignties: Redefining Political Community*. Boulder, Colo.: Lynne Rienner.

Chapter 17

Recent Developments in the Theory of the State and the Changing Canadian Metropolis:
Implications of Each for the Other

Alan Smart
The University of Calgary

Changes in Canadian cities, particularly when they are negatively evaluated, raise issues of public policy. Within many discussions of public policy there are two distinct tendencies. The first is to assume that changes are generated externally and are essentially inevitable; the most public policy can do is respond to these changes and perhaps ameliorate their effects. This assumption is perhaps most common in discussions of demographic and global economic changes. The second tendency is to assume that policymakers are free to design, adopt, and implement whatever policies seem to be technically optimal.

These two tendencies share at least one common feature: no attempt is made to identify how much freedom and power (in other words, autonomy) local governments actually have to react to challenges or initiate new developments. One of the arguments of this chapter is that determining the degree and nature of the autonomy of Canadian local governments is critical for both a theoretical appreciation of the ways in which Canadian cities are changing and for more effective practical responses to such changes. A review of recent developments in the theory of the state will provide support for this claim and a conceptual framework with which to explore the issues. This chapter discusses these issues as they have been raised in and are relevant to the articles contained in this volume. First, it explores how developments in state theory can illuminate the dynamic developments in contemporary

Canadian metropolises and generate new questions or insights. Then, the logic of inquiry will be reversed in order to examine how the distinctive features of Canada's metropolises may raise new questions for the theory of the state, or even undermine taken for granted assumptions. These tasks, of course, can at best be achieved only sketchily in the space available.

THE THEORY OF THE STATE AND URBAN STUDIES

If one theoretical development could summarize the changes in urban studies during the 1970s and 1980s, it must surely be the intense theoretical concern with the state and its interventions at the local level. Although initiated by neo-Marxian incursions into the mainstream of urban theory, notably by Manuel Castells and David Harvey, the resulting debates produced a proliferation of studies of the state from other perspectives as well.

Concern with the state did not spring from nowhere in the 1970s. Indeed, the field of urban politics has a long heritage. The alternative positions were the pluralist view of local politics as essentially a neutral input-output device responding to a diversity of political pressures, and the elitist view that local government was controlled by a small number of influential members of the economic elite (Melling 1980; Clark and Dear 1984).

Neo-Marxian critiques were not intended to support either of these positions but to argue that the questions being asked were far too narrow; that they neglected too many crucial issues. Both Harvey (1973) and Castells (1977, 1978) attempted to broaden the sights by focusing on the relationship between the city, its politics, and the dominant mode of production. Neither pluralists nor elitists were correct, they maintained, because both approaches focused upon individuals and their strategies and ignored the critical role that the state, both centrally and at the local level, played within capitalist social formations.

Castells, following a structuralist epistemology developed primarily by Louis Althusser, concluded that the state was more than just "the executive committee of the bourgeoisie" as depicted in Stalinist orthodoxy. Instead the state possessed "relative autonomy" that allowed it to look beyond the immediate demands of the dominant capitalist class in order to ensure the longer-term interest of the capitalist mode of production. In a formalistic manner that has garnered a great deal of justifiable criticism (Saunders 1981; Gottdiener 1985; Magnusson 1985),

Castells concluded that the basic feature of the "urban" was to provide for collective consumption in order to reproduce labour power for the capitalist mode of production. As a result, the study of urban politics would focus on disputes over the provision of objects of collective consumption and resistance to the ways in which they were provided (urban social movements).

The structuralist conception of the state has numerous problems but it also has made some important contributions. It certainly is an improvement on any Marxian analyses that treated the state simply as a tool of the capitalist class. (Marx himself avoided such a view in his substantive work, though not always in his programmatic statements.) More significantly, it raised important questions about the relationship between the state and the mode of production. It became clear that government could not simply act in any way that local pressures might combine to push it; that there were formidable constraints upon it; and that it performed critical functions that had heretofore received insufficient critical attention. The key to this contribution was the concept of "relative autonomy" that simultaneously indicated, on the one hand, the freedom of action the state possessed and needed if it were to intervene in ways often opposed to the short-term interest of dominant economic actors and, on the other hand, the constraints on this freedom. Unfortunately, it is also partly because of the weakness of this concept that the structuralist project collapses.

Relative autonomy is used in structuralist Marxism as a way of avoiding naive views of the state as a tool but also of keeping the state metaphorically on a leash. The state has autonomy, but only because state autonomy is functional for the capitalist system. Although the autonomy of states is undoubtedly limited, the concept of relative autonomy has been compromised by the tendency of theorists to use it in a totally ambiguous sense that allows them to argue that whatever the state may do will fit within their theories (Saunders 1979, 187; Glucksmann 1974, 134). If the state expands welfare programs, it does so because program expansion is functionally required; if it dismantles them, then this also must be functionally required. A structuralist explanation of any state intervention relates it to the functional requirements of the system. The explanatory task is simply to show that the intervention is in fact essential for the reproduction of the social system and why this is the case. The assumption is that the intervention will follow, since the role of the capitalist state is to act in the general interest of capital.

These issues have been worked on in great detail in what has come to be known as the "state derivation debate" (Holloway and Piccioto 1979). One strain in this debate attempted to derive the need for a state from the logic and dynamics of capital. The problem with this is that the state predated capitalism and played a major role in its emergence. It thus became clear that what was necessary was an "historical derivation" of the state, showing how the state was transformed into its current form and investigating whether and how the state actually does intervene in the long-term interests of capitalism (rather than assuming that it does) and, if it does, what forces produce this intervention (Gerstenberger 1979).

The attraction of relative autonomy is its avoidance of the twin pitfalls of "reductionism" (the state as a tool of capitalists or capitalism) and "autonomism" (the state as totally independent, unconstrained, and undetermined by the mode of production) (Urry 1981, 2). A theoretical resolution of this conflict cannot be adequately achieved, however, by a concept characterized by post-hoc rationalization that allows theorists to argue that anything fits within their theories. The challenge is rather to specify the degree of autonomy achieved by states in particular societies at particular times and the conditions that make this degree of autonomy possible (Skocpol 1985, 8). This challenge has been addressed by a group of neo-Weberians, most prominently Theda Skocpol, who attribute an independent influence to the state, arising out of actions based on its own interests and resulting in a dynamic not simply attributable to the society of which the state is a part.

Skocpol argues that most analyses are society-centred and that there is a need to develop a state-centred approach The point is not to see the state as truly autonomous and free of influence from civil society, but to investigate the real degree of autonomy states possess. Skocpol (1985, 9) sees state autonomy as the ability of states to "formulate and pursue goals that are not simply reflective of the demands or interests of social groups, classes, or society."

There are also tendencies in this direction from theorists working in the Marxian tradition. Clark and Dear (1984, 33), for example, argue that "the state can be analyzed as a separate institution and given an agenda conceived in the social relations of production; however, once it is formed as an historical entity, the state also has qualities of an autonomous actor."

While useful, this argument still implies that the state is formed under capitalism and only subsequently develops autonomy, whereas in fact the state pre-existed capitalism and influenced its emergence. Gottdiener (1987, 190) incorporates this insight:

> Precapitalist social relations, or the "historical substratum," . . . articulates with the developing capitalist mode of production and produces the idiosyncratic elements that then comprise the social formation; that is, the particular historical product of such development that varies from nation-State to nation-State.

The outcome of this historical process is not predetermined nor uniform, and states can differ in their degree of autonomy as a result of it.

This perspective seems to avoid most of the theoretical problems discussed above, but it still needs to be more clearly elaborated. Migdal (1988, 4), in an excellent comparison of the relative strength of a number of Third World states, identifies the critical dimension of state capacities as their ability "to penetrate society, regulate social relationships, extract resources, and appropriate or use resources in determined ways." These capacities are the outcome not only of domestic processes but also of the place of a state in the world of states (Migdal 1988, 21) or what Wallerstein (1974) calls the interstate system.

Thus far, the analysis has dealt with developments in the theory of the state in general. More work must yet be done in the next section to relate this body of theory specifically to cities and local governments, which have important limitations on their autonomy not shared by nation-states.

LOCAL GOVERNMENT/LOCAL STATE

Although nation-states and provinces or states are intimately involved in cities, when we consider state actions or responses from the perspective of a particular city, we tend to discuss local governments. Because of their subordination to superior governments, local governments have a whole set of limitations on their autonomy that do not apply to sovereign nation-states. As a result, when we discuss the autonomy of cities or municipal governments, we need to distinguish between two types of limitations on their freedom. Gurr and King (1987, 56) call these Type I and Type II autonomy. They define Type I autonomy in this way:

> The local state is autonomous to the extent that it can pursue its interests without being substantially constrained by local economic and social conditions (p. 57).

The conditions that most commonly constrain local governments in Type I (which, for clarity, I will subsequently refer to as socio-economic autonomy) are limits on the revenues that can be extracted from the local economy, resistance of dominant local interests, and the activities of local political organizations and social movements (Gurr and King, 1987, 57).

> Type II, or political autonomy, involves autonomy from higher governments. The local state is autonomous to the extent that it can pursue its interest without substantial interference by the national state (p. 63)

In Canada this needs to be expanded to recognize that the *provincial* government is the primary source of legal limits on local governments (Smith and Bayne, this volume), and this level of legal control is often the case in federal systems.

While the Marxian literature on the theory of the state has concentrated on socio-economic autonomy, discussions of Canadian cities have tended to focus on the autonomy of local governments *vis-à-vis* higher levels of government. To comprehend the true freedom of movement and capacities of local governments, however, it is necessary to examine both in conjunction, since one can influence the other.

The term "local state" has been used as an alternative to "local government" as a way of avoiding the narrowness of the latter concept and the resulting limitations common in examinations of urban politics (Magnusson 1985; Cockburn 1977). Local government consists of institutions and the political groups controlling them that are embedded in the local state. The definition of what is and what is not part of the local state is a difficult and as yet unresolved challenge. Inasmuch as one can legitimately talk about entities acting, however, it seems to be the local government that can most usefully be discussed in terms of its degree of autonomy, and this usage will be followed below.

It is clear from Gurr and King's ideas discussed above that the degree of autonomy of local governments is not fixed even within a particular nation-state. The state of play in federal and provincial politics, the size of an urban settlement, the vitality of its economy, the strategy and strength of its power-holders, the efficiency of its institutional organization: all these factors and more may increase or decrease its degree of autonomy (see, for example, Smith and Bayne's article in this volume). Furthermore, all of these are influenced by changes in external factors. It has been argued that contemporary changes, most notably the centralization of power in higher levels of government and the increasing interdependence of the world economy, have produced a trend toward a steady reduction in local government autonomy. This issue will be addressed in the next section.

Finally, it is necessary to avoid reifying the concept of autonomy or state capacity. Autonomy or capacity is not an absolute or unidimensional characteristic. Ultimately, the question must be asked: "capacity to do what?" One state may be better able to intervene in one sphere while another has greater capacity in another. Canadian local governments have tended to engage to a greater (though still very limited) extent in land-use planning than their counterparts in the United States because of the lack of legitimacy accorded to planning in the U.S. (Frisken 1988, 3). Hong Kong can more easily intervene in housing than Toronto because all of Hong Kong's land is crown land.

CONSTRAINTS IN CANADIAN METROPOLISES

Most of the literature on municipal autonomy in Canada is concerned with the relationship with higher levels of government. What municipalities can legally do, the resources with which they can do it, and what they are required to do whether they wish to or not are all determined by higher levels of government. In Canada, municipalities are constitutionally under the control of the province in which they are situated, and their powers are essentially determined by that province (Smith and Bayne, this volume; Higgins 1977, 52). This means, of course, that the powers and limitations of municipalities will vary from province to province, and generalization is not easy. One critical question is whether or not there has been a trend toward a centralization of power and a reduction in the autonomy of municipalities (Gurr and King 1987, 181; Frisken 1991). The expansion of welfare programs and fiscal transfers (see Nolan, this volume) may reduce the bargaining power of local governments, although this is not necessarily the case. Local governments may actively promote such transfers, although they generally try to avoid receiving them as "tied grants" (committed to particular types of expenditures).

Regardless of the situation with respect to the political autonomy of Canadian municipalities, other questions remain. Local autonomy can be constrained in many ways other than by formal legal authority. Among the most important of these is what was termed above "socio-economic autonomy." The power of local elites or the demands of competition in a rapidly changing economy may undermine the freedom of movement of decision makers by making only one or a few options available to them.

Fiscal austerity and its impact on urban centres has received a great deal of attention in the last decade. In Britain and the U.S. in particular municipalities have encountered much tighter restraints on their spending due to a complex interaction between restraints at higher governmental levels, global economic restructuring, and resistance by voters and enterprises to higher levels of taxation. It is in fiscal austerity that the two main constraints upon local autonomy become intertwined, since austerity is the outcome of both political and socio-economic processes.

A major coordinated global research program has been launched to examine the political responses of urban governments to fiscal austerity (Clarke 1989). Two relevant questions addressed are: (1) How do responses relate to the degree of autonomy of municipal governments?; and (2) Is innovation more likely with greater or lesser autonomy? One might expect that as financial constraints become tighter local autonomy will decrease. The results of the studies suggest the opposite. Fiscal austerity seems to provide opportunities for innovative manipulation of relationships "among corporate and competitive sectors, central and local government institutions, and economic and social policy concerns in such a way as to increase their relative autonomy from these pressures" (Clarke 1989, 26). The preferred coping strategies tend "to be those that allow policy-makers to retain their flexibility and sustain their legitimacy for future decision situations" (Clarke 1989, 27). The ambiguity of the situation may lend itself to uncovering the ability of local autonomy to make a difference, since fiscal austerity programs very often "grant local officials more autonomy over fewer resources" (Clarke 1989, 247). Such claims are supported by the conclusion of Andrew (this volume) that Canadian intergovernmental relations in an era of restraint "may offer certain opportunities for the large cities to become more important participants in federal policy-making."

Variations found by these studies suggest that the degree of autonomy found initially is an important influence on municipalities' responses to fiscal austerity. Most interestingly, they indicate that the relationship between political and socio-economic local autonomy is not a straightforward one. It was discovered that "Local officials in more centralized systems are more likely to make 'hard choices' on expenditure strategies" (Clarke 1989, 240). This is likely due to the ability of local managers to blame the central authorities for the disruptions, and this may increase their autonomy from local social and economic influences, although at the cost of decreased autonomy from higher levels of government.

Local autonomy *vis-à-vis* higher levels of government may be of less importance, however, if Magnusson (this volume) is correct in suggesting that trends toward the globalization of the economy are reducing even the ability of nation-states to follow distinctive paths. For this reason, it is critical to examine the constraints placed on their cities by their position within the world economic system and to examine what degree of autonomy they may still have within this system and what factors may allow them to increase it.

It is not simply that cities are interconnected parts of larger economies, nor that they are strongly affected by changes occurring elsewhere. The critical point is that the scale of these larger economies may be increasing, and the scope for independent action decreasing. According to Clark and Dear (1984, 170-1):

> the scale of the economy has shifted from local to state, to national, and even to international dimensions. Of course this has meant that the ability of any one local government to regulate its local economy has drastically shrunk. Local economic growth and decline respond to forces outside the immediate area. Also, by virtue of this expansion in scale, local governments have become direct competitors in the sense that their abilities to attract and hold industry have come to depend upon their comparative policies and inducements. . . . Policies are increasingly set in reaction to the requirements of private (and global) capital.

The basic problem is that capital is mobile, and increasingly so, partially as a result of international efforts to liberalize world trade. While capital becomes "hypermobile," labour is much more tied to particular places and cities are "increasingly reduced to the status of a labour pool" (Urry 1985, 33). Hypermobile capital is a force that cities require but cannot command, so the bargaining power of capitalists is increased and the socio-economic autonomy of cities is reduced. Cities come to compete for investment, and policies and programs are created, discarded, or modified to increase their attractiveness to investors (Peterson 1981; see also Nolan, this volume). The effect of this, it is claimed, is "to discipline any urban-based class alliance to common capitalist requirements" (Harvey 1989, 126).

These comments suggest a very pessimistic view of the potential for local autonomy in a global economy of hypermobile capital increasingly able to tempt/extort concessions from local and even national governments that can at best respond by trying to attract a share at the expense of their neighbours. But is this view not overplayed? Autonomy is perhaps reduced, but does that make it insignificant? We need to ask to what extent local governments can still make distinctive choices that may not be precisely what capitalists would want. Daly's comparison of government responses to homelessness in Britain, Canada, and the U.S. (this volume) shows the differences that can exist in reactions to similar challenges. To what extent can political action based upon locality manage, for example, to get the maximum benefit from the capital that is attracted or is already in place? Is some kind of balancing act possible for local governments? As Leo (this volume) discusses, to what extent are such possibilities limited by a city's position in urban hierarchies? Can we identify different strategies that have been adopted to deal with this challenge, and does position in the global spatial division of labour determine the chance of success of a particular strategy? These questions lead us to ask to what extent local autonomy is still significant, even if it might be reduced. Horan (1991) suggests that local politics still has considerable potential and that "the economic imperative" is simply a political myth that supports the continued dominance of local politics by a "pro-growth coalition."

Indeed, it has been argued that despite global economic restructuring, local autonomy is of critical importance in managing many of the changes that are occurring and are still needed. Savitch (1988, 287) argues that in the construction of "postindustrial" cities[1] in the developed countries, government is of critical importance: "Despite neoconservative efforts to reduce government, postindustrialism entices its expansion." This is because one condition of successful postindustrial cities based upon the service sector is the complex task "of building a brand new physical environment. . . . Whether they want it or not, politicians are handed the consuming task of making it all work" (Savitch 1988, 286). He argues that precisely because of external competition, urban politics will tend to be internally less competitive and corporatist, since "To compete effectively, the post-industrial city needs to harness its internal resources" (Savitch 1988, 285).

Although from this point of view urban politics is of critical importance in determining the degree of success of postindustrial cities' bids for economic investment and growth, the direction in which

---

[1] I follow Savitch's term "postindustrial" here with reluctance. It seems that discussions of postindustrialization often simply put a positive spin on what in practise is little more than a process of de-industrialization.

successful politics moves is still constrained. Beauregard (1989, xiv-xv) goes somewhat farther and sees urban officials as *mediating*

the relation between economic restructuring and spatial transformations. These mediating agents transmit shifts in production
and exchange to rearrangements of the built environment and, in
turn, transmit the constraints and opportunities inherent in that
environment back to the economic sphere.

Thus, although political actors and decision makers are still important,
they cannot act successfully in any manner they choose. The result of
this is an ubiquitous instability of cities' "economic structure and social
dynamics, as a consequence of the volatility of movements in the
international economy" (Castells 1989, 346). The outcome of this
process, which is not yet complete, is that local governments become less
and less capable of acting upon the "basic mechanisms that condition the
daily existence of their citizens" (Castells 1989, 347). The decline of
urban politics, examined in detail by Gottdiener (1987), may not be
surprising in this context, as these politics may become little more than
a way of optimally using a city's resources to increase its ability to attract
and retain capital.

The article by Magnusson (this volume) makes clear the importance
of political process in the transformation of Canadian metropolises. He
sees the metropolis as intrinsically spilling across all boundaries
constructed to contain it, as does the increasingly global economy.
Traditional municipal politics in Canada, constrained between the state
and the market, has spawned new forms of politics, both on the right and
the left, which challenge the boundaries of what local politics is supposed
to do. Magnusson locates the capacity of politics to breach the boundaries of established political spaces to the linkages created with broader
social movements. His analysis is carefully balanced between pessimism
and optimism. Precisely because of this uncertainty, it convinces us that
urban politics do retain a great capacity to make a difference. The
discussion of the Oka crisis also identifies a new element of Canadian
local politics (native self-government), which may be a forerunner of
developments in other nations.

Harvey (1989), while recognizing the increasing constraints upon
cities and regions, suggests that significant local autonomy is still
necessary and critically important. Capitalist accumulation relies upon
social and political innovation, and this, Harvey argues (p. 158), can only
be achieved in the restructuring of cities through autonomous urban
politics, created by processes in which "the confusions and instabilities

of class-alliance formation create a political space in which a relatively autonomous urban politics can arise" (Harvey 1989, 152). This relative autonomy is critically important because stable control by a local capitalist class would not necessarily serve its long-term interests and is unlikely to produce the innovative policies that might attract new investment. Local autonomy is disciplined, however, since

> We can view the urban region as a kind of competitive collective unit within the global dynamics of capitalism. . . . Each urban region has the autonomy to pursue whatever course it will, but in the end each is disciplined by the external coercive laws of competition (Harvey 1989, 158).

What Harvey neglects here, however, are the constraints placed upon local governments by superior governments, discussed above. The basic point is crucial, however: there is not just one way to prosper within a global division of labour. Urban politics can act as a mechanism for identifying those paths that may be collectively most acceptable for a city's residents, rather than just mechanically copying the incentive programs of other urban regions. It should be kept in mind that some progressive reforms may increase a city's competitive advantage; that in fact this has occurred in the past. Such reformism may be particularly important in those cities at the top of the urban hierarchy, where the transition to a service-based economy may place a premium on liveable, vibrant cities as places of residence for highly skilled information workers. In practice, of course, these concerns coupled with fiscal austerity are tending to produce cities that are increasingly polarized between the affluent and the poor, although not yet to the extent found in the United States.

The above discussion has raised a large number of questions that should be answered about Canadian cities in the light of theoretical debates about states. There is a confluence of forces that are changing the basic features of cities' economic base and political opportunities. What worked for local governments in the past may not work now. They seem to need to do more and to be under ever-greater conflicting pressures, yet they have fewer resources and less flexibility to pursue solutions to their problems. To see how Canadian cities are responding to these challenges, it is useful to start with an exploration of the degree of autonomy possessed by various cities, the capacities they have to accomplish certain tasks, and the political circumstances that may increase their capacities.

LESSONS FROM CANADIAN CITIES

At the beginning of this chapter, I suggested that a dialectical consideration of the theory of the state and recent changes in Canadian metropolises should be able mutually to inform each other. The analyses produced for this volume and the workshop on which it is based support this suggestion. They indicate that a fuller understanding of state capacities is of central importance to an understanding of the past, present, and future development of Canadian cities.

The broader significance of Canadian metropolises for state theory is generally less explicitly developed in this volume's contributions, probably because of the specific focus upon Canada rather than upon comparison. There are some specific references, however, and many of the topics raised are also relevant to this broader theoretical context.

As the review above indicates, most of the theoretical work on the theory of the state within urban studies has been developed in work on American and European cities. There is always an advantage in comparative analysis, particularly in extending comparison to areas previously left out (for a methodological discussion, see Smart 1989). Doing so may allow theorists to check the validity and generality of their abstractions and to undercut common assumptions that may not apply in different cases.

Canada is a particularly interesting case for consideration, since it shares certain similarities with the United States (federal system, common social and economic patterns), as well as having a high level of interdependence with that country. It is also more similar to European nations in certain other characteristics, notably the higher respect paid to planning, the greater power of the state *vis-à-vis* individual rights, and higher density cities due to development restrictions (Goldberg and Mercer 1986; Feldman and Goldberg 1987). As a result, Canada may offer the possibility of the combination of "most similar systems" and "most different systems" comparative analysis that Pickvance (1986) suggests can be very productive.

The work of Goldberg and Mercer (1986) is very relevant here. They have argued in detail that, despite socio-economic similarities and intensive contact between Canada and the United States, there are pervasive differences between the cities of the two countries. These differences cannot be accounted for by reference only to size or regional variation, but seem to derive primarily from differences between the political systems and political cultures. Canadian political culture has consistently placed a greater emphasis on the rights of collectivities and state-generated solutions to problems than that of the United States, where constitutional primacy is accorded to individual rights and the predominance of the private sector. They argue that even urban form varies between the two countries as a result of these differences, with Canada having generally higher urban densities, which in turn influence the feasibility and costs of efficient public transportation systems. Canada thus shares many elements of social and economic organization with the United States, yet has a political system that shares many features found in European market economies.

Christopher Leo's chapter indicates the potential for reconsidering certain aspects of the theory of the state by examining the experiences of Canadian cities. Leo addresses ways in which the economic position of cities influences the power of the local state and its ability to implement planned policies. He suggests that an overarching system of economic power "strongly influences or perhaps even determines the political power that is capable of being wielded by, and in, individual communities . . . ." Applying these ideas, Leo examines the history of development planning in Vancouver and Edmonton, showing how planning controls have been progressively abandoned in Edmonton but have been much more effective in Vancouver. Edmonton, having only seven head offices of the top corporations, is much more vulnerable to movements of corporate capital than Vancouver, a city with 38 head offices and "inundated in development proposals," which give it a greater ability to set conditions for development. However, while the economic position of the metropolis influences the power of the local state, Leo also argues that local culture and politics are major influences on the outcome. He points out that Calgary shares some of Vancouver's advantages but has planning policies more like those of Edmonton than of Vancouver.

Charbonneau, Hamel, and Barcelo (this volume) present a case study of planning policies related to urban sprawl (see also Sancton and Montgomery, this volume) in the Montreal area, a metropolitan area that unlike Vancouver has experienced a serious "shrinking of its economic space." One of their conclusions is that the policies adopted by the Quebec government did not succeed in redirecting the logic of urban development. Among the reasons for failure were local government resistance to the policies and lack of consensus and coordination within the Quebec government itself. This case study, then, raises serious questions for discussions of the capacities of central states to implement their policies.

Ley's contribution indicates the importance and potential efficacy of local politics in a very effective way. The discussion of DERA shows the way in which effective development controls and the provision of needed social services can be pushed and to a certain extent achieved, despite the reluctance and even antagonism of government officials. What is missing in Calgary is probably precisely this kind of citizen activism, which can be a critical resource for those representatives of the local state who want to influence the character of development in their city.

A central question for Canadian cities is therefore "how much do politics matter?" If we accept the claim that the power of capital *vis-à-vis* localized states has increased, what can political activity achieve? Is it simply a matter of being able to deliver efficiently the services required to attract and retain investment? While politics would still matter in such a situation, as Harvey suggests, they would be constrained dramatically in what they could achieve.

Louise Quesnel (this volume) examines the role of political parties in local government politics and asks what difference they make. This is indeed an important question. Does partisan politics provide a more efficient mechanism for mobilization that might increase the bargaining power of municipalities, at least against those enterprises that wish to locate there? Can parties avoid the divide and conquer techniques that developers and others can use against city halls controlled by unstable coalitions and temporary alliances? Since the short-term advantages of individual capitalists may be in conflict with the long-term interests of capitalism as a system of political economy, we can avoid some degree of fatalism by recognising that some progressive reforms may increase the competitive advantage of cities. It is arguable, for example, that the limited successes of reform politicians in Toronto managed to improve the "liveability" of this urban setting, making this one of its locational advantages. Ironically these very successes have led to the poor and middle classes being progressively priced and squeezed out of the city centre (Magnusson, this volume). Successful innovations may be most achievable in the area of environmental initiatives, due to the rapidly growing potential for popular mobilization and the need for changes, as Paehlke's chapter in this volume indicates.

Fallis's article draws on Paul Peterson's *City Limits* (1981) to suggest the limits on redistributive public policy in "small, open economies." However, in his examination of housing policy, he argues that features of the Canadian political system reduce the limits upon subordinate governmental action and increase the set of policy instruments available to them. As other contributors have also pointed out, the provinces can effectively block certain types of federal intervention. Second, "Canadian cities are less limited than American cities, because we have stronger metropolitan and regional governments. . . . Canadian metropolitan structures are stronger because they are less limited and therefore their politics and policy will be more amenable to the redistributive issues of housing policy."

Smith and Bayne's contribution suggests, however, that the development of postmodern patterns and attitudes are undermining regional planning and governmental structures, as a result of an emphasis upon local initiative and control. With postmodernity comes a collapse of beliefs in rational planning by the state (the classical bearer of Enlightenment values). Regional governments seem to suffer most, since they represent neither democracy nor market. The result may bring Canadian cities closer to the pattern described by Peterson (1981).

The view of local governments as being limited by higher levels of government, while important, is only one side of the story. The actions of the higher governments are also limited, in practice if not always in theory, by subordinate governments. Caroline Andrew's chapter clearly demonstrates this in its account of the constraints on the development of any new federal policies that are openly directed at cities as such. Such limitations often become apparent only when we examine the actual practice of policy implementation and not just the theory and text of formal institutions and division of powers. She suggests that what is more important than explicit policies *about* cities is what the federal government is actually doing *in* cities. Leo and Fenton's (1990) examination of federal involvement in specific urban redevelopment corporations shows that the federal government is in fact actively involved and that the form of involvement is crafted to maximize their credit and minimize their financial commitment. These activities take a kind of "end-run" around provincial blockages but support the view that provincial governments constrain federal action and help to channel it in particular directions.

Frisken's chapter on transportation policies contends that in effect the provinces now constitute the metropolitan governments of cities like Toronto and Montreal that have sprawled beyond their metropolitan boundaries. This article and some of her earlier work (1991) demonstrate that theory and practice can diverge quite dramatically. The formal realities of Canadian municipalities, that they are creatures of the provinces and agencies for administering provincially delegated responsibilities, has led to a common view that "local policy-making has little significance for an understanding of domestic policy-making in Canada . . . " (Frisken 1991, 352). The practice, Frisken argues, is often very different, as she found in an analysis of the Ontario government's efforts to reform the property tax. Many theorists argue that there is a trend to increasing centralization of authority (Frisken 1991). Yet the failure of the Ontario government to implement its planned reforms of the property tax indicates that "local interests, acting through local political officials and directly on provincial decision-makers, can effectively counteract provincial attempts to bring local policy into conformance with provincial and even national policy objectives" (Frisken 1991, 377). Despite the province's clear authority over municipalities, local politics managed to prevent the changes being made in the way the province desired: theory and practice are distinct. This is a point that unfortunately is too often neglected. In general there is an imbalance in the literature: analyses of policies and formal descriptions of institutions are plentiful while works that consider what actually happens in these institutions, how policies are implemented, and how local responses may modify what actually results are in scarce supply.

The chapter by Smith and Cohn on urban paradiplomacy helps to correct the balance by examining the difference between the constitutional theory of the governmental division of labour and the reality of municipal practice. They demonstrate that municipal governments may act in ways not formally sanctioned by higher governments and that global changes are encouraging, even demanding, such responses.

The work carried out thus far indicates the utility of examining Canadian cities in terms of their autonomy and capacity to achieve different kinds of objectives. It also suggests, however, how much more effort is needed to fulfill the promise of such an endeavour. Changes in Canada and in the world are steadily producing new pressures on Canadian metropolises but may also be providing new opportunities for them, if they can respond effectively. If Harvey is correct in his vision of local politics creating an innovative capacity that responds to external constraining forces, we must ask if Canadian cities are accomplishing this, and if not, what can be done to facilitate it?

REFERENCES

Beauregard, R. 1989. "Preface." In *Atop the Urban Hierarchy*, ed. R. Beauregard, Totowa: Rowman and Littlefield, xiii-xx.

Castells, M. 1977. *The Urban Question*. Cambridge: M.I.T. Press.

_____. 1978. *City, Class and Power*. London: Macmillan.

_____. 1989. *The Informational City: Information Technology, Economic Restructuring, and the Urban-Regional Process*. Oxford: Basil Blackwell.

Clark, G., and M. Dear. 1984. *State Apparatus*. Boston: Allen & Unwin.

Clarke, S. 1989. "Urban Innovation and Autonomy: Cross-National Analyses of Policy Change." In *Urban Innovation and Autonomy*, ed. S. Clarke, Newbury Park: Sage, 21-30.

Cockburn, C. 1977. *The Local State*. London: Pluto Press.

Feldman, E., and M. Goldberg. 1987. "Introduction." In *Land Rites and Wrongs*, ed. E. Feldman and M. Goldberg, Cambridge: Lincoln Institute of Land Policy, 1-20.

Frisken, F. 1988. *City Policy-making in Theory and Practice*. London: University of Western Ontario, Local and Regional Government Program.

_____. 1991. "Local Constraints on Provincial Initiative in a Dynamic Context: The Case of Property Tax Reform in Ontario." *Canadian Journal of Political Science* 24 (June): 351-78.

Gerstenberger, H. 1979. "Class Conflict, Competition and State Functions." In *State and Capital: A Marxist Debate*, ed. J. Holloway and S. Picciotto, Austin: University of Texas Press, 148-59.

Glucksmann, M. 1974. *Structuralist Analysis in Contemporary Social Thought*. London: Routledge and Kegan Paul.

Goldberg, M., and J. Mercer. 1986. *Continentalism Challenged: The Myth of the North American City*. Vancouver: University of British Columbia Press.

Gottdiener, M. 1985. *The Social Production of Urban Space*. Austin: University of Texas Press.

_____. 1987. *The Decline of Urban Politics*. Newbury Park: Sage.

Gurr, T., and D. King. 1987. *The State and the City*. Chicago: University of Chicago Press.

Harvey, D. 1973. *Social Justice and the City*. Maryland: John Hopkins University Press.

_____. 1989. *The Urban Experience*. Baltimore: Johns Hopkins University Press.

Higgins, D. 1977. *Urban Canada*. Toronto: Gage.

Holloway, J., and S. Picciotto. 1979. "Introduction: Towards a Materialist Theory of the State." In *State and Capital: A Marxist Debate*, ed. J. Holloway and S. Picciotto, Austin: University of Texas Press, 1-31.

Horan, C. 1991. "Beyond Governing Coalitions: Analyzing Urban Regimes in the 1990s." *Journal of Urban Affairs* 13(2): 119-35.

Leo, C., and R. Fenton. 1990. "Mediated Enforcement and the Evolution of the State." *International Journal of Urban and Regional Research* 14(2): 185-206.

Magnusson, W. 1985. "Urban Politics and the Local State." *Studies in Political Economy* 16:111-42.

Melling, J. 1980. *Housing, Social Policy and the State*. London: Croom Helm.

Migdal, J. 1988. *Strong Societies and Weak States*. Princeton: Princeton University Press.

Peterson, P. 1981. *City Limits*. Chicago: University of Chicago Press.

Pickvance, C. 1986. "Comparative Urban Analysis Assumptions about Causality." *International Journal of Urban and Regional Research* 10(2): 162-84.

Saunders, P. 1979. *Urban Politics: A Sociological Interpretation*. London: Hutchinson.

_____. 1981. *Social Theory and the Urban Question*. London: Hutchinson.

Savitch, H. 1988. *Post-Industrial Cities*. Princeton: Princeton University Press.

Skocpol, T. 1985. "Bringing the State Back In: Strategies of Analysis in Current Research." In *Bringing the State Back In*, ed. P. Evans, New York: Cambridge University Press, 3-37.

Smart A. 1989. "Extreme Case Comparison: Housing Provision and the State." *City and Society* 3(1): 40-54.

Urry, J. 1981. *The Anatomy of Capitalist Societies*. Atlantic Highlands: Humanities Press.

_____. 1985. "Social Relations, Space and Time." In *Social Relations and Spatial Structures*, ed. D. Gregory and J. Urry, London: Macmillan, 20-48.

Wallerstein, I. 1974. *The Modern World-System*. New York: Academic Press.

Chapter 18

Party Politics in the Metropolis:
Montreal 1960-1990

Louise Quesnel
Laval University

For decades the story of cities in Canada has been about development and the provision of public utilities to accommodate a rapidly increasing urban population and industrial expansion. Developmental issues became even more acute in major metropolitan areas as suburbanization rapidly supplemented urbanization as part of a process of global restructuration of urban space that is still underway.

An immediate response to the rapidly changing social and economic situation of the post World War II period was the adoption of administrative solutions like opening up the decision-making process and reorganizing staff and line arrangements in the public sector. The politics and policies of the early 1950s were considered piecemeal and parochial, however, and more modern and progressive solutions were sought. In Quebec, this fundamental reorientation happened first at the provincial level. In the late 1950s and early 1960s, a wind of change and modernization swept the province, bringing with it new political actors moved by a will to strengthen the collective instruments of welfare and progress. The foci of this movement were two urban centres: Montreal, the major metropolitan centre, and Quebec, the provincial capital.

This research is sponsored by the Social Sciences and Humanities Research Council of Canada. Background material was collected in collaboration with Serge Belley, Johane Charbonneau, and Pierre Nolin. It consisted of documentary research, including files of the municipal parties, and interviews with actual and past officials of the parties.

In these two cities, the formation of municipal parties appeared to be the best way to cope with problems of modernization and development. As astonishing as the idea may be, this approach was seen as a solution to the over-politicization of local politics. The party was seen as a facilitator of policy formation and as a way to end short-sighted political confrontations. One must remember that Canadian municipalities had not experienced the party machine politics known to many American cities. Thus the idea of parties in city hall did not cause criticism as it did in the American context, at least not in Quebec's progressive circles.

Who were these people who promoted the idea of an organized politicization of city hall? What kind of political party did they have in mind? The answers to these questions are conditioned by the urban context of the 1950s and by the place that these local actors wanted to confer on the province's urban centres. But these conditions changed over the years, and new issues imposed a redefinition of the political scene and of the strategies needed to operate within it. However, municipal parties remained a privileged strategy.

This chapter focuses on the city of Montreal where the first municipal parties were formed in the 1950s and 1960s. In these years, Montreal was Canada's first metropolis, striving to keep this prestigious position in the face of the ascendancy of other urban centres in the Canadian urban system. The struggle was not an easy one, as many factors influenced the competition. Changing social conditions, modernization, and internationalization influenced the political confrontations in which municipal parties got involved. In the remainder of the chapter, this argument is developed in three sections. In the first, the major concepts are defined and discussed. In the second, the emerging context is described, and the factors that determined the creation and evolution of parties in Montreal are identified. The third part presents an analysis of the behavior of the municipal party system over the last 20 years. The analysis makes it possible to see how the parties fared over that period and under which conditions they succeeded in keeping up with rapidly changing social conditions.

MUNICIPAL PARTIES AND REFORMISM

The current understanding of the term "political party" refers to a stable organization whose main objective is to influence policy through the election of representatives to decision-making bodies. Differences from country to country appear if the analysis considers the origins of the parties, their patterns of activities, or their impact on policy (Castles 1982; Gagnon et Tanguay 1989; Brodie and Jenson 1980; Lemieux 1985; Rose 1984). Our attention is not focused on international comparisons, however, but rather on a case study. This approach has been little used, because of an assumption that there is relative continuity in partisan lines stretching from local to national politics, inasmuch as the same parties are active at the central and at the decentralized political levels of many countries (the U.S.A. the Scandinavian countries, and many European countries). In Canada, however, the partisan system has some regional features and the province of Quebec is no exception. Moreover, the appearance of strictly municipal parties in this province presents a special case, insofar as these organizations have been stable and strong for a few decades.

It is our contention that strictly local groupings of people who aim to run for municipal elections and hold political office are political parties. The fact that they are nominally, structurally, and financially separate from provincial or national political parties does not deny them that status in theoretical terms. Moreover, the individuals who founded the first generation of these municipal organizations, in the early 1960s, used the term "party" to stress the collective and coordinated action expected from this type of political mobilization. As will be seen in this chapter, a different terminology was used by the second generation of parties, in the 1970s, which labelled themselves "rassemblements" or gatherings. Notwithstanding the image projected by this term, these organizations also have the theoretical characteristics of political parties: an effective party apparatus, members, leaders, resources, programs. In some cases, these characteristics can even be said to hold more significance in relation to local issues than is the case with some provincial or national parties in relation to provincial or even wider issues. So let us consider that the term "municipal parties" refers to political parties present on the local municipal scene.

How do these municipal parties compare with the coalitions that in some interesting cases (e.g., Stone 1989) have a significant presence at the municipal level? Stone makes a distinction between the "electoral coalition" that involves political candidates and the electorate at election time, and the "governing coalition" that is formed as a mode of cooperation between elected officials and those in the community who have appropriate resources to achieve common goals. In the American southern city of Atlanta, Stone found these resources to be in the business sector of the community. Informal arrangements between business people and elected officials, which Stone labels an "urban regime," are a way to bolster the formal capacity to act in a situation where formal authority is weak (Stone 1989, 5).

At first sight, municipal parties combine the characteristics of the electoral and the governing coalitions. They have an active electoral component, and getting elected or re-elected is one of the most, if not the most imperative of all their objectives. Once elected, either on the majority side or as the opposition, the parties form coalitions with some sectors of the community.

Our observation of the municipal scene in Montreal suggests that where there is an active party system there is more than one coalition, and coalition forming is paramount. There is not just *one* city governing alliance but also an opposition alliance that contributes, in its way, to the governance of the city. Hence considering a "counter-coalition," or an opposition party in the parliamentary sense of the term, introduces an interesting dialectical dimension to the analysis of local politics as an ongoing process of social and political change.

Municipal parties in Quebec do not restrict their activities to the electoral process. They also participate in the governance of the city. By combining the electoral and the governing roles, they may not be governing coalitions in Stone's terms, but they are urban coalitions in a broader sense.

Because much of the Canadian writing on local government deals with the reform movement, some remarks are now necessary to clarify the positions of municipal parties on reform issues, since parties were actually created to bring about some kind of social and political change. First, let us refer to a few criteria that have been used to characterize reformism in Canadian cities.

Reformism in Canadian cities initially followed the experimentation of the American reform model based on the introduction of new management techniques and an ideal of a democratic decision-making process (Linteau and Artibise 1984, 31). In the first part of the century in urban planning, new ideas were stimulated by the rapid development of major infrastructures and core areas. According to Kaplan (1982, 312), the city of Montreal did not follow this pattern to the same extent as Toronto and Winnipeg did, although some reform took place (Linteau and Artibise 1984, 31).

This differentiation did not appear in the reform movement of the late 1960s. In all major Canadian cities, including Montreal and Quebec, strong opposition to the "destructive consequences of post-war city building on the ambience of the built urban environment" (Caulfield 1988, 108) occurred. But the reform movement of the 1960s also followed another path. It was animated by a demand for increased participation in city affairs on the part of local groups, which stressed housing needs and the reorientation of urban development policies in favor of core residents.

As Caulfield mentioned (1988, 107), there is not *one* reform platform but many avenues of change, all of which did not follow the social-democratic paradigm. In this broad sense, reformism can be identified with different groups and individuals who supported social change at the urban level in various and even opposite ways. Hence, the first generation of municipal parties in Montreal can be considered as agents of social change and as instruments of reform. Opposition to the managerial type of reform that these parties put forward came from the second generation of municipal parties, in the 1970s.

Municipal parties are, each in its way, connected to reform ideals, be they of left (social democratic) or of new right (quality of urban life) orientation. Therefore, to describe municipal parties as reformist does not provide a clear semantic way of discriminating among them. We try to avoid using this term by adopting a typology based on three criteria:

1. the *pro and anti development* criteria cannot be put aside, but

2. attention must also be drawn to the type of development, thereby introducing a *pro business versus pro citizen interest* component, and, finally,

3. ideas about the *political process*, whether they embrace the closed-executive model or the participatory model.

These criteria will be used to differentiate among the municipal parties and to examine how each type of party responded to specific social and economic conditions in its political platform.

EMERGING CONTEXT

The context of the development of party politics in Montreal goes back to 1945-50. Urban growth during that period brought about a very rapid opening up of urbanized territory. The central city was busy responding to public service demands while suburbs were on the increase and would soon challenge the stability of the urban core.

In the 1940s, the city of Montreal with some 900,000 residents, already had almost its present size of population. As the core of Canada's largest metropolitan area, Montreal was a major economic centre where firms had their headquarters, where a large majority of the region's business activities took place, and where almost all tourist and cultural activities occurred.

Although industrial expansion had shifted to the suburbs, the central city still had a strong and diversified economy, with a dominant tertiary sector (transport, communication, professional services, business). According to these criteria, Montreal was then a rich and healthy city containing 81 percent of the metropolitan population.

Moreover, Montreal presented a very singular characteristic in comparison with all other Quebec cities. Its rising immigrant population amounted to 17 percent of its population in 1961. Predominantly francophone (around 62 percent of the population), Montreal received numerous ethnic groups while its English-speaking community lost importance (from 24 percent in 1941 to 18 percent in 1961).

But Montreal was also heavily struck by the negative impacts of the 1930s depression and had more than its share of unemployed and poor. The numerous beneficiaries of the federal government's newly created family allowances and welfare programs were located largely in the city of Montreal. They were in need of low-cost housing and social services that the municipal authority was incapable of providing. Collaboration with the provincial government was made difficult by a long lasting confrontation between municipal and provincial authorities, based on a disagreement about the extent of the province's responsibility for sharing the cost of Montreal's fiscal burden. The issues of social housing and other social services caused growing dissatisfaction, as elected officials strove for other types of development. City council was then dominated by representatives of the landlords and ratepayers (Germain 1991, 50) although more than 70 percent of households were occupied by tenants.

The municipality was very busy regulating rapid urban development. A major feature of municipal intervention was that the city government used its own financial resources to pay for street construction and water and sewage infrastructures. Under these conditions a large number of small promoters got involved in real estate and housing construction with promises of public investments. A climate of corruption and patronage characterized city politics at this time, posing serious difficulties to the efficient functioning of civic affairs (Linteau, Durocher, Robert, Ricard 1986, 267).

In 1954, a young visionary lawyer by the name of Jean Drapeau became head of a new group, the Ligue d'action civique, and was elected mayor for a three-year term. Drapeau then had to face what was seen as federal "interventionism" in the field of housing. The new federal housing program favoured slum clearance and urban renewal, while Drapeau opposed this program. Moreover, the mayor of Montreal refused to pay tribute to the overwhelmingly powerful premier of the province, Maurice Duplessis, who in return organized strong opposition to Drapeau in the 1957 municipal election and contributed to his defeat.

Drapeau was back with another group, this time called the Parti civique de Montréal, (Montreal Civic Party, or MCP), in 1960. Due to more favourable circumstances, following Premier Duplessis' death and the election of the Liberal party government in the 1960 provincial elections, Drapeau went back as mayor and held this position until his retirement in 1986.

The first decade of Drapeau's reign was punctuated by world-renowned achievements such as the 1967 world exhibition. During this period of "grand design" (Kaplan 1982), the central district of the city was restructured. Place Ville-Marie and other new high rises symbolized the new international status of the metropolis (Léveillée 1988, 46). To solve the city's urgent transportation problem, and in preparation for the 1967 exhibition, the subway was built in the early 1960s.

But Drapeau and his political party were not partisans of the welfare state at the municipal level. They were much too busy with prestige projects to elaborate an economic development policy, let alone enter the growing field of social policy. Drapeau was "blind" as regards housing in general, and even more so as regards social housing (Léveillée 1990, 214).

Drapeau's blindness to the decreasing quality of living conditions in Montreal led to growing unrest and to the formation of citizens' organizations. Popular mobilization around social issues such as unemployment, poverty, and the need for low-cost housing was supported by the city's growing labour movement. Social democrats were disillusioned with the traditional political parties in Quebec and soon found out that even the newly formed Parti Québécois was more committed to the promotion of independence than to social policy (David and Maheu 1982, 201; Quesnel 1990, 41).

In April 1970—a pivotal year in the political life of Montreal—the liberal government was elected at the provincial level. The election results showed a shift of partisan support in Montreal, with a third of the vote going to the new party, the Parti Québécois. Despite this important support for the PQ, this election also indicated a new realism on the part of inner-city citizen groups, which severely criticized the PQ for its unwillingness to promote social policies and antipoverty programs.

There was a sense of a vacuum on the left side of the political arena, and a strictly local political alliance appeared to be the only avenue for real social change. During the summer of 1970, the Front d'action politique (FRAP) actively prepared to oppose Drapeau and the MCP in the coming October 25 municipal election. For the first time, the well-established Civic party faced an organized opposition, which benefited from the awesome support of an active part of the labour movement and of many militant groupings such as students, feminists, nationalists, the unemployed, and socialists (Cardin 1990, 59).

These groups along with FRAP were asking for change, at all levels of society, as is shown by FRAP's publication entitled *Les salariés au pouvoir*. FRAP's political platform was formulated almost concurrently with the demands of the Front de libération du Québec (FLQ). A tendency for the public to confuse the two political forces was exploited by the establishment and by the MCP. In fact, the FLQ was animated by a twofold ideology, based on radical *socialist* and *independentist* values. For them, as for the FRAP, Drapeau and the MCP were instruments of the bourgeois establishment and should be defeated in the October 1970 election. On this basis, the FRAP was identified with the FLQ during the dramatic October crisis of that year.

THE OCTOBER CRISIS

The third determining moment of this period is what is now referred to as the "October crisis." This crisis was punctuated by a series of dramatic events that occurred during the municipal electoral campaign. A summary of some of these events is presented here:

October 5, 1970	British diplomat J. R. Cross was kidnapped by the FLQ.
October 8, 1970	The FLQ "manifesto" was read over CBC television and radio channels.
October 10, 1970	The Quebec Minister of Justice announced that the provincial authorities would not negotiate with the FLQ. Immediately after this announcement, the Quebec vice premier, Pierre Laporte, was kidnapped by the FLQ.

October 14, 1970	Sixteen well-known personalities representing the major sectors of Quebec society (the labour movement, the cooperative sector, the nationalists—including René Lévesque—eminent university professors, and Claude Ryan from the newspaper *Le Devoir*) made a public appeal for negotiation with the FLQ. A view somewhat sympathetic to this solution to the crisis developed in Quebec (Cardin 1990, 99-100).
October 16, 1970	On the basis of "apprehended insurrection," the War Measures Act was implemented by the federal cabinet in agreement with the provincial authorities and Jean Drapeau in Montreal. The immediate impact of this decision was the occupation of Montreal's inner-city districts by the armed forces, and the arrest of many labour leaders and nationalists. From this point on, the municipal electoral campaign was overwhelmed by issues pertaining to the crisis, as the FRAP was identified with the FLQ. For the leaders of the labour movement, such a judgment represented the "sabotage of democracy" (Cardin 1990, 113).
October 17, 1970	Pierre Laporte was found dead. Sympathy toward the government's hard strategy developed in the public and within the rank and file of the labour unions.
October 25, 1970	Jean Drapeau was reelected as mayor, along with all 52 MCP candidates as councillors. FRAP ended up with 30 percent of the vote cast and no elected candidate.

The importance of the October crisis on the municipal scene must be stressed here. In fact, for the most part, the repression was most apparent in Montreal, and it severely limited the mobilisation capacity of the FRAP. While the importance of the general circumstances of the crisis cannot be underestimated because of the prominence of the issue of nationalism, we suggest that local circumstances were also of high strategic relevance.

The October crisis took place in the midst of Montreal's municipal election. In this election, Drapeau and the MCP faced what could seem in their minds to be alarming circumstances, that threatened the hegemonic situation in which they had been over the previous 10 years. For the first time electoral suffrage was extended to all residents of the city with Canadian citizenship, and the voting age was lowered from 21 to 18. Nearly 700,000 persons were eligible to vote, a constituency that considerably exceeded the traditional political network of the MCP.

Even if the FRAP did not have any mayoralty candidate, it had a very noticeable presence in the election campaign. Its platform was strongly focused on a realignment of municipal and national policy in favour of the needy, while being marked by a strong nationalist vision of politics. This program, together with a list of well-qualified candidates, stimulated enough support to represent a very serious threat to the MCP. A third of the FRAP's candidates was identified with the labour movement, not a traditional field of electoral activity for the MCP.

In these conditions, the implementation of the War Measures Act and the repression in Montreal were instrumental for Drapeau and the MCP. They contributed to the electoral outcome, in which Drapeau secured 90 percent of the vote cast and MCP candidates were elected to all the seats in city council. Electoral participation moved up to 53 percent (from 33 percent in the preceding election, in 1966).

The political climate emphasized the distance between the two major parties. The FRAP's program appeared more radical and harder to vote for under the circumstances. A vote for Drapeau was "safe," and very few people were looking for risky situations on October 25, 1970.

EXOGENOUS FACTORS IN THE EMERGENCE
OF MUNICIPAL PARTIES

The preceding argument shows that postwar economic conditions cannot explain everything about the municipal party formation process in Montreal. Local political conditions were also determinant. At this point, we wish to add to these factors some larger political conditions, mainly those pertaining to the relationship between provincial and federal parties and local political forces.

By 1970, the main features of Montreal's local political scene were in place for the coming 20 years. The two major political forces were established: on the right side of the spectrum, Drapeau and his Parti civique de Montréal, and on the left side, FRAP and its grassroots action committees. This scheme underwent many interesting modulations over the following decades as other forces positioned themselves in the political arena. However, the basic configuration of forces was in place. Up to this point we have analysed local or endogenous factors to explain the formation of the political structure that would shape the next decades of municipal political activities. But we must now point to some no less significant exogenous political factors that contributed to the emergence of municipal parties in Montreal at that time.

The first of these factors was the relationship between local political elites in Montreal and provincial authorities. Until 1960 the province was governed by the Union Nationale party headed by Maurice Duplessis. With a very strong rural constituency, this party was less popular in Montreal where antitraditional trends were operating at a rate unknown in the nonmetropolitan areas of the province. Montreal urged a redefinition of public policy, in favour of the growing needs of the urban population. Duplessis's party did not offer an acceptable framework for the political activism of those who wished to promote Montreal's economic development.

The political alternative might have been possible with the other major party, the Parti libéral, which held power at the provincial level from 1897 to 1935. But that party's approach had not been more favourable to the metropolis during that period. Like the Union Nationale, the Parti libéral supported a traditional political culture that was increasingly cut off from what was happening in Montreal (Lemieux 1976, 58). Thus the metropolis' political elite was not comfortable with either of the provincial parties' programs and commitment to the challenges of urbanization. Moreover, they felt the need to keep some distance from the provincial authorities for strategic reasons.

For years, the provincial government had imposed regulations on Montreal's municipal institutions. These interventions, which reduced the power of the mayor and reinforced that of nonelected members of the city council, were opposed by the city's political officials. Local officials were also dissatisfied with what they saw as a lack of understanding of the city's problems on the part of the provincial government. The perceived inadequacy of provincial policies was constantly referred to as the cause of the deterioration of Montreal's economic and social conditions. Under these circumstances, provincial political parties could not be seen as adequate allies in the search for the solution of the metropolis' urgent problems.

As the two provincial political parties did not represent relevant instruments to promote the expansion of the metropolis and the modernization of its political and administrative apparatuses, Drapeau and those with him who wished to change Montreal and to open the city to a more global environment decided to constitute their own political force. For many reasons the most relevant formula for political action at the local level appeared to be the municipal party.

The municipal party was also considered by the emergent political leaders as an effective instrument of organization and policymaking. This perception was decisive since Drapeau and his colleagues aimed to end the corrupt administrative and political tradition of the city and to install a rational and "clean" decision-making process under the strong leadership of the mayor. Drapeau also sought the kind of legitimacy that would allow him to be recognized by provincial and federal authorities as the primary spokesman for the metropolitan city. These objectives came together in the creation of a highly centralized political party, in which the mayor, as chief of the party, was the central figure.

The MCP did in fact realize a series of prestigious projects, thereby succeeding in maintaining the city's position of major metropolis. But this policy left unaddressed some urgent local problems such as poverty and housing. A large political space was opened to the formation of an alternative form of mobilization and numerous citizen and community groups moved in to occupy it. The second generation of parties appeared with the formation of FRAP in 1970. As in the case of the formation of the MCP 10 years before, a strictly local political format was adopted. But the model was entirely different and unique to this moment. First, let us see why the changing forces did not operate within the framework of existing provincial or federal parties.

At the provincial level, the political scene had changed since 1960. The Union Nationale party was disappearing, the Parti libéral was back to power in the spring of 1970, and the new Parti Québécois was rising with force in the Montreal area. But none of these parties appeared to the community action groups as possible vehicles of change. The Parti libéral, with strong roots in the metropolitan area, was seen as an establishment party with no central concern for the workers and no commitment to any alternate form of urban development. Its orientation was closer to that of the MCP than to that of the opposition forces. As to the Parti Québécois, its first goal was the independence of Quebec and not the reform of urban policies. Though part of its membership was drawn from Montreal community groups and labour associations, the latter preferred to separate the issues and to create a strictly local political force.

Because of the social democratic orientation of the groups and of the political action committees in Montreal, the New Democratic Party could have been an ally. In fact, however, this party was hardly present in Quebec then, and its difficulty in reaching the political sensibilities of Quebecers was known in Montreal as elsewhere. As in the case of the Parti Québécois, or even of the Parti libéral, there were some supporters of the New Democratic Party in the community groups. But the need to define a precise though encompassing approach to urban problems required the creation of a new political force in which progressive members of different provincial or federal parties could work together.

This strictly urban approach was already present with the formation of the MCP in 1960, but to a much lesser degree because of dissatisfaction with the two traditional and rural based parties that then existed. In 1970, the provincial parties had become aware of the impact of urbanization. They both needed electoral support in the Montreal area. But the community groups' radicalism and dissatisfaction with the existing parties could find an outlet only in a new local opposition force.

Their critical views of politics and parties led the community groups to gather in what they preferred to call a "front d'action politique," an *alliance* but not a *party*. The terminology was chosen for ideological reasons, given the negative connotation of the term party when applied to the traditional political parties. In functional terms, however, the FRAP's organization resembled that of a party. It had an electoral program, a list of candidates, and a strong desire to introduce significant changes in policies after the election. But the outcome of the election left the party with no elected candidate and having to deal with the serious aftermath of the October crisis. Despite the negative electoral outcome for the FRAP, this period was essential in structuring the city's evolving political and party system.

THE POST 1970 PARTY SYSTEM

For Jean Drapeau and the Montreal Civic Party, the 1970 election represented a total victory. The mayor strengthened his control over the city council. City councillors, all members of the MCP, were not allowed to ask "insidious" questions and were expected to support executive recommendations without reservation. These rules were quite acceptable to the councillors who were used to business type management (two thirds of the MCP councillors were entrepreneurs or businessmen).

The MCP administration continued its megaprojects in the 1970s in preparation for the 1976 Olympic games to be held in the city. While huge redevelopment projects occasioned the demolition of thousands of low-cost housing units in the east part of the city, investments did not always follow demolition, and a large number of vast parking lots appeared in the city's core area.

Drapeau was greatly concerned with the city's international image, and he wisely entertained city residents and community groups with this topic. His strategy was partly successful since he was able to realize his projects while still benefiting from constant support in the opinion polls at that time. However, the opposition forces that had supported the FRAP were still present outside city hall.

Coming out of the October 1970 crisis was not easy for the FRAP and its supporters. In the following years, strong debates saw partisans of a strictly ideological movement opposing partisans of a more action-oriented movement. The leftist and the moderate factions dominated the organization in turn, thereby creating conditions for a weak out-of-council opposition to the Drapeau administration.

City officials refused to focus their policies on street-level problems and increasingly difficult conditions in the central neighborhoods. In this context, the action-oriented component of the FRAP got together with some other reform groups to create a new organization whose main concern would be the city neighbourhoods. In 1974, the Montreal Citizen Movement (MCM) was formed, partly from some of the still burning ashes of the FRAP.

The MCM was created by a group of activists coming from different origins: labour union activists, Parti Québécois militants, members of the Quebec branch of the New Democratic Party, and supporters of the urban progressive movement. These people had one major objective: to defeat Drapeau and the MCP in the November 1974 municipal election. The chosen instruments in this electoral strategy were threefold. The first was to form a mass party, based on a large number of members in all districts of the city. In doing so, the MCM showed itself to be very different from the MCP at the outset. In fact, the MCP's only members were actual and former elected officials. The second instrument was the program, a 30-page document that opened with the party's views on democracy and its basic proposal to put in place neighbourhood councils with decentralized powers. The second of the program's seven themes was housing, and the last was . . . the 1976 Olympic games. In striking contrast, the MCP did not adopt a formal program but presented a platform published as a one-page electoral advertisement in the newspapers. The MCP based its message on its past achievements in the fields of expressways and redevelopment and introduced no specific commitments concerning housing or local democracy.

The MCM's third electoral instrument was a list of candidates whose profile strongly contrasted with that of their opponents. At the mayoralty level, the MCM candidate was an almost unknown Jesuit with no political background. At the councillor level, candidates mainly came from the professional class, while the business class was almost completely absent.

Despite serious differences in electoral experience and the absence of a known figure as candidate opposing Drapeau for mayor, 18 MCM candidates were elected, and Drapeau's support went down to 55 percent of the vote, an unprecedented low score since his election in 1960. These 1974 results were seen as a victory for the MCM, which enthusiastically assumed its opposition role in city hall while keeping up with its demanding internal rules of democracy.

Again the electoral versus ideological dialectical struggle emerged as the leftist faction of the MCM met with some opposition inside the party. Following the party's 1976 annual convention, a radical majority took the lead in the party organization, while the elected branch of the MCM appeared to be moderate. The party reaffirmed its willingness to keep its distance from the provincial parties by refusing to reintegrate two of its former councillors who had resigned to run in the 1976 provincial election. These individuals, along with some other MCM members who were rebuffed by the radical orientation of the party following the 1976 convention, united to form a new party, the Municipal Action Group.

Internal divisions weakened the MCM and reduced its militants' will to engage in strong electoral organization as the 1978 election rapidly approached. Meanwhile the newly formed Municipal Action Group, led by a well-known member of the federal Liberal party, asked the MCM to form a united opposition to Drapeau and the MCP. The MCM rejected this proposal, and each of the two opposition parties ended up with one elected councillor while getting altogether 44 percent of the vote.

The 1978 municipal election in Montreal was particularly meaningful inasmuch as it finally focused attention on economic issues and the city's fiscal problems. The outgoing municipal government's major decisions concerning the Olympic games had been kept out of the election by the establishment of a provincial commission of inquiry. The MCP was left to boast about its record in city hall, while the two opposition parties offered competing views concerning the future of the city.

These two parties were strong enough to threaten Mayor Drapeau's seat. For the first time—but not the last—the incumbent mayor announced a few months before the 1978 election that he was thinking of retiring. Such a threat provoked a wind of support for Drapeau and strengthened the spirit of his troops.

Opposition forces also influenced the MCP's policy orientation. After the 1976 Olympic games, which had been used to justify a concentration of municipal and private-sector intervention in the city's central district, Drapeau still had an international project on which to ride out the 1978 campaign. The announcement of an international floral show reinforced the image of Montreal as an *international city*. But the status of Montreal as a *metropolitan centre* was collapsing as economic and urban development moved outside the boundaries of the city itself. Moreover Montreal's position appeared to weaken considerably in comparison with that of the other major Canadian metropolis, Toronto (Naylor 1990; Chorney 1990). Something had to be done to regenerate the economy and stop the city's demographic erosion. Hence, the MCP became more aware of the importance of Montreal's neighbourhoods and started implementing some economic development as well as housing programs there. The MCP government thus moved into some of the major policy fields of the MCM and, later, of the MAG. It was forced to pay attention to the metropolis and not only to the international city.

By 1978, Montreal's position in the North American urban structure was changing fundamentally and this trend had an impact on the configuration of local socio-political forces (Léveillée 1988, 58-60). Municipal governments had to adapt to a changing external context not only by remodelling their administrative apparatus, but also by redefining their democratic institutions. In fact, under the leadership of Y. Lamarre, chair of the city council's executive committee and right arm of Mayor Drapeau, new consultation devices were put in place, including a more intensive process of public hearings. The issues of social and economic development touched on the interests of different groups: community groups, downtown business people, neighbourhood merchants, international corporate managers, etc. The questions at stake called for new leaders to jump into the political arena and establish the necessary consensus to maintain Montreal's metropolitan status.

The MCP was unable to meet this challenge under the leadership of Drapeau, who maintained his 1970s types of policies. A new leader would have to come from outside the MCP. He would preferably possess the capacity to listen to a complex variety of local and international interests and to maintain the prestigious image of Montreal. However, individual qualities would not be enough to cope with this situation because the new leadership would have to be supported by a strong and experienced organization. The MCM, on the other hand, was ready for this challenge in 1982.

But the MAG's ongoing presence in 1982 threatened to divide the opposition forces as it had done in 1978. This time, the MCM initiated a collaboration scheme with MAG that would allow the two parties to have a common mayoralty candidate running against Jean Drapeau. MAG withdrew from these negotiations following H. P. Vignola's decision to run for the party. Vignola was a very prestigious candidate, with a well-known career as chief of the Montreal Urban Community police force.[1] But his party was much less well organized than the MCM. Moreover, with a very active neighbourhood presence, the MCM had developed a well-articulated party program. In addition, the MCM had opened up to the middle class and local entrepreneurs as issues of local economic development intensified with the crisis of the 1980s (Léveillée 1982, 24).

The MCM chose a young lawyer, Jean Doré, to run as its mayoralty candidate against Jean Drapeau of the MCP and H. P. Vignola of the MAG. J. Doré had been amongst the founders of the MCM in 1974. Professionally active in the cooperative and in the labour movements, he had completed his law requirements in 1977.

After a very long campaign that started in the early months of 1982, Drapeau was reelected with 49 percent of the vote. During the election campaign the MCP referred mainly to past experiences and still capitalized on the 1967 world exhibition, the construction of the subway and the Olympic stadium, etc. The MCP campaign showed that Drapeau still exercised strong control over the party's platform. However, the

---

[1]There is a resemblance here with the 1991 election in Toronto. A former chief commissioner of police, June Rowlands, ran for election against a well-known New Democratic Party candidate, Jack Layton. Candidates with the "law and order" profile, such as J. Rowlands in Toronto and H. P. Vignola in Montreal, tend to a form of electoral discourse that is seen as very relevant in the metropolitan city where crime and violence are part of everyday life. The electoral ratings of these two candidates were quite different, however, as J. Rowlands was elected in 1991, and Vignola finished in third place in 1982. The author will analyze this situation fully in a future work.

opposition parties forced the MCP to put forward some proposals for the future. These were essentially undertakings to limit tax increases, as the traditional prestige projects could not reasonably be proposed in this period of recession. Nevertheless, Drapeau came up for the first time with the idea of a rapid transit system between Montreal and New York.

From the opposition parties, projects and critical views abounded. There were proposals for shelter homes, services to immigrants, daycare centers, and women's employment programs. There was also severe criticism of the incumbent municipal government's housing policy. In fact, the MCM and the MAG were definitely putting these items on the future agenda of the city. The attractiveness of this platform contributed to the election of 15 MCM candidates and three MAG candidates out of 57. Doré came in second place for mayor with 35 percent of the vote, while Vignola, of MAG, got 16 percent.

The content of the 1982 election bore upon the MCP policies for the following term of office. Social justice and neighbourhood life gained importance within the city's internal affairs (Léonard and Léveillée 1986, 55-68). But the city's external affairs were still highly centralized in the mayor's hands, thereby maintaining the already established bipolar relationship within the city's portfolios, that of the metropolis and that of the international city.

In 1982, the MCM positioned itself as the alternative to the MCP and to Drapeau. Following its defeat, MAG disappeared and left the opposition field wide open to Doré and the MCM. In 1984, the MCM's leading representative in city council resigned in order to open his seat to Jean Doré. Following a by-election, Doré entered city hall as leader of the opposition and devoted his full energies to preparing for the 1986 election.

THE BEGINNING OF A NEW ERA

As expected, Drapeau announced his decision not to run for a ninth term at the beginning of 1986. Opinion polls were already predicting a victory for Doré and the MCM. The MCP entered a new era, marked by the absence of a strong leader and a remarkable reduction of central control over the party. For the first time a complete program, adopted by the party's enlarged membership, proposed four priorities: (1) economic, social, and cultural development, (2) "healthy" management of civic affairs, (3) quality urban environment, and (4) an international role for the city.

Despite this well-articulated program, the MCP was not able to make up for its great leader's departure, and Drapeau's absence was felt deeply by the traditional Civic Party militants. There was a loss of interest in this side of the political scene and growing enthusiasm for the opposite side where the MCM stood.

The MCM had been preparing for this decisive moment since 1984 with a sequence of important steps. In addition to choosing a well-known and promising leader, it had established cordial relations with the city's business sector and convinced the economic elite of its ability to take over. By holding to its initial commitments to grass-roots democracy and a largely defined social-democratic platform, the MCM maintained its popularity in the neighbourhoods and community groups. Moreover, the MCM continued to attack the incumbent city government for its maintenance of an anachronistic administrative process, its lack of an economic development policy, or, to put it globally, its incapacity to impose a vision of Montreal as a metropolis. A striking summary of these points was published by Jean Doré in his book entitled *Pour Montréal* (1986) just a few months before the election.

In this context, Doré's election as mayor of Montreal was no surprise. With 67 percent of the vote, Doré and the MCM held 55 out of the 58 seats on city council and the MCP ended up with only one elected representative, although its mayoralty candidate got 30 percent of the vote.

The basis of the MCM's strategy as a governing party, after having acted as a party in opposition since 1974, was its program and its culture. The program resulted from debates within the party and represented the MCM's stand on major issues of the time. Housing, health, economic development, public transportation, environment, women's issues, security, and, above all, local democracy, were among the 12 themes that structured the MCM program from 1974 to 1986.

As the importance of some of these issues was highlighted by the economic situation as well as by political pressure from the opposition forces, the MCP also adopted some of these themes in its electoral discourse (Belley 1991). Despite ongoing fundamental differences in the approaches to local government and democracy, the MCP and the MCM were closer to one another in 1986 than in 1974. Both of these major parties agreed on the need to reconcile economic and social development and to reinforce the economic structure of the neighbourhoods while keeping a strong business center. In so doing, neither of the two parties alienated the business community, a point that seemed essential in establishing one's legitimacy to govern a metropolitan city.

Each party's culture was very particular however. Despite the new leader's efforts to open up the MCP's decision-making process and make a place for membership participation, this party remained deeply influenced by 30 years of Jean Drapeau's iron hand. It could not reasonably project the image of a party devoted to the type of democratic process for which the MCM had been struggling over the last 12 years in and outside city hall. Even a meaningful nucleus of the business class in Montreal believed the city government should adopt new democratic values, thereby justifying some implicit support to the MCM in 1986.

While the MCM could not ignore its program and culture as it established its strategy for action during the 1986 electoral campaign, the new city government faced some additional constraints once in city hall. With limited local resources and with a deteriorating economic situation in the city, the MCM government witnessed a rapidly increasing rate of closing down of industries and of unemployment. The city not only got its share of wealth in periods of affluence but got more than its share of poverty in periods of economic restructuring and depression.

Finding solutions to these structural problems was not an easy task, particularly with the high level of expectations raised by the MCM. In some cases, the management of issues was clearly awkward, as in the case of Overdale (Jensen 1990);[2] in other situations, the MCM was criticized for giving too much consideration to promoters and not enough to residents; in other cases, its slowness was condemned, for example in the establishment of parks and green areas, and in ending the practice of forbidding referenda in the city.

Despite these criticisms, the MCM's overall achievements were quite impressive: complete reorganization of the municipal administrative apparatus, creation of an information network in the neighbourhoods, creation of consultative commissions on planning issues, a policy for ethnic communities, a woman's access to equality program, creation of

---

[2]In 1987, the MCM administration announced that the residents of 100 housing units in the Overdale area in the Montreal core would be relocated to make space for a one hundred million dollar condominium project. The issue produced the first major resident opposition to the MCM. Despite the extensive mobilization that took place, the housing units have indeed been torn down. New construction is still awaited.

a new program for waste recycling, etc. Without any real difficulty, the MCM and Doré were reelected in 1990 for another four-year term.

The new city government introduced changes that should have been adopted many years before but were delayed because of the previous city government's lack of commitment to social and environmental issues. While Doré and the MCM did tackle these questions, the problems still exist. This situation is partly due to an underassessment by central authorities of the city's critical problems. Doré has not been more successful than his predecessor, Jean Drapeau, in his effort to intensify the provincial and the federal authorities' commitment in the city. The central city, if left to the care of strictly local authorities without particular support from the country's central authorities, cannot by itself muster the necessary resources.

In 1970 the MCM's "ancestor," FRAP, had perceived this problem of institutional fragmentation of responsibilities and proposed a global program and an overall change of social policies, notwithstanding existing institutional barriers. A significant part of the mayor of Montreal's job has been to try to convey this vision to the upper levels of government so they will share the costs of services with the city government. The state and the metropolis cannot be seen as two different spheres of the public realm.

THE "THIRD" PARTIES

This presentation has dealt exclusively with the interaction of two municipal parties in Montreal, the Montreal Civic Party and the Montreal Citizens Movement. However, from 1960 till 1990, 18 other parties existed, more or less influencing the local political scene sporadically (Table 18.1). We now turn to these parties to see how they can be positioned in relation to the two major parties.

First it is clear that a two-party system has not been able to accommodate all the political forces in Montreal over the last 30 years. On two occasions, four other parties were formed (in 1970 and in 1990). In all other elections, one or two additional formal municipal parties were active during the campaigns, but almost all of them failed to get some elected representatives in city hall. The exceptions were the Municipal Action Group in 1978 and 1982 and the Municipal Party of Montreal and the Montreal Democratic Coalition in 1990 (Table 18.2).

Second, it is interesting to observe that the emergence of these parties was not strictly a reactionary process. They were of course formed to

Table 18.1.   *Political Parties Present in Municipal Elections, City of Montreal, 1960-1990*

	1960	1962	1966	1970	1974	1978	1982	1986	1990
Ass. de la réforme Municipale	x								
Ligue d'action civique	x	x							
Parti civique de Montréal	x	x	x	x	x	x	x	x	x
Parti des citoyens de Montréal		x							
Parti de libération de Montréal			x						
Parti démocratique de Montréal			x						
Conseil du travail de Montréal				x					
Parti de Montréal				x					
Parti réaliste ouvrier & professionnel de Montréal				x					
Réveil de Montréal				x					
Front d'action politique de Montréal				x					
Démocratie Montréal					x				
Ligue socialiste ouvrière					x				
Rass. des citoyens de Montréal					x	x	x	x	x
Groupe d'action municipale						x	x		
Alliance démocratique de Montréal								x	
Coalition démocratique									x
Parti écologique									x
Parti éléphant blanc									x
Parti municipal de Montréal									x

Table 18.2. *Composition of City Council Following Each Election, Montreal, 1960-1990*

	Total[1]	MCP	MCM	Other parties	Independents
1960	66[2]	45	---	0	21
1962	45	41	---	0	4
1966	48	45[3]	---	0	3
1970	52	52	---	0	0
1974	55	36	18	0	1
1978	54	52	1	1[4]	0
1982	57	39	15	3[5]	0
1986	58	1	55	1	1
1990	50	1	42	6[6]	1

[1]Due to a changing electoral map and to changes in the voting system, the number of seats varies from 1960 to 1990.

[2]In 1960, the city council consisted of the mayor, 66 elected councillors, and 33 members nominated by a set of established pressure groups.

[3]Out of 45, 33 were elected with no opposition.

[4]This councillor was a member of the Municipal Action Group.

[5]All three successful candidates were from the Municipal Action Group.

[6]There were three successful candidates from the Municipal Party and three from the Democratic Coalition.

criticize the incumbent city government and the major opposition party, and they were also in a position to react to past programs or to proposals for future action. But they often took a more pro-active position when they explored new ideas and even showed more innovative concerns than the major parties. For example, the Parti de libération de Montréal was the first party to present a female candidate in 1966 and to oppose Drapeau and the MCP's megaprojects openly and drastically. In the same way, the Montreal Party was the first party, in 1970, to define itself as the voice of ethnic groups in the city. In these times, such topics were far from creating consensus. The more electorally oriented parties, such as the MCP or even the MCM in 1974, did not dare adopt innovative positions that could alienate a fair number of voters.

Third, these parties have introduced a very wide variety of issues over the 1960-1990 period. The *issue of businesslike city management* was put forward in 1960 and again from time to time until 1990 when the Municipal Party of Montreal came close to the MCP's position. The *decision-making process* was emphasized in the more openly democratic approach adopted by the Municipal Action Group in 1978 and 1982. But this issue was primarily put forward by FRAP in 1970 and by the MCM from 1974 until 1986. While being in power weakened the MCM's once very strong views on the subject, local democracy became the main concern of the Democratic Coalition, a party formed by dissenting MCM representatives in city hall in 1990.

The *issue of development* also structured some party formation during this period. Some parties have been strongly and unconditionally prodevelopment, as was the Réveil de Montréal in 1970 and the Ligue d'action civique in 1960 and in 1962, along with the Montreal Civic Party throughout the period. Other parties have been radically antidevelopment, like the clearly leftist Ligue socialiste ouvrière, which proposed to put an end to "capital domination in city hall" in 1974. In this same category could be placed the Democratic Coalition and the Montreal Ecological Party in 1990. But these two parties' positions on development were based on different logics. The Democratic Coalition condemned the exploitive nature of development while the Montreal Ecological Party proposed a green type of development.

The most popular issue in all parties over the 1960-1990 period, however, was the democratic process and local leadership. In this sense, politics were very strongly influenced by reaction to Drapeau's political style and, as some put it, by his "municipal dictatorship" (the expression is borrowed from the Parti de libération de Montréal, in 1966). Many aspects of the democratic process were discussed, some concerning the decision-making process in city hall (including the excessive discretionary power given to the executive committee, lack of freedom of speech for the Montreal Civic Party's elected representatives, lack of relevant information for the opposition members of council), some about the representation of local interests (lack of concern for residents as opposed to overwhelming concern for real estate promoters and the business class, the absence of women or of representatives of ethnic groups in political institutions), and some about the barriers to grass-roots participation (the impossibility of holding referenda on local issues, the absence of information and of consultation of neighbourhoods and of community groups).

Issues as well as processes have been at the heart of the Montreal multiparty system over the last 30 years. It is commonly known that, unlike regimes based on proportional representation, regimes based on majority vote do not guarantee adequate representation to third parties or marginal parties in situations where two major parties dominate the political arena. Therefore it is not surprising that these marginal parties were almost totally absent from city hall over the period under study. However, our observations suggest that these parties influenced the political and the electoral processes as they intervened directly and often quite strongly between elections and during electoral campaigns. Their main contribution has been to raise new issues and to force these issues on the electoral agenda.

In conclusion to this point, let us summarize the major findings of this research.

1.   Under a two-party dominated system, other smaller parties have a short existence and can therefore be called marginal parties.

2.   Marginal parties are activated by a weaker sense of electoral imperative and therefore tend to be more programmatic. This leads them to adopt more radical and critical views than do the major parties. Such views can be on the right as well as on the left side of the political spectrum.

3.   Marginal parties hold views that are as diverse and as relevant to the political realm as are those of the major parties. The main difference between the two types of party lies in their level of organization and of resources and in the political experience and prestige of their leadership.

4.   The emergence of municipal parties in Montreal has been less conditioned by government regulation and more by specific conditions in the city. While provincial legislation adopted in 1978 (see Appendix) certainly influenced the management and the funding of municipal parties, it did not occasion an increase in their number. When six parties ran for election in 1970 and in 1990, the political interests at stake were the reelection of a still powerful local leader and resourceful party as well as strong discontent with many aspects of the local system. Therefore, the formation of municipal political parties is intensely related to the state of the local political and socio-economic system as a whole.

CONCLUSION

In the early 1950s, modernization of the administrative apparatus and of the decision-making process inspired the Montreal Civic Party. Its leader, Jean Drapeau, campaigned against corruption and presented himself as the champion of Montreal's new international role. Drapeau's major policy instrument was his party, which assured him of the necessary support and control inside city hall and in his relations with provincial and federal authorities. The party therefore was essential to the establishment of strong formal authority in Montreal, as opposed to the weaker type of local authority that had been kept in place by provincial Premier Maurice Duplessis. The party was an effective instrument of control under Drapeau's centralised leadership.

But this party was not convinced of the benefits of participatory democracy, nor was it concerned with social and cultural development. It had been formed as a pro-economic development coalition in the 1950s and failed to consider the impact of this ideology on residents of inner-city districts and on the overall equilibrium of the city.

The emergence of a counter-movement, at the end of the 1960s, made space for the formation of the FRAP in 1970 and of an impressive number of smaller parties. Because these parties usually did not survive the electoral defeat of all their candidates in one municipal election, they can be labelled "electoral coalitions" (Stone 1989). However, the case of Montreal shows that there are many coalitions in a single city of the dimension of this metropolis.

Despite the variety of their appellations and the evolution of their electoral platforms, these coalitions represented relatively stable manifestations of persistent sets of interest. Their values relating to business as opposed to resident interests, economic as opposed to social and cultural development, and executive as opposed to participatory decision making helped to define the position of each party throughout the 30-year period under study. Other issues were raised more sporadically, particularly the adequacy and the cost of the city government's prestige projects under Jean Drapeau. But the core of the parties' platforms focused on the impact of modernization and internationalization on either one or many of the three sets of values mentioned previously.

The findings of this research show that the traditional pro- and antidevelopment model used to classify local political forces must be expanded to take into consideration at least two other components of local party platforms: the type of interests that should be dominant in civic affairs and the openness of the decision-making process.

The pro- and antidevelopment model was defined on a right-left paradigm that was relevant before the emergence of economic development alternatives at the local level (Hamel 1991, 149-76) and before the appearance of issues, such as women's issues, ethnic plurality, and environmental issues, that can hardly be melded with the traditional prodevelopment/antidevelopment question. Furthermore, the right-left dichotomy, based on each party's commitment to social-democratic values, fails to make place for differences in opinion concerning the democratic process, which is of very high concern in the local political arena.

In the face of the complexity of the metropolitan situation and of the rich variety of organized political and social interests within the metropolis, confrontations and coalitions call for long range and multiform analysis. Within such an analytical framework, primary attention should be given to the democratic process as it relates to the issues of economic and social development.

Over the last years, Montreal has been interesting to researchers in the social sciences for many reasons. As a metropolis, the city was badly hurt by a loss of industry and manufacturing activities. The solution to problems of economic globalization was sought in the pursuit of a prestige strategy that put Montreal on the international map as it hosted an impressive series of world famous events.

But this strategy was unable to cope with Montreal's declining importance as a central city in the metropolitan area and in the Canadian urban system. With high rates of unemployment and increasing social dependency, Montreal needed a social policy. Despite the awkwardness of this situation, the city government was reluctant to respond to the issues and even opposed the implementation of social housing programs put forward by the federal government. This insistence on a limited role for city government in social issues, and on the wholesale promotion of local economic development, characterized Jean Drapeau and the Montreal Civic Party until the end of the 1970s. With the deterioration of the economic situation and of living conditions in Montreal, social unrest led to political mobilization and multifaceted electoral confrontations. Political parties gave voice to new forces in city politics and made it possible to raise new issues. The dynamics of the political and partisan system caused an exchange of influence between the major parties, the MCP and the MCM, and between these parties and the many so-called marginal parties.

The emergence of a new generation of parties, particularly FRAP in 1970 and the MCM in 1974, but also the smaller parties formed in 1962, 1966, and especially in 1970, brought about drastic changes in the local political system as well as in the policy field. There was an opening up of discussion about the issues, which forced the MCP city government to introduce some important up-to-date modifications in the administrative apparatus. Moreover, the MCP addressed local economic development concerns in the early 1980s. But the question of the democratic process was responsible for the high expectations that accompanied the MCM's election as majority party in city hall in 1986. For the moment, it is too early to observe the real impact of the 1986 change in city government. The 1990 election has, however, shown that much criticism is still focused on a perceived lack of improvement in the local democratic process and in economic conditions in the city.

In the metropolis of 1990, as in the metropolis of 1960, democracy and development remain the major issues and represent the challenges with which the political forces have to deal. Municipal political parties have contributed to the discussion of these issues and to the emergence of alternate forms of solution.

REFERENCES

Belley, Serge. 1991. "Les partis politiques municipaux et les élections municipales de 1986 à Montréal et de 1989 à Québec." Communication présentée dans le cadre du 59e congrès de l'ACFAS, Sherbrooke.

Brodie, Janine, and Jane Jenson. 1980. *Crisis, Challenge and Change: Party and Class in Canada*. Toronto: Methuen.

Cardin, Jean-François. 1990. *Comprendre octobre 1970. Le FLQ, la crise et le syndicalisme*. Montréal: Méridien.

Castles, Francis G. 1982. *The Impact of Parties: Politics and Policies in Democratic Capitalist States*. London: Sage.

Caulfield, Jon. 1988. "Reform as a Chaotic Concept: The Case of Toronto." *Urban History Review* 17(2): 107-11.

Chorney, Harold. 1990. "Le défi du plein emploi: lubie ou objectif réalisable à Montréal?" In *Politique urbaine à Montréal*, ed. J. H. Roy and B. Weston, Montréal: Guernica, 133-47.

David, Hélène, and Louis Maheu. 1982. "Problèmes sociaux, contradictions structurelles et politiques gouvernementales." In *Les mobilisations populaires urbaines*, ed. P. Hamel, J. F. Léonard, R. Mayer, Montréal, Nouvelle Optique (Original version 1970), 191-215.

Doré, Jean. 1986. *Pour Montréal*. Montréal: VLB Éditeur.

Gagnon, Alain B., and A. Brian Tanguay. 1989. *Canadian Parties in Transition*. Scarborough: Nelson Canada.

Germain, Annick. 1991. "La Métropole à l'aube de la modernité." *Cap-aux-Diamants*, no 27: 48-51.

Hamel, Pierre. 1991. *Action Collective et démocratie locale: les mouvements urbains Montréalais*. Montréal: Presses de l'Université de Montréal.

Harris, Richard. 1989. "A Defence of Urban Reform." *Urban History Review* 17(3): 209-10.

Jensen, Lisa. 1990. "L'affaire 'Overdale': la grande trahison." In *Politique urbaine à Montréal*, ed. J. H. Roy and B. Weston, Montréal: Guernica, 47-70.

Kaplan, Harold. 1982. *Reform, Planning, and City Politics: Montreal, Winnipeg, Toronto*. Toronto: University of Toronto Press.

Lemieux, Vincent. 1976. "Les partis provinciaux du Québec." In *Partis politiques au Québec*, ed. R. Pelletier, Montréal, Cahiers du Québec/Hurtubise HMH, 53-68.

_____. 1985. *Systèmes partisans et partis politiques*. Québec: Presses de l'Université du Québec.

Léonard, J. F., and J. Léveillée. 1986. *Montréal after Drapeau*. Montreal: Black Rose Books.

Léveillée, Jacques. 1982. "À la veille des élections Montréalaises de novembre 1982." *Conjoncture politique au Québec*, No 2: 19-30.

_____. 1988. "Pouvoir local et politiques publiques à Montréal: renouveau dans les modalités d'exercice du pouvoir urbain." *Cahiers de recherche sociologique* 6(2): 37-63.

_____. 1990. "Habiter Montréal: version fiscale ou sociale? "*Relations*, No. 563: 214-16.

Linteau, Paul-André, and Alan F. J. Artibise. 1984. *L'évolution de l'urbanisation au Canada: une analyse des perspectives et des interprétations*. Cahier 5, Winnipeg: Institute of Urban Studies, University of Winnipeg.

_____, René Durocher, Jean-Claude Robert, and François Ricard. 1986. *Histoire du Québec Contemporain. Le Québec depuis 1930*. Montréal: Boréal.

Naylor, Tom. 1990. "Le déclin économique de Montréal: d'un empire industriel à une boutique bon chic." In *Politique urbaine à Montréal*, ed. J. H. Roy, B. Weston, Montréal: Guernica.

Quesnel, Louise. 1990. "Political Control over Planning in Quebec." *International Journal of Urban and Regional Research* 14(1): 25-48.

_____, and Serge Belley. 1990. *Partis politiques municipaux: une étude de sociologie électorale*. Montréal: Éditions Agence d'Arc.

Rose, Richard. 1984. *Do Parties Make a Difference?* 2d ed. London: Macmillan.

Roth, Roland. 1991. "Local Green Politics in West German Cities." *International Journal of Urban and Regional Research* 15(1): 75-89.

Stone, Clarence N. 1989. *Regime Politics: Governing Atlanta 1946-1988*. Lawrence, Kan.: University Press of Kansas.

APPENDIX

Note on provincial regulations concerning municipal political parties and municipal elections in Quebec.

1968   The provincial legislature adopted a law lowering the voting age from 21 to 18 and extended the right to vote and to run for election to all residents of the city with Canadian citizenship.

1978   The provincial legislature adopted a law recognizing the existence of municipal political parties. Under this new regulation, municipal parties must be accredited by a provincial authority and must report annually to this authority. From then on, all municipalities of 20,000 or more are obliged to have council members elected on the basis of electoral districts. The electoral map must be approved by the provincial authority.

The new legislation also makes it possible for a mayoral candidate to run as "fellow candidate" (in french "colistier") with a city council candidate of his party.

1984   Municipal parties were given the right to receive municipal public funding.

These new institutional arrangements have had a huge impact on politics in Montreal. The number of electors increased very significantly for the first time in 1970, from 150,000 to some 660,000. The 1978 legislation put a stop to open corporate funding of parties and elections and allowed some public scrutiny of the sources of party revenues. It also facilitated party-based voting with the identification on the ballot of each candidate's party affiliation, thereby allowing less-well-known individuals to get more electoral support because of their party affiliation.

The new electoral map increased the number of districts from 19 to 54 in 1978. This last minute change affected the electoral organization of the MCM and of the MCP, and seems to have contributed to an increase in popular interest. Electoral participation indeed went back up to its 1970 level, i.e. 53 percent, after falling to 38 percent in the previous (1974) municipal election.

The original "fellow candidate" disposition was introduced to facilitate the election of a defeated mayoral candidate to a seat held by a successful council candidate of his or her party. The purpose of this procedure was to encourage the implementation of a more parliamentary type of process in city hall by providing for the presence of an opposition leader. This will be achieved in 1990 when one of the opponents to the elected mayor will take the seat of his elected "fellow candidate" and become leader of the opposition in council.

Chapter 19

International Cities and Municipal Paradiplomacy:
A Typology for Assessing the Changing Vancouver Metropolis

Patrick J. Smith
Theodore H. Cohn
Simon Fraser University

One of the most significant changes in the contemporary Canadian metropolis has been the rise of municipal international relations. Canadian cities have become global cities. They have established an increasingly activist and sophisticated international paradiplomacy; they have done so with either the encouragement or benign neglect of senior constitutional authorities; they have contributed to changing perceptions about the role of subnational actors in international relations, and they have been a factor in the emergence of new "intermestic" issues that are "simultaneously, profoundly and inseparably both domestic and international" (Manning 1977, 309).

Municipal internationalism has also changed the Canadian metropolis: it has altered municipal intergovernmental relations, and it has challenged existing understandings of urban public policymaking in Canada. Indeed, some authors have argued that we are witnessing the emergence of a "new international cities era" (Fry, Radebaugh, and Soldatos 1989). This expansion of subnational internationalism has been a byproduct of the globalization of politics and economics. In Kenichi Ohmae's terms, we have moved toward a borderless world, with substantial interlinking of economies (Ohmae 1990). For Keohane and Nye, this interdependence has created both risks and opportunities for nonnational jurisdictions and their economies (Keohane and Nye 1977). Seelig and Artibise have concluded that in this new global setting "traditional boundaries between countries . . . become increasingly meaningless, . . . cities (become) independent of their countries and deal directly with other parts of the world, . . . (and) city and regional interests . . . will be far more important than national or provincial economic policies" (Seelig and Artibise 1991).

This chapter focuses on explanations for these changes and on their implications for the policy roles and activities of contemporary Canadian cities. We begin by providing some background on the constitutional/political setting in which Vancouver operates. This legal/domestic component is then placed in the context of a typology of municipal internationalism developed to assess the changing intermestic linkages of cities. While this typology can be used to classify and assess the global activities of Canadian cities in general, we provide examples primarily from Vancouver's experience for several reasons. First, we did extensive interviewing of Vancouver officials and can therefore provide in-depth (rather than anecdotal) illustrations of the city's global involvement. Second, Vancouver has been in the forefront of municipal internationalism in some important respects, and it has therefore engaged in the entire range of activities covered in our typology. In the final part of the chapter, we use the typology to examine Vancouver's involvement with global relations in greater detail. In some instances, we discuss the activities of other large Canadian cities and of smaller municipalities in British Columbia to provide a comparative perspective.

VANCOUVER'S CONSTITUTIONAL/POLITICAL SETTING

Constitutionally, foreign policymaking has been a primary responsibility of national governments, and in all jurisdictions local authority derives from a senior level of government. Thus, Victor Jones has demonstrated that "at common law, and under the constitution . . . Canadian and American local governments . . . are . . . 'tenants at will' of the provinces or states" (Jones 1988 90).[1] Under Section 92(8) of Canada's Constitution Act 1867 "municipal institutions in the province"

---

[1]This "tenants at will" definition of the local-state relationship derives from the landmark decision by Judge Dillon in the *City of Clinton v. Cedar Rapids and Missouri River Railroad Company* (1868), 24 Iowa 455,475.

are exclusive provincial concerns. In the Vancouver case, three legislative enactments flowing from this provincial authority are particularly germane:

1. The Municipal Act, under which most local authorities in B.C. are constituted and governed. In Greater Vancouver the act covers 18 municipalities and three electoral areas.

2. The Vancouver Charter, created in 1886, provides for the separate governance of the city of Vancouver.

3. Regional District legislation, added to the Municipal Act in 1965, governs the operation of the Greater Vancouver Regional District (GVRD).

When one moves from constitutional relationships to political realities, however, the difference between authority and power becomes particularly relevant. As Jones argued, the right of senior governments "is only a legal authority to act. Even though the right may be plenary, it must be distinguished from power, or the ability of the authority to act in full or in part, to exercise unfettered choice, to act at any one time, any place, or to any extent it chooses" (Jones 1988, 91). Political restraints on the ability of senior governments to act may stem from a variety of factors, including their recognition of Swainson's "frustration thesis." Swainson concluded that there is "a growing recognition . . . that each [level of government] has a considerable capacity to frustrate the other and yet, in the long run, is likely to derive little advantage from this type of behaviour" (Swainson 1983, 263). Additional constraints on national governments emerge from the interlocking linkages of global interdependence and the simple bypassing of central authorities by international actors, state and private.

Despite the constraints on senior government behaviour, the central questions to emerge out of Jones' research are "when, how and where will the [senior] governments exercise their will against their recalcitrant or innovative children." It would appear that the exercise of senior authority—and power—against local governments is substantially correlated with the extent of local frustration of senior governmental policy intentions (Smith 1988). Recent British and British Columbian examples offer a warning to local governments that the game of policy conflict and recalcitrance with their senior governmental partners is fraught with significant dangers. Margaret Thatcher's ongoing conflicts over policy direction with Britain's major metropolitan governments throughout the 1980s led to her abolition of the Greater London Council and the six major Metropolitan County Councils. The 1985 dismissal of recalcitrant locally elected school boards in Vancouver and Cowichan by the British Columbian government, and the subsequent 1989 suspension of GVRD authority over its watershed, also reflected "the nuclear option" to policy-conflict resolution rather than the more conventional warfare that is the intergovernmental norm (Smith 1985). These examples remind intergovernmental participants that constitutional-legal relationships can affect local-senior governmental relations, and that the powers implicit in such relationships are central where frustration and policy disputes persist.

In this comparative context, there are particular systemic differences in local-senior governmental relations worth noting: In the U.K., such relations are local-central, with the national Parliament supreme; in the U.S., "multiple cracks" in the political system allow local authorities "to play a more active and influential role in intergovernmental relations and in the formulation of national and state policies" (Jones 1988). In Canada, the province has dominated local-senior governmental relations, both in constitutional (authority) and political (power) terms (Smith 1986, 1988). What is interesting about the changing internationalist stance of Canadian cities is that much of the jurisdictional intrusion has been local to national, with the federal government normally encouraging the cities' development of global economic linkages.

In view of these constitutional-legal dimensions, the key dilemma for senior governments is how to encourage local governmental policy innovation and change that is not in conflict with senior governmental agendas. From the perspective of municipal governments, the dilemma is how to implement reforms that would provide them with policymaking instruments and authority coordinate with their responsibilities. Thus, the Federation of Canadian Municipalities' (FCM) brief to the 1983 Royal Commission on the Economic Union and Development Prospects for Canada maintains that

in Canada, as elsewhere, the overall scope of government has expanded enormously . . . [And] while the formal division of authority between [senior] levels of government has been modified only slightly since Confederation, the actual scope of their respective activities has changed considerably, with consequent changes in their relations with one another and with municipal governments, and in the means available to them to discharge their added responsibilities. Nonetheless, for municipal-ities, the growing complexity of their functions has yet to be matched by the changes necessary to enable them to perform these functions (FCM 1983).

Four points emerge from this contention:

1. Canadian municipalities have argued that the gap between what they are expected to do and their authority to act "is growing insurmount-ably." What Canadian municipalities have requested is more formal authority, clearer constitutional standing, and broader financial capacity. Through reports such as *Puppets on a Shoestring: The Effects on Municipal Government of Canada's System of Public Finance* (Canadian Federation of Mayors and Municipalities 1976) and FCM submissions, like the one to the Macdonald Royal Commission and arguments for a Local Government Bill of Rights, as proposed to the FCM by Vancouver Mayor Gordon Campbell (1991), cities have argued their need for these reforms.

2. Even when local governing units have exercised authority granted to them, where their decisions are in substantial policy conflict with a senior (particularly provincial) jurisdiction, they operate at some risk. For example, in British Columbia, where the Greater Vancouver Regional District has exercised its functional authority (in land-use planning or water quality control) the provincial government has removed the regional powers that conflicted with the province's agenda (Oberlander and Smith 1993).

3. What is most interesting about the substantial growth in international policy roles for Canadian cities is that it has occurred without any formal grant of authority by either level of senior govern-ment.

4. What is equally interesting about such municipal international activities is that cities have been able to undertake such a broad spectrum of global policymaking with so little provincial or federal opposition. In the case of the federal government, where external jurisdiction is clearest, the response has generally been positive and encouraging. Despite the supposedly "hands off" approach of the federal government to urban affairs in Canada since the demise of the Ministry of State for Urban Affairs (MSUA), federal trade and immigration officials have been directly helpful to city international efforts. Other federal departments and

agencies have been equally supportive. For example, the Canadian International Development Agency (CIDA) has enlisted direct city assistance in furthering federal foreign aid policy objectives, and the Department of Finance has supported the designation of Vancouver as an international banking centre. The most obvious rationale for this positive federal government response to local international initiatives is that municipal efforts to encourage foreign trade, investment, immigration, and economic development are in congruence with the senior authority's policy objectives. Such policy coincidence produces intergovernmental harmony.

Since much of current city international activity is devoted to local economic development, there has been little inclination by the provincial government to curtail municipal efforts. Indeed, there is evidence that the province has been actively encouraging municipal-based expansionism. The efforts of the B.C. Ministry of International Business and Immigration (MIBI) to encourage twinnings through Sister City symposia, etc. is a case in point. And even where city global initiatives appear to run counter to existing federal government policy, the province has sometimes weighed local (and provincial) economic benefits above national governmental diplomatic interests. For example, B.C. pointedly did not concur with the federal government's condemnation of Maple Ridge's twinning with a city in Taiwan.

From a local government perspective, the policy response municipalities would like from senior governments is sufficient legislative authority to allow local governments to participate more constructively in global activities and relationships. For local governments that would mean appropriate legal/constitutional changes to permit decision making in areas of local concern and to provide for alternative (e.g., regional) governing structures.

The evidence from actual local government global activities suggests an alternative: appropriate action may simply mean that senior authorities not exercise their existing jurisdictional ascendancy over their innovative global local partners. Despite the array of reconfederation arenas in post-Meech Canada, the formalization of new local authority would not appear to be a short-term reality (Smith 1990). The more likely reality is that in an increasingly borderless world, cities will continue to recognize the challenges of global change and respond to them. Senior governments might seek to place impediments to this activity in the name of jurisdictional formality, but just as "watertight" definitions of federalism (e.g., see Black 1975) gave way to more porous reality, so too has global change created more "cracks" of opportunity for local governing actors to operate in the international realm formerly dominated by nation states. This becomes obvious when the global activities of various municipal governments are examined in the context of a typology of subnational internationalism.

A TYPOLOGY OF MUNICIPAL INTERNATIONALISM

The scope of international relations has expanded dramatically as global interdependence has increased, encompassing issues such as environmental pollution, human rights, immigration, monetary and trade instabilities, and sustainable development. Interdependence implies "mutual dependence" in which "there are reciprocal (although not necessarily symmetrical) costly effects of transactions" (Keohane and Nye 1977, 8-9; Cohn 1990a, 23-28). It has contributed to the rise of intermestic issues, since the "ordinary citizen" is increasingly affected by global problems:

The economic interdependence of the modern world is more than international. It is also inter-local . . . every jiggle in the pattern of the international economy is likely to pinch some local group . . . and convert it immediately into a vocal group (Manning 1977, 309).

The concepts used in theories of interdependence can be applied to the changing global relations of cities. Of particular relevance are Keohane and Nye's definitions of transgovernmental and transnational relations. Transgovernmental relations are "direct interactions between agencies (governmental subunits) of different governments where those agencies act relatively autonomously from central governmental control" (Keohane and Nye 1976, 4). While Keohane and Nye viewed transgovernmental relations as occurring primarily among subunits of national governments, their definition can also include provinces or cities that act relatively autonomously from senior governmental control. Cities are "hybrid international actors" because they lack the qualities of sovereignty normally associated with higher levels of government. Nevertheless, they are governmental subunits since "they are linked by various means into the network of governmental and administrative processes" (Hocking

1986, 483). In terms of Vancouver's international activities, the "senior government" may be either the British Columbian or the Canadian government. Transnational relations are "interactions across the border in which at least one actor is nongovernmental" (Keohane and Nye 1976, 4). This definition can be used to describe cross-border interactions of a municipal government with a nongovernmental actor such as a transnational corporation, or even an international organization. The transnational and transgovernmental activities of cities are increasingly concentrated in the economic area. However, cities have also been involved in a wide variety of cross-border cultural, social, and political activities.[2]

Figure 19.1 of our global cities typology provides an illustration of the transgovernmental and transnational interactions of municipal government as a primary actor. Subnational governments are primary actors when they engage directly in global relations (Hocking 1986, 484). As Figure 19.1 shows, a city's cross-border interactions may be egressive flows, which are initiated "from the inside out," or ingressive flows, which are channelled "from the outside in" (Duchacek 1986). Alternatively, the flows can occur in both directions; for example, two municipalities might engage in reciprocal efforts to establish a sister-city link.[3]

Major cities such as Vancouver may be involved in cross-border relations with governmental and private actors at a number of levels. At the local level, Vancouver has sister city linkages (Smith 1991) with Odessa, Yokohama, Edinburgh, Guangzhou, and Los Angeles. Neighbouring cities within the metropolis also have their own global linkages. Under its two most recent mayors, Vancouver has in addition instituted a rather well-developed strategic cities policy (Smith and Cohn 1989a, 1989b).

The Strategic Cities policy option refers to the city of Vancouver's policy of designating selected cities as significant "gateways" into important regional or national economies with which Vancouver intends to develop strong economic and other links. Once so designated, these cities become the subject of more intense Vancouver activity. It is interesting to note that Vancouver is unique among Canadian cities in

---

[2]See Cohn, Merrifield, and Smith 1989, for a comparative review of these activities.

[3]For a more detailed discussion of the typology see Cohn and Smith 1990.

Figure 19.1. *Intermestic Interactions of Municipal Government: Municipal Government as a Primary Actor*

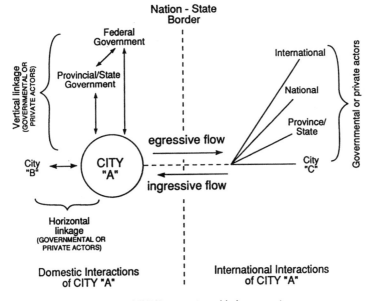

* In this Figure, CITY "A" represents municipal government.

Source: Theodore H. Cohn and Patrick J. Smith, "A Typology of City-Based International Involvement: The Case of Vancouver," in *Processes d'Internationalization des Villes*, Groupe Nice, Lyon, France, 1990.

having a well-developed strategic cities policy.[4] Strategic cities are not necessarily aware that they have been so designated by Vancouver, since there is an absence of the more formal protocol requirements involved in sister city linkages. As Table 19.1 indicates, Vancouver considered 13 cities as potentially strategic to its needs. Apart from the existing European sister cities of Odessa and Edinburgh, the rest were in the

---

[4]The uniqueness of Vancouver's policy became evident to the authors in the exchange of views at conferences on global cities at Brigham Young University, Provo, Utah, and Centre Jacques Cartier, Lyon, France.

Table 19.1. *Assessment of Vancouver's Relationship with Selected Cities*

	Accords with Federal Priorities	Potential Niche for Vancouver Businesses	Potential Niche as Asia-Pacific Gateway	Keen Organizations Exist	Frequent Personal Contact Potential
Guangzhou*	●	●	●	●	●
Yokohama*	●	●	●	●	●
Tokyo	●	●	●	◒	●
Osaka	●	●	●	◒	●
Los Angeles*	●	●	●	●	●
Odessa*	○	○	○	○	○
Edinburgh*	○	○	○	○	○
Shanghai	●	◒	●	○	○
Chongqing	●	◒	○	○	○
Hong Kong	●	●	●	●	●
Kuala Lumpur	●	○	○	◒	○
Singapore	●	◒	●	◒	◒
Bangkok	●	◒	○	◒	◒

```
                    LEGEND
    ● = Strong
    ◒ = Emerging
    ○ = None at this time
    *   Denotes Vancouver Sister Cities
```

Source: City of Vancouver, Economic Development Office.

Pacific Rim. As discussed below, a number of these were eventually designated as "strategic."

The cross-border linkages discussed in this chapter are primarily government-to-government, but it is important to note that our typology also includes linkages involving private actors. As discussed, these transnational ties are a fundamental aspect of the growth in interdependence. One case of city-to-city linkages at the private level is the joint venture between the *Vancouver Sun* and *Hong Kong Standard* newspapers to distribute the "Asia Pacific Report," a quarterly paper that was first published in October 1989. The *Sun's* editor-in-chief has described this joint venture as "an important step in bridging the two business communities and cultures" (*Vancouver Sun*, October 5, 1989).

While the cross-border ties of governmental subunits are usually cooperative in nature, they may at times be conflictual. For example, some major differences have arisen over the Los Angeles City Council decision in July 1989 to ban the construction of new wood shingle roofs. The ban was adopted (at least in part) to protect houses from damage caused by forest fires, but the shakes and shingle industry claims that wood roofing can now be made fire resistant. British Columbia exports about $250 million worth of shakes to the United States annually. The joint suit by American and B.C. manufacturers against the Los Angeles ordinance is a prime case of a dispute involving governmental subunits. The shakes and shingle dispute also highlights the metropolitan or city-region dimension of urban global relations. While Vancouver was only indirectly affected by the Los Angeles ban, it was fully cognizant of the impact on neighbouring municipalities dependent on shakes and shingle production and of the serious implications for the provincial government. Thus, the September 1989 issue of Vancouver's Sister City News (the Newsletter of the Vancouver-Los Angeles Sister City Committee) began with the headline, "LA Ban on Wood Roofs Hurts BC."

Figure 19.1 shows that cities may also have cross-border relations with international actors such as the United Nations (UN). In 1986 the UN Secretary-General designated Vancouver as one of 62 "Messenger of Peace" cities, thus making it a member of the World Union of Cities for Peace headquartered in Verdun, France. Initially called the World Union of Martyr Cities, this association was founded in 1982. Membership in the union was originally limited to cities that had been direct victims of war, but the association's name was changed in 1985, and other cities were permitted to become members. The objectives of the association are "based on the principle that cities represent local powers in the service of peace." Vancouver was asked to join the association because of its long-standing involvement in the international peace movement, its declaration that the city is a Nuclear Weapons Free Zone, its Annual Walk for Peace, its 1986 Peace and Disarmament Symposium, its Expo '86 theme, and the dedicated work of its numerous peace groups.

On a less positive note, the UN Environmental Program and the World Health Organization (WHO) are sponsoring a "Global Environment Monitoring System," which is a continuing project to monitor air pollution. According to a project report published in 1988, about 30 of the 50 cities monitored regularly exceed WHO standards set for sulfur dioxide, dust, lead, nitrogen oxide, and carbon monoxide. The three largest Canadian cities, Toronto, Montreal, and Vancouver, were all found to have "excessively high concentrations of carbon monoxide levels, particularly in rush hours" (Shulevitz 1989, 29).

Vancouver also has relations with private international actors such as transnational corporations, and these ties are not always amicable. In September 1989 the Vancouver City Council narrowly approved a motion barring the city from purchasing Shell products until the Royal Dutch Shell Group "completely withdraws from South Africa" (*Vancouver Sun*, October 12, 1989, B2). However, Shell Canada Ltd. succeeded in overturning the city council's decision in the courts.

Figure 19.1 shows that cities have cross-border relations with actors at the national as well as international levels. Indeed, Duchacek notes that

noncentral contacts with national governments are . . . to be expected in our era of welfare/warfare nation-states; they are unavoidable in contacts with socialist authoritarian systems in which one-party and central government authority is fully in charge of all aspects of the national economy. During trade-promotional trips to the People's Republic of China, for example, both the New York City mayor and the British Columbia premier primarily negotiated with the central government and its agencies in Beijing (Duchacek 1986, 247).

Finally, cities may be involved in cross-border linkages with (U.S.) states or (Canadian) provinces. The promotion of trade and tourism in an urban context has acquired greater importance and "in some U.S. cities, there are two or three Canadian provincial houses in addition to and in cooperative and sometimes competitive relationships with the consulates of Canada" (Duchacek 1986, 247). In 1984, Premier William Bennett responded to British Columbia's ailing economy by travelling to meet business and government leaders in San Francisco, Los Angeles, and Sacramento, California (Duchacek 1987, 15). However, city-provincial relations are not always cooperative. The province of Ontario launched a court action against the city of Detroit, for example, because of the latter's new garbage incinerator. The incinerator is only a few kilometres north of Windsor, and the province maintains that Detroit's emission control standards are inadequate. More recently, American municipalities in the Puget Sound region have sought assistance from Washington state and the U.S. Secretary of State to pressure B.C. cities such as Victoria— through state-province and nation to nation links—to undertake more than primary sewage treatment and limit the pollution impacts on the Sound waters (*Vancouver Sun*, March 7, 1991, B2).

In contrast to Figure 19.1, Figure 19.2 illustrates the intermestic interactions of municipal government as a mediating actor. Cities as mediating actors "seek to influence the formulation of national policies" and in Canada also of provincial policies in the international arena. For example, a mediating actor may attempt to promote federal policies "that are beneficial to local conditions in such areas as trade and foreign investment" (Hocking 1986, 484).

Municipal governments can assume the roles of primary and mediating actors simultaneously. American cities such as Seattle were primary actors when establishing sister city ties in Nicaragua, but some of these cities were also attempting to influence U.S. government policies toward the Ortega government. In a Canadian context, Winnipeg, Manitoba, and the small municipality of Maple Ridge, British Columbia, both have sister cities in Taiwan. The federal government in Ottawa has no official relations with Taiwan and tends to frown upon this city-based activity. The comments of Maple Ridge Mayor Bill Hartley indicate that cities establishing links with Taiwan may be assuming the dual role of primary and mediating actors:

> I know there are some problems from a Canadian diplomatic point of view. But at the same time the province of B.C. and, I believe, the Canadian government are very interested in Taiwan investment (*Vancouver Sun*, May 26, 1989, B7).

Figure 19.2.   *Intermestic Interactions of Municipal Government:*
                     Municipal Government as a Mediating Actor

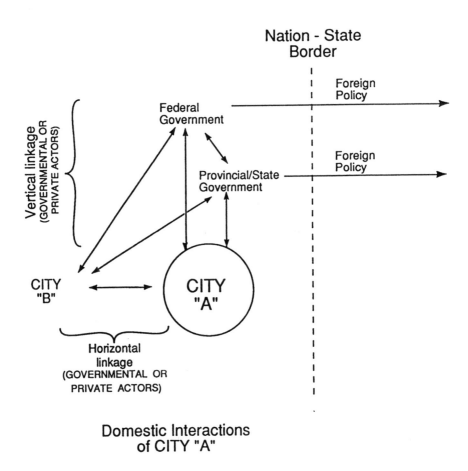

Domestic Interactions
of CITY "A"

* In this Figure, CITY "A" represents municipal government.

Source: Theodore H. Cohn and Patrick J. Smith, "A Typology of City-Based International Involvement: The Case of Vancouver," in *Processes d'Internationalization des Villes*, Groupe Nice, Lyon, France, 1990.

Canadian cities sometimes compete with each other as mediating actors. For example, former Vancouver Mayor Mike Harcourt helped to promote the city's case as Canada's Pacific "gateway." These efforts involved work with the new (1984) Conservative Government in Ottawa to establish Vancouver as one of Canada's international banking centres and to strengthen its Pacific links. However, Toronto sought to maintain its preeminence and tried to prevent the Canadian government from establishing Montreal and Vancouver as international banking centres. While Toronto could not prevent the passage of the necessary legislation, it did succeed in weakening the provisions and thus in limiting Vancouver's and Montreal's competitive advantages (*The Globe and Mail,* October 3, 1989, C7).

The international banking legislation case demonstrates the need to examine domestic as well as cross-border interactions. Figure 19.1 shows that a city has both horizontal linkages with other cities and vertical linkages with its senior governments. These linkages may be cooperative, competitive, and/or conflictual in nature.[5] Horizontal linkages may involve the efforts of several cities to coordinate their planning for a trade mission, or the competition/conflict among cities attempting to attract a foreign company's plant. Vertical linkages may involve a city's cooperation with senior governments in attracting foreign investment and expanding trade. Conflict may also result from the city's efforts to act too autonomously, or to adopt policies that are viewed as detrimental to senior governmental interests. To date, most municipal global activity has not proven conflictual.

Vancouver normally has cooperated with other municipalities in the city-region in promoting international relationships. When Vancouver delegations visit sister and strategic cities, individuals from neighbouring municipalities are often included, and Vancouver frequently helps its neighbours to establish linkages with visitors from abroad. In March 1985 a delegation from Vancouver's sister city of Guangzhou was taken to see

---

[5]Cooperation and conflict often co-exist in a relationship. Furthermore, some competitive situations are "friendly" while others are more closely associated with conflict. For a detailed examination of the relationship among these three variables, see Cohn 1990a, Chs. 1 and 8. For a discussion of Vancouver's cooperation with a "filial rival" (Seattle) see Cohn, Merrifield, and Smith 1989, 105-06.

the large Dairyland plant in Burnaby, B.C.; and in the summer of that year a Vancouver delegation visiting Guangzhou included the president of Dairyland and someone dealing with cattle embryos from Langley, B.C. The manager of Vancouver's Economic Development Office maintains that it is natural for the city to adopt this broader vision of its domestic relationships:

> When you start talking about the economy you can't put the blinders on and say that anything beyond my borders doesn't exist. . . . [On sister city delegations] we'll take people from the rest of B.C. We'll take people from Victoria, from Alberta even. We're not that narrow in thinking. The friendship and the camaraderie is between the two cities [in a sister city relationship], but we have friends, we have cousins, we have other people (Interview, Sid Fancy 1989).

Unlike Vancouver, smaller B.C. municipalities are more likely to compete with each other for plants of offshore industries, and they also tend to be suspicious of their larger neighbours (Smith and Cohn 1989a). Nevertheless, there is so much good will generated that conflict between large and small municipalities usually does not become a major issue. It should be added that Vancouver's cooperation with other cities is not limited to municipal governments in western Canada. For example, Shanghai is a sister city of Montreal, and a Vancouver official on a 1986 mission reported that "we got red carpet treatment in Shanghai because we were a cousin of Montreal and a sister of Guangzhou" (Interview, Sid Fancy 1989).

With regard to Vancouver's vertical linkages, the most obvious "external" factor is the constitutional framework of local governance in Canada. Given a history of some intergovernmental jealousy in matters federal-provincial and a pattern of provincial efforts to predominate over their municipal "creatures," it would be easiest to predict a political environment that is hostile to Vancouver's international forays.[6] Nevertheless, there is little evidence to support this contention. According to Mayor Gordon Campbell, the city "is not curtailed in any way at all by the province or the feds" (Interview, Gordon Campbell 1988). Senior city

---

[6]See for example, Simeon 1972 and 1986, and Smiley 1987. On such patterns of local-senior government relations in B.C. see Smith 1986, 6-20.

staff tend to feel that Vancouver's special position gives it added opportunity for international activity:

> Certainly, the City of Vancouver, although it is a creature of the province, has never felt that to the same extent that any other city in B.C. does (Interview, Ted Droetboom 1988).

> Certainly, we've never had any indication whenever we've entered into an [international] arrangement that either the province or the federal government would not agree with what we've done. . . . On the recent trip to Odessa, the External Affairs Department assisted us. . . . When we were in Tokyo last year, we went and met with the Provincial Government House in Tokyo, and they were very helpful in terms of providing us with information and assistance (Interview, Maria Kinsella 1988).

There are several reasons for the low level of conflict between cities such as Vancouver and senior governments. First, cities generally lack jurisdiction on matters international. While a city's establishment of a nuclear weapons free zone may create some resentment, such an action is usually considered largely symbolic and does not pose a major threat to national priorities. Second, as earlier discussed, cities and their senior levels of government are inclined to act with restraint since both sides "are likely to derive little advantage from" frustrating each other (Swainson 1983, 263). Third, local officials are often concerned with global activities such as the promotion of foreign investment and trade, in which they have common interests with their senior governmental counterparts.

In the Vancouver case, there are many instances of vertical linkages that are cooperative in nature. One example of municipal-provincial cooperation involves activities with Vancouver's sister city of Los Angeles. In March 1989 Premier William Vander Zalm officially opened a B.C. government office in the Los Angeles area. The Vancouver-Los Angeles Sister City Committee used the goodwill associated with this event and sent a 50-member business/cultural delegation to the California city. The organization of "Sister City Symposia" in Vancouver by the B.C. Ministry of International Business and Immigration in October 1989 and September 1990 is another instance of common provincial and municipal interests.

The strategic cities program that Vancouver developed in 1987 is an example of municipal-federal government cooperation. Indeed, Vancouver's Economic Development Office recommended that the city should concentrate on strategic relationships that "complement the priorities of the federal government's trade and development program" (City of Vancouver Manager's Report 1987c, 3). The cities that Vancouver identified as "strategic" were generally in accord with federal government priorities.

Federal government assistance has not involved large amounts of funding but Vancouver's assistant city manager has noted that "there is a willingness to facilitate" (Interview, Ted Droetboom 1988). For example, the Canadian embassy in China planned to raise Canada's profile in that country by staging special events in May 1989. As part of the preparations, Canada's ambassador wrote to the Vancouver mayor that "given the dynamic relationship you have developed with your twin city of Guangzhou . . . you may wish to participate and initiate some event to occur next May" (City of Vancouver Strategic Cities Program Budget 1989, 4). The Canadian International Development Agency has also given grants for the FCM's Municipal Professional Exchange Project (FCM Municipal Professional Exchange Project, 1988c). This project funded an exchange where Guangzhou officials responsible for traffic control spent time in Vancouver, and equivalent staff from Vancouver visited Guangzhou. Despite the June 1989 events in Beijing's Tiananmen Square, the sister city linkage continues—albeit on a slower track—again in keeping with federal policy.

While Canadian cities and the federal government normally cooperate on trade and investment issues, tensions do arise. Cities and provinces in particular Canadian regions have at times felt the need to take more local initiative because of a perceived lack of interest by the federal government. Thus, a former premier of Alberta maintained that "many Western Canadians are tired of going to Asian countries and meeting with well-meaning, but Eastern-Canadian-oriented civil servants who can relate the name of every major company doing business in Montreal or Ottawa or Toronto, but who have never heard of some of the international concerns of Winnipeg, Regina, Edmonton, Calgary or Vancouver" (Johannson 1978, 364).

In Vancouver, the International Trade Advisory Group (ITAG) is an example of three-way cooperation between the municipal, provincial, and federal governments. Although Vancouver formulates many of its own trade and investment-promotion strategies, the manager of the Economic

Development Office notes that there are continuous efforts to promote coordination with senior governments:

> We're trying to be sensible and not trip over the Province or have them trip over us. In that regard . . . there is a small group that meets periodically. We call it ITAG, the International Trade Advisory Group. . . . The Board of Trade is there . . . it's in their offices. Federal people who have worked on trade missions. . . . There are usually two representatives from the Province, two from the Board of Trade, and one of my staff. We just talk about what we're up to, and pool information (Interview, Sid Fancy 1989).

Another example of municipal-provincial-federal cooperation is "the Asia Pacific Initiative." In December 1986, British Columbia signed a Memorandum of Understanding with the Canadian government to jointly develop projects that would promote Pacific Canada as a centre for trade, commerce, and travel. The first major result of this effort was announced in June 1987, with the formation of the Asia Pacific Initiative Advisory Committee (APIAC). One of the five task forces established under this committee, the task force on international trade and finance, is to develop recommendations on how to enhance Vancouver's role as an "international city." It is focusing on how more Canadian and foreign trade-based organizations, financial institutions, and other firms— particularly those with Asia Pacific interests—can be encouraged to locate offices and do business in Vancouver (Government of Canada [Treasury Board] and Government of British Columbia, n.d.).

The intermestic relationships depicted in Figures 19.1 and 19.2 are so numerous and complex that it is impossible to examine all of them in detail here. In this chapter we focus mainly on Vancouver's role as a primary actor in cross-border relations with other cities.

MUNICIPAL PARADIPLOMACY AND
THE VANCOUVER METROPOLIS

Municipal governments in Canada have undertaken a wide array of city-based global activities of a cultural, social, educational, economic, and political nature. Examples from British Columbia, metropolitan Vancouver, and the city of Vancouver illustrate the nature and range of such activities; the organization of municipal international activity; and the results of this global involvement.

If senior governments are going to harness their cities to respond to growing international interdependence and to find solutions to major concerns such as global warming, they will have to look to the public policy literature and to the growing experiential base of municipal internationalism. The public policy literature offers several suggestions, the most basic of these being to dive deep rather than spread thin (Pal 1987, 249-53). The experience of cities like Vancouver supports the contention that it is better to concentrate global relationships on fewer ties than to spread them across a broad number of city-based twinnings (Soldatos 1989, 39).

The problems with spreading city-based global activities too thinly are administrative, financial, and political. Vancouver established a "quiet moratorium" on new sister city twinnings after it had added Guangzhou, China, in 1985 and Los Angeles, USA, in 1986. The reasons for the moratorium related to the city's capacity to cope with the formal undertakings involved in such relationships. Vancouver receives up to several requests a week for twinning arrangements and turns down such proposals "all the time," according to city staff. The same pattern repeats itself in other large and small municipalities. In a survey of B.C. local governments, we found that many mayors/senior city staff listed limitations like "the need to establish some standards and criteria, plus more funding, before seeking more sister cities"; or "staying with one sister city because of costs/limit of resources"; others cited "no more linkages at the present time. Current linkage is only one year old—needs to be consolidated"; and "perhaps other sister cities, but cautious of spreading too thin;" or "No! Because of possible municipal costs." As an example, the costs of the August 1990 Burnaby, B.C., visit to its Japanese sister city of Kushiro to celebrate the 25th anniversary of its twinning relationship was $50,000 (Information from Office of the Mayor, Burnaby, January 24, 1991).

At least three types of municipal diplomacy have been established in British Columbia. These include municipal twinning/sister cities, municipal foreign aid linkages, and strategic cities. Strategic city relations in particular tend to be confined to major city regions, and they appear most advanced in the Canadian experience in the city of Vancouver.

Municipal Twinning—Sister Cities

The first sister city established by a Canadian municipality was Vancouver's 1944 twinning with the (then Soviet allied) city of Odessa. The local rationale was rooted in humanitarian assistance to a war-devastated sister port. There was also, and continues to be, a cultural link between the Jewish communities in both cities. Cold War relations after 1945 limited further contact but the sister city link was never broken. This linkage highlights one feature of such formal exchanges—as with families, these relationships may stray and be strained, but they are not broken. Indeed, with the major policy shifts in the Soviet Union under Gorbachev, Odessa provided a basis for Vancouver's entry into the strategic Soviet market. More recent Vancouver-Odessa exchanges involved such areas as peace, culture, and education; however, the continuing importance of the city's economic linkages with Odessa, Ukraine, in a post-Soviet setting are less certain.

The Federation of Canadian Municipalities' Guide to Municipal Twinning suggests four broad types of criteria for developing sister city links:

1. General characteristics such as geographic location, size, existing linkages, local ethnic population mix, comparable key industries, and humanitarian assistance.

2. Cultural/civic/educational characteristics such as cultural institutions, civic organizations, media outlets, sports group links, educational institutions, and medical/health institutions.

3. Political/economic criteria such as similar economic conditions or investment climates/levels, language/cultural links or impediments, levels of government bureaucracy, branches of banks/factories/airlines and number of foreign residents.

4. Commercial factors such as invisible trade (education/high tech/services/experts), airlinks, diplomatic presence, tourism, local businesses engaged in international activity, and trade exchange potential.

While all these factors apply to B.C. municipalities, it has not been unusual for municipalities to enter into sister city relations in an ad hoc, incremental manner. Without a more institutionalized and rational basis, these relations often languish for long periods of time. Vancouver's experience highlights this pattern—and problem. After the 1944 exchange with Odessa, Vancouver added Yokohama in 1965 and Edinburgh in

1978. In each instance, the pattern was the same: intense initial involvements by parts of the community and the municipality, followed by lengthy periods of relative neglect.

Central to any formal municipal twinning is the support and participation of the mayor, because of his/her leadership and recognizability. The mayor of an international city is instantly recognizable and understood in the political firmament. Regional government officials may be important participants, but they cannot "carry the flag" as effectively as the mayor on foreign trade and investment missions; that is certainly the view in Vancouver:

> It is hard to sell the idea of a Chairman of the Greater Vancouver Regional District as the leader of a mission. The reason [is] that the title means nothing to them overseas. . . . When people receive the Mayor of Vancouver, they feel that they are receiving the Mayor of the whole of the Lower Mainland. And that's what counts. . . . The people that the cities overseas really seem to take notice of are: the prime minister of the country; very high profile cabinet ministers, and then comes the mayor of a major city.

> In terms of recognition, premiers have a hard time compared to the mayors of large cities. And the reason for that is that most people have difficulty understanding what a province is all about and where it fits in the order of things. . . . It doesn't mean that the mayor of the city really has more power; it's just that others are certain what power is invested in that person. That is why the mayor is so effective in opening doors" (Interview, Sid Fancy 1989).

Beyond mayoral involvement, programs that have generally worked well have also involved one or more local councillors. Successful sister city programs invariably have a strong community base, whether cultural, social/educational, political, or economic/commercial. Not surprisingly, such programs work best when they are based on a combination of these factors. For example, Vancouver's 1985 decision to twin with Guangzhou stemmed from a broad range of common interests and needs. Many citizens of Chinese ancestry in Vancouver had emigrated from the Canton region, and some of them have business connections with both Guangzhou and Hong Kong (which are very near each other). Some prominent members of Vancouver's Chinese community, including a city alderman, therefore favoured twinning with Guangzhou instead of another Chinese city such as Shanghai. The Guangzhou connection facilitates the maintenance of social, cultural, and economic contacts as well as maintaining an "open door" with Hong Kong.

The limitations of sister city twinnings relate to the capacity of a local administration to manage the protocol requirements of such formal linkages. As noted, Vancouver felt it necessary to establish a "quiet moratorium" on new sister city links in 1986 despite receiving requests from "more than 50" possible twins:

> You have to ask yourself how many sister cities can you afford to have, because a sister city involves you in a great deal more relationships than perhaps a strategic city program does. . . . You get involved in visits back and forth. You do this for me and then I'm obliged to do that for you. I mean you inherit obligations and so on. It's much more time-consuming. There's an awful lot more work involved . . . [and] you have to ask yourself, can you twin effectively with fifty cities (Interview, Sid Fancy 1989)?

In summary, Vancouver's experience suggests that twinnings (and indeed, strategic links) work best when they are limited in number, broadly based in the community, with an economic component and focused in policy terms (Federation of Canadian Municipalities, n.d.).

Municipal Foreign-Aid Linkages

In the 1980s, the Canadian government began to use local governments as vehicles for foreign aid to less-developed countries (LDCs). The reasons are understandable, given that many LDC problems are urban-based, but the use of cities for this purpose is unique, at least in the Canadian experience. The FCM has noted that "the problems of communities in the developing world are both more basic and more extensive than in Canada," and the trend to more urbanized and growing populations has made these predicaments more pressing (Federation of Canadian Municipalities, June 1989). Being able to solve these city-based problems has been recognized as crucial:

> The shortage of shelter is a fast deepening crisis. . . . The disposal of waste is as central a problem as the supply of clean water. The reality of urban transportation typically lags genera-

tions behind the need. Poverty, crime, disease, and drugs are usually problems of daunting proportions.

For the United Nations, the fundamental fact is this—only if the Third World urban challenge is met, will sustained economic advance in developing countries be possible (Federation of Canadian Municipalities, June 1989).

The federal government has therefore sought to utilize the expertise of Canadian cities in its foreign aid activities to achieve senior governmental policy goals. These national initiatives grew out of international programs. For example, the UN's "Global Strategy For Shelter to the Year 2000" encouraged national governments "to create an environment of incentives and facilitating measures." The government's role was to be primarily "an 'enabling' one, mobilizing the resources of other actors and facilitating their deployment" (United Nations 1987). In Canada, this facilitating role translated into several city-based aid programs. The Canadian International Development Agency made the Federation of Canadian Municipalities the "executing agency" for a number of foreign aid initiatives, including the Chinese Open Cities Program, municipal professional exchanges, and Africa 2000.

The Chinese Open Cities Program: As part of its modernization efforts, China designated 14 Coastal Cities, four Special Economic Zones, and three Delta areas to be "open" to the outside world for foreign trade, joint business ventures, and foreign investment. China also requested Canadian assistance to increase its municipal capacity. CIDA provided $7 million over five years through FCM to assist in developing the human resources of Chinese local government through training activities, study tours, staff exchanges, educational exchanges, and joint human resource development projects of linked municipalities. The projects undertaken— as between Vancouver and Guangzhou on transportation planning, Toronto and Sao Paulo, Brazil, on housing, or the study tour of Canada by mayors/vice mayors from Shandong Province—include urban land-use planning, the urban environment, urban management, urban economic development, foreign trade and investment, and information on Canadian political institutions (Federation of Canadian Municipalities 1987).

In the process of providing such assistance, local managers in Canadian cities have developed a broader view of municipal issues. Thus, Ray Spaxman, Vancouver's Director of Planning for 15 years, recently noted that people who manage cities don't know how other cities deal with problems on a large scale. Planners may ask one another about individual situations, but they don't take the big picture. The trick to solving a city's problems is comprehensive planning, not with vision focused on single issues (Lecture, University of British Columbia, November, 1989; cited in Jamie Lamb, "Uptown, Downtown," *Vancouver Sun*, November 25, 1989, A5).

Projects such as China Open Cities permit Canadian municipalities to develop "a deeper understanding of local government . . . [and] new perspectives on municipal problems . . . from an international perspective" (Federation of Canadian Municipalities 1987). Finally, foreign assistance relationships often further the economic interests of the donor as well as the recipient in such areas as trade and foreign investment linkages. Since the Tiananmen Square actions of June 1989 there has been less interaction under the Canada-China programs, but the linkages remain. The exception to this is the suspension of Toronto's sister city link with Chongqing, China, following June 1989, events.

The Municipal Professional Exchange Project: The FCM has also developed a "program . . . for professional exchange of senior municipal managerial and technical staff between Canada and the Third World. . . . [to] complement twinning activities" (Federation of Canadian Municipalities 1988b). In 1986, CIDA had provided funding for an exchange of officials from seven cities in Canada—including Vancouver—with cities in Brazil, Columbia, Ghana, India, Senegal, and Zimbabwe. The success of that initial trial exchange produced the Municipal Professional Exchange Program (MPEP) project in 1987. Under the MPEP, municipalities contribute staff time for external exchanges, and arrange for foreign managers to work in Canadian municipalities. The FCM, with CIDA funds, supports basic travel and subsistence. The projects may be initiated by municipalities of any size but all are to include

a commitment to long-term collaboration; joint planning implementation and evaluation; responsiveness to the needs identified by the Third World community involved; strengthening of the professional capacity of municipal institutions and staff [and] contribution of staff time by Third World and Canadian participants (Federation of Canadian Municipalities 1988c).

Funding under the professional exchange program provided for Vancouver's assistant city manager to spend time in the sister city of

Guangzhou working on traffic/transportation planning and management. It also allowed Guangzhou officials to work on similar problems within the Vancouver city administration. From these initial exchanges a variety of practical projects developed on establishing an environmentally acceptable sewage system, emergency health services coordination, city vehicle maintenance, transportation management, computer mapping, training of rural citizens in fish breeding, vegetable growing and chicken farming, and data analysis systems development for urban planning (FCM Municipal Professional Exchange 1988c).

Africa 2000: The Municipal Response: The Canadian International Development Agency requested FCM assistance for city-based aid in Africa as well. FCM is involved with an Africa 2000 project that

> shifts aid from a country-to-country basis to a community-to-community exchange. This should allow for better monitoring, and more sensitive grassroots responses to programming. It also emphasizes human resource development as an essential and often underrated ingredient in the development process (Federation of Canadian Municipalities 1988b).

Under the Africa 2000 plan, five cities in English Canada were tied to five municipalities in nonfrancophone Africa. Saanich—a municipality in the Victoria Capital Region District in British Columbia—was linked to Zomba, Malawi. The municipality's chief engineer, Department of Public Works, and the Finance Department have had technical exchanges, and a Zomba Public Health official will work in Canada on an exchange project. The Malawi High Commissioner to Canada has also visited Saanich as a result of the program.

The Saanich-Zomba connection has received funding through several provisions of the Africa 2000 plan. Under the "Small Capital Expenditure" provisions of the CIDA funding, the Saanich visit to Zomba produced proposals for basic equipment such as calculators to be purchased for the African municipality's Finance Department. Under the "Community Based Projects" component, Saanich voluntary organizations raised $20,000, matched with a CIDA grant (to that maximum) to provide a roofed-in public market in Zomba. And finally, under "New Initiatives" provisions, $5,000 was provided through CIDA for an exchange of video tapes between the Universities of Victoria and Malawi—on programs depicting the character of life in the two communities. The Saanich contributions to date have been in staff time "and perhaps $1,000 in municipal functions and gifts." Although the project has "just started," officials have recognized the "enormous amount of goodwill for Saanich and Canada and the personal growth of those members of municipal staff involved in exchanges" (Sturrock 1989).

One footnote is worth mentioning in the context of changing municipalities and the Africa 2000 experience. The program also involved five cities in Quebec being linked to five francophone African cities. The exchange of Quebec's five municipal governments with francophone African communities was delayed for constitutional reasons. As with much of Canadian constitutional history, Quebec has been most sensitive to federal intrusions into areas of provincial jurisdiction. Since Africa 2000 involved direct grants from the Canadian government to municipalities, the Quebec government objected on the basis of its jurisdictional ascendancy. It did not oppose the program itself but insisted that the money be given to the province, which would then pass it on to municipalities. This has now been done. One of the enduring lessons of Canadian federalism is that when Quebec stakes out such constitutional positions, other provinces often follow.

The FCM/CIDA international programs have normally not been conflictual in nature because they represent areas of significant agenda agreement. However, Quebec's response to the Africa 2000 program suggests that this may not always be the case. For senior governments anticipating programs to involve their municipal "partners" more actively, and for local governments considering their global policy options, there are important questions to ask and useful experiential lessons to be learned. These are perhaps most obvious in the development of a strategic cities policy.

Strategic Cities

The experience of Canadian municipal governments in the range of global activities described above is essential to understanding the significance of the strategic city policy initiative undertaken by Vancouver in 1987. It remains a rather unique approach to municipal global diplomacy, from which other major Canadian and international centres are keen to learn (Smith and Cohn 1989b, 1990b).

Vancouver emerged in the 1980s with three sister cities—one each in the Soviet Union, Britain, and Japan—as a result of ad hoc policy

decisions over 20 years. This incremental approach was consistent with
the idea of municipal twinnings as a basis for cultural and other forms of
exchange. The program was relatively low-key and at times almost
ignored when local community interest waned. In 1980, a new mayor
(Mike Harcourt) began promoting Vancouver as Canada's Pacific
Gateway. Harcourt utilized the FCM and the major Canadian cities
forum to develop more pro-active policy stances on intergovernmental
and international matters; for example, to exert municipal pressure on
both the provincial and federal governments to provide $15 billion to
rebuild the nation's urban infrastructure, or to designate Vancouver as a
nuclear weapons free zone. Under the Harcourt administration, Vancouver's sister city programming took on a new look. In keeping with the
new Pacific economic priorities, two Pacific Rim cities were added—
Guangzhou in 1985 and Los Angeles in 1986. The policy focus also
became more rational—with the objective of establishing the city's place
in Canada and *vis-à-vis* the Asia-Pacific area. In administrative terms, the
laissez-faire, incremental approach was also replaced by a more coordinated, rational form. Beginning with this policy shift, a confluence of
several factors that significantly altered this reality emerged throughout
the 1980s:

1. The increasing interdependence of the world economy affected
national and city/regional economies. As a result, cities became central
as catalysts of economic growth (Castells 1983, Part 3; Jacobs 1984).

2. The shift from incremental to more rational global policymaking
and the institutionalization of international activity in Vancouver emerged
during the 1980s.

3. The expanded role of the city's Economic Development Office,
and the addition of U.S. and Chinese sister cities coincided with a new
provincial and federal focus on Pacific Rim trade and investment.

4. The 1986 election of a business-oriented mayor, Gordon
Campbell, and a business-oriented council majority, was the final step in
the policy shift.

Within months of his November 1986 election, Campbell (in a March
1987 memo to Council) provided his policy response to the new
directions established by his predecessor:

A sister city rationale for the 1980s must recognize that in
addition to friendship, economic and cultural opportunities must
be reinforced. It is vital that governmental and non-governmental

institutions co-ordinate their efforts to optimize economic benefits (Mayor's Report to City Council, March 1987).

Campbell also recommended "that Vancouver establish 5 Citizen Committees and a Sister City Commission . . . [and] that the Mayor and the Manager of Economic Development . . . prepare a strategy paper to integrate Council's economic strategy with our Sister City goals, and to further our goal to become the centre of Canada's Pacific Region."

In April 1986, the previous council had approved the first of these components—an economic strategy for the city entitled "City of Vancouver: Economic Goals, Objectives and Principles." In August 1987, the first outline of a strategic city program emerged in a Report to City Council by the manager, Economic Development. Since the program has become an important part of Vancouver's economic development strategy, some detail on its features is of interest.

The strategic city program combined economic and trade missions, the economic development strategy (approved in 1986), the sister city program, and the new Sister City Commission into a single integrated plan. The program was to have enough flexibility to establish new and differing relationships with foreign cities. "Vancouver's special relationship with . . . 'key' cities in the Pacific Region" was viewed as "a natural foundation for such an initiative." While Vancouver was to solidify its business ties throughout the world, all of these links could not be strengthened at the same time. The program would therefore "focus on those that offer the best and most immediate benefits" (City of Vancouver 1986).

On determining which cities were "strategic," Vancouver assessed its existing interactions. Here Hong Kong stood out, despite a lack of formal twinning. For Vancouver this link was based on a large Chinese population and a 400-member Hong Kong-Canada Business Association formed in 1985. Vancouver's links to the fast-growing ASEAN (Association of Southeast Asian Nations) economies also held considerable potential, and Singapore was designated as "the major gateway city within that region." Montreal's twin in Shanghai and Toronto's in Chongqing both offered a basis for "cousin-based" opportunities as well. Vancouver's other significant links were with Kuala Lumpur and Bangkok (see Table 19.1).

As with sister cities, Vancouver recognized that it could not develop effective programs with all 13 cities identified as possibly strategic. Thus, the staff recommended that the council concentrate on those cities that would complement the priorities of the federal government's trade development program (i.e., to maintain market share, increase value added, encourage investment, enhance Canadian technology growth, focus on U.S.A., Japan, South Korea, and Australia); provide a significant niche for the Vancouver business community; have potential as gateways to other cities and national and regional economies, with particular emphasis on the Asia-Pacific; possess organizations—in Vancouver and the other city—with a keen desire to foster a cultural and commercial relationship; and have the potential for generating frequent contact between considerable numbers of business people.

Of the 13 possible strategic cities, staff recommended that the city concentrate on the five sister cities as well as on Hong Kong and Singapore. Vancouver also maintains close links with Tokyo and Osaka via its Yokohama link. In concluding the report, council was reminded that "Vancouver's contacts with these cities would encompass cultural as well as business relationships because an understanding of each other's perspective is an important prelude to mutually satisfactory business arrangements."

To coordinate this strategic city policy initiative, there would be citizen sister city committees established, as well as citizen committees focusing on Hong Kong, Singapore, and the ASEAN area. Each would include cultural representatives "to maximize the potential for economic and cultural development." To make sister city activity "part of a more comprehensive activity," the manager's report recommended that the Sister City Commission be recast as the Strategic City Commission. Membership on the new commission would include the chair/vice chair, aldermen appointed by the mayor, citizen committee representatives appointed by council on the mayor's recommendation, senior staff (from the city clerk, director of social planning and manager of economic development), and a Vancouver School Board representative. Staff support would reside in the city clerk's office (for protocol) and the Economic Development Office (for day-to-day policy coordination).

The February 1989 Strategic Cities Program (SCP) budget proposal to city council contained an updated description of the SCP. Strategic links were to be with cities having "potential as gateways to other cities, and regional and national economies"; cities with organizations (including Vancouver) "with a keen desire to foster a cultural and commercial relationship"; and cities providing "a discernable niche for the Vancouver business community, and the potential for frequent contact (networking) between Vancouver and the overseas business people."

The 1988 SCP budget was $92,000, plus a one-time $200,000 city contribution to the sister city Yokohama Exposition (Yokohama had participated in Expo '86 in Vancouver). Despite the limited funding (the total city budget was $335 million), the impact of its "seeding" in global relations is much greater when private sector multipliers and government grants are added. For example, Vancouver's $200,000 grant for the Yokohama Exotic Festival was matched by $200,000 from B.C. and $200,000 from the federal government's Western Diversification Fund. The Vancouver-Yokohama Society was able to raise an additional $900,000 privately for a total of $1.7 million. When a 1989 budgetary request for $76,500 (a decrease of $15,000 from 1988) was submitted to city council with Strategic City Commission support, the Strategic City Program budget was cut to $30,000 (Interview, Sid Fancy 1989). In an election year, heightened political sensitivity to possible local resistance was a significant factor in these cuts (See Kincaid 1989). The two most active sister city societies—for Yokohama and Los Angeles—have succeeded in becoming significantly self-sufficient in financial terms. The city's seeding is more important for less active sister-city efforts, particularly in the settings of Odessa and Guangzhou. However, city sponsorship and mayoral involvement remain key conditions for any successful twinning.

Interestingly, the more rational footing for the policy, and the stronger business/economic base, have left the program less at risk than a 60 percent budgetary cut might indicate. With a reasonable community base, citizen committees, and established economic-cultural links at least partially developed, all linkages have been maintained. Some have reached the point of organizational "take-off," according to senior city staff. The Vancouver-Los Angeles link is a good case in point. Though established only in 1986, it has a strong network of self-funded interactions; these include bringing groups of independent film producers to

B.C. and arranging for groups that include provincial cabinet ministers to visit Los Angeles to promote foreign investment.[7]

Despite the Strategic City Program emphasis on the Asia-Pacific area, there is a continuing interest in other areas. In view of changing East-West relations, Vancouver's sister city of Odessa provides a basis for entry into the Soviet market. When Soviet President Gorbachev chided Canadian Prime Minister Mulroney in November 1989 about Canada's tardiness in responding to Soviet reforms, Vancouver felt that its 1944 twinning with Odessa and the city's earlier 1980s visit to its Soviet twin following years of cold-war neglect provided Vancouver with an important national and global advantage *vis-à-vis* the opening Soviet market. There is also the issue of ties with the European Community, since the EC's planned consolidation in 1992 will provide major new opportunities for trade and investment linkages (Cohn 1990b). According to a November 1989 interview with B.C.'s Agent-General in London, the community is "the most major economic initiative and economic alliance in the history of the world," and "Canada is asleep at the switch." Vancouver has a sister city link with Edinburgh, though it has been more cultural than economic. It also has unofficial links between city staff and federal government trade staff formerly in the Pacific region, but now in postings such as Bonn. It appears that Vancouver is beginning to heed the advice from B.C.'s Agent-General, even though the EC represents a "harder" market. The province is also directing more attention to Europe with its newly established European Community Advisory Committee. In this task, Vancouver is far behind Toronto, where most of the global focus is on Europe. Last, but certainly not least, the implications of the Canada-U.S. Free Trade Agreement for B.C.'s and Vancouver's cross-border trade have only begun to be felt. B.C. is relatively less

---

[7]See Smith and Cohn 1989b and 1990a for a more complete discussion of these factors. In some respects this is a daunting task, given the relatively infamous reputation of the Vancouver Stock Exchange. Thus, the 1989 issues of Forbes and Barons business magazines suggested that the Exchange was no better than an unstable casino. Presumably the October 20-26, 1989 Vancouver visit to Los Angeles, which included B.C.'s Minister of Finance, and a seminar on the Vancouver Stock Exchange, were designed to counter the negative U.S. press coverage. See *Sister City News*, Newsletter of the Vancouver-Los Angeles Sister City Committee, September 1989, Issue, p. 2.

dependent on U.S. trade—and more dependent on trade with Asian states—than other Canadian provinces, but the free trade agreement will nevertheless have a significant impact. Canadian-American-Mexican Free Trade, if put into effect, would appear to simply compound any such impacts.

The uncertainty these changes represent has led to more city-based global—and strategic—choices, and there is every indication that this will continue. It is therefore important to determine the policy lessons—for senior and local governments—that emerge from these changes.

POLICY LESSONS AND PROSPECTS FOR THE CHANGING GLOBAL METROPOLIS

Each component of Vancouver's changing internationalism contains elements that assist us in weighing appropriate policy responses by senior governments and in understanding the implications of particular policy choices. A number of factors stand out, the first being context. In his text on Canadian foreign policymaking, Kim Nossal has contended that

foreign policy, properly speaking, is concerned with the explanation of the behaviour of those who have the capacity to exercise supreme political authority over a given set of issue areas, for a given people in a given territory. That is why we exclude the external policies of governments like that of Toronto. The members of the City Council of Toronto may declare their city a nuclear weapons free zone, as indeed they have done. But their declaration commands no authority, and has no effect—for the simple reason that municipal governments are not empowered to decide such matters, even for those who live within their boundaries. Such a decision can be, and has been, overridden by the legitimate authority on such matters, the federal government (Nossal 1989, 2-3).

Our findings indicate, however, that there is a major difference between a city's formal authority to act internationally on the one hand and its capacity to do so on the other. In dismissing an external policy of the city of Toronto—the designation of itself as a nuclear weapons free zone—Nossal misses much about the changing context of global relations. His one example is a strategic security issue that is clearly within the purview of the federal government. The most important international actions of major municipalities today are, in fact, in socio-economic policy areas, which are far more intermestic in nature. Furthermore, globalization has meant that significant areas of trade, investment, immigration, development, and the environment are now beyond the capacity of national governments to contain. It is this very limitation on senior governmental capacity that explains much of the growing globalism of Canadian city regions. Just as much of London's global interconnectedness is no longer tied to Britain, so too is this beginning to be the case with some of Canada's larger metropolitan centres. Nossal may be correct about the minimal impact of city nuclear weapons free policies on Canadian foreign policymaking. Increasingly, however, the same can no longer be said for city-based international activities in such areas as trade and foreign investment.

The second feature that emerges is the necessity vs. sufficiency differential—the slippage between what local governments have traditionally felt they needed with regard to constitutional, institutional, financial, and policy reform, and what is actually required to sustain and support local internationalism.

In their 1983 Brief to the (Macdonald) Royal Commission on the Economic Union and Development Prospects for Canada, Canadian municipalities identified and called for reform of seven key factors limiting the capacity of local governments to contribute to national policymaking and economic development: lack of direction; lack of cohesion; lack of cooperation; lack of consultation; lack of information; lack of authority; and lack of appropriate instruments (Federation of Canadian Municipalities 1983).[8]

In assessing the global policy roles of city regions like Vancouver, the lack of positive response by senior governments to the most significant of these reform needs—authority and financial capacity—has not proven a major impediment to municipal paradiplomacy. This does not mean that all metropolitan regions in Canada have embraced this global policy expansionism equally. At one extreme is the city of Halifax, where the mayor feels that such activity is inappropriate, since it is beyond the jurisdiction and traditional role of local government (Interview, Ron Wallace 1990). In the middle range are cities such as

---

[8]See Smith and Cohn 1989b and 1990a for a more complete discussion of these factors.

Winnipeg, which has nine current twins, but whose international activity in economic and financial areas is rather limited (Interview, Jim Beaulieu 1990). At the other extreme are the more activist cases of Toronto and Vancouver. These two cities have sought to place their international involvement on a more focused level, with much more intergovernmental involvement with senior authorities and greater impact on their policy agendas.

The city of Toronto now has eight formal twinnings, with Amsterdam, Frankfurt, Lisbon, Barcelona, Warsaw, Thessalonika, Volgograd, and Kiev. Its relationship with Chongqing, China, was suspended following events in Tiananmen Square in June 1989, and its linkage with Sao Paulo, Brazil, is under the CIDA/FCM funded Municipal Professional Exchange Program. While not all city councillors had positive views of the city's increased involvement (Polanyi 1990) in international programs, Mayor Art Eggleton felt they had brought "significant benefits to Toronto, in the areas of urban technology, economic development, education and cultural exchanges" (City of Toronto International Office 1990). Toronto's International Office stated in the same report that its global expansion was "in response to worldwide trends of increasing urbanization and economic globalization."

More importantly, Toronto has developed close intergovernmental ties with the Province of Ontario and the federal government. This has helped overcome the policy and attitudinal impediments of lack of consultation, cooperation, cohesion, direction, and information. As a result, Toronto has become an international city (see Appendix for characteristics). It is home to over 60 foreign banks and is seen by the province as "a key . . . in attracting business, not only to the city, but to the rest of Ontario."[9] Firms also directly solicit Toronto "introductions" to sister city officials to further their business interests. For example, IMAX Systems requested an introduction to "leading city officials in Lisbon in order to develop a business relationship that could lead to the establishment of an IMAX/OMNIMAX theatre in that city."[10] The city of Toronto has also joined 10 other cities from three continents in working to develop a blueprint for dealing with greenhouse gases. As the only Canadian city in the Urban

---

[9]Letter from Minister of Industry, Trade and Technology, to Toronto Mayor Art Eggleton, August 3, 1990; cited in City of Toronto, 1990, appendix.

[10]Letter from IMAX to City of Toronto, in City of Toronto, 1990.

Carbon Dioxide Project, Toronto hopes that other jurisdictions will follow the project cities' example.[11]

In 1989, Toronto spent at least $674,000—out of a total city budget of $553 million—to maintain its international office and the city's global activities. In Vancouver, the figure is less than $100,000. Yet with a clear focus and a substantial Pacific Rim orientation, officials have maintained that the city need only provide "seed" funding in most instances. The examples cited earlier of Vancouver's Los Angeles Sister City Committee and the Yokohama Festival work support this view. Significant multipliers emerged from senior governments and from the private sector with small amounts of initial city support. The use of the city's auspices for these ventures, however, was essential. As discussed, Vancouver has been one of the most activist Canadian cities internationally. The Vancouver case would support the conclusion that the motivation of municipal officials (especially the mayor), and the encouragement (or at least indifference) of senior governments are more important factors in stimulating municipal internationalism than financial capacity and formal transfers of authority. Globalization has meant that the latter are no longer a necessity.

The third feature is prospects for global policy enhancement. The Vancouver case and the experience of other Canadian international cities, support the contention that city regions will continue to grow as important elements in economic, environmental, and related policy fields.[12] How cities confront livability, how they contribute to economic prosperity, and the kinds of international linkages they establish will have significant impacts on senior government policymaking and on the relative well-being of their citizens. The need for city regions to develop their own global policies is an inevitable consequence of the growth of global interdependence, and it will occur with or without senior government support. In Canada, the era of the changing global metropolis has clearly arrived.

---

[11]"Cities Join to Fight Global Warming," *Vancouver Sun*, June 13, 1991, A10.

[12]See Fry, Radebaugh, and Soldatos 1989 for a discussion of Montreal, Toronto, Calgary, and Vancouver.

INTERVIEWS

Beaulieu, Jim, Deputy Minister of Urban Affairs, Government of Manitoba, October 20, 1990.

Campbell, Gordon, Mayor, City of Vancouver, October 17, 1988.

Droetboom, Ted, Assistant City Manager, City of Vancouver, September 30, 1988.

Fancy, Sid, Manager, Economic Development Office, City of Vancouver, October, 27, 1989.

Kinsella, Maria, City Clerk, City of Vancouver, September 30, 1988.

Wallace, Ron, Mayor, City of Halifax, February 14, 1990.

REFERENCES

Black, Edwin. 1975. *Divided Loyalties: Canadian Concepts of Federalism.* Montreal: McGill Queens University Press.

Campbell, Gordon, Mayor of Vancouver, 1991. "Local Government Bill of Rights." FCM Presentation. St. John's Newfoundland. Sept 4.

Canadian Federation of Mayors and Municipalities. 1976. *Puppets on a Shoestring.* Ottawa: C.F.M.M. April.

Castells, Manuel. 1983. *The City and the Grassroots: A Cross-Cultural Theory of Urban Social Movements.* Berkeley: University of California Press.

City of Toronto International Office. 1990. "International Linkages: The Benefits to Toronto." August.

City of Vancouver. 1986. *Economic Goals, Objectives and Principles.* April.

_____. 1987a. "Mayor's Memo to Council." March.

_____. 1987b. *Mayor's Report to City Council.* March.

_____. 1987c. *Manager's Report.* Vancouver: Economic Development Office. August 29.

_____. 1989. *1989 Strategic Cities Program Budget.* February.

Cohn, Theodore H.   1990a. *The International Politics of Agricultural Trade: Canadian-American Relations in a Global Agricultural Context.* Vancouver: University of British Columbia Press.

_____. 1990b. "Canada, Europe, and the Politics of International Trade." Paper presented to symposium on "Canada and Europe" at Ruhr-Universitat Bochum, Bochum, Germany. October 29.

_____, David E. Merrifield, and Patrick J. Smith. 1989. "North American Cities in an Interdependent World: Vancouver and Seattle as International Cities." In *The New International Cities Era: The Global Activities of North American Municipal Governments*, ed. Earl Fry, Lee Radebaugh, and Panayotis Soldatos, Provo, Utah: Brigham Young University, 73-117.

_____, and Patrick J. Smith. 1990. "A Typology of City-Based International Involvement: the Case of Vancouver." In *Processus d'Internationalization des Villes.* Lyon, France: Groupe Nice, MRASH.

Cohn, Theodore H., and Patrick J. Smith. 1993. "Developing Global Cities in the Pacific Northwest: The Cases of Vancouver and

Seattle." Paper for the New International Cities Era Conference, Brigham Young University, Provo, Utah, October; proceedings publication forthcoming, Earl Fry, et al., eds.

Duchacek, Ivo D. 1986. *The Territorial Dimension of Politics: Within, Among, and Across* Nations. Boulder: Westview.

_____. 1987. "Toward a Typology of New Subnational Governmental Actors in International Relations." Institute of Governmental Studies Working Paper, University of California, Berkeley, 1987-2.

Federation of Canadian Municipalities (FCM). 1983. *Brief to the 1983 Royal Commission on the Economic Union and Development Prospects for Canada*. November.

_____. 1987. *China Open Cities Pamphlet*. Ottawa: FCM.

_____. 1988a. *Africa 2000: The Municipal Response*. Ottawa: FCM. May.

_____. 1988b. *A Practical Guide to Municipal Twinning*. Ottawa: FCM. May.

_____. 1988c. *Municipal Professional Exchange Project*. Ottawa: FCM. May.

_____. 1989. *Meeting the Challenge: Urban Development in the Third World*. Ottawa: FCM, International Program. June.

_____. n.d. *International Program Pamphlet*. Ottawa: FCM.

Fry, Earl H., Lee Radebaugh, and Panayotis Soldatos, eds. 1989. *The New International Cities Era: The Global Activities of North American Municipal Governments*. Provo, Utah: Brigham Young University.

Government of Canada (Treasury Board) and Government of British Columbia (Economic Development Ministry). n.d. *Opportunities for Pacific Canada: The Asia Pacific Initiative*. Pamphlet.

Hocking, Brian. 1986. "Regional Governments and International Affairs: Foreign Policy Problems or Deviant Behaviour?" *International Journal* 41: 477-506.

Jacobs, Jane. 1984. *Cities and the Wealth of Nations: Principles of Economic Life*. New York: Random House.

Johannson, P. Roff. 1978. "Provincial International Activities." *International Journal* 33: 357-78.

Jones, Victor. 1988. "Beavers and Cats: Federal-Local Relations in the United States and Canada." In *Meech Lake: From Centre to Periphery—The Impact of the 1987 Constitutional Accord on*

Canadian Settlements: A Speculation, ed. Hilda Symonds and H. Peter Oberlander, Vancouver: U.B.C. Centre for Human Settlements.

Keohane, Robert O., and Joseph S. Nye, Jr. 1976. "Introduction: The Complex Politics of Canadian-American Interdependence." In *Canada and the United States: Transnational and Transgovernmental Relations*, ed. Annette Baker Fox, Alfred O. Hero, Jr., and Joseph S. Nye, Jr., New York: Columbia University Press.

_____, and Joseph S. Nye. 1977. *Power and Interdependence: World Politics in Transition*. Boston: Little, Brown and Co.

Kincaid, John. 1989. "Rain Clouds Over Municipal Diplomacy: Dimensions and Possible Sources of Negative Public Opinion." In *The New International Cities Era: The Global Activities of North American Municipal Governments*, ed. Earl Fry, Lee Radebaugh, and Panayotis Soldatos, Provo, Utah: Brigham Young University, 223-49.

Manning, Bayless. 1977. "The Congress, the Executive, and Intermestic Affairs." *Foreign Affairs* 55: 306-24.

Nossal, Kim. 1989. *The Politics of Canadian Foreign Policy*, 2d edition, Scarborough, Ontario: Prentice-Hall.

Oberlander, H. Peter, and Patrick J. Smith. 1993. "Governing Metropolitan Vancouver: Regional Governance, Public Policy Making and Intergovernmental Relations in British Columbia." In *Metropolitan Governance: American/Canadian Intergovernmental Perspectives*, ed. Donald Rothblatt and Andrew Sancton, Berkeley, Calif. Institute of Governmental Studies Press.

Ohmae, Kenichi. 1990. *The Borderless World: Power and Strategy in the Interlinked World Economy*. New York: Harper Business.

Pal, Leslie. 1987. *Public Policy Analysis: An Introduction*. Toronto: Methuen.

Polanyi, Margaret. 1990. "Politicians Query Value of Twinning: Benefits of International Links Debated." *Globe and Mail*, Oct. 22, p. A6.

Seelig, Michael Y., and Alan F. J. Artibise. 1991. *From Desolation to Hope: The Pacific Fraser Region in 2010*. Vancouver: Vancouver Board of Trade.

Shulevitz, Judith. 1989. "Pollution: The Risks for Travellers." *The New York Times*, August 6: 29.

Simeon, Richard. 1972. *Federal-Provincial Diplomacy*. Toronto: University of Toronto Press.

_____. 1986. *The Political Economy of Canadian Federalism, 1940-84*. Vol. 71 of the Royal Commission on the Economic Union and Development Prospects for Canada. Toronto: University of Toronto Press.

Smiley, Donald. 1987. *The Federal Condition in Canada*. Toronto: McGraw-Hill Ryerson.

Smith, Patrick J. 1985. "Policy Conflicts Between Local and Senior Governments: Canadian, British and American Comparisons." Paper for the International Political Science Association, Paris. July.

_____. 1986. "Regional Governance in British Columbia." *Planning and Administration* 13 (2): 1-20.

_____. 1988. "Local-Federal Government Relations: Canadian Perspectives, American Comparisons." In *Meech Lake: From Centre to Periphery—The Impact of the 1987 Constitutional Accord on Canadian Settlements: A Speculation*, ed. Hilda Symonds and H. Peter Oberlander, Vancouver: U.B.C. Centre for Human Settlements.

_____. 1990. "Whiplash and Spirals: The Canadian Re-Confederation Talks: Constitutional Life After Meech." Paper for the American Political Science Association, San Francisco. August.

_____. 1992. "The Making of a Global City: The Case of Vancouver." *Canadian Journal of Urban Research*, Vol. 1, No. 1 (July): 93-112.

_____. 1993. "Policy Phases, Subnational Foreign Relations and Constituent Diplomacy in the United States and Canada: City, Provincial, and State Global Activity in British Columbia and Washington." In *Foreign Relations and Federal States*, ed. Brian Hocking, London: Leicester University Press, 211-35.

_____. 1994. "Beyond Lotusland and Fantasyland: Public Policy and Perceptions of Governance in British Columbia." In *Canadian Politics and Introduction to the Discipline*, ed. James P. Bickerton and Alain-G. Gognon, 2d ed., Peterborough, Ontario: Broadview.

_____. 1994. "Globalization and Fragmentation: Governance and the Changing Public Policy Agenda in Greater Vancouver." *Urban Policy and Research: An Australian Guide to Urban Affairs*, Vol. 11.

_____. 1994. "Labour Markets and Neo-Conservative Policy in British Columbia: 1986-1991." In *Continuities and Discontinuities: The Political Economy of Social Welfare and Labour Market Policy in Canada*, ed. A. F. Johnson, S. McBride, and P. J. Smith, Toronto: University of Toronto Press, 291-305.

_____, and Theodore H. Cohn. 1989a. "Municipal Diplomacy and City-Based Policy Making in Canada: Global Relations and British Columbia Municipalities." In B.C. Ministry of International Trade and Immigration Report, *Sister Cities in British Columbia*. Victoria, B.C.: Ministry of International Trade and Immigration.

_____. 1989b. "Strategic City Policy Making: Canadian Cases, Intermestic Perspectives." Paper for "Quelles Strategies Internationale Pour Les Villes?" Seminaire International par Triade France et L'Institut d'etude des villes internationales— Canada. Paris, France.

_____. 1990a. "Municipal and Provincial Paradiplomacy and Intermestic Relations: British Columbia Cases." Paper for the Canadian Political Science Association. Victoria. June.

_____. 1990b. "Municipal Diplomacy in British Columbia: Theory, Practice and Comparative Lessons." B.C. Ministry of International Business and Immigration. Second Sister City Symposium Report, Vancouver. September.

Soldatos, Panayotis. 1989. "Atlanta and Boston in the New International Cities Era: Does Age Matter?" In *The New International Cities Era: The Global Activities of North American Municipal Governments*, ed. Earl Fry, Lee Radebaugh, and Panayotis Soldatos, Provo, Utah: Brigham Young University, 37-72.

Sturrock, H. F. 1989. Presentation on "Saanich-Zomba, Malawi Exchange under Africa 2000 Project," to B.C. Sister Cities Symposium. Vancouver: B.C. Ministry of International Business and Immigration, SFU— Harbour Centre. October 21.

Swainson, Neil. 1983. "Provincial Municipal Relations." In *The Reins of Power: Governing British Columbia*, ed. T. Morley, N. Ruff, N. Swainson, J. Wilson, and W. Young, Vancouver: Douglas and McIntyre.

United Nations. 1987. *Global Strategy for Shelter to the Year 2000*. New York: UN.

Vancouver Sun.

APPENDIX

Main Characteristics of an International City

A. The city has a geographically international exposure.

B. It is receiving, from abroad, factors of production (e.g., foreign capital, foreign manpower, foreign services, etc.) and is engaged in various economic transactions (e.g., trade).

C. It is hosting foreign and/or international institutions and their representatives (e.g., foreign firms of MNCs, foreign banks, foreign consulates, foreign or binational—foreign-domestic— chambers of commerce, foreign trade or tourist offices, trade commissioners, etc.).

D. Its firms and other economic institutions are present abroad.

E. It has direct transportation links with foreign countries.

F. It is significantly engaged in social communications activities with foreign countries (tourism, mail, student exchanges, trade missions, etc.) and has a strong telecommunications network.

G. It has an outward-looking supporting services network (e.g., convention halls, exhibition halls, hotel facilities, office parks, research parks, etc.).

H. Its mass media have an international presence and/or audience abroad.

I. It hosts, regularly, major international events (e.g., exhibitions, festivals, sport events, etc.).

J. It is the locus of national, regional, or even local institutions with an international scope, reputation, or impact (international relations' clubs and associations, international divisions of local chambers of commerce, universities, research centers, museums, etc.).

K. Its public or private institutions have agreements of cooperation with foreign or international institutions (sister cities agreements, economic cooperation agreements, etc.).

L. Its local government (municipal, county, etc.) has the requisite administrative apparatus to conduct in a systematic manner a city paradiplomacy.

M. Its population make-up has an international composition.

Source: Soldatos 1989, 39.

Chapter 20

The Urban Economy and the Power of the Local State:
The Politics of Planning in Edmonton and Vancouver

Christopher Leo
The University of Winnipeg

The relationship between a city's economic power and the power of the local state is a subject much written about and yet inadequately understood. It seems beyond doubt that such a relationship exists, but its actual contours remain unclear. A substantial literature tells us that cities everywhere are becoming integrated into a network of producers, consumers, and service-providers whose possibilities and limitations are shaped by finance and markets that operate on a world scale, and that this integration has an impact on local decision making. Often, the literature invokes or implies a hierarchical metaphor: markets force cities to specialize almost as individuals do, it suggests, and stratifies them into

I am grateful to Warren Magnusson, John Marshall, Frances Frisken, and, Vitomar Ahtik for exceptionally challenging and useful critiques of an earlier draft of this chapter. I have not always done what they wanted me to do, and the shortcomings of the article remain my responsibility. Thanks also to Andrew Thompson, Barbara Burr, Eileen Sheridan, and Gabriela Sparling for their very helpful research assistance, to the Social Sciences and Humanities Research Council of Canada for financial support, and to the Institute of Urban Studies at the University of Winnipeg for seed money. Last but not least, my warm thanks to the numerous politicians, officials, academics, and business people—most of whom would prefer not to be named—who have taken the time to share with me their understanding of the politics of planning in Edmonton and Vancouver.

a hierarchy reminiscent of human society. The most favoured cities—the urban *crème de la crème*, as it were—concentrate on producer services, i.e., serve as corporate decision-making centres, while others labour in the sparser fields of industrial production, tourism, or housing for retired people, and still others languish in the "slums" of the urban hierarchy, where communities compete for the ignominy of hosting prisons or waste disposal facilities, lest they be consigned to the outer darkness of economic stagnation. In the words of Logan and Molotch (1987, 290), "Metropolitan areas . . . are driven . . . to make their deals for growth. Success or failure in these endeavours helps shape the status of place in the system—and helps determine how various indigenous subgroups will fare." An ongoing process of economic growth in some cities and decline in others has the effect of "developing a specialized space-economy that restructures industries at different times and communities with different degrees of severity" (Beauregard 1989, 228).[1] Economic growth and decline, it is alleged, forge a hierarchically patterned urban system.

---

[1]Beauregard 1989, 228. The title of the Beauregard volume, *Atop the Urban Hierarchy,* makes the hierarchy metaphor explicit, as do Logan and Molotch in a passage in which they recommend a political programme of forcing firms to move "down the place hierarchy . . . " (295) from more powerful cities to others less powerful. Smith and Feagin (1989) refer to multinational corporations as creating "an integrated, worldwide network of production, exchange, finance and corporate services arranged in a complex hierarchical system of cities." Many other writers seem to assume the existence of an urban hierarchy, even when they do not refer to it explicitly. For example, the widely discussed idea of "uneven development," a staple of the Marxist literature in geography and sociology, points to the existence of economic distinctions that raise and lower the status of cities in relation to each other and thus seems to define a hierarchy. Smith (1984) offers a systematic attempt to come to terms with this concept. The notion of hierarchy is also implicit in writing about the competitive struggle among urban centres for economic development (Cox and Mair 1988, 315-20; Logan and Molotch 1987, 34-35, 52, 57-62; Peterson 1981, 27-29) and is well understood by commentators oriented to economics and policymaking. Noyelle and Stanback, for example, offer an elaborate scheme for the classification of cities, also without making the concept of hierarchy explicit, but clearly showing that cities occupy advantageous or disadvantageous positions in relation to each other (Stanback and Noyelle 1982; Noyelle and Stanback 1984). Hanson, seeking to draw out the policy implications of this scheme, develops a typology in which cities are classified into two tiers, referred to as "command and control centres" and "subordinate centres" (Hanson 1983).

Anyone who has observed the decline of some cities and the rise of others, especially in the United States and Britain but elsewhere as well, will see the truth in these characterizations. They give us a clear picture of rusting industrial areas and the social dislocation and personal misery they cause, of burgeoning high-tech industries contracting for labour around the world, of factories relocating to small towns, and of "urban villages" springing up at the peripheries of metropolitan areas, while the city centre decays. Certain stereotypical cases stand out in sharp relief: Los Angeles, the ultimate urban village complex; Duluth, the quint-essential victim; Boston, the rust-belt centre that came back; and in Britain, the stagnant north, the booming south. The political implication is clear: An overarching system of economic power strongly influences or perhaps even determines the political power that is capable of being wielded by, and in, individual communities over a wide range of social and economic issues.

But what is the significance of these generalizations for individual cities? It is one thing to recognize a large picture painted in broad brush strokes, quite another to imagine what we will see if we magnify one part of it. Knowing what is going on globally and how it affects stereotypical cases is not at all the same as understanding the effect upon individual communities. Most communities do not fit neat hierarchical pigeonholes: they are neither industrial slums nor centres of high technology or producer services. Their situation is less clear-cut, their prospects more mixed. Even the stereotypical cases differ from each other in ways that cannot be read directly from an understanding of the global situation. There is a need to develop a much more concrete understanding than we now have of how cities are affected politically by their economic situation—to cultivate an eye for local variation while maintaining a sensitivity to the global and economic contexts.

This need is only one specific case of a more general shortcoming in the urban literature, and one that is attracting increasing attention. In fact, there are at least two urban literatures, both lively and productive but still largely isolated from each other. One yields insight into the rich variety of local politics while another examines the global context, or the economic context, within which individual states can be seen to be working out the fates of the cities governed by them. As each of the two literatures becomes more sophisticated in its own sphere, the limitations of that sphere become more obvious. Writers oriented to political economy and to global structural change have been insightful in charting the impact of the global economy upon local communities, but suffer from a recurrent tendency to treat the communities themselves as interchangeable units. By the same token, those oriented to the diversity of local politics tend to lose sight of overarching economic forces.

Peter Saunders offers a particularly telling instance of limitations of the global orientation precisely because he is more attuned to local variation than most such writers and yet tends to lose sight of local nuance. In *Urban Politics: A Sociological Interpretation* (1983), for example, he is alive to the economic differences among cities caused by the global forces of uneven development but apparently does not see them as having any implications for the political autonomy of cities. "Both France and Italy," he notes, "are characterized by a stark division between highly industrialized areas and underdeveloped areas of peasant agriculture. Britain, too, . . . has its 'regional problem' . . . here the imbalance is between the new industrial sectors located in areas like the Midlands and the southeast, and declining industrial areas in the northeast . . . " (132-33). But in summarizing the current sociological understanding of city autonomy, a little more than 50 pages farther along (189-97) he treats the local state as a single entity, offering little or no hint that different local states might find themselves in different situations. The local state, he argues, faces a variety of constraints on its exercise of autonomy, including ecological, political, and economic ones. But from a reading of the section one might well conclude that these constraints are the same for all local states. Any suggestion that states in different economic circumstances might face different constraints is absent from the discussion. National economies are characterized by stark divergencies, but the local state is just a local state.

What is missing from Saunders' discussion, and is hard to find elsewhere in the urban literature, is a plausible connection between the admirable body of broad-brush urban theory and the concrete realities of actual communities. Other commentators have noted this shortcoming. For example, Clarke and Kirby (1990, 394) complain—a bit hyperbolically perhaps—of

> deductive views of capitalist development and the nation-state [that] presume that in most important respects impacts [of world economic change] are similar across communities and, consequently, attention is shifted away from localities toward analysis of "the unfolding logic of capital accumulation processes." This diversion is compounded by theoretical frameworks that portray the state and the local state solely as arenas for the struggle between capital and labour rather than as a set of entities with

distinctive and important characteristics that influence political outcomes.

Clarence Stone tries to address that shortcoming but falls into the opposite trap of stressing local variety over theoretical uniformity. His account is particularly significant for the same reason Saunders' was: just as Saunders stands out among commentators taking a global perspective as being more than usually concerned with local variation, so Stone is more concerned than many students of local variation with identifying the impact of economic power on politics. And yet in *The Politics of Urban Development* (Stone and Sanders 1987, 5) he seems almost reluctant to acknowledge the existence of overarching economic forces and their impact on local politics and inclined to minimize their importance. In his words:

> ". . . as we look at a variety of cities . . . we can expect certain continuities. Those who control investment capital are bound to be important actors, along with those who control public authority. These two sets of actors must reach an accommodation. We can also expect differences—variations in how that accommodation is reached.

The problem with that formulation is that it all but loses sight of supra-local economic forces in the clutter of local variety. In the place of capital operating on a world scale to reshape urban space we are shown a babble of local business people, interest groups, politicians, and public servants negotiating and jockeying for position—a political life that seems bereft of any economic logic beyond the constellation of local powers. In reality, it seems likely that both accounts are exaggerated. In all probability, capital does not reshape urban space with quite the facility and uniformity that is suggested in some accounts, nor are local outcomes quite as contingent as others would have us believe. But that is speculation. What is needed either to confirm it or to prove it wrong is more investigation of local politics from a perspective attuned to global political economy. The present study is a contribution to that effort.[2]

---

[2]Among other writers who seek, as I do in the present article, to derive insight from a juxtaposition of the global economy with local politics are Feagin (1988), whose study of Houston reveals the interplay between the local ruling group and the oil industry; Smith and Feagin (1989), who seek to unearth the local ramifications of economic restructuring; Horan (1991) who poses the problem of local political response to global forces, offers a framework for addressing it, and undertakes a survey of relevant American literature; and

TWO CASES

We pursue our subject by means of a comparative case study of two local states,[3] similar in many ways and pursuing a similar objective, but distinguished by clearly identifiable economic differences. The local states are those of Edmonton and Vancouver, and the objective they were both pursuing was that of establishing a system of control over the character of downtown development. Although the initial objectives were the same, the results were completely different, for reasons that—as the evidence makes clear—were related to the differing economic circumstances of the two states. We will examine the evidence,[4] reach the conclusions it allows us, and explore the further implications of the conclusions.

My central contention, based on a comparison of development controls in Vancouver with those in Edmonton and of the processes that produced them, is that different degrees of economic power imply not only a difference in bargaining power in dealing with particular developers but also different conditions for the development of a planning system, hence different planning systems. The evidence suggests that these differences, in turn, are related to different citizen perceptions and demands—a different political culture. In short, a different degree of economic power is associated in Vancouver and Edmonton with the existence of two substantially different local states.

The data make a second important point, however: The relationship between the global economy and local politics is complex. Although a

---

Pickvance and Preteceille (1991), whose six-country comparison of the effects of state restructuring on local power proceeds with a sharp eye on changes in the global economy, while at the same time being attuned to local variation. The variations the Pickvance/Preteceille study looks for however, are found more at the national than the local level.

[3]"Local state," is used in different ways by different writers. Compare, for example, Gurr and King 1987, 49-55 and Magnusson 1985a, 121-25, 1985b, 577-81. As it is used in these pages, the term is largely synonymous with "local government," in that it refers to locally elected and locally appointed bodies that take decisions on public matters and exercise control. The reason for preferring "state" to "government" is that, in both the Marxist and non-Marxist literature using the term, governance is conceived of as part of a nexus of interrelated social and economic forces and not just as a decision-taking machinery responsive to public opinion. That is how it is conceived in this article as well.

[4]Drawn from government documents and interviews with officials, politicians and representatives of the development industry, as well as secondary sources.

city's economic situation clearly sets limits upon the local state's freedom of action, those limits leave substantial space for community action and for the forging of unique community identities through political action. In the cases examined in these pages, local politics has played an active role in shaping the impact of capital on the two localities. In the final analysis, these cases suggest that the impact of global economic forces upon the locality is contingent not only on the configuration of those forces but also on the character of the local political response to them.

Vancouver and Edmonton:
The Global Context of Local Politics

The global economic context for a comparison of politics in the two cities is readily grasped: Vancouver is located "above" Edmonton in the "hierarchy" of Canadian cities. Even the most avid Edmonton booster would readily concede that. Edmonton is a modestly prosperous provincial capital while Vancouver is the major urban centre in western Canada. In the area of downtown development, the main focus of this study, the differences are especially pronounced. Vancouver city planners are besieged by development proposals for the downtown area while the city centre of Edmonton, referred to as Deadmonton by detractors, is struggling with decline. At this writing (1991), it has yet to recover from the damage to the downtown retail trade inflicted by the development in the early 1980s of the colossal, suburban West Edmonton Mall, and vacant store fronts and offices are a recurring embarrassment to Edmonton boosters.

What is the significance of these economic differences? If we draw on the literature about global economic change and its impact on cities, we can readily construct an answer to that question. The answer runs as follows: both Vancouver's and Edmonton's downtown core are afflicted by the decentralizing forces characteristic of North American suburban development—the suburbanization of industry, housing, and routine administration (Scott 1988; Kantor 1987). At the same time, however, corporate headquarters have become more concentrated in a smaller number of major urban centres, centres that are deemed by corporate decision makers to be attractive locations, capable of sustaining the urban "lifestyle" of the affluent professionals—the lawyers, accountants, and financial advisers—upon whose services corporate headquarters rely (Noyelle and Stanback 1984; Knight and Gappert 1989). Vancouver is capable of attracting more corporate headquarters and of sustaining more of the kind of "sophisticated" retail trade that tends to gravitate to city centres rather than suburbs. Perhaps the single most telling statistic to sum up the comparative economic positions of the two cities comes from the listing in *Canadian Business* of Canada's 500 top corporations. According to data culled from that list, the head offices of 38 of the top corporations are in metropolitan Vancouver, while only seven are located in Edmonton (*Canadian Business*, June 1989).[5] Judged by that statistic, Vancouver is a modestly attractive location for major corporate headquarters while Edmonton is a backwater. That is the global economic context within which the two cities are located. What is the local political significance of that context? We turn to our comparative case study of the politics of planning for an answer.

Edmonton

The envelope system incorporated into the downtown area redevelopment plan in 1981 was inspired by the kinds of city planning ideas popularized by Jane Jacobs (1959) and William H. Whyte (1988), both of whom advocate the use of urban design to achieve environments that invite people to make use of the streets in order to keep them lively, attractive, and safe. According to these ideas, attractive street environments are ones that benefit from sunlight and offer wind protection—especially protection from the accelerated winds that high rise towers funnel to the street surface; that are not overwhelmed by the blank walls and impersonal-looking show windows often found at the street level of office towers; that are roomy enough to accommodate pedestrian traffic in comfort; and that provide spaces where people are able to interact informally. In pursuit of these objectives, the plan bylaw (Edmonton, City of, 1981) provided for 10 building envelopes, each setting design parameters for buildings in specified areas of the central city. The envelopes specified such things as relationship of building lines to property lines, width of sidewalks, height and dimensions of canopies and arcades, depth of front yards, and angling of building silhouettes to allow for sky exposure. Character area regulations specified which

---

[5]The top 500 rankings are based on sales, net income, and total assets. A comparable use of similar data can be found in Friedland 1983 where the locations of the largest 1,000 industrial corporations as listed in *Fortune* magazine are used as the basis for a wide-ranging categorization of American cities.

building envelope or envelopes applied to each part of the central city. The purpose of the envelopes was to ensure the maintenance of view lines, sky exposure, and wind protection and to provide for the suitability of buildings to the character of areas in which they were located (91-100). Also integrated into the Envelope System was the concept of Mixed Use Areas, in which density bonuses and other concessions would be made available to developers in return for their including residential units in their developments.

The envelope system was evolved in the late 1970s and early 1980s, when Edmonton's economy was buoyant. It was part of a wider downtown planning process that called for street improvements and the development of more attractive public space. The city planning department played an activist role, publicly making the case for the various components of the downtown plan even when it was not yet clear how much support the plans would win on council, in the business community, and among the public. The department carried out and commissioned numerous planning studies—dealing with such matters as parks, open spaces, and pedestrian malls, wind conditions on downtown streets, and pedestrian circulation, as well as economic evaluations, tests of the envelope system, and evaluations of the reactions of business people.[6]

This flurry of activity climaxed in a series of public hearings, meetings, and communications by letter with representatives of a wide range of local groups, including Building Owners and Managers Association of Edmonton, landowners from affected areas of the central city, developers' associations, the Edmonton Chamber of Commerce, the Alberta Association of Architects, the provincial government, heritage preservation and environmental protection groups, the Edmonton Social Planning Council, and a municipal reform organization, the Urban Reform Group of Edmonton. The wide range of participation enabled the planners to demonstrate that allegations of too much state intervention by one group were often balanced by assertions by another that the degree of regulation was insufficient. At the same time, considerable pains were taken to meet as many objections as possible by making modifications. Special care was taken to introduce modifications to ensure the economic viability of the plan. Throughout, the plan was presented on the one hand as an initiative to improve the attractiveness of the central city and on the

---

[6]For a sampling of these studies, see the 1979-81 publications listed under Edmonton, Planning and Building Department in references.

other as an economic development initiative.[7] In the end, council was persuaded to pass the area redevelopment plan bylaw, and with it the envelope system.

Thus, while the bylaw sought to impose standards of development, pains had been taken to avoid a regime of regulation that would unduly discourage developers. Building envelopes did not dictate designs; rather, they were intended to set parameters within which design would take place. Visually, the envelope, as set out in the plan bylaw, took the form of a partial building silhouette and a top-view schematic of the sidewalk (see Figures 20.1 and 20.2). But these outlines did not mandate a particular shape for the building. "The Building Envelopes define the maximum volume of space within which buildings may be designed, and do not dictate the final form of the building." Additional flexibility was allowed for in the following provision: " . . . the Development Officer [a planning official], may, at his discretion, approve developments which do not comply with the provisions of the specified Building Envelopes . . . " (90). Thus, if an architect could make the case that a design not in conformity with the envelope nevertheless met the objectives of the bylaw, then an exemption was readily obtainable.

Business Reaction

To anyone who has remarked unfavourably on the street environment created by a canyon of office towers, the bylaw would hardly appear as an onerous statist imposition. But in the early 1980s it did begin to appear so to many in Edmonton's business community. As we saw, the regulations in the bylaw had been formulated with participation from the business community. But that was in 1981 in the final days of a business boom. When the boom ended not long afterward and downtown development stalled, business people began to perceive matters differently. In 1983 Mayor Cecil J. Purves appointed a Task Force on the Heart of the City, chaired by Joe Shoctor, a prominent local business person. In its report, published in August 1984, the task force, noting that "Edmonton's economic situation has reversed," recommended that the

---

[7]The public participation programme, or communication programme as it was dubbed, is summarized in Edmonton, Planning and Building Department 1981c.

Figure 20.1. *Building Envelope E*

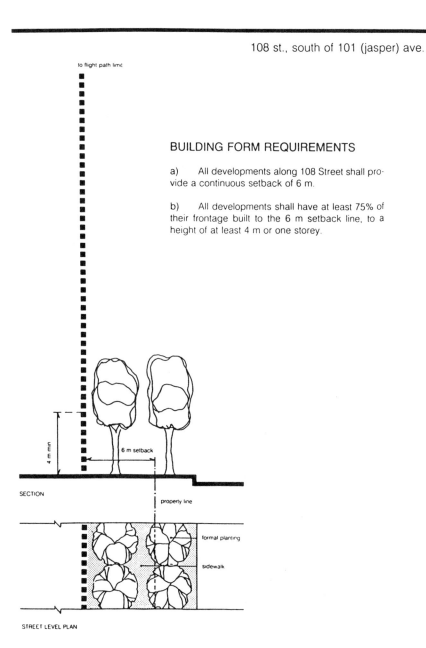

108 st., south of 101 (jasper) ave.

to flight path limit

BUILDING FORM REQUIREMENTS

a)   All developments along 108 Street shall provide a continuous setback of 6 m.

b)   All developments shall have at least 75% of their frontage built to the 6 m setback line, to a height of at least 4 m or one storey.

4 m min

6 m setback

SECTION

property line

formal planting

sidewalk

STREET LEVEL PLAN

Source: Edmonton 1981, Section 20.

Figure 20.2.   ***Building Envelop D***

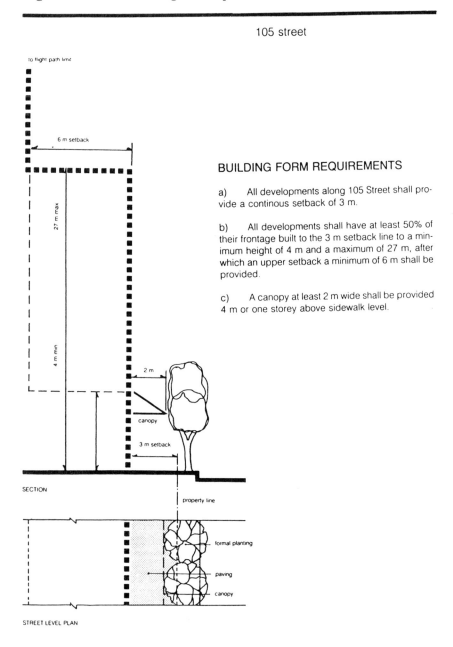

105 street

to flight path limit

6 m setback

27 m max

4 m min

2 m

canopy

3 m setback

SECTION

property line

formal planting

paving

canopy

STREET LEVEL PLAN

BUILDING FORM REQUIREMENTS

a)   All developments along 105 Street shall provide a continous setback of 3 m.

b)   All developments shall have at least 50% of their frontage built to the 3 m setback line to a minimum height of 4 m and a maximum of 27 m, after which an upper setback a minimum of 6 m shall be provided.

c)   A canopy at least 2 m wide shall be provided 4 m or one storey above sidewalk level.

Source: Edmonton 1981, Section 20.

city's planning department and the business community join forces in "a joint review of the Downtown Area Redevelopment Plan Bylaw to evaluate its effectiveness and to prepare revisions if necessary" (Edmonton, Mayor's Task Force 1984, 24). The perception that Edmonton needed a quicker, easier development approvals process to attract interest in the central city was widespread. For example, an official of the Edmonton Downtown Development Corporation, which was created at the behest of Shoctor's task force, noted in a 1987 interview that planners would have preferred a more controlled development process, but added that such a process takes time, while for Edmonton speed was of the essence.[8] Business people and politicians alike were urgent in their calls for action. "Our biggest task," Alderman Lyall Roper was quoted as saying, "is to make the downtown atmosphere attractive enough so that the businessman, the entrepreneur, the large and small developers will want to come back downtown. . . . " Shoctor raised the spectre of interurban competition, maintaining that Edmonton had, in the past, lost development to Calgary because of delays (*Edmonton Journal*, September 24, 1984).[9] That sentiment reflects trepidation, which is widely shared in Edmonton, about Calgary's more buoyant economy.

These ideas were rapidly translated into action. Already in early 1984, a joint committee of the City Centre Association, a business group, and the city planning department was formed to review the Downtown Area Redevelopment Plan bylaw. The committee found "universal objection to the built form requirements [i.e., the envelope system]" and concluded that "The changing economic situation in the city has forced the re-evaluation of other plan policies" (Edmonton, Planning and Building Department, n.d.). Clearly, the economic downturn had evoked a panic reaction in the business community. In November the City Centre Association, in a letter to recently elected mayor Laurence Decore, suggested repeal of the building envelope regulations. The business group obviously expected a serious hearing and quick action because it added, "We would hope that the Planning Department would be able to present [the bylaw revision] to Council by January 1, 1985 [a little more than a

---

[8]Interview, May 4, 1987.

[9]Shoctor was quoted as saying, "We have an awful lot to answer for. We're the city that wrangled so long over the Husky Tower project that Husky said 'Forget it' and took its tower to Calgary."

month later]."[10] The letter included "a list of those individuals who had input into the above." Of 23 names on the list, at least 18 were from the business community, including four people involved in land development, and representatives of six retail businesses, three major banks, two hotels and an insurance company. Three representatives of the city were also on the list.

A year later, revisions of the Downtown Area Redevelopment Plan Bylaw were complete, and Bylaw #6477 (Edmonton, City of, 1985) was passed, with a variety of changes. A careful comparison of this bylaw with the 1981 plan bylaw shows that the system of design control had been gutted. To be sure, one or two of the changes could be defended as having been based on other considerations. For example, the deletion of ¶18.2.1 in the old bylaw eliminates a requirement that "high-rise buildings be designed as a podium-plus-tower composition, or as a variation thereof." It could be argued that this change removes some rigidity from the regulations, leaving more room for architectural creativity, though it is more plausible to see it as giving developers a free hand to build towers straight up from the sidewalk, thus overwhelming pedestrians even more than a tower with a podium would. Another change, which might actually be seen as a strengthening of design controls if it were read uncritically and without considering the rest of the bylaw, was a provision calling for compatibility of a new development with neighbouring buildings. In this provision ¶18.2.1 of the new version of the bylaw, the design of a new building must "complement" neigh-bouring buildings, whereas the earlier version of that requirement only referred to the podium portion of the building. Less significantly, the 1985 version of the bylaw adds to the overall plan objectives a new provision, ¶3.1.6, not present in the 1981 version, namely to "Encourage the re-use and renovation of existing buildings in the Downtown by providing for variances to parking, loading and amenity area requirements of the Land Use Bylaw." The preservation of heritage buildings is likely to work in the best interests of design control. However, a close examination shows that changes in the provisions in the "Heritage Conservation" subsection, which sets out the detailed regulations, are limited in ¶16.2.2.4 to relaxation of the requirements developers must meet in the case of older buildings (Edmonton, City of, 1981, 64-72;

---

[10]City Centre Association to His Worship Mayor Laurence Decore, November 26, 1984.

1985, 46-50). Undoubtedly there is a case to be made for such changes, but they are being made at the expense of design controls.

In any case, the overall thrust of the changes in the bylaw is unambiguously in the direction of freedom for developers at the expense of protection for the streetscape. The building envelopes are deleted and replaced by much more limited, and more cosmetic, canopy and arcade requirements (Edmonton, City of, 1981, 80; 1985, 65). A change to ¶18.2.2 eliminates a guideline calling for the creation of "a streetscape at a human scale within which the pedestrian can feel comfortable." The deletion of ¶18.2.5 eliminates a policy calling for "the high-rise or tower portion of a building [to] be designed in scale model form not only for purposes of micro-climate testing but to easily evaluate the relationship of its form and materials to those of other towers on the skyline." The deletion of ¶18.2.8 removes wording designed to assure that the upper or tower portion of a high-rise be set back from the building line "in order that the podium will be able to deflect winds from the sidewalk, and to allow more sunlight to reach the street." In short, the changes limit the ability of the city of Edmonton to control wind velocities at street level, to ensure that sunlight can reach the street, and to require street-level design on a human scale.

The planners' own explanation of the changes makes it explicit that the abolition of envelopes drastically limits development control:

With the deletion of the built form requirements, the Land Use Bylaw will only contain the floor area ratio's [sic], uses, parking and loading and amenity area requirements. [Deletion of the envelopes] will put a greater onus on the developer and the City to ensure that the Plan objectives of improved street amenities and good design result. *The development officer's ability to influence urban design will be greatly reduced.* Providing the developer meets the requirements of the Land Use Bylaw, *the Development Officer would be required to issue a development permit even if urban design factors are not considered. . . . The responsibility for good design in the Downtown will fall on the private sector* (Edmonton: Planning and Building Department, n.d. italics added).

Changing Development Strategy

Having been compelled to abandon the envelope system, the planners found themselves grasping at the straws of volunteerism and public pressure. In an internal document dated December 19, 1984, a member of the planning department, seeking a means of responding to the loss of control, recommended that

> the Planning Department . . . prepare design guidelines. These guidelines would be voluntary and could only be implemented with the support of the developer. The planning department will also work with the City Centre Association to investigate the establishment of a volunteer design panel. . . . [A] development permit cannot be denied on the advice of the design panel,

the planner acknowledged, but he added: "It is hoped that this panel could provide public pressure. . . . " In the absence of political will on the part of elected representatives, planners were left with nothing to fall back on but the hope that the public itself would act in council's stead. That hope was in vain. The design panel, which was not established until the end of 1986, consists of representatives of the development industry and such development professionals as architects or engineers. A planning official involved with the panel observed that the group's influence depends very much on timing. It meets four times a year and, if a major project gets underway between meetings, "it won't be held up waiting for their next meeting."[11] The panel is strictly advisory, and its role is persuasive rather than regulatory. Its mandate is to encourage good design, not in any sense to require it.

Business Dominance

In the meantime, the abandonment of the envelope system marked the beginning of an era of more aggressive business leadership in the supervision of downtown development. It soon became obvious that the change in planning regulations was much more than simply a decision about planning; it signalled a major change in the character of the local state.

The downtown area was designated a Business Revitalization Zone (BRZ), an arrangement whereby businesses in the area are subjected to a municipally administered tax that is turned over to a private sector organization that may spend the money on promotion and local improvement. In explaining the reasons for the change, John Hickey, executive director of the City Centre Association, told a journalist, "It is clear that

---

[11]Interview on June 6, 1990.

the strong, 'hands on' direction required to help revitalize downtown and provide the critical liaison between civic government and the private sector can only be achieved by complete participation of all downtown businesses" (*Edmonton Journal*, September 9, 1983). With the establishment of the BRZ, the City Centre Association was replaced by the Downtown Business Association of Edmonton, formed in 1986 to administer BRZ revenues, grants from the provincial and city governments, corporate donations, and parking revenues (Downtown Business Association of Edmonton 1986). Thus as the role of the local state in downtown development weakened, leaders of the business community were able to constitute themselves as a private quasi-state agency, which filled the power vacuum with control of a very different character.

The Downtown Business Association was not the only quasi-state agency created to facilitate private-sector leadership in the development of the city centre. The mayor's Task Force on the Heart of the City, which as we noted above was in the forefront of demands for the deletion of the envelope system, also proposed the establishment of a "'for profit corporation' that would initiate and participate in development projects (by itself or in joint ventures with others) in the downtown area . . . " (Edmonton, Mayor's Task Force 1984, 48). The corporation, to be named the Edmonton Downtown Development Corporation (DDC), was to be jointly funded by the city and by privately purchased shares. Armin Preiksaitis, a former planner, was appointed president of the corporation. By his own account,[12] Preiksaitis, in the process of deciding how the DDC should be structured, considered examples from across the country—most of which were some form of crown corporation—but decided to opt for the U.S. model of business leadership, as practised in Denver, Minneapolis, and Milwaukee. Shares were priced at $5,000 per year, and prospective shareholders were asked to make a three-year commitment.

To facilitate the search for members, the Westin Hotel sponsored a series of luncheons for local business people, who garnered pledges. Later, it was decided to try to sell Toronto head offices of major corporations on membership. Molson's breweries sponsored another luncheon, and Toronto business people were urged, on the one hand, to put something back into the community from which they drew profits and, on the other, to consider that they, as landowners, had a strong

---

[12] Interview, May 4, 1987.

interest in a vibrant downtown. They were also reminded that a contribution gave them a chance to get involved in decision making. Preiksaitis noted that, unlike Minneapolis and Denver, where major corporations had also been persuaded to make a commitment to local development corporations, Edmonton is largely devoid of head offices. It was no mean feat, he felt, to get national headquarters to make a commitment of this magnitude to a branch plant city.

The selling job included assurances that local government would maintain a low profile. According to a newspaper account, Alderman Lyall Roper, returning from a Toronto meeting with major corporate executives, reported, "At the outset, they were cautious about the idea. They had concerns about the corporation being completely dominated by government." The fact that the majority of the board would come from the private sector allayed their fears, he added (*Edmonton Journal,* March 3, 1985).   When the recruitment was complete, the DDC board of directors had 40 founding members, 33 representing business concerns, including, among national corporations, Eaton's, Sun Life Assurance Company, Trizec Equities, Imperial Oil, Campeau Corporation, and Marathon Realty (Edmonton Downtown Development Corporation, n.d.). A 1988 DDC document also lists the Toronto Dominion Bank, the Bank of Nova Scotia, Olympia and York, the Royal Bank, the Bank of Montreal, the Canadian Imperial Bank of Commerce, and the Manufacturers Life Insurance Company among the corporation's members (Edmonton Downtown Development Corporation 1988).

As business dominance of downtown development intensified, business leaders also became more overtly involved in political affairs. In late 1985, a newspaper account referred to a plan, originating with principals of the City Centre Association, the DDC, and the chamber of commerce, to run candidates against city councillors "who oppose the mayor" and a "'hit list' ... drawn up by Chamber of Commerce members aimed at getting 'negative' councillors off council" (*Edmonton Journal,* December 22, 1985).   Whether or not one takes that report seriously, it was clear from city council's assent to the gutting of design controls and to the establishment of the DDC and the BRZ that an enhanced business role in the control of development was gaining widening acceptance, not only in the business community but also in the local state. The abandonment of the envelope system was part of a wider pattern of weakening the state and strengthening the business community in hope of attracting investment to the central city.

Evaluation

There are at least three lines of defence that can be invoked in support of the abandonment of the envelope system and the private sector-dominant development strategy that went with it. The most obvious, but also least plausible, is to argue that the unregulated market is the best arbiter of urban design and that interference, whether from the state or from the public, is only likely to make things worse. In moments of extreme subjectivity, business people and others have been known to argue along these lines, but in fact few people are so enamoured of the ordinary run of modern (or postmodern) architecture and design as to hold seriously to such an argument. In any case, the unregulated market is at best a distant ideal for Edmonton. Both the DDC and the Downtown Business Association are subsidized by the state, and the development strategy that was pursued under their auspices involved heavy concessions to individual developers—in effect, state inverventions in the market to stimulate private investment—concessions that were still coming back to haunt city council at this writing.[13]

A second line of argument, which sounds more plausible at first blush, is that the envelope system introduces an undesirable element of bureaucratic rigidity that hampers both the development process and the creativity of architects. As an official in Mayor Decore's office argued,[14] the regulatory approach to development is what made Edmonton into "a downtown full of flash cubes"—a phrase often invoked in discussions about Edmonton's downtown. Any amount of nonsense can be perpetrated while complying with regulations, she argued. Under the business-dominant system, business people talk to each other, propose innovative ideas, and work with counter-suggestions. Substantive, as opposed to apparent, coordination of different points of view and different approaches is better under the new system than it was before.

Beguiling as it sounds, that argument too is difficult to credit. In the first place, the envelope system was neither intended to be, nor did it work out as, a set of rigid regulations. It was intended simply as a means of setting some minimum standards for such things as availability of sunlight, wind protection, and pedestrian comfort and amenity. Exceptions to the rules were provided for wherever a plausible case could be

---

[13]The concessions issue are dealt with in Leo 1993.
[14]Interview on May 6, 1987.

made that a different approach would work better.[15] Indeed, it could as readily be argued that the "downtown full of flash cubes" was a result of too little rather than too much regulation. Certainly the development community cannot claim to have had no part in bringing it about and seems poorly placed now to offer itself as Edmonton's saviour from a flash cube-infested future. In any event, Edmonton has not substituted a more flexible or less bureaucratic regulatory regime for a rigid one. That, as we will see, is what happened in Vancouver. The envelope system was not replaced by anything else. It was simply abandoned, and the idea that Edmonton as a community has the right to exercise control—bureaucratic or otherwise—over the appearance of streets and the design of buildings in the central city was abandoned with it.

In the final analysis, there is only one real reason for Edmonton's changed development strategy: the perception that the city's economic position mandates business dominance, for better or worse. To an outside observer—on admittedly impressionistic evidence—one of the most pervasive features of the local political culture is a contradictory mixture of love for Edmonton, ambition to make it "great" in some ill-specified sense, and nagging inferiority over its relatively slow growth. This psychology provides a fertile ground for the promises and threats of developers, and some of them have become practised in the art of gaining public compliance for unpopular developments by a deft combination of promises of investment, threats to go elsewhere, and high estimates of the cost of alternative proposals.[16] Indeed, the threats may not always be idle, and it may be true that Edmonton would grow more slowly, or on a different scale, or in a different way, if it placed less emphasis on a speedy, compliant development process. What is clear is that Edmonton's place in the interurban system of economic differentiation is far more than just a set of statistics. It is a major influence in shaping its style of governance, its political culture, and the actual content of local state regulations.

---

[15]In practise many exceptions were made and some of those exceptions went on to become the most widely detested developments. Examples are the Bank of Montreal and the Eaton Centre (Leo 1993).

[16]For example, reluctant public acceptance of demolition of the Tegler Building was secured by release of a much-disputed estimate of the cost of preserving it. In other cases, numerous concessions, on both monetary and design issues, have been secured by implied or open threats to withhold investment.

Vancouver

The reader will recall that one of the purposes of this chapter is to cast a jaundiced eye upon broad theoretical generalizations about cities and local states that tend to reduce them to an unwarranted uniformity. The story of Edmonton seems to confirm one of those generalizations, perhaps most pithily expressed by Logan and Molotch in the words, "Cities, regions and states do not compete to please people; they compete to please capital . . ." (1987, 42). In a discussion of British urban planning, Kirk expressed a similar conclusion: " . . . though it is ostensibly concerned to control commercial development, land-use planning in Britain can only do this to a limited extent, and in general terms supports the interests of big business and landowners" (1980, 181). And summarizing an article that documents the power of large corporations to shape cities as they will, Rimmer (1988, 417) says:

Keen for the economic benefits and political spin-offs, the [Australian] states . . . are prepared to override the usual planning role performed by local government of directing development into preferred locations to meet economic, social and spatial preconditions. Job creation is paramount. Hence, the prime aim of the states has been to get super-projects started at almost any social cost. . . .

All that sounds just like Edmonton and to some degree is undoubtedly true everywhere, but it is not the whole story, certainly not in Vancouver. Vancouver's case opens the door to a more nuanced view of the relationship between the state and capital than that put forward by Kirk and the others, because in comparing it with that of Edmonton, we find that corporate power stands in a very different relationship to the two local states.

From Envelopes to Discretionary Zoning

Vancouver started with an envelope system similar to the one Edmonton decided to abandon, but instead of a weakening of control over development, the objective in Vancouver was a substantial strengthening, combined with greater flexibility. Attitudes toward development were influenced by a strong public attachment to the city's spectacular natural setting, with the ocean or ocean inlets never far away and mountain vistas in the background. In the 1960s there was a building boom, and towers began to sprout in front of the water and the mountains.

For the first time, the people of Vancouver felt the impact of the built environment on the natural setting. The special views to the mountains and water which they once took for granted began to disappear. New developments started to overshadow the waterfront and hinder public access. Many new developments also blocked off valuable sunlight to public streets and open spaces, and in return, provided windswept plazas on the street (*Quarterly Review* 1984).[17]

High-rise apartment development was already dominant in the city's West End and was spreading. In the words of a planning document, "The only alternative form of higher density housing being built was the repetitive three storey frame apartment. In the downtown underground shopping malls and 'black towers' appeared." There were growing fears that Vancouver would be overwhelmed and cut off from the mountains and the ocean by ranks of pedestrian high-rise buildings and cloned shopping malls (See Figure 20.3). The 1972 election of city councillors belonging to The Electors' Action Movement (TEAM), a reform party oriented to the idea of a "livable" city, signalled the growth of public pressure for greater control over development. When TEAM replaced the conservative Non-Partisan Association (NPA), it became obvious that a sea change was in the offing. Officials, pondering the existing control system, sought a way of modifying it to meet the growing public pressure without creating a crisis of disaffection among developers and architects. The answer they found was a system of flexible controls, called design guidelines, based on firmly established principles that could be implemented in various ways, depending on the outcome of negotiations involving developers, citizens, and the local state. "The objective of the new zoning can be summed up in the word 'neighbourliness.' Sunlight preservation, view protection, privacy, topographic adaptation, tree preservation, social and recreational amenities, safe parking garages—all these things are deemed to be part of this neighbourliness."[18] Flexibility and neighbourliness necessarily involve bureaucratic discretion in the interpretation of guidelines and entail sometimes protracted negotiations

---

[17]*Quarterly Review* is a publication of the Vancouver Planning Department.

[18]Both quotations in this paragraph are from Vancouver, Planning Department 1981 (unpaginated), Introduction.

Figure 20.3.

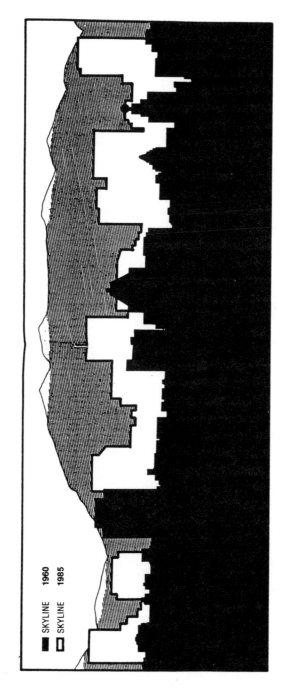

Source: Quarterly Review 12(2) 1985. Reprinted in Vancouver 1986, 135.

involving citizens' groups, developers, and the local state. All of this has proven acceptable—not without grumbling on all sides, to be sure—and it appears now to have become part of Vancouver's regular way of doing business.

Guidelines

The design guidelines replaced Vancouver's version of the envelope system, which regulated the size and configuration of yards and included light angle controls and requirements designed to minimize obstruction of daylight. The guidelines are both more stringent and more open to interpretation than the rules they have replaced because they stress the importance of the neighbourhood context of a development and thus necessarily produce different results in different places. In the words of a planning document, they "do not require literal interpretation in whole or in part." But they are taken into consideration in the process of deciding whether to grant a development permit. This decision is made by the Development Permit Board, which "may, in its discretion, refuse or require modification to a Development Permit Application proposal, for failure to meet the standards of [the] guidelines in whole or in part" (Vancouver 1985a, 1).[19] The guidelines are extensive and detailed. Following are some of the main ones:

Public open space.
A development should include varied, accessible, and, where appropriate, interconnected open spaces to be used by a wide range of people throughout the year. . . . Spaces should be varied [and] interesting. . . . Elements such as level changes, plant material, and pattern should be carefully related (Vancouver 1985a, 2).

Social and cultural amenities.
. . . an attempt should be made to preserve as much of the historic townscape of the City as possible. . . . Where viable communities exist . . . downtown, their presence should be maintained and reinforced. . . . To strengthen these communities, it is advisable to encourage the presence of people working or

---

[19]As of July 1990, this document was the current version of the downtown design guidelines.

living downtown during the full 24-hour day and to attract a wide
range of visitors and users throughout . . . (Vancouver 1985a, 6).
Specifics covered in this section include the location of day-care centres;
of cultural facilities such as cinemas, theatres, and community halls; of
recreational amenities; of facilities for the accommodation of motor
vehicles; the preservation of historic structures; the orientation of
developments in relation to the street and to view corridors, and what
kinds of activities should be located at street level and what kinds at
other levels.

Views.

Existing views should be protected and, wherever possible,
new views should be created . . . [including]

Views of the mountains and the water from street level and
especially from street-ends ending near the waterfront.

Views of landmark buildings, art works. . . .

Views and vantage points for viewing major pedestrian
activity, and views of the most important activities of the city,
such as the port . . . the pleasure-boating community . . . the
commercial fishing fleet and . . . railroad activity (Vancouver
1985a, 9).

To maximize views, developers may be encouraged to provide such
things as higher than usual ceilings at ground floor, minimization of
columns at building perimeters, and slender building cores. "All new
development proposals should consider [views] of adjacent . . . public
areas, of surrounding buildings [and] of the proposed building itself"
(Vancouver 1985a, 10).

Environmental guidelines cover such things as shadows cast by
buildings, amounts of sunlight in public spaces within developments,
weather protection for pedestrian routes, shelter for transit stops, wind
currents caused by new buildings. ("New developments should attempt
to integrate into their design outdoor spaces of relative calm.") A section
on noise conditions calls for incorporation of "quiet outdoor spaces" into
the designs of new buildings, and another section deals with the
"introduction of nature," including the preservation of existing mature
trees, the introduction of large trees and other plants, as well as "[w]ater
basins, fountains and . . . waterfalls . . . " (Vancouver, 1985a: 12-13).

Physical design guidelines call for "a very high quality . . . urban
environment . . . ," buildings that "observe energy-conserving principles
. . . " and "a pedestrian environment along . . . major sidewalks which is
attractive to, and in scale with the pedestrian." Meeting these objectives

involves, among other things, the avoidance of "impersonal façades" as well as

> sensitive proportioning and dimensioning of building elements . . . choice of materials, detailing, textures, colours, lighting, street furniture, landscaping and signage. In addition, the transparency of the façades and frequency of entrances contributes significantly to the interaction between building and pedestrian street traffic.
>
> Tower portions of downtown buildings should be evaluated with respect to their compatibility with surrounding structures, their contribution to the . . . skyline, their adherence to other guidelines and the intrinsic excellence of their form . . . their colour, reflectivity, shape, fenestration, materials, detailing and ease of maintenance will receive careful scrutiny" (Vancouver 1985a, 14-15).

Enforcement

The enforcement of this highly detailed set of rules takes the form of a quasi-political, administrative review process designed to ensure that the various relevant points of view—those of neighbours, developers, city officials, and design professionals—are brought to bear on the final decision, which is made administratively.[20] The object of the process is, as we have noted, the issuance or refusal of a development permit. The process begins with the filing of a development permit application, which details the proposal and outlines how it is intended to comply with the design guidelines. The application is referred to an advisory body called the Urban Design Panel, consisting of architects and engineers nominated by their professional associations as well as representatives of the planning bureaucracy. At the same time, it is referred to city departments with an interest in the proposal, and citizens in the area are notified and given an opportunity for input. The process is an interactive one, and the application may be changed to meet objections before it goes forward for a decision.

If at this point the application is judged to be noncontroversial, it can be approved by the director of planning. If not, it goes to a public hearing

---

[20]Details on the process can be found in Vancouver 1981, Vancouver 1985b, Vancouver 1987a, and Vancouver 1987b.

before the Development Permit Board, the voting members of which are the director of planning, the director of social planning, and the city engineer. The board is assisted by a seven-member, nonvoting advisory panel including developers, citizens, and design professionals. At the conclusion of the hearing, the voting members of the board render a decision. However, the applicant may revise the application to meet objections and start over again.

The discretionary zoning system creates a decision-making arena within which a wide variety of participants—citizens, architects, city officials, and the developers themselves—can vie for their interests. Planning documents explaining how the system works are at pains to emphasize the degree to which all parties, including developers, can gain concessions, and they are undoubtedly right to insist that developers continue to wield real power. But it is clear that the discretionary zoning system imposes significant constraints on developers and has a real impact on the appearance of the developments that result, thus giving a serious measure of influence, independent of developers, to citizens, citizens' groups, and the local state.

Balance of Forces in the Local State

We have seen that the abandonment of the envelope system in Edmonton was not just a planning measure but had wider significance for the character of the local state, for the emerging balance of forces within it, and even for the local political culture. The discretionary zoning system is similarly pregnant with significance for Vancouver politics. It clearly grows out of a very different political consciousness and is part of a politics of development that is distinct from that of Edmonton.

Evidence of the political consciousness associated with the rise of discretionary zoning is less impressionistic than that cited above for Edmonton because a study of locational conflicts is available that covers the period during which the discretionary zoning system was established. Ley and Mercer (1980) analysed all locational conflicts reported in the *Vancouver Sun* from the beginning of 1973 to the end of 1975. In examining the reasons for the actors' involvement in locational disputes, the authors found that both social and aesthetic factors were cited more often than economic factors.[21] Commenting on these and other findings, they say:

> the dominant status of social factors is notable. So too is the relative standing of aesthetic factors. . . . Broadly social criteria were cited both by community interests and city hall officials in half the controversies that they joined. For these groups, economic grounds were mentioned in only 10-20 percent of issues, no more frequently than aesthetic criteria. This demotion of the primacy of economic arguments is surprising and perhaps rare among politicians. The same trend was evident in the outcome to conflicts, where entrepreneurial lobbyists with their economic arguments were the least successful of the competing groups (Ley and Mercer 1980, 100, 107).

In a related article, Ley (1980) implied that the emphasis in Vancouver politics upon noneconomic issues was not particularly characteristic of Vancouver but was part of a wider social trend that involved "passing from an emphasis on growth to a concern with the quality of life. . . . " He saw this trend as being associated with the growth of white-collar technical, administrative, and professional occupations and characterized it as a "new liberalism" that could be "recognized less by its production schedules than by its consumption styles." Affluent white-collar workers, "[w]ith a secure economic base . . . represent the present day counterparts of Veblen's leisure class, displaying the canons of good taste, intent upon the aesthetic" (Ley 1980, 239, 242-43). Although there is undoubtedly much truth in that interpretation, it exaggerates in suggesting the predominance of aesthetic considerations in Vancouver's politics of development. As we found in Ley and Mercer's own study, social factors were seen to be dominant political motivators while aesthetic ones were much less prominent. More to the point of the present study, the evidence of our comparison with Edmonton shows that the political trends Ley and Mercer identified are not general to the society as a whole but are more in evidence in some urban centres than in others. It may well be true, as the authors suggest, that the kind of development politics found in Vancouver requires the backing of affluent voters, but it is not true—at least not in all cities—that the growing prominence of white-collar occupations mutes the local state's concern with economic issues while

---

[21]Social factors included need for improved services, compatibility with neighbourhood, impact on traffic, safety, and availability of housing (Ley and Mercer 1980, 98-99).

bringing about a greater emphasis on social and aesthetic questions. Certainly it has not happened in Edmonton. But it was happening in Vancouver in the mid-1970s, and it continues at this writing.

As we noted, the rise of discretionary zoning was associated with the eclipse of the conservative NPA by the reform-oriented TEAM party. The period of TEAM's pre-eminence was followed by a period of dominance by the NDP and COPE, parties located to the left of TEAM on the political spectrum. In 1986, the NPA returned to power, and Vancouver politics underwent another sea change, but discretionary zoning has so far proved too durable an institution to be dislodged by a new conservative regime. Indeed, it was clear that many of the controversial premises first advanced by TEAM in the late 1960s had become part of the conventional wisdom of Vancouver politics. For example, a 1985 planning study confirmed, indeed strengthened, an earlier finding (Vancouver 1980) that the preservation of views of the water and mountains was a top priority for Vancouver residents. As Vancouver planners reported, "The powerful cluster of goals surrounding the unique natural environment of Vancouver was reaffirmed [by the 1985 study], but was now viewed as something that should be taken for granted, a 'given' and constant background for City policy" (*Quarterly Review* 13(4), October 1986, 10).

The NPA-dominated city council has confirmed that position. In 1989, council voted to accept a report on views preservation that, according to a newspaper account, "will form the basis of an interim policy on view preservation and require some restrictions on building heights in the commercial core." Before they voted, they heard from 17 architects and developers opposing acceptance of the report. Mayor Gordon Campbell, a member of the NPA—who, significantly, has in the past been associated with TEAM—was quoted as commenting: "I don't believe council's obligation is to try and maintain potential profit on land in the downtown core" (*Vancouver Sun,* December 13, 1989, A9).[22] That statement rated page A9 of the *Sun.* In the Vancouver context, there is nothing remarkable about it. In Edmonton, such a remark, coming from a conservative mayor, would be unthinkable.

---

[22]Compare the following quotation from Edward Koch, mayor of New York: "The main job of government is to create a climate in which private business can expand in the city to provide jobs and profit" (Katznelson 1981, 4).

Evaluation

If anyone thinks that the existence and vigorous enforcement of the design guidelines lead to a noticeably higher level of satisfaction with the government's performance in this area, they should disabuse themselves. What we find, rather, is a more competitive political environment, marked by higher expectations, greater uncertainty on all sides as to the outcome of political disputes, and, therefore, more vociferous dissatisfaction with the outcomes. Vancouver's political woods are full of criticisms of the design guidelines and of the development permit process. Indeed, sometimes it is difficult to find anyone with a good word to say about it. It is worth our while to take a look at some of the most important criticisms.

The objections of developers are not far to seek. They are faced with a process that can take a long time if there are major objections to their proposal from citizens or the local state—and time is of the essence to them because delays cost money and eat into their profits. The subjective element of design guidelines that respect the physical surroundings of a proposed building, and that put a great deal of weight on the opinions of neighbours, is also a thorn in the developer's flesh. Clearly developers are not happy with the system. Ley's judgement, published in 1980, and benefiting from day-to-day observation of the system, was as follows:

> The Planning Director . . . consistently supported citizens rather than business interests in rezoning controversies; he resisted granting a redevelopment permit to one proposed residential tower in a high amenity central location on the grounds of it being 'unneighbourly' in its intrusion on existing properties. . . . The assault on high density living and particularly high rise developments was conducted with vigour and in four years council . . . achieved residential down-zonings in every major apartment district in the city. In almost every instance the downzonings were supported by local citizens' groups and opposed by the land development industry. Nor were downtown commercial interests more successful in gaining council backing; repeatedly their viewpoint was rebuffed at public meetings in the council chamber (Ley 1980, 252).

Undoubtedly the conservative regime of the late 1980s has been less severe toward developers, but it is far from having satisfied them.

Another set of criticisms, widely voiced, converges with the developers' dissatisfaction over the subjectivity of the guidelines. One version of those criticisms targets the former director of planning, Ray Spaxman, maintaining that he used the discretionary character of the guidelines to impose his personal vision. As one architect remarked, when a developer or the architect was seeking a development permit, "you didn't talk to [planning] staff, you tried to get an appointment with Ray."[23] Spaxman's successor, Tom Fletcher, is widely characterized as seeking to depersonalize the decision-making process, shifting decision making downward in the hierarchy and encouraging the development of departmental, rather than personal, policies for enforcement of the design guidelines. That, however, brings with it a new problem. As the architect quoted above sagely remarked, Fletcher's approach is "good and bad, because now you have to deal with the quality of the individual at the lower level." It seems clear that such criticisms cannot be met to everyone's satisfaction. As we have seen in the case of both Edmonton's and Vancouver's envelope systems, a set of impartial guidelines is open to the criticism that it leaves insufficient flexibility and room for individual creativity. Any attempt to achieve greater flexibility in the enforcement of guidelines is bound to lead, sooner or later, to suggestions that the system is being applied arbitrarily.

More substantially, the discretionary zoning system is vulnerable to the charge that, on one hand, it helps to promote Vancouver as a corporate headquarters and a residential area for the rich and the near-rich while on the other it shirks the far weightier problem of how the metropolitan area as a whole will accommodate population growth and house the poor. The development permit system is proving to be a powerful lever for well-to-do neighbourhoods that wish to avoid densification, while the problem of homelessness intensifies and urban sprawl continues at the periphery of the metropolitan area, beyond the reach of city council's authority. As Ley (1980) and Knight (1989) point out, cities that wish to accommodate corporate headquarters must also make themselves attractive to highly paid professionals whose "life style," in Logan and Molotch's acerbic characterization, "emerges as an alternative American ideal; low-fat cuisine and BMW replace the dour gothic imagery of knitting needle and pitchfork . . . this vision of urban 'rebirth' helps justify . . . the subsidized destruction of old neighbour-hoods for the sake of the rent-rich uses that will replace them" (Logan

---

[23]Interview, May 24, 1990.

and Molotch 1987, 287). To be sure, in Vancouver's Canadian variation on this American story, the neighbourhoods are being preserved rather than destroyed. It is fair to add too that, in such new developments as Coal Harbour and the North Shore of False Creek, the city is insisting on the inclusion of moderate- and low-income housing. But serious doubts remain as to whether these and other efforts are enough, and certainly design controls by themselves do little or nothing to address them.

Our main concern in these pages, however, is not the outcome of policies but the contrasting capacities of different local states. Therefore, we are less concerned with deciding just how good, or inadequate, or wrong-headed, the design controls are than with observing that there are controls, that they are taken seriously and enforced vigorously, and that they exert enough control over development to elicit cries of pain from the development community. It is important to notice the capacities of the local state even if we do not approve of the way Vancouver's government has used its power. If the local state has found a way of achieving substantial leverage in its dealings with developers, it is reasonable to suppose that the leverage is available to serve a variety of purposes. One can readily imagine, for example, a COPE-dominated city government deciding to lay less stress on views or maintenance of low densities and more on affordable housing. That suggestion is implicit in the following quotation from Kantor:

> Cities that own dominant market positions face limited competition from other cities, a relationship that increases their economic independence in the process of inducing capital investment. Potentially at least, they may be more responsive to popular control because of the diminished "exit" opportunities of economically important population groups (1987, 496; see also Kantor with David 1988).

Two different positions on the urban hierarchy are associated with the existence of local states and of local political cultures with sharply different capacities.

CONCLUSIONS AND MORE QUESTIONS

Like many studies, this one makes some contributions to our understanding while at the same time raising a host of new questions. A contribution that can be drawn from it is that it offers a fresh look at local political alignments, offering a substantially different picture of the line-up of political forces, especially in Vancouver, than that which is conventional in the current literature. The questions it raises have to do with the relative importance of economic and cultural factors in determining the character of the local state. The answers to these questions, in turn, will influence the individual reader's judgment of whether Vancouver, and especially whether Edmonton, could have pursued a different course than the one described in these pages. We can take up each of these subjects in turn, starting with local political alignments.

Political Alignments

It has become conventional in recent studies to see the politics of Vancouver as marked by a radical subordination of the local state to the forces of capitalist development.[24] These findings echo those of a variety of other commentators on the politics of other cities, including Logan and Molotch (1987), Kirk (1980), and Rimmer (1988), whose analyses are discussed in the introduction to the section on Vancovuer. The picture that emerges from these studies suggests, contrary to our findings, that there is not much to choose between local states as regards their relationship to capital—or, as applied to our cases, that Edmonton's and Vancouver's local states are very similar in their subordination to developers. In the case of Vancouver, the conventional analysis is arrived at by dismissing as inconsequential the essentially liberal restrictions designed to promote "livability" and "neighbourliness," which form such an important part of local state policy in Vancouver, on the grounds that they are in reality responsive to the objectives of developers and the business community. Business people, so the argument runs, are interested in enhancing Vancouver's status as a centre for producer services and thus welcome the imposition of controls that will have the effect of making the city more attractive to the kinds of professionals who purvey producer services. Having thus been encouraged to discount Vancouver's most significant exercise of local state power, the reader is left with the impression that Vancouver and Edmonton are roughly equal in their subordination to the forces of capitalist development. In support of this interpretation, both Magnusson and Gutstein are at pains to emphasize the similarities between conservative and liberal programmes. This emphasis originates from a well-intentioned attempt to underline the

---

[24]See especially Gustein 1983 and Magnusson 1990.

importance of left-wing issues, but it is too theoretically sophisticated by half.

To be sure, it is fair comment to point out that TEAM was essentially a liberal, establishment party, concerned with middle-class issues, with at best a limited concern for such matters as affordable housing, inner-city education, homelessness, racism, and women's issues. It is no more than reasonable to point out, therefore, that TEAM devoted little or no attention to a long list of social questions. It is equally reasonable to charge, as Magnusson does, that the consensus in favour of "livability" in Vancouver in the 1980s grew out of the NDP acceptance of a liberal program. What is problematic about that emphasis, however, is that it blurs the distinctions between TEAM and the even more conservative, development-oriented approach to city planning that TEAM succeeded in striking from Vancouver's political agenda. In point of fact, even if it is true that "livability" is in the long-term interests of the development community, developers themselves appear to be blissfully unaware of this convergence of their interests with those of the political centre and the left and are distinctly ungrateful for the bounty being bestowed upon them by the local state in the form of onerous restrictions that they must observe. In the process of blurring the distinction between the centre and the right, the conventional view of Vancouver politics loses sight of the very substantial exercise of state power that TEAM initiated and made respectable. It is fair to point out that the achievement of "livability" leaves many important problems unsolved, but it makes little sense—especially in North America, the home of so many bleak and ruined urban landscapes—to dismiss it as inconsequential.

This tendency, widespread in the literature, to erase the distinctions among the various kinds of conservatives (or classical liberals), moderates, and social democrats is a symptom of the paucity of political perspective that we observed in the introduction to this chapter, in that part of the urban literature oriented to global political economy rather than to local variation. It mirrors the equally distorted attempt by right-wing political forces to reduce local politics to a simplistic sparring match between "free enterprise" and socialism—long a staple of western Canadian, and especially British Columbia, politics. In that version of the political world, all forms of liberal and moderate politics are conflated with the dreaded socialism, and the forces representing the business and development communities are portrayed as our saviours from the dead hand of the state. One version blurs distinctions between the right and the centre, the other between the left and the centre. Both serve an ideological end, but neither conveys an accurate picture of the political spectrum. Since a substantial proportion of the actual political clashes in Canadian cities, and cities throughout the capitalist world, pit liberal and conservative forces against each other—as opposed to unifying them against radicals—we are too often missing the point. Our analyses are in danger of expressing our aspirations rather than explaining the politics of cities.

In practical political terms, it makes a great deal of sense to link the issue of livability with such issues as housing because this increases the size of the constituency for resistance to capital. Experience in Canadian cities suggests that either type of issue by itself is insufficient for a durable political offensive designed to secure critical scrutiny of development proposals, but that a coalition of forces concerned, in various mixes, with both liberal and left issues is capable of developing some staying power (Magnusson 1991, 185). We have seen how the TEAM regime in Vancouver in the 1970s, followed by that of COPE and the NDP in the early 1980s, constituted a liberal-left coalition that addressed issues of livability. We noted briefly that they also devoted some attention to such concerns of the left as affordable housing, day-care, and, it could be added, tenant rights. Another example of joint liberal-left political action that achieved results can be found during the period in the 1970s when Civic Action (CIVAC) held the balance of power in Toronto and instituted a regime of downtown development controls with support from the left while yielding to left-wing pressure to promote affordable housing through the development of the St. Lawrence Neighbourhood and the creation of Cityhome, a municipal housing corporation. In recent years in Montreal, the regime of the Montreal Citizens' Movement (MCM) is yet another example of a liberal regime that draws on left-wing support and pays some attention to left issues.

The left has had plenty to complain about during all these regimes, and with good reason. Liberals have probably, on the whole, done somewhat better during these periods, but that is neither here nor there. The point is that, while even a casual student of city politics could cite a number of examples of effective joint action drawing on both liberal and left support, it is much harder to think of examples of either group realizing a program of reform without support from the other. In addition, the unhappy example of Edmonton's supine political culture points to the psychological importance of the belief—seemingly absent in Edmonton—that there are feasible alternatives to the proposals put forward by developers, and thus the importance of keeping all the alternatives alive instead of taking the position that some of them are insufficiently radical to be worthy of notice.

Economics, Culture, and the Character of the Local State

Our findings point to a strong correlation between the "location" of Vancouver and Edmonton on the "urban hierarchy," the political cultures of those two cities, and the different characters of the two local states. Since Edmonton's submissive political culture is clearly conditioned by a belief, widely held locally, in Edmonton's economic inferiority, while Vancouver's is marked by a fine disdain for economic considerations, it seems clear that the economic situation of the two cities is the independent variable, to resort to behaviourialist jargon, and that the different cultures and differently constituted local states are results of their differing economic circumstances.

Even if that somewhat speculative finding is accepted, however, it begs a more interesting question. Do the economic conditions of the two cities *determine* their political cultures and their different local states? Is it the case that Vancouver's economic circumstances effectively mandate a local state policy of strict control over development and that Edmonton's "lower" position on the urban hierarchy leaves no choice but to allow developers to work their will? The likely answer to those questions is, No. If Vancouver's political "clout" originates in its attractiveness as a corporate headquarters, as we have suggested in these pages, its degree of "clout" is by no means a necessary accompaniment of its degree of attractiveness. One could cite numerous examples of American cities as attractive, or more attractive, to capital than Vancouver—New York, Los Angeles, Miami, and Houston spring to mind—where controls over the quality of downtown development are minimal by Vancouver's standards, or absent altogether. In Canada, Calgary, which is comparable to Vancouver in its attractiveness as a corporate headquarters,[25] is governed

---

[25]According to a listing in Canadian Business, the headquarters of 41 of Canada's top 500 corporations are located in Calgary, compared with 38 for Vancouver. (It is worth noting in passing that these figures may make it worth reconsidering the common perception, cited above, that Vancouver is western Canada's major urban centre. The figures do not, however, affect our conclusions about the relative positions of Vancouver and Edmonton and are therefore peripheral to the argument in these pages.)

by a local state that cheerfully eschews any serious attempts to control the quality of downtown development.

By the same token, numerous European cities, and even the occasional North American city, at least as "provincial" as Edmonton manage to sustain workable city centres, unmarred, or at least less marred than Edmonton, by empty storefronts or wind-swept streetscapes. To name only one of many examples in Europe, Geneva's renown as one of the most beautiful cities in the world is such that few people are aware that it is a secondary city with a metropolitan-area population of less than 400,000—substantially smaller than Edmonton. Clearly it has succeeded despite (or perhaps even in part because of) the fact that it does not enjoy the status of an economic powerhouse. In the U.S., Portland, Oregon, is widely cited as a success story in the establishment and maintenance of an attractive city centre. In Canada, St. John, New Brunswick, a city that lost its economic importance in the 19th century and remains a backwater today, has done much, through renovation of older buildings and intelligently conceived new development, to re-establish the attractiveness and viability of its city centre.

To be sure, these are impressionistic examples, not backed by careful investigation. But a detailed study is unnecessary to establish the point that a city's place in the "economic hierarchy" does not, in any simple way, determine the degree of political will, or even necessarily the ability, of the local state to exercise control over development. As Michael Peter Smith and Joe R. Feagin comment in the introduction to *The Capitalist City*, community responses to global economic forces "are not mere by-products of [global] economic and state restructuring; the everyday activities of people living in households and communities . . . are constitutive elements in the process of urban transformation; they shape as well as reflect the global flows of labour and capital and the character of state policies." In short, if we want to achieve a full understanding of the differences between Edmonton and Vancouver, or to understand any other local state, we must move beyond global economic forces and theories of political economy to a much more specific assessment of the local culture and local politics. Economic factors are a primary influence, but they are not the only influence.

Indeed, it seems likely that Edmonton's local culture and the character of its local state are conditioned less by objective economic circumstances than by a panicky misreading of its economic situation. Edmonton is not a major drawing card for corporate headquarters, and it undoubtedly lacks a significant concentration of the producer services necessary to accommodate corporate headquarters, but it is a major centre of government administration as well as health and education facilities,[26] which are considered by students of urban economies to be important bases for the generation of prosperity (Noyelle and Stanback 1984; Stanback, 1984). Edmonton's objective economic circumstances hardly seem to justify the seemingly hysterical reaction of the local business community to the threat that even small delays in the development approval process would lead to withdrawal of investment. What we seem to have in Edmonton is not a business community and a public that has made a sober assessment of their economic circumstances and reacted to that assessment, but a business community that has been mesmerised by a subjective judgment that it occupies an insufficiently "elevated" position in the "urban hierarchy," and that has seized control of the local state to implement a program of capitulation to corporate demands, regardless of the cost to the community. Seemingly, the Edmonton business community, and with it the local state, has taken the "urban hierarchy" simile a bit too seriously for the city's own good.

It seems reasonable to conclude, then, that a balanced understanding of the circumstances of both Vancouver and Edmonton, while it must be based on a sensitivity to the global economic context, also requires a nuanced awareness of the particular circumstances of each city, including local political cultures and the political forces that comprise the local state and control the directions it takes. As we suggested in the opening paragraphs of this chapter, a full assessment of the circumstances of the two local states is, in the end, impossible without both elements. The same is undoubtedly true for other local states. A major task confronting students of urban politics, therefore, is the production of more studies that forge a plausible link between the uniform pressures exerted upon communities by global economic forces and the infinite variety of local political responses to those pressures.

---

[26]Including the University of Alberta, Athabasca University, Grant MacEwan College, the University of Alberta medical complex, the provincial government, and a significant federal government presence.

REFERENCES

Beauregard, Robert A. 1989. *Atop the Urban Hierarchy.* Lanham, Md.: Rowman.

Canadian Business.

Clarke, Susan E., and Andrew Kirby. 1990. "In Search of the Corpse: the Mysterious Case of Local Politics." *Urban Affairs Quarterly* 25 (3): 389-412.

Cox, Kevin R., and Andrew Mair. 1988. "Locality and Community in the Politics of Local Economic Development." *Annals of the Association of American Geographers* 78 (2): 307-25.

Downtown Business Association of Edmonton. 1986. *Annual Report.*

Edmonton, City of. 1981. *Downtown Area Redevelopment Plan Bylaw 6477.* Edmonton: City Hall.

_____. 1985. *Downtown Area Redevelopment Plan Bylaw 6477* (consolidated edition, December 1985). Edmonton: Planning and Building Department.

Edmonton Downtown Development Corporation. 1988. *Launching the Decade of Development.*

_____. n.d. *Edmonton Downtown Development Corporation.* Brochure.

Edmonton Journal.

Edmonton, Mayor's Task Force on the Heart of the City. 1984. *Final Report: A Blueprint for the 21st century.*

Edmonton, Planning and Building Department. n.d. "Summary of the Effect of Bylaw #7801."

_____. 1979a. *Downtown Retail Study.*

_____. 1979b. *Considerations for Pedestrian Level Wind Conditions in Downtown Edmonton.*

_____. 1979c. *Regulation of the Form of Development and Public Spaces.*

_____. 1980a. *Downtown Commercial Parking Study.*

_____. 1980b. *Downtown Area Redevelopment Plan Draft: Background Information Report.*

_____. 1980c. *Downtown Pedestrian Circulation System.*

_____. 1981a. *Plan for Public Development.*

_____. 1981b. *Building Envelope Testing.*

_____. 1981c. *Report on the Communication Programme: a Public Review of the Downtown Area Redevelopment Bylaw Draft.*

Feagin, Joe R. 1988. *Free Enterprise City: Houston in Political and Economic Perspective.* New Brunswick: Rutgers.

Friedland, Roger. 1983. *Power and Crisis in the City: Corporations, Unions and Urban Policy.* New York: Schocken.

Gurr, Ted Robert, and Desmond S. King. 1987. *The State and the City.* Chicago: University of Chicago Press.

Gutstein, Donald. 1983. "Vancouver." In *City Politics in Canada*, ed. Warren Magnusson and Andrew Sancton, Toronto: University of Toronto Press, 189-221.

Hanson, Royce, ed. 1983. *Rethinking Urban Policy: Urban Development in an Advanced Economy.* Washington, D.C.: National Academy Press.

Horan, Cynthia. 1991. "Beyond Governing Coalitions: Analyzing Urban Regimes in the 1990s." *Journal of Urban Affairs* 13(2): 119-35.

Jacobs, Jane. 1959. *The Death and Life of Great American Cities.* New York: Random House.

Kantor, Paul. 1987. "The Dependent City: The Changing Political Economy of Urban Economic Development in the United States." *Urban Affairs Quarterly* 22 (June): 493-520.

_____, with Stephen David. 1988. *The Dependent City: the Changing Political Economy of Urban America.* Glenview, Ill.: Scott, Foresman, Little Brown.

Katznelson, Ira. 1981. *City Trenches.* New York: Pantheon.

Kirk, Gwyneth. 1980. *Urban Planning in a Capitalist Society.* London: Croom Helm.

Knight, Richard V. 1989. "City Development and Urbanization: Building the Knowledge-based City." In *Cities in a Global Society*, ed. R. V. Knight and Gary Gappert, Newbury Park, Calif.: Sage, 223-42.

_____, and Gary Gappert, eds. 1989. *Cities in a Global Society.* Newbury Park, Calif: Sage.

Leo, Christopher. 1993. "The Subordination of the Local State: Developer Dominance and Regime Politics in Edmonton." New Orleans: Association for Canadian Studies in the United States, biennial conference.

_____, and Robert Fenton. 1990. "'Mediated Enforcement' and the Evolution of the State: Urban Development Corporations in Canadian City Centres." *International Journal of Urban and Regional Research* 14 (2): 185-206.

Ley, David. 1980. "Liberal Ideology and the Postindustrial City." *Annals of the Association of American Geographers* 70(2): 238-58.

_____, and John Mercer. 1980. "Locational Conflict and the Politics of Consumption." *Economic Geography* 56 (2): 89-109.

Logan, John R., and Harvey L. Molotch. 1987. *Urban Fortunes: the Political Economy of Place.* Berkeley: University of California Press.

Magnusson, Warren. 1985a. "Urban Politics and the Local State." *Studies in Political Economy* 16: 111-42.

_____. 1985b. "The Local State in Canada: Theoretical Perspectives. *Canadian Public Administration* 28(4): 575-99.

_____. 1990. "Regeneration and Quality of Life in Vancouver." In *Leadership and Urban Regeneration: Cities in North America and Europe*, ed. Dennis Judd and Michael Parkinson, Newbury Park: Sage, 171-87.

_____. 1991. "Progressive Politics and Canadian Cities." In *Challenges to Local Government*, ed. Desmond King and Jon Pierre, Newbury Park: Sage, 173-94.

_____, and Andrew Sancton, eds. 1983. *City Politics in Canada.* Toronto: University of Toronto Press.

Mayor's Task Force on the Heart of the City. 1984. *Final Report: A Blueprint for the 21st Century.* City of Edmonton.

Noyelle, Thierry J., and Thomas M. Stanback. 1984. *Economic Transformation of American Cities.* Totowa, N.J.: Allanheld and Rowman.

Peterson, Paul. 1981. *City Limits.* Chicago: The University of Chicago Press.

Pickvance, Chris, and Edmond Preeteceille. 1991. *State Restructuring and Local Power: A Comparative Perspective.* London: Pinter.

Quarterly Review.

Rimmer, Peter J. 1988. "Japanese Construction Contractors and the Australian States: Another Round of Interstate Rivalry." *International Journal of Urban and Regional Research* 12(3): 404-24.

Saunders, Peter. 1983. *Urban Politics: a Sociological Interpretation.* London: Hutchinson.

Scott, Allen J. 1988. *Metropolis: From the Division of Labour to Urban Form.* Berkeley: University of California.

Smith, Michael Peter, and Joe R. Feagin, eds. 1989. *The Capitalist City: Global Restructuring and Community Politics.* Oxford: Basil Blackwell.

Smith, Neil. 1984. *Uneven Development: Nature, Capital and the Production of Space.* Oxford: Basil Blackwell.

Stanback, Thomas M., Jr. 1984. "The Changing Fortunes of Metropolitan Economies." In *High Technology, Space, and Society,* ed. M. Castells, Beverley Hills: Sage, 122-42.

_____, and Thierry J. Noyelle. 1982. *Cities in Transition: Changing Job Structures in Atlanta, Denver, Buffalo, Phoenix, Columbus (Ohio), Nashville, Charlotte.* Totowa, N.J.: Allanheld, Osmun.

Stone, Clarence N., and Heywood T. Sanders, eds. 1987. *The Politics of Urban Development.* Lawrence, Kansas: University Press of Kansas.

Turner, Robyne S. 1990. "New Rules for the Growth Game: The Use of Rational State Standards in Land Use Policy." *Journal of Urban Affairs* 12 (1): 35-47.

Vancouver, Planning Department. 1976. (Cited as Vancouver 1976). *Development Permit Applications: Central Area.*

_____. 1980. (Cited as Vancouver 1980). *Goals for Vancouver.*

_____. 1981. (Cited as Vancouver 1981). *Eight Years After: Case Studies under Discretionary Zoning in Vancouver.*

_____. 1985a. (Cited as Vancouver 1985a). *Downtown Design Guidelines.*

_____. 1985b. (Cited as Vancouver 1985b). *Zoning and Development Permits in Vancouver.*

_____. 1986. (Cited as Vancouver 1986). *The Vancouver Plan: the City's Strategy for Managing Change.*

_____. 1987a. (Cited as Vancouver 1987a). *The Development Permit Process.*

_____. 1987b. (Cited as Vancouver 1987b). *Development Permits for Major Developments.*

Vancouver Sun. December 13, 1989, A9.

Vogel, Ronald K., and Bert E. Swanson. 1989. "The Growth Machine versus the Antigrowth Coalition: The Battle for our Communities." *Urban Affairs Quarterly* 25(1): 63-85.

Whyte, William H. 1988. *City: Rediscovering the Centre.* New York: Doubleday.

Chapter 21

Social Polarisation and Community Response:
Contesting Marginality in Vancouver's Downtown Eastside

David Ley
The University of British Columbia

Over the past several years I have been studying the gentrification of Canadian central cities, that is, the movement of middle-class households into new or renovated dwellings in neighbourhoods occupied, sometimes by blue-collar workers, but more often by small households including students, the elderly, and poorly paid service workers.[1] A full interpretation of this process draws the researcher into a range of interwoven contexts, including the growth of the downtown service sector (the labour market for the new inner-city housing market), the rise of the so-called new middle class, the movement of women into the professional labour force, the aestheticisation of the urban landscape, and the often ambiguous currents of reform politics. But no less are we drawn into the underside of these urban transformations, to an equally unfamiliar ecology in the Canadian city, to the world of food banks and homelessness, to narcotics and juvenile gangs, in short to the urban dispossessed.

The reciprocal relations between these two realms are focused around what in a number of Canadian cities has been the decade-long crisis of

---

Part of this chapter is developed in greater detail in Ch. 6 of S. Hasson and D. Ley, *Neighbourhood Organizations and the Welfare State* (1994).

[1]See Ley 1986, 1988, and 1992. The literature in this field is growing substantially; among recent contributions see Rose 1987; Mills 1988; and Caulfield 1989.

affordable housing. For the embourgeoisement of a Don Vale, a Plateau Mont-Royal, or a Kitsilano is associated at best with the replacement, more commonly with the displacement, of affordable rental units. The changing occupational status of inner-city residents provides some measure of this displacement (Table 21.1). Over the 1971-86 period a substantial number of managerial, administrative, professional, and technical workers entered the inner-city housing market in Canada's largest cities. This cohort in the quaternary or advanced service sector showed an increment of some 116,000 in the six cities, doubling their relative presence. In contrast the remainder of the employed labour force resident in the inner city declined by 215,000. There are a number of further intricacies in these data that I will not delay over here, though it is worth noting that despite recession, the pace of gentrification quickened during the early 1980s.[2] It should be emphasised, though, that these figures refer only to inner-city residents in the labour force and ignore groups more vulnerable to housing displacement such as the elderly, students, and single parents without paid employment.

A second illustration of the restructuring of the housing market is the plight of those on the bottom rung of the housing ladder in rooming houses and residential hotels. This submarket has shown extraordinary contraction in the past two decades: in Ottawa in a torrid market 40 percent of the city's rooming houses were lost in a three-year period; the losses were clustered in districts undergoing gentrification. One Vancouver estimate indicated a depletion of over 60 percent of single-resident occupancy buildings adjacent to downtown between 1975 and 1981. Over a longer, 15-year time period, the stripping of affordable housing in Vancouver shows the geographical association with gentrification. The Kitsilano, Fairview, and West End neighbourhoods all had substantial listings of rooming houses in 1971 as they experienced the classic downfiltering cycle of older dwelling units. But Kitsilano and Fairview contain the census tracts that experienced the most intense gentrification between 1971 and 1986, and by the latter date listed rooming houses had virtually disappeared from these districts. In the West End, the transition process has been more complex, but gentrification has certainly been a principal cause of the erosion of rooming houses. In Vancouver's inner city, the last reserve of this bottom end of market accommodation is

---

[2]For further discussion of this section, see Ley 1985, 1988.

Table 21.1. *Changes in the Occupational Status of Inner-City Residents in Six Canadian Cities, 1971-86*

	Quaternary Occupations % Change		Non-Quaternary Occupations % change	
	1971-81	1981-86	1971-81	1981-86
All six cities	35	20	-20	-8
Halifax	36	10	-27	-3
Montreal	31	17	-28	-16
Ottawa-Hull	29	25	-25	-6
Toronto	31	27	-20	-3
Edmonton	27	6	-3	-16
Vancouver	58	17	-8	-1

Source: Author, based on calculations derived from the Census of Canada, 1971, 1981, 1986.

located in the Downtown Eastside, the district to which I shall be turning shortly.

The considerable transformation occurring in Canadian inner cities since 1971 has impacted neither cities nor neighbourhoods equally, a point that will become clear in the first section of this chapter that examines the variable geography of social change in inner districts across metropolitan Canada. Nonetheless, these changes provide a dominant context for the social and housing pressures experienced within neighbourhoods. The second, and major, part of the chapter examines one such neighbourhood, Vancouver's Downtown Eastside, and documents the remarkable struggle by community groups in the city's poorest district to promote housing quality and affordability over a period of almost 20 years, in an inner-city setting where a dominant theme of the 1980s has been the embourgeoisement of an aspiring world city.

SOCIAL CHANGE IN THE INNER CITY

What, then, are the dominant processes as one tries to make sense of the Canadian inner city at the beginning of the 1990s?[3] Recently, researchers have been cautioned not to follow the media in exaggerating gentrification to the neglect of other inner-city processes (e.g., Bourne 1989). Indeed, there are some who would conclude that *pauperisation* remains a major characteristic of inner cities, an interpretation reinforced by the American underclass thesis that sees an intergenerational transmission of poverty in the inner city. This thesis might have some partial insights to offer in small sections of some cities in Atlantic Canada, Quebec, and the Prairies. Less controversial social indicators include homelessness estimates, which range between 100,000 and 250,000 across Canada, with the total for Toronto, the nation's wealthiest city, said to be in the vicinity of 20,000 (Dear and Wolch 1993). Despite emerging suburban nodes, the city's poverty population remains concentrated in the inner city, illustrated by the clustering east and west of downtown of the more than 75 food banks existing in Metro Toronto in 1989 (Relph 1990).

Pauperisation is, however, only part of the story, for the presence of gentrification is too pervasive to deny. A second interpretation of the inner city points to the growing *social polarisation* of the 1980s accompanying a decade of market-based policies. Most brilliantly and starkly these contrasts are drawn in Tom Wolfe's *The Bonfire of the Vanities*, a novel that moves audaciously between the wealthy hustlers of Wall Street and the poorer hustlers of Harlem (Wolfe 1988). The polarisation argument invokes the dual labour market associated with a service economy, with a minority of high-waged professionals and managers and a majority of low-waged clerical and service workers. The erosion of unionised middle-income jobs in blue-collar and public sectors is then tied to the diminution of the traditional middle class. Bourne (1990) has assembled a set of income data that offer some support for the polarisation thesis within the central city. A comparison of average and median household incomes gives a rough measure of the skewness of income distributions and thus the range of income inequalities (Table 21.2). This skewness index shows, first, the greater income inequality of

---

[3]The three-fold typology of inner-city change that follows is taken from Hamnett 1990.

Table 21.2. *Income Disparity as a Measure of Social Polarisation, Toronto CMA, 1986*

Municipality	Household Income		Index of Income Disparity	
	Average	Median	1985	1970
Toronto CMA	43,025	36,890	16.6	11.9
Central CMA				
City of Toronto	39,118	29,177	34.1	22.8
East York	34,828	29,970	16.2	
York	32,418	27,799	16.6	
Mature Suburbs				
Etobicoke	44,058	37,589	17.2	
North York	43,258	34,797	24.3	
Scarborough	41,010	37,840	8.4	
New Suburbs (over 50,000 population)				
Brampton	45,289	43,196	4.8	
Markham	60,407	52,625	14.8	
Mississauga	46,781	42,204	10.8	
Oakville	53,205	47,479	12.0	
Vaughan	55,060	48,329	13.9	

Note: Index of income disparity = (Average - Median Income)/Median Income x 100%
Source: Bourne (1990)

the city over the metropolitan area and, second, the marked increase of differentials within the city over the 1970-1985 period, indicative of greater social polarisation. Extending the analysis to the census tract scale shows that a deepening of trends has occurred in Toronto: whereas in 1950 the average income of the wealthiest district was three times that of the poorest, by 1980 the differential had widened to nearly 14 to 1.

Some observers see social polarisation itself as a transitional stage to a growing *professionalisation* of the central city in the large metropolis, an embourgeoisement that would return the innermost districts to the elite status they enjoyed in the pre-industrial city. This is Hamnett's (1990) conclusion in examining recent social change in London. Perhaps more relevant to large cities in Canada are two striking maps of income change in the Sydney metropolitan area in the early 1980s (Horvath et al. 1989). In patterns that show remarkable geographical coherence, net gains of high-income families have been made in a solid block of districts in the inner city, with net losses in the distant suburbs; for low-income families the pattern is reversed. While this intrametropolitan gradient cannot be detected in Canadian cities at present, some intriguing tendencies point in the same direction. Although the city of Toronto held its ground in relative income terms between 1970 and 1985, average incomes in the surrounding inner ring of mature suburbs fell relative to the norm for the CMA (Bourne 1990). Looking at the innermost districts alone in 12 cities, the process of embourgeoisement is most evident (Table 21.3).

One should be cautious with this data source for the demarcation of the inner city is very conservative and includes some incongruities. Nonetheless, the clear trend is a sharp reduction of low-income families, a slight decline of middle-income families, and a marked rise of high-income families in the residential districts adjacent to the CBD. These trends are most evident in Toronto and Ottawa-Hull and give some substance to the remark of a Toronto planning commissioner that the inner city is becoming "a ghetto for the rich" (Weston 1982). It is clear that professionalisation has continued since the 1986 census. A survey of Toronto's Central Area indicated that nearly 40 percent of residents had entered the district between 1986 and 1989 (City of Toronto 1990). Sixty percent of these new residents were employed in managerial or professional occupations, a figure well in excess of the level of those with a longer tenure in the Central Area. The break-up of the affordable rental market in the inner city indicates that in Toronto, as in London, lower-income households are increasingly isolated in clusters of government-assisted housing (Bourne 1990; Hamnett 1990).

But one further issue needs to be addressed. Just as there is an increasing social differential within the central city, so too there is growing variation within the urban system. A glance at Table 21.3 confirms the diverging experience of Winnipeg and Toronto, or Saint John and Saskatoon. Indeed, in Winnipeg there is some evidence that, despite the considerable expenditures of the Core Area Initiative,[4] pauper-

---

[4]The Core Area Initiative, 1981-91, has been a coordinated effort by the three levels of government to revitalise the depressed inner city.

Table 21.3. *Percentage of Inner-City Families in Selected Income Groups, 1970 and 1985, (constant 1985 dollars)*

Inner City	Less than $20,000		$20,000 - $60,000		Over $60,000	
	1970	1985	1970	1985	1970	1985
Toronto	43	33	48	45	9	22
Montreal	54	42	39	42	7	16
Vancouver	46	43	50	48	4	9
Ottawa-Hull	39	28	55	53	6	19
Edmonton	42	32	53	55	5	13
Calgary	47	41	50	49	3	10
Winnipeg	54	56	44	41	2	3
Quebec	50	45	45	45	5	10
Halifax	56	42	43	50	1*	8
Saskatoon	47	37	52	50	1*	13
Regina	51	39	48	49	1*	12
Saint John	51	55	48	51	1*	1*
All Inner Cities	47	39	47	46	6	15
Rest of CMAs	24	21	67	60	9	19

*Approximate figure (data suppressed)
Source: Ram, Norris, and Skof 1989

isation is a dominant theme in the inner city, with an aggravation of income, unemployment, and affordability problems both absolutely and relative to the metropolitan area. Charette (1990) concludes that "inequities between the inner and non-inner city are increasing. Moreover, those groups which are already the most disadvantaged—Natives and single parents—are experiencing the greatest level of worsening conditions." These disadvantaged groups are also growing most rapidly in number.

Broadway's (1990) comparative study of seven cities sharpens the thesis of a growing divergence among metropolitan areas. The critical divide seems to be an urban economy with a resilient service sector (compare Ley 1986). In Winnipeg, Regina, and Saint John inner-city pauperisation is evident from a range of variables during the 1970s, whereas Halifax, Toronto, Edmonton, and Vancouver show clear evidence of inner-city upgrading. A still broader profile is gained from a factorial ecology across 24 metropolitan areas (CMAs) using 1981 census data (Davies and Murdie 1993; see also Davies and Murdie, this volume). A factor labelled impoverishment was derived from the analysis, which included high loadings against female, lone-parent households, and low income. For the whole population of CMAs, some 19 percent of tracts had extreme impoverishment scores, but there was considerable variation around this mean. In Saint John, Quebec, Trois-Rivières, and Montreal the incidence of extreme impoverishment was twice this level or more; in Toronto, Vancouver, and Calgary the number of impoverished tracts fell well below the national average. The story of the past 20 years seems to be the accentuation of social gradients at all geographical scales.

CONTESTING CHANGE IN THE DOWNTOWN EASTSIDE

With the upgrading pressures from an expanding downtown service sector, the inner city of Vancouver is characterised by social polarisation or even, in the early 1990s, by the process of professionalisation (compare Table 21.1). The rapid erosion of rooming houses is only part of a larger stripping of the affordable rental market. The role of the state in providing affordable housing to lower- and middle-income households has become critical at precisely the time when the state is partially withdrawing from its role in social housing. The poor in Vancouver's inner city confront the double jeopardy of increased pressure on the existing housing stock and diminishing options. The entire metropolitan area has experienced an inflating residential market, so no short-range relocation of the poor is feasible. The absence of alternatives brings a sense of desperation to the protection of existing affordable units. These circumstances are not of course unique to Vancouver, but what is unusual is the emergence of an effective neighbourhood organisation in the city's poorest district which, since 1973, has been contesting the terms of social and land-use change.

As we saw earlier the last major stock of bottom end of market housing is in the Downtown Eastside, a district of lodging houses and residential hotels, and including the poorest census tract in the metropolitan area. It meets admirably Michael Dear's characterisation of the public city, that is, a district that is heavily service-dependent and receives substantial transfer payments from the state. The typical resident is an elderly male Caucasian perhaps with an industrial injury, on some form of social assistance, though Native and Chinese residents have been long-standing minorities, and recently single-parent households, teenage runaways, and the deinstitutionalised mentally ill have added growing diversity. In 1986, 90 percent of individuals and 70 percent of families fell below Statistics Canada's low-income threshold.

The Downtown Eastside, then, contains a cross-section of the nation's most vulnerable households. It is not hard to understand why such a population, as it confronts in everyday life the massive problems aggravated by the economic and political restructuring of Canadian cities in the 1980s, should be portrayed in a discourse coloured by an existential fatalism and a theoretical passivity. But in fact the Downtown Eastside offers a powerful corrective to such functionalist thought, for it exemplifies the capacity of poor and marginal communities to contest the terms of change. For almost 20 years, the district has been championed by the city's most feisty neighbourhood organisation, the Downtown Eastside Residents' Association (DERA), which has engaged in a multifaceted campaign with symbolic, political, welfare, and territorial objectives. It has challenged all three levels of government, as well as such public and private corporations as Expo 86, the Port of Vancouver, and Li Ka-shing's Concord Pacific Corporation. Both in terms of theory, and also of political strategy, this example of community resistance offers some important lessons. By 1990 DERA claimed 4,500 members, and two former leaders have, since 1982, been elected to the 11-person city council. The same year DERA's community organizer, Jim Green, ran as a mayoralty candidate in the civic election and received 45 percent of the popular vote.

Among DERA's multifaceted objectives, I shall limit discussion to the organisation's housing initiatives, its most abiding preoccupation (for a fuller treatment, see Hasson and Ley, 1994). After several years of reaction to individual crises, by 1978 a housing strategy had been assembled that included three components: (1) a struggle for housing rights, including code enforcement and the legal redefinition of hotel residents as tenants, with full tenants' rights; (2) the targeting of renovation and the upgrading of rooms; and (3) a strategy to build social housing through nonprofit housing corporations. In general these goals represent a progression from a reactive to a proactive strategy, and have seen the evolution of DERA from a protest organisation in the 1970s to one engaged in a relation of coproduction with the state in the 1980s.

DERA AND THE HOUSING QUESTION

> A man lies huddled in an old grey blanket on the bed in the
> corner. He ignores the cockroaches crawling down the wall and
> across the grey sheets. A tap drips into a sink with grime so
> embedded it's hard to tell it was once white. The floor, where
> you can see it, is filthy. Bottles, glasses, cigarette butts, leftover
> crusts and a red liquid—you can't tell if it's blood or wine—fill
> the rest of the floor . . . (Shaw 1983).

Conditions in the Travellers Hotel on Cordova Street for a room with a
sink at $170 a month were not unusual in Downtown Eastside hotels in
1983. But a decade earlier conditions had been worse, and there were no
alternatives to the private market.

In the early 1970s bylaw standards were lax and irregularly enforced.
Fire was a serious hazard, and during 1973 10 men perished from hotel
and rooming house fires. Over the course of the year, no fewer than 107
fires occurred in skid road hotels; the Cobalt Hotel was in flames on
seven separate occasions.[5] Following a fatal October fire in the Commercial Hotel, DERA picketed city hall and attended Council chambers en
masse demanding the upgrading and enforcement of fire standards. A
flurry of activity by the city followed, with new fire regulations and a
new promise of enforcement; 10 hotels were said to have been closed
down in the previous year for violating the existing code. But hotel
owners confronting a significant bill were slow to comply, and the fires
continued. Following a further fatal fire at the end of October 1974, a
demonstration of 150 DERA supporters issued a statement to council:

> You have succumbed to the whims of landlords when they
> threaten to close down their premises rather than comply with
> health and fire standards. . . . We urge Council to assume the
> responsibility it was elected with. You are playing with people's
> lives and we will not stand by and watch it happen any longer.

Thereafter compliance and enforcement were practised, and with sprinkler
systems the fire hazard almost disappeared.

---

[5]Unless otherwise stated, material is derived from the minutes of DERA
meetings, interviews with DERA leaders, or the organisation's newspaper,
Downtown East (1973-80). In the interests of space, full citations to sources are
omitted (see Hasson and Ley, 1994, from which this section is taken, for a fuller
discussion).

One reason why hotel owners hesitated in upgrading was the economics of operating residential rooms. While this is a controversial question, the frequent closures and conversions to other uses suggest that some operations at least were marginal. The critical variable in a hotel's profit margin was its beer parlour. It was said that in 1982 the Europe Hotel earned revenues of $550,000 from its pub, but management was not prepared to transfer its profits into repairs and maintenance. Before it was converted into social housing units, the owner of the architecturally distinct Europe Hotel had plans to capitalise on its heritage designation and Gastown location with an upmarket renovation. But these improvements would not benefit existing tenants. Despite a net income of $220,000 in 1982, the Europe had complied with only a quarter of the improvements ordered by the city up to three years before. "I have held off the improvements waiting for this (renovation) plan" observed the owner. "You don't think I would restore it for the derelicts living there now, do you?" (Power 1982).

It was this prejudice that DERA confronted in its attempt to improve living standards, and with it a laggardly pattern of code enforcement plus a forgiving judiciary. Following success with the fire bylaw, DERA directed its attention to the Standards of Maintenance code. Here it confronted a foot-dragging civic bureaucracy, which was challenged by a prolonged campaign in 1978. DERA noted that the Warren Hotel had been visited 17 times by inspectors before orders were issued, while the Cascade Hotel was visited 18 times in a year, given a list of orders seven pages long, and then granted a license before these were followed up. The scale of violations was staggering. In an exhaustive joint investigation of 23 hotels by DERA and city inspectors in 1978, close to 10,000 code violations were detected, an average of 7-8 violations per room. Yet attacking code enforcement simply released a hydra's head of attendant problems. First, the effort and expense of prosecutions produced no deterrents in the courts. The Warren Hotel was found guilty of infringing bylaws and fined $100; the Cascade Hotel was found guilty on 12 counts and fined $600, the minimum penalty. In a DERA-supported action, 37 tenants, primarily Chinese pensioners, at the East Hotel took their landlord to Small Claims Court on breach of contract for not providing heat or hot water and not cleaning filthy premises. This promising precedent was torpedoed by the court's response; after an 18-month struggle it found in the tenants' favour and awarded each of them damages of $25.

Code enforcement also raised the risk of closure. A defence of the East Hotel was that it was losing money and could not afford a sprinkler system and other mandated improvements; refused a redevelopment permit, it was still empty in 1982. By the autumn of 1974, 21 hotels faced closure notices for noncompliance with the new bylaws; two years later over 1,500 rooms had been closed. Closures for noncompliance of bylaws and summary evictions of tenants have continued through the 1980s. The carrying out of improvements has also proven a two-edged sword, accompanied as it often has been by rent increases and evictions. In one instance, 63 tenants of a rooming house fought successfully to turn back rent increases of up to 118 percent, after the owner had spent $50,000 on a sprinkler system and new wiring.

So the enforcement solution raised a new series of problems. DERA addressed each of these in turn, but also, as we shall see, turned to a broader housing strategy. Rent increases and summary evictions were a daily fact of life in the Downtown Eastside because occupants of residential hotels had no legal protections, falling outside the terms of the Landlord and Tenant Act passed by the New Democratic (NDP) government in the early 1970s to establish tenants' rights. DERA files are full of the human cost of nonprotection—for example, a case thrown out by the courts against the Columbia Hotel for evicting a tenant of 20 years' standing with one day's notice on Good Friday—though worse was to come with the evictions and rent increases accompanying Expo in 1985-86. A subsequent Residential Tenancy Act required each resident of a hotel or rooming house to apply separately for designation, and thus protection, as a tenant. It was a hopeless task, but DERA staff gamely aided residents on an individual basis to seek designation. After intensive lobbying, picketing of government agencies, and mounting frustration over 15 years, some measure of success was finally attained with the passage of amendments to the Residential Tenancy Act in 1989, extending normal tenant protections to hotel and rooming house residents by right.

But the difficulties with code enforcement also prompted a broader vision of necessary change. Strong and enforced bylaws and tenant protection were important, but so too was some protection from the vagaries of a purely market-driven housing stock. The role of the state was critical, not only as regulator, but also as housing supplier. In the summer of 1976, DERA's organiser, Bruce Eriksen, took the Federal Minister for Urban Affairs plus the constituency Member of Parliament on a walkabout and proposed to them that the new Residential Rehabilitation Assistance Programme (RRAP), with loans and grants for targeted older neighbourhoods, be extended to rooming houses and residential hotels. Six months later the new minister announced an amendment to RRAP incorporating this proposal, with the Downtown Eastside serving as the first area to be designated. An advantage of RRAP-funded renovation was its linkage to rent controls, thus precluding arbitrary rent increases. The program has proven a useful one, and by the end of 1986, 1,200 units in the Downtown Eastside had been upgraded using RRAP funds.

The third leg of DERA's housing strategy was new social housing. This initiative was already afoot in the early 1970s primed by Vancouver's liberal reform councils. The United Housing Foundation purchased and renovated three hotels in the Downtown Eastside for low-rent housing. These were followed by three lodges with 381 units built with funding from all three levels of government over the next three years; promises of a total of 10 projects were made. DERA, assisting in the settling of tenants, accumulated a waiting list of 1,100 applicants. But then shifts in government policy, particularly at the provincial level, eroded the funding sources. DERA had strongly endorsed this building program and continued to lobby for it: "the real solution must be massive construction of low cost housing in our area." But its appeal fell on deaf ears at the city. Following its vigorous enforcement campaign in 1978, DERA presented a policy document to council in September 1978 with its three point plan to "eliminate slum housing": (1) bylaw enforcement, (2) renovation, and (3) new housing. The proposal was opposed by 20 hotel owners and a city staff report rejecting new housing. An unfriendly council, now with a conservative majority, eventually disapproved DERA's proposal by a 6-2 margin. The following spring a newly constituted group of city staff, the Downtown Housing Implementation Committee, issued its report with no mention of new housing; its principal author was quoted as claiming that "Non-profit housing would directly compete with private owners." The report had its genesis in the meeting of council members with DERA and hotel owners the previous September, and there was no doubting which interest group had caught the ear of council and its staff.

There was only one avenue to pursue. If the city and province would not sponsor social housing, then DERA would form its own corporation and build the units. There was considerable skepticism at this initiative, and the Canada Mortgage and Housing Corporation (CMHC) forwarded a grant of only $500 for the development of a nonprofit housing proposal.

As it did so often, DERA broke the rules with a bold and innovative application to purchase and renovate the Stratford Hotel. Room sizes would be doubled and profits from the beer parlour used to subsidise rents. CMHC's regional office was "stumped" at this finessing of due process, and after long deliberations the application was turned back. It was a deeply demoralising defeat. A full year's work—and hopes—had borne no fruit, and the DERA office had been shut for six months without funds. But within a few months the organisation had been turned around. Its leaders, Bruce Eriksen and Libby Davies, were elected alderman and parks commissioner in the 1980 civic election, and Jim Green had been appointed DERA organiser. The next major phase in its housing strategy was underway.

As Jim Green remembers it, DERA backed into the sponsorship of social housing. In the early 1980s, a huge victory was won in persuading the provincial government to close its profitable but troublesome liquor store at Main and Hastings. But the DERA members were not satisfied, and, in Green's words, "wanted to seek retribution for what the liquor store had done to the neighbourhood all those years": they demanded the site from the province for social housing. This was not forthcoming, but the city's Social Planning Department promised that if DERA would relinquish this demand there was a good chance that a better site on city-owned land would be available. Passage of this proposal through council was more difficult than anticipated as old enmities were bared, and it was approved at an in-camera session in early 1983 (with, of course, the presence of councillors Eriksen and Davies, who had both been returned in 1982) by a narrow 6-5 majority. With a lease on city-owned land and CMHC funding, the DERA executive could announce jubilantly to its membership that the 56-unit DERA Co-op would be completed in 1984. Symbolically it includes a six-storey mural of the history and struggles of the Downtown Eastside and the Vancouver Waterfront.

The DERA Co-op powerfully extended the achievements of the past into the present and provided precedents for the future. In Jim Green's estimation,

> The DERA Co-op was of tremendous symbolic significance in showing what could be done with no Board, no staff, entirely self-sufficient. The City and the Feds said this is impossible that people in this district manage a $5 million budget. The Co-op is a shining example of what is possible. We just went on from

there. We had a large number on the waiting list and experience
that should be re-used.

The second project was equally audacious. The long recession following
1981 combined with the erosion of affordable housing had brought
families to the Downtown Eastside, and the 153-unit, Four Sisters Co-op,
was the first project in the district planned to include families as well as
seniors. Once again the proposal ran into heavy criticism, from council
and some city departments, but again, thanks to the advocacy of the two
DERA councillors, it was narrowly approved, was completed in 1987,
and has a long waiting list. Two further renovations have been undertak-
en since, with joint federal-provincial funds, and by 1990 DERA is
among the largest landlords in the Downtown Eastside, with 413 units in
its four buildings, administration of an additional 76 units, and with
further plans under discussion. A current thrust is to introduce the
nonprofit hotel model, which has worked effectively in several American
cities, to Canada, through the purchase and renovation of existing hotels.
This initiative would introduce competition to market hotels, and also
provide better management of beer parlours, a major neighbourhood
problem. Reminiscent of DERA's proposal for the Stratford Hotel in
1980, the pubs could also generate subsidies and working capital for each
structure.

While these achievements have been enabled by funds from various
levels of the state, the record indicates that initiatives and innovation have
typically originated in the community. It was pressure from DERA that
influenced bylaw revisions in the 1970s and led to the formation of the
Downtown Housing Implementation Committee in 1978 at the end of a
concerted lobbying campaign. Initially DERA's three-point housing
programme of bylaw enforcement, rehabilitation, and new building was
resisted by council and staff, but in the 1980s it became official policy.
During Mayor Harcourt's tenure, 1980-86, the city acquired 10 sites for
nonprofit housing societies, and in total 1,244 society-operated units were
built in the Downtown Eastside. A further 1,200 market units were
renovated through the rent-controlled RRAP programme, and 1,500
others, renovated for Expo, have been returned to the local market. In
1989 revisions to the Rental Tenancy Act gave tenants' rights to
Downtown Eastside residents after a 15-year campaign. And even the
notion of using a beer parlour as a profit centre to subsidise room rentals,
suggested by DERA in 1980, is now part of city-provincial-DERA
negotiations over purchase of a downtown hotel. Repeatedly, if not

without a struggle, the community has succeeded in impregnating the state, and has come to set the housing agenda.

TERRITORIAL STRUGGLES:
EXPO AND THE NEW URBAN REALITY

But this argument should not be pressed too far. Community control is contested and far from total. Indeed by the late 1980s, there was an air of crisis as to whether the Downtown Eastside could survive the forces of embourgeoisement, with incursions of mega-projects encircling it on three sides: from the east and north the threat is the redevelopment of the waterfront by the Port of Vancouver; from the west the pressure comes from Gastown-induced gentrification and, behind it, the expansion of downtown functions, including Simon Fraser University's new downtown campus and the convention and leisure business associated with Canada Harbour Place; and to the south, on the site of the Expo lands, the beginnings of the vast Concord Pacific redevelopment by the Hong Kong entrepreneur, Li Ka-shing, complete the encirclement. DERA's organiser sees the capacity for displacement to be substantial:

We've got major high-rise developments coming in on three sides of us in the next few years, an invasion of well-off people, and nobody is giving a thought to the effect it will have on this neighbourhood. . . . Expo was bad, the worst year of my life. But this will be worse because the evictions will be more massive, and more long-term—in fact, permanent (Sarti 1988).

Expo '86, the World's Fair, marked the transition to this new urban reality, as DERA's dealings shifted from local slumlords to national and international public and private corporations. With its well-honed local knowledge, the organisation was not caught off guard. Indeed when Jim Green began as organiser in 1981, his terms of reference included, as first priority, relations with B.C. Place, the provincial crown corporation that acquired the Expo site in 1980. Equally vigilant was the First United Church, which in June 1981 anticipated hotel upgrading in the Downtown Eastside for Expo visitors leading to evictions of "at least 800" residents, a remarkably prescient estimate (Olds 1988). By the following January, an alliance of DERA, the Carnegie Centre and First United Church had formed a coalition, the Save the Downtown Eastside Committee, which had begun lobbying in earnest, and by early 1983 various departments of the city were also considering housing and other impacts, leading to a request by Mayor Harcourt to the federal government for a special disbursement of offsetting housing funds.

Meanwhile DERA had assembled its own housing strategy to divert the worst case scenario of neighbourhood impacts. Early in 1984, DERA joined a coalition of First United Church and the Chinese Benevolent Association and approached the Expo 86 Corporation with a proposal to build 450 units of housing in converted warehouses near the Expo site, to be rented for Expo use during the fair, and then turned over to nonprofit groups afterwards. This offer was declined by the corporation, which instead built delegate housing at the University of British Columbia, six miles away from the site. The lobbying campaign then went into high gear with a walking tour for 42 politicians from the three levels of government of the Downtown Eastside, and DERA's eight point proposal to secure the stability of the district in the face of megaproject threats. Two of the proposals were for a rent freeze in Downtown Eastside hotels during the Expo period, and, once again, full tenancy rights for residents, thereby protecting them from summary eviction. These items were developed further and presented to the city in a report requesting that a rent freeze and no evictions during the course of the fair be incorporated in a new bylaw. At DERA membership meetings, the mood was grim: "What we will get from Expo are tourists, more crime, more traffic and less housing. We will not benefit from Expo one bit." The bylaw was an essential base to a preventative strategy. "A major fight coming up is for the bylaw for Expo '86—August 13, 1985. If we don't get the bylaw, gloves are off for Expo. . . ."

A similar strategy was doing the rounds of the Social Planning department at city hall, and the department endorsed DERA's proposal before council—one of many examples of a more cooperative relationship between the association and city staff in the 1980s. The bylaw's history before council was one of prolonged frustration, in the face of tied votes, the sickness and absence (twice) of a key supporter on council, and wrangling over legal wording. Aldermen opposed to the bylaw had a long history of hostility to DERA, and charged that the association was rumour-mongering and exaggerating Expo impacts. Finally, in February 1986, with the undisputed evidence of Expo evictions now underway, council supported DERA's reapplication for a bylaw enforcing a rent and eviction freeze for established residents, and petitioned the provincial government for enabling legislation.

Not surprisingly that legislation never materialised, for both ideological and personal barriers separated DERA from the right-wing Social

Credit administration. The province had been steadily drawing in its welfare net for several years, under the rubric of a restraint programme, and social impacts in the Downtown Eastside were far from its list of Expo priorities. Indeed in a radio interview, Premier Bennett declared that the exposition had achieved what the city had been unable to accomplish, to "get rid of the slums" (Olds 1988). There were also acerbic personal relations between cabinet members and DERA stretching back to tenants' and welfare rights campaigns in the 1970s. More recently, Jim Green had sued B.C. Place for misleading advertising in its public relations and had been a member of a group who had occupied the premier's Vancouver office in a demonstration that was a part of the Solidarity Coalition's campaign against the government's restraint programme.[6] DERA's task became one of treatment rather than prevention as it facilitated the rehousing of many evicted tenants.

Events were moving to a higher level of politicking. In Victoria, the NDP member for Vancouver Centre was removed from the legislature for accusing the premier of lying over Expo impacts. Leaders of the main opposition parties in Ottawa visited the Downtown Eastside, and questions were raised in Parliament over the evictions. Indeed, much to the embarrassment of the provincial government, the evictions became a cause célèbre and were widely reported in the national and American press and even beyond.[7] The evictions themselves increased steadily and with them exorbitant rent increases, with room charges inflating from $200-$250 a month to $45-$65 a night in some hotels. The total number of evictions is unknown, but the best estimate suggests a figure between 500 and 850 residents in the period immediately prior to the opening of the fair (DERA 1987; Olds 1988).

The Expo evictions represented the struggle of the previous decade writ large to protect a fragile community of the poor, the elderly, and the disabled against more powerful and destructive external forces. DERA's

---

[6]The Solidarity Coalition was a loose alliance of unions and community and professional associations opposed to the social policies of the Social Credit government of British Columbia. In 1983 escalating differences led to the verge of a general strike in the province

[7]For example, see the lengthy article in the *Toronto Star*, March 10, 1986, by Rosemary Eng: "Expo Greed Blamed as Transients Lose Homes." The death of Olaf Solheim, aged 88 years, two weeks after his eviction from the Patricia Hotel, his home for 62 years, was reported on the front page of dailies in his native Norway: see DERA 1987.

local knowledge proved more reliable in the projection of impacts than the intuition of unfriendly aldermen or the predictions of a wavering Social Planning Department, and its solution of a rent and eviction freeze, juggled by council for six months, was finally supported only when DERA's dire predictions were proven correct. But Expo also marked a transition. The escalation over the evictions brought the group added prominence, nationally and internationally, as champion of the district in numerous interviews for radio, television, and newspapers. *The Los Angeles Times, Detroit Free Press,* and other foreign newspapers, all promoted the association and thus enhanced its power. So did a feature on Australian television, mindful of its own Exposition in 1988 on an inner-city site in Brisbane.

CONCLUSION: THE RECOVERY OF URBAN POLITICS

Enough has been written on the limits of local struggles and of the possibilities of agency *vis-à-vis* structure to prevent both the theoretical and political error of overidealising DERA. Yet neither should the opposite error be made. Political struggles at the level of locality need not preclude coalition-building and a broader vision, indeed they concretise sometimes abstract and intangible issues (Magnusson and Walker 1988). DERA has participated in citywide housing and welfare rights' initiatives, while also active in peace and labour movements including the Solidarity Coalition that brought the province to the verge of a general strike in 1983. Besides raising neighbourhood issues, telegrams to the prime minister have included protests aimed at cruise missile testing in Canada, and in 1983 advised the prime minister to "demand the immediate withdrawal of all foreign troops from Grenada." Nor should a view of political passivity before massive societal forces be upheld. Despite the unrelenting hostility of the provincial government between 1975 and 1986, and only a six-year window with a slim majority of allies on municipal council, DERA has succeeded in securing important victories from the welfare state including, but far beyond, the housing achievements outlined in this chapter.

Indeed DERA's ideology and actions effectively challenge functionalist theory (of both the left and the right) that sees only passive and dependent victims in the public city. Against the theoretical charge of localism is a view of society that is systemic and treats the local as an instance of a broader constellation of forces. The association has since its early years distanced itself from agencies that limit themselves to treating the symptoms of victims, without examining systemic inequalities. The Downtown Eastside on Vancouver's waterfront has strong trades union roots. Both Eriksen and Green have been union members, and the union model of democratic socialism has offered an interpretive schema as well as a tactical precedent for DERA's activity.

DERA's view of human agency dispels the mistaken theoretical view of dependency and passivity. In July 1973, the month before DERA was formally incorporated, Bruce Eriksen wrote a letter in which he outlined "The purpose of the Downtown Eastside Residents' Association." Its objectives would include:

1. To help the people of the Downtown Eastside gain control over the forces that affect their lives.

2. To inform the people as to how to go about demanding change and/or preventing disruption in the community.

3. To make the people aware of their own power to make changes of political importance.

These objectives of local power have been sustained to the present. They explain, for example, the extraordinarily hostile view of social workers and other outside professionals, particularly in the early years: "It's time we told City Hall we have no use for expensive hired hands. We have competent workers of our own" (Libby Davies 1973). The objectives illuminate also the critical symbolic, as well as material, significance of local achievement. The successful development of the DERA Co-op was an important object lesson on the possibilities of local control and thus a means of identity formation. In perhaps as clear an illustration as one may find of the recursive nature of structuration, Jim Green (1985) reflected on the symbolic meaning of the DERA Co-op: "The resident control model can lead to the creation of new people . . . a new type of human being, who have pride in themselves, know they can change things."

A confirmation of the capacity of human agency has been intimated not least by DERA's leadership, for like other poor people's movements the presence of charismatic leadership is a powerful resource. As a candidate in Community Resources Board elections in 1975, Bruce Eriksen described himself as a Downtown Eastside resident for over 20 years and "Tough, outspoken and never gives up," an assessment fully endorsed by his frequent presence before council in the 1970s. Picket lines and well-publicised delegations led by Eriksen became an unwelcome experience of aldermen: "We raised hell with City Council if we didn't get what we wanted." Following the election of Eriksen and Libby

Davies in 1980, Jim Green joined the association as organiser. While sharing Eriksen's union and neighbourhood background, and with a tough style and appearance, negotiation has become a larger part of DERA's strategy, as it has moved from a conflict model in its dealings with the state to one that alternates between conflict and coproduction. But despite a group of dedicated and able co-workers, Green's powerful presence has continued the pattern of "a big man" leading the association.

Part of DERA's success and longevity derives from its sophisticated understanding of power. It has consolidated its own base in the Downtown Eastside through local programs and services derived from funding sources as disparate as the city police, the Royal Bank, and the Department of Health and Welfare. It has pursued a union negotiating model: while not compromising principles, negotiations and even coalitions are joined for specific goals. As a result of its strategic coalition-building an impressive array of allies can be assembled: in 1983, in a setting that approached high farce, it overwhelmed city council by amassing 150 delegations to present briefs to support its appeal for an annual operating grant, a grant that a less politically astute council had denied.

The education of the public and of politicians has been an important strategy. Politicians of every stripe have been invited, and have undertaken, walking tours of the district to view conditions and needs at first hand. During the early years grants from experimental and innovative programmes in Ottawa sustained the organisation, but by the late 1980s a proven track record led to joint projects with even the long-hostile provincial government. At the same time an electoral strategy has been pressed to make access to power more direct. As Jim Green has observed: "More can be accomplished in one election than DERA can accomplish in 10 years" (Hume 1986), a statement that might restore, to some jaundiced minds, the significance of the electoral process. Eriksen was elected to council on his fourth try, Libby Davies on her third, while Jean Swanson a long-time DERA and antipoverty worker, garnered 37 percent of the popular vote in the 1988 mayoralty race; Green himself ran for mayor in 1990 and captured 45 percent of the vote. In a city with at-large elections, the success of Eriksen, Davies, and Harry Rankin, a lawyer and an old DERA ally with a Downtown Eastside office, has meant that since 1982 the 11-person council has included three councillors with roots in the Downtown Eastside, a district with 2-3 percent of the city's population.

If the Downtown Eastside has benefited from a particular geography of representation, there is a second context in which geography and politics have combined. Unlike Toronto or Montreal where poor households are more scattered, the spatial concentration of poverty households in the Downtown Eastside has aided the building of a local base and the establishment of a politics of turf. The discourse of neighbourhood resonates strongly through DERA's pronouncements, and has been part of a lengthy cultural and symbolic struggle to deconstruct the oppressive label of skid road, and show it for what it is, the construction of outsiders: "They have invented 'Skid Road' and they intend to sustain the invention" declared an early article in the association's monthly newspaper in September 1974.

The struggle over the meaning of place has gained some considerable success. In 1983 a civic citation from a friendly mayor declared that "The Downtown Eastside Residents' Association has helped to change the concept of an area of our city formerly known as 'Skid Road' to the Downtown Eastside" (City of Vancouver 1983). But perhaps as significant is the pronouncement by a conservative mayor in 1990 that office expansion into the Downtown Eastside should be checked, a pronouncement that left downtown merchants "mad as hell" (Buttle 1990). If not yet a dialogue among equals, social change in Vancouver's eastside has become a political, not just a natural, process. Even Li Ka-shing, a member of an international power elite, discovered that development was a process, a protracted one at that, which required compromises, including reserving 20 percent of dwelling units on the Concord Pacific site for social housing.[8]

It is important to remember the simple proposition that social change is socially constructed and may therefore be socially contested. A survey in 1982 of social agencies in and around the Downtown Eastside asked them to assess the impacts upon the housing of their clients of massive development on the Expo lands over a five-year period. While a majority anticipated major negative spillover effects, one in six anticipated slight positive impacts, as a direct result of political bargaining between the community and the (then) crown corporation. Just as a label like skid row requires deconstruction, so there is an urgent need to denaturalise such reified categories as the pauperisation or professionalisation of the inner city, or indeed the broader categories of privatisation or globalisation, and recover the social, and thus contestable, relations bound within them.

---

[8]It should be added that to date funds to build this reserved housing have not been provided by senior government.

Otherwise the "is" becomes not simply the "ought" but the "must"; the words unproblematically create worlds. There is both a theory and a practice that prefers that these categories remain unexamined. In an era of theoretical functionalism and practical instrumentalism, DERA's broader contribution is its rescue of urban politics, both practically and intellectually.

REFERENCES

Bourne, L. S. 1989. "Are New Urban Forms Emerging? Empirical Tests for Canadian Urban Areas." *The Canadian Geographer* 33: 312-28.
_____. 1990. "Worlds Apart: The Changing Geography of Income Distribution within Canadian Metropolitan Areas." Paper presented to the annual meetings of the Canadian Association of Geographers, Edmonton.

Broadway, M. 1990. "Social Upgrading and Inner City Deprivation: An Analysis of Seven Canadian Cities." Paper presented to the annual meeting of the Canadian Association of Geographers, Edmonton.

Buttle, J. 1990. "Row Brews Over Victory Square Plan." *Vancouver Sun*, April 16 .

Caulfield, J. 1989. "Gentrification and Desire." *Canadian Review of Sociology and Anthropology* 26: 617-32.

Charette, C. 1990. "Inequities Between the Inner and Non-Inner City." Institute of Urban Studies, University of Winnipeg: Newsletter No. 31:3.

City of Toronto. 1990. *The Central Area in Transition: Findings of the Central Area Residents' Survey, 1989.* Toronto: City of Toronto Planning and Development Department.

City of Vancouver. 1983. "Proclamation: Downtown Eastside Day." Vancouver: City of Vancouver, Office of the Mayor.

Davies, L. 1973. "More Hired Hands." *Downtown East* 1(3): July 1-15.

Davies, W., and R. Murdie. 1993. "Measuring the Social Ecology of Canadian Cities." In *The Changing Social Geography of Canadian Cities*, ed. L. Bourne and D. Ley, Montreal and Kingston: McGill-Queens University Press.

Dear, M., and J. Wolch. 1993. "Homelessness in Canada." In *The Changing Social Geography of Canadian Cities*, ed. L. Bourne and D. Ley, Montreal and Kingston: McGill-Queens University Press.

DERA (Downtown Eastside Residents Association). 1987. *Expo '86: Its Legacy to Vancouver's Downtown Eastside.* Vancouver.

Green, J. 1985. Address to the Conference on Affordable Housing In B.C. Vancouver.

Hamnett, C. 1990. "London's Turning." *Marxism Today* (July): 26-31.

Hasson, S., and D. Ley. 1994. *Neighbourhood Organisations and the Welfare State.* Toronto: University of Toronto Press.

Horvath, R., G. Harrison, and R. Dowling. 1989. *Sydney: A Social Atlas.* Sydney: Sydney University Press.

Hume, M. 1986. "The Notoriety Helps DERA." *Vancouver Sun*, April 23.

Ley, D. 1986. "Alternative Explanations for Inner-City Gentrification: A Canadian Assessment." *Annals, Association of American Geographers* 76: 521-35.

_____. 1988. "Social Upgrading in Six Canadian Inner Cities." *The Canadian Geographer* 32: 31-45.

_____. 1992. "Gentrification in Recession: Social Change in Six Canadian Inner Cities, 1981-1986." *Urban Geography* 13: 230-56.

Magnusson, W., and R. Walker. 1988. "De-Centring the State: Political Theory and Canadian Political Economy." *Studies in Political Economy* 26: 37-71.

Mills, C. 1988. "Life on the Upslope: The Postmodern Landscape of Gentrification." *Society and Space* 6: 169-90.

Olds, K. 1988. *Planning for the Housing Impacts of a Hallmark Event: A Case Study of Expo 86*. Unpublished thesis, School of Community and Regional Planning, University of British Columbia.

Power, B. 1982. "Ailing Landmark in Peril." *Vancouver Sun*, July 19 .

Ram, B., M. Norris, and K. Skof. 1989. *The Inner City in Transition*. Ottawa: Minister of Supply and Services for Statistics Canada, Catalogue 98-123.

Relph, E. 1990. *The Toronto Guide*. Department of Geography. Scarborough College, University of Toronto.

Rose, D. 1987. "Un aperçu feministe sur la restructuration de l'emploi et sur la gentrification: le cas de Montréal." *Cahiers de Géographie du Québec* 31: 205-24.

Sarti, R. 1988. "Residents' Organizer Fears New Evictions." *Vancouver Sun*, October 27.

Shaw, G. 1983. "Skid Road: The Flop Side and the Flip Side." *Vancouver Sun*, April 16 .

Weston, J. 1982. "Gentrification and Displacement: An Inner City Dilemma." *Habitat* 25(1): 10-19.

Wolfe, T. 1988. *The Bonfire of the Vanities*. London: Pan Books.

Chapter 22

The Issue of Local Autonomy in Edmonton's Regional Plan Process:
Metropolitan Planning in a Changing Political Climate

Peter J. Smith
Patricia E. Bayne
The University of Alberta

The issue underlying this chapter concerns a critical aspect of metropolitan governance that can be stated most directly as a question: "Is it possible, within individual metropolitan planning systems, to make effective arrangements for regional or areawide planning purposes while extending a high degree of autonomy to constituent communities?" On the one hand, given the spatial characteristics that are typical of most metropolitan areas—notably a dispersed form of development and a fragmented pattern of local government units—superordinate authorities have long been considered essential if areawide needs and problems are to be adequately addressed and the "dissonance" of interjurisdictional conflict overcome (Evenden 1978, 192-94). On the other hand, the belief that planning is most properly a task of local communities—indeed, is one of the most vital ways in which they express their independence and individuality—is an even more venerable and powerful one, buttressed as it is by the democratic ideals of responsible self-government (Hodge 1986). It is obviously difficult to reconcile such contrary ideas. The establishment of any form of authority with jurisdiction over an entire metropolitan area automatically undercuts the autonomy of the constituent communities. That is the crux of the issue.

Conventional planning theory tends to gloss over the inherent contradiction between local autonomy and regional planning (see, for example, Hall 1970; McDowell 1986; Branch 1988). Most critically, because it focuses on the functional logic of regional integration and control, it presents regional planning in an essentially apolitical light. There is a strong sense, in fact, that regional planning ought to be above politics, a way of dealing with needs and problems on their functional merits rather than leaving them to the uncertain hand of parochial self-interest. There is also a tacit assumption that the benefits of a regional approach will be so apparent and so compelling that individual communities, through their local governments, will willingly forgo some degree of autonomy for their mutual gain.

The reality, it is almost unnecessary to add, is altogether different. Particularly as practised in our major metropolitan areas, regional planning is a thoroughly political proceeding and could not be otherwise. The very act of creating a regional planning organization, which entails a restructuring of powers within the metropolitan polity, has large political ramifications. It apportions responsibilities between the regional level of authority and the local, and so shapes political relations both between the regional agency and the local communities and among those communities themselves. It involves tradeoffs between regional and local control as well as finding an appropriate balance between them in whatever institutional arrangements are made for metropolitan planning—and "appropriate" here has less to do with the functional abstractions of regional planning theory than with the limits of acceptability in the local political context. It naturally follows that these limits will change as the political context changes.

Here we come to the specific theme of this chapter which rests on the argument that there has been a significant change in the overall climate of opinion affecting planning in Canada. One important manifestation of this change, perhaps the most important, has been a deliberate and pronounced shift in favour of local control, both in the structure of planning systems and in their regular operations. This shift suggests that the approach to regional planning has had to change as well, particularly in the metropolitan domain, where the tension between local and regional interests is always likely to be most acute.

To amplify this general line of argument, we present a case study of Edmonton's metropolitan planning authority as it went through the exercise of preparing its regional plan between 1981 and 1984. Although the Edmonton events were in many respects unique, reflecting peculiarities of the local situation, they were also indicative of a process caught up in much larger currents of political and cultural change. The import of these currents was not appreciated at the time, least of all by those planners who were charged with the technical responsibility of producing the Edmonton plan, but we can now see them to have been typical of the general condition that has come to be known as postmodernity. As Harvey (1989, vii) has put it, the 1970s brought a "sea-change" in cultural and political-economic practices, including the practices of urban and regional planning. Canada could not escape these global tendencies, and the Edmonton case study captures a critical moment in their development.

POSTMODERNISM, LOCAL AUTONOMY, AND REGIONAL PLANNING

The notion of postmodernity—this "highly problematic term," as Boyne and Rattansi (1990, 19) describe it—is complex, ambiguous, and vast in its scope. It is commonly posited as a reaction to modernism, though the nature of the modern/postmodern antithesis is a matter of much dispute (Goodchild 1990; Curry 1991). With respect to urban and regional planning, however, the central point is clear enough. Through most of the 20th century, planning developed as a "modernist project" (Beauregard 1989), not just in theory but in its institutional forms and procedures, and hence in its social relations. But while modernist sentiment still dominates planning theory, and continues to have a strong hold on the minds of planners, it has fallen out of harmony with the political realities of contemporary society and cannot satisfy the diverse interests that the planning process must somehow accommodate. Since the late 1960s, modernist planning has been under persistent attack and erosion. Although this has not yet resulted in a radically reconstructed planning, and may never do so, planning as it came to be practised in the 1980s was sufficiently different from earlier decades that it can fairly be described as having taken on a new style (Dear 1986; Goodchild 1990; Sholberg 1991).

And what, exactly, are the characteristics of the postmodern style of planning? Put most simply, postmodernism stands for diversity, fragmentation, and localism. It rejects totality, uniformity, centralized control, and all the other qualities of comprehensiveness, that great pillar of modernist planning doctrine. Instead, it favours local initiative and local control, offering a vision of individual communities taking charge of their own futures and their own affairs, meeting their own needs in their own ways rather than following standardized rules and prescriptions. This is defended in the name of democracy and translates into a much more open planning process, grounded in the norms of participation and popular control rather than those of technical rationality. Postmodernism also stands for decentralization, not in the narrow administrative sense where effective control is retained by a central authority but in the sense of democratic decentralization, "conceived as a means of increasing the powers of elected local government or of community groups" (Goodchild 1990, 123). In these terms, decentralization is a manifestation of local autonomy, defined here as the power of a community to act on its own behalf.

Pragmatically, as far as organizational structures for planning are concerned, the issue of centralization versus autonomy can never be reduced to a simple either/or choice. It is inevitable in any large organization that there will be forces pulling simultaneously in both directions (Brooke 1984). Planning organizations are no exception, as Figure 22.1 illustrates. It is a matter of balance, once again: "How much authority and what kinds of powers will be concentrated in the centre, and what will be delegated to subunits of the whole organization?" The answer to this question depends on judgements that every jurisdiction must make for itself, in the circumstances of its own time and place, but that makes it all the more significant when different jurisdictions appear to be moving simultaneously in the same direction. In Canada, for instance, several provinces have completed major revisions of their planning legislation since the mid-1970s, and the desire to strengthen local autonomy was stated as a major motive in every case. This can reasonably be interpreted as a common response to general changes in the climate of opinion within which planning must operate—changes that were manifest most forcibly in the rising tide of populism and protest, and the consequent politicization of the planning process.

How were these pressures accommodated in the reformed legislation in relation to the overall aim of strengthening local autonomy? There were two aspects to this issue. In the first place, to meet demands for more responsive planning local planning authorities were generally required to provide more opportunities for the public to be involved in planning exercises of all kinds. In no case, however, did this extend to a requirement for formal power sharing. The ruling principle was stated most precisely by Nova Scotia's Planning Act Review Committee (quoted in Grant 1988, 262):

> There must . . . be a careful balance between the role of the
> public as participator and the responsibilities of government as

Figure 22.1. *Pressures for Centralization and Autonomy in a Provincial Planning System*

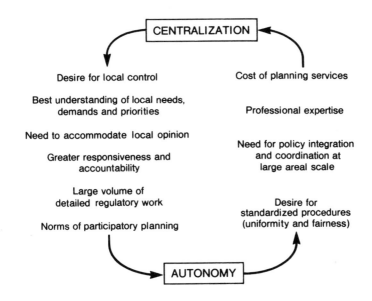

decision maker. Public participation must be recognized as a requirement for good decision making, not as a transfer of decision making from, and accountability of, elected representatives.

Exactly the same view was expressed in Alberta, where the governing statute was rewritten in 1977 (Alberta 1980, 11). Participation in planning matters was definitely facilitated as never before; but equally, as never before, the act was at pains to establish that the responsibility for local planning decisions rests with municipal councils. That is the essence of local autonomy as it is conceived under planning law.

In the second place, there was a general concern to clarify and strengthen the role of municipal governments relative to their respective provincial governments. The aim was to establish that planning is first and foremost a municipal responsibility. Whether that made any difference to the actual or achieved autonomy of the local authorities is a moot point, since there are so many ways in which provincial governments and their agencies can intervene in land-use and development matters from outside the statutory framework of planning procedures

(Robinson 1979). But at least in terms of ascribed autonomy—that is, of the powers that are legally extended to municipal governments by planning statutes (Hoggart 1981)—the purpose of the legislative reforms was clear: they were meant to enhance the decision-making authority of municipal councils and, with that, their political accountability. Such reforms, it was argued, would lead to more responsible decisions by local planning authorities and would simplify and clarify the operations of planning systems that were all too complex and confusing. Both planning and municipal government, it was thought, would become more effective as a consequence (Bossons 1978, 4-6; Alberta 1980, 9-10).

In general, then, Canadian planning systems are highly decentralized, certainly with respect to the relationship between provincial and municipal levels of government. But where does that leave regional planning, the in-between level of planning organization? Does it reflect centralizing tendencies or decentralizing ones, particularly in those provinces like Alberta where there is no system of regional government or regional municipalities? From one perspective, which has generally been favoured by planners since Patrick Geddes introduced the concept some 80 years ago, the region is a special kind of locality (Gertler 1972; Sussman 1976; Mumford 1986). A rather large locality perhaps, but one possessing an intrinsic unity for all that—a unity at once more vital and more real than that of any of its subunits, especially if the region is a metropolitan area and the subunits are an arbitrary and archaic patchwork of municipalities. This after all has been the gist of the metropolitan reform argument for 60 years or more (Wichern 1986). From the municipal perspective, by contrast, any regional authority will be seen as a form of centralization and may well come to be regarded as a local agent of the central state, one of the instruments by which provincial government policies are imposed on the "real" localities, the municipalities (Magnusson 1985). The general point to be drawn from this is that regional planning commonly operates in an ambiguous environment, which in turn creates uncertainty about its role and powers. A "remarkably elusive" concept is how the noted American planner Harvey Perloff (1957, 71) once described it, and time has not made that any less true.

In the current climate, there is a double strike against regional planning. Not only is it liable to be undermined by any move to strengthen municipal autonomy as the accepted institutional expression of localism but it also epitomizes the ideals of comprehensiveness and functional rationality that postmodernism rejects. There is considerable evidence that Canadian planning practice is turning away from comprehensive visions and comprehensive solutions, a trend having particular significance at the metropolitan scale. What else, to take one well-known case, is the government of Ontario's "retreat from regional planning" in the Greater Toronto Area but a retreat from comprehensiveness (Frisken 1982, 1990)? The Toronto-centred region plan was by far the boldest attempt yet at fixing the overall form of a whole metropolitan region, but the difficulties of implementation—the political difficulties above all—were too great to be overcome (Bordessa and Cameron 1982; Macdonald 1984). Nor was this an isolated experience, though it may have been one of the more extreme. Regional planning organizations in Canada have never had the powers they need to be effective agents of large-scale growth management. In practice, they have been allowed to do little more than "local land-use planning written large" (Robinson and Webster 1985, 29), a reality that both clouds their relationship with lower-tier municipalities and diminishes the purpose of regional planning as a public responsibility. It also suggests a vulnerable institution that could readily be sapped when the climate of opinion shifted in favour of a stronger local voice in public affairs. By the early 1980s, the feeling of disenchantment was palpable (Cullingworth 1987, 293-373). In British Columbia, for instance, the regional planning system was emasculated in 1983; the stated reason was to free municipalities from the regulatory authority of regional districts (Rashleigh 1983; Cameron 1984). Even in Alberta, long held up as a Canadian exemplar of regional planning, a major reorientation was under way, primarily to meet municipal complaints about reduced autonomy (AAMDC/AUMA 1980; Dale and Burton 1984).

THE INSTITUTIONAL FRAMEWORK FOR
REGIONAL PLANNING IN
ALBERTA UNDER THE 1977 ACT

Before the case study of Edmonton's regional plan process can be presented, it is necessary to describe the institutional context in which it occurred (Laux 1990). We therefore begin by summarizing those features of the Alberta planning system, as it has been constituted since 1977, that help to shape the relationship between regional planning and local autonomy. Their structural implications are highlighted in Figure 22.2.

1. The responsibility for regional planning in Alberta is vested in ad hoc commissions whose powers and duties are stringently delimited by the planning act. In essence, the commissions exist to do three things:

Figure 22.2.   *Inter- and Intra-authority Relations in Albertan Regional Planning Organizations*

(1) to prepare regional plans; (2) to provide technical planning assistance to member municipalities whenever they request it; (3) and to act as subdivision approval authorities for those municipalities that do not have such authority themselves. This last duty is especially valued by the commissions because it provides them with their only regulatory power and their only direct means of implementing development policies. In 1977, however, the government of Alberta granted municipal councils the right, under certain conditions, to act as their own subdivision approval authorities. This represented a potentially significant transfer of power from the regional planning commissions; its sole justification was the desire to strengthen local autonomy.

2.   Most of the real power in the Alberta planning system is explicitly vested in municipal governments, whose ascribed autonomy is correspondingly great. In Clark's terms, they score highly on both the power of initiation (i.e., the power to determine their own actions) and the power of immunity, or "the power of localities to act without fear of the oversight authority of higher tiers of the state" (Clark 1984, 198). The statutory instruments of municipal planning all become legally binding when they have been adopted as bylaws; none of them has to be approved by any external authority, either provincial or regional; and the grounds for intervening in any decisions taken under the bylaws are extremely limited. The most important constraint on municipal governments—and it is a weak one—is that they must "conform" with the regional plan. Yet even here the regional planning commissions do not have powers of enforcement. Rather, disputes must be referred to a central agency, the Alberta Planning Board, for adjudication.

3.　Planning regions are aggregations of municipalities compelled to join together for one special purpose, a situation that is ripe for conflict, especially in the competitive environment of a fragmented metropolitan area. In the Edmonton area there is a history of conflict going back some 40 years (Smith and Diemer 1978; Batey and Smith 1981). In the main, the city of Edmonton has been pitted against its neighbours, but the regional planning commission was often seen to be part of an alignment against Edmonton as well. This perception came down to the fact that until 1982 Edmonton had only three out of 22 votes on the commission.

4.　The voting members of regional planning commissions are municipal politicians appointed by their councils as their representatives. Needless to say, it is a rare commissioner who is able to put the regional interest first, especially when it conflicts with the interests of the home municipality. Instead, the regional perspective is represented most strongly and most consistently by the technical staff, who are also most likely to view the region as a superior kind of locality. This creates a definite tension between planners and commissioners—tension that will be at its greatest during the preparation of a regional plan, the one formal exercise in which all parties are required to think about the meaning of the region.

5.　Unlike municipal planning instruments, regional plans have to be approved by provincial authorities, first by the Alberta Planning Board and ultimately by the Minister of Municipal Affairs. The scope of their jurisdiction is vague, however. Early published documents appeared to limit it to two matters: ensuring that statutory procedures were followed and that the substance of a plan did not conflict with provincial policies (Alberta 1980)—but the statute itself sets no such limitations. The board therefore set out to clarify the situation in 1982 by issuing "guidelines" for the preparation and approval of regional plans (Alberta 1982a ,1982b). These guidelines did not remove all the uncertainties about the province's "oversight authority" (or about the purpose of regional planning, for that matter), but on one point there was no doubt: a regional plan would not be permitted to override the autonomy of municipal councils. It was to provide a general policy framework and no more. In the board's own words, "A properly-framed policy plan, at the regional level, will permit municipal governments the degree of flexibility they require to meet the requirements of the Act and *to satisfy local aspirations*" (Alberta 1982a, 3; emphasis added).

THE CASE STUDY

Now we turn to the case study proper, which we treat in three parts. First, we outline the sequence of key events; then we consider how the issue of local autonomy affected the regional plan process; and, finally, we discuss the implications for regional planning as an evolving institution. The material base throughout is the documentary records of the Edmonton Metropolitan Regional Planning Commission, supplemented by semistructured interviews with seven staff planners and 11 municipal politicians, all of whom were involved in the preparation of the plan. (For a full account see Bayne 1986.)

Key Events 1974-1984

When the Alberta planning system was revamped in 1977, the preparation of regional plans was made mandatory for the first time, and regional planning commissions were given five years, to December 31, 1982, to complete the task. This was a great spur to regional planning activity, although it had been anticipated in most jurisdictions. In the Edmonton case, the commission had embarked on a regional growth studies project in 1974, as the first step toward replacing a so-called "preliminary plan" that had been in effect since 1958. This was essentially a regulatory instrument. It prescribed a general land-use pattern to which the municipalities were required to conform in their zoning bylaws and against which the commission exercised its own subdivision approval powers.

The growth studies report was completed in 1977 and was followed, in 1979, by a draft regional plan (Edmonton Regional Planning Commission 1977, 1979). The central policy issue in both documents, and the primary source of conflict, concerned the distribution of growth between Edmonton city and the surrounding municipalities. What the plan actually proposed was that 50-55 percent of the region's population increase should be allocated to the city of Edmonton, and 65-70 percent to the whole of the inner metropolitan area, which included the dormitory suburbs of St. Albert and Sherwood Park (Figure 22.3). Edmonton never did accept this apportionment, however. Its position was that the inner metropolitan area should be consolidated under the city's jurisdiction and all future development contained there. That, in turn, was totally unacceptable to the region's municipalities, whose voting power on the commission allowed them to reject Edmonton's arguments. Detached

Figure 22.3. *The Edmonton Metropolitan Regional Planning Commission and its Constituent Communities*

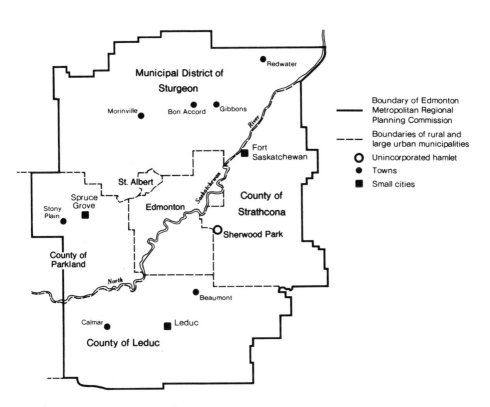

suburbanization had become a significant phenomenon in the Edmonton area by the 1970s, and the municipal councils were largely controlled by people who wanted that trend to continue. The regional plan seemed to offer them a means of realizing their wishes, and they meant to take full advantage of it.

These were the immediate circumstances in which Edmonton finally decided to proceed with a massive annexation application that it had long been considering (Plunkett and Lightbody 1982; Smith 1991). It turned out to be the fiercest and most expensive annexation fight in Alberta's history, dominating intermunicipal relations in the Edmonton area for the next two years. For all intents and purposes, the regional plan went into limbo and could not be resuscitated until cabinet issued its annexation order on June 10, 1981. Three main decisions were delivered then. They attempted, with only partial success, to strike a new balance in the metropolitan polity, giving Edmonton enough additional territory to ensure its acquiescence far into the future without unduly sacrificing the interests of any other municipality (Smith 1982).

1.   Effective January 1, 1982, the Edmonton Regional Planning Commission was reconstituted. Its rural western territory was detached to form part of a newly organized Yellowhead region, while the more densely populated eastern section became the Edmonton Metropolitan Regional Planning Commission (EMRPC, see Figure 3). The system of representation was changed as well. The new commission was to have 27 voting members, nine of them from the city of Edmonton, a proportion determined by the fact that the planning act requires a two-thirds majority vote for the adoption of a regional plan. This greatly strengthened Edmonton's hand. Although it could not dominate the commission, it was now in a position to prevent the adoption of a plan to which it was opposed if it could win the support of one outside representative.

2.   Edmonton's territory was increased by roughly 50 percent, adequate it was believed for at least 50 years of growth. At the same time, cabinet expressed in the plainest language its determination to protect the autonomy of the existing communities of St. Albert and Sherwood Park. The cabinet order actually authorized them to plan on doubling their size, to populations of 70,000 each, as a means of ensuring their long-term viability.

3.   In its most controversial ruling, cabinet directed that 75 percent of the metropolitan area's population growth should be accommodated within Edmonton's enlarged boundaries. This became known as the 75/25 rule. Its most obvious implication, when taken with the enhanced growth prospects of St. Albert and Sherwood Park, was that there would be little development left to distribute among the dozen or so communities in the outer metropolitan area.

With the territorial and jurisdictional issues clarified at last, and only 18 months until the statutory deadline, it was imperative to resume work on the regional plan. The outgoing commission struck an interim committee to review the implications of the cabinet order but it was the staff planners who carried the primary responsibility for rewriting the plan document. That continued to hold true even after the EMRPC came into effect in January 1982. A new regional plan committee was appointed, but it gave little formal direction to the staff planners, who were left to interpret their task according to their own professional lights. Over the next 12 months they wrote a major position paper on issues and goals, generated and evaluated alternative growth scenarios, and finally, in December, issued a new draft plan (Edmonton Metropolitan Regional Planning Commission 1982). The statutory public hearings were held in January 1983, and written comments were received from the member municipalities and the Alberta Planning Board over the next several weeks. Their tone was overwhelmingly negative and frequently hostile.

At this point, in May 1983, the regional plan committee decided that it had to take on the responsibility of redrafting the plan to meet the various criticisms. In fact, a rift had been developing between the committee and the planners for several months, but now it was deep and open. The committee's version of the plan was approved unanimously by the EMRPC in September 1983. After some further revision, carried out in consultation with the Alberta Planning Board, it was ratified by the minister a year later.

In Defence of Local Autonomy:
Conflicts in the Regional Plan Process

The central policy issue in 1982 and 1983, as it had been in 1979, was growth management, not just in the substantive sense (that is, how growth should be distributed within the Edmonton metropolitan area), but in procedural terms as well; that is, how closely the distribution pattern should be regulated and by whom—above all, by whom. The 1979 draft plan had addressed these matters in its own highly prescriptive way, but regional planning had to operate under quite different ground rules by 1982. The annexation order was a critical factor here, both because of its profound effect on the local Edmonton context and, more fundamentally, because it compounded the uncertainty that already existed about the nature and purpose of regional planning under the 1977 planning act. It was one thing to set out to strengthen local autonomy in the Alberta planning system, but what implications did that have for the regional planning function? Edmonton's regional plan episode highlighted the importance of this question in particularly graphic fashion. In a real sense, the "mandate" for regional planning, as it came to be described locally, was the primary issue in dispute.

For its part, although not directly engaged in plan preparation activities, cabinet was guilty of sending a mixed message to the protagonists. To the extent that it protected St. Albert and Sherwood Park by refusing Edmonton's annexation bid, the cabinet order could be interpreted as supporting local autonomy, and it was proclaimed in that light. At the same time, by laying down the 75/25 rule and by authorizing greatly enlarged growth targets for St. Albert and Sherwood Park, cabinet interfered in growth management policy to a degree that was quite unprecedented for Alberta. This meant that the order was bound to be controversial on several grounds. For one thing, as the planners were quick to point out, it ran counter to development trends within the region (which would make it difficult to implement) and to the dispersed growth scenario that had been approved in 1977 as the basis for the first draft plan (which made it politically unpalatable). Still more fundamentally, it could be viewed as an attack on values that the regional municipalities held dear. In particular, to direct that growth be so strongly concentrated in Edmonton was to deny all other jurisdictions the right to compete freely for new development. In a governmental system in which growth—industrial growth in particular—translates into tax revenues, the ability to attract development affects a whole range of issues at the local level, the quality of services not least among them.

These concerns were heightened by the city of Edmonton's behaviour. It goes without saying that the city's representatives were well pleased with the promise of an enlarged growth share. They supported the 75/25 rule wholeheartedly and voted for it en bloc at every opportunity, although that brought them into open conflict with the representatives of the other municipalities. Indeed, the growth management controversy continued to fuel the animosities that had exploded during the annexation hearings. It bears emphasizing, however, that this conflict was not just an expression of intermunicipal rivalry and competition for development. It was, at a more basic level, a mark of the municipalities' fear that some part of their right to self-determination had been taken away from them.

On the face of it, given that it was such a clear-cut directive, the cabinet order might have been expected to simplify the regional plan process. Instead, by appearing quite arbitrarily to deprive so many municipal governments of their right to make decisions on matters of fundamental importance to them, it threw affairs into turmoil, to the extent that the process itself came to be seen as a threat to local freedoms. Nor was the situation eased by the actions of the Alberta Planning Board, which, like cabinet, was guilty of sending mixed signals. On the one hand, the board cast itself as the defender of municipal autonomy under its own guidelines; on the other, on three separate occasions between October 1982 and April 1983, it instructed the commission that the 75/25 rule had to be incorporated into the plan. As far as staff planners were concerned, this left them no choice: they were obliged to honour the order, which they did by devising an elaborate growth allocation scheme based on a functional classification of all the settlements in the metropolitan area. In the event, it was precisely these aspects of the draft plan that drew down the fiercest firestorm in the early months of 1983, when the municipalities came to appreciate the implications of the annexation order for each of them individually. All of them (except Edmonton) voiced their opposition to the overall growth limitation; many of them protested their classification under the planners' scheme, as an even more severe limitation on their growth prospects and freedom of choice; and some argued that the 75/25 rule should not appear in the plan at all because it was a policy of the provincial government. To frame development strategy around such a directive, it was claimed, would be tantamount to endorsing it. This point was taken up at meetings of the regional plan committee as well, and a motion to delete all references to a 75/25 growth allocation, and to treat the cabinet order as an appendix to the plan, was actually approved in April 1983.

At this stage, in the period March-May 1983, the Alberta Planning Board began to change its signals. First, in a move that had the effect of deflecting criticism from cabinet, the board joined in the chorus of objections to the draft plan. The planners, the board said, had erred in their operationalization of the 75/25 rule. Cabinet's wish, the planners were now told, was for "long-term estimates of future population," not specific population targets and growth allocations. The staff planners were also charged with having usurped municipal authority by producing such a prescriptive plan:

> In general, we feel that the draft severely extends into municipal autonomy particularly in the areas of land use designation, allocation of growth, and creation of hierarchies of communities.
> The Regional Planning Commission should be a facilitator of development in all communities by establishing policy parameters within which an individual municipality can, to a large extent, determine its own destiny (letter from the Alberta Planning Board, May 10, 1983).

Here, of course, the board was acting as the protector of municipal autonomy in accordance with its own guidelines for regional plan approval. But how were the planners supposed to reconcile those guidelines with an apparently firm order from cabinet? The board gave no help with this dilemma, other than to reiterate that the 75/25 rule had to figure in the plan. Then suddenly, in May 1983, the board changed its position, informing the regional plan committee that it would be permissible to remove the cabinet order to an appendix, where it would have no legal force and would not appear to have been sanctioned by the EMRPC. This, in turn, allowed the committee to substitute a general "statement of intent," to the effect that "Edmonton should maintain its present proportion of the region's population," followed by a rather more open planning goal: "To maintain the city of Edmonton as the dominant community in the region, while providing the opportunity for all other existing municipalities to share in the accommodation of the region's population and economic growth" (Edmonton Metropolitan Regional Planning Commission 1984, 13, 15). Thus, by relaxing its attitude towards the 75/25 rule, the board was able in a single stroke—a single inconsistent stroke—to live up to its self-imposed criteria, to assuage the fears of the region's municipalities without provoking Edmonton to fresh outrage, and to cast the staff planners as the villains of the piece. By acting as it did, the board made it appear that it was rescuing the regional plan committee from an untenable position that the planners had created.

The committee, for its part, behaved equivocally throughout. In principle its role was vital, because it was the official liaison between the commission's political and technical arms and was supposed to direct staff during policy formulation. In fact, that did not happen. Staff presented position papers to the committee, which then endorsed them, despite the serious reservations of some members. Similar reservations were expressed when the draft plan was submitted for the committee's review, but again no changes were made and the plan was allowed to proceed to public hearings. Not to put too fine a point on it, the committee abdicated its responsibility. In part this might be seen as a consequence of the dilemma posed for municipal government representatives by wearing two hats; that is, by being expected to take a regional as well as a municipal point of view and not being sure how to balance the claims of the two perspectives (see Aron 1969; Lim 1983). It has also been observed that participants in an interagency process are likely to react to situations of conflict and divergent opinions by avoiding commitment to any one stance (Skelcher 1982). In this case, the committee's passive endorsement of staff positions can certainly be interpreted as avoiding commitment. But when faced with a deluge of criticism from their own municipalities and forced to defend policies that most of them (wearing their local hats) did not support, the committee disavowed the plan. Again, then, staff became referred targets for criticisms that should more properly have been directed elsewhere, this time at the regional plan committee for failing to give direction when it was most needed. By failing to commit to policies they were prepared to defend, committee members exacerbated the conflict over the regional plan process and isolated their technical staff, who had at least tried to represent the regional perspective.

This is not to suggest, however, that the planners were entirely innocent victims of a process in which self-serving municipalities were eventually able to get their own way in the name of local autonomy. The planners were as guilty as anyone of failing to face up to the political realities of the context in which they were operating. More guilty perhaps, because they were well aware of the long record of conflict among the local municipalities and should have understood its implications. But although EMRPC documents characterized the commission as a forum for intermunicipal negotiation and compromise, and hence an appropriate body for resolving disputes, the regional plan exercise was not approached in that light. In terms of the classic dichotomy between technical and political planners (Howe 1980), the EMRPC staff were unquestionably on the technical side. Their task, as they saw it, was a problem-solving one (Baum 1980), which meant they had to show how growth could best be managed within the constraints of whatever policy directives were issued by the political decision makers. In the absence of firm instructions from the regional plan committee, that came down to the cabinet order. Yet by being so closely associated with the 75/25 rule, the planners lost the confidence of the member municipalities and so became, to a large degree, the specific focus of conflict. From the planners' perspective, socialized as they were by modernist planning theory, they were the only ones dealing with the needs of the overriding locality, the region, and the only coherent voice for the regional interest. From the members' perspective, however, staff members were acting more like agents of the provincial government and so were part of the attack on local autonomy—the most exposed and accessible part.

Discussion and Implications

At one level, the Edmonton events afford a particularly rich demonstration of the political reality of metropolitan planning. The situation bred conflict of quite unusual kind and degree, especially after the regional plan process became conflated with the most aggressive annexation attempt in Edmonton's long history of territorial expansion. This gave rise to the most unusual circumstance of all, in that it forced the Alberta cabinet to become involved, at least indirectly, in a regional planning exercise. Although cabinet could not be an active participant in the business of preparing the plan, its annexation order reshaped the context for regional planning in the Edmonton area and thus became a major factor in the disputes that attended the planning process.

At the same time, it must be emphasized that Edmonton's regional plan process did not become political *because* of cabinet's actions. While the particular forms and intensity of political activity were certainly a consequence of the cabinet order, conflict was inherent in the situation. The structure of the regional planning organization, the institutional framework provided by the 1977 planning act, and the attitudes of the Edmonton area municipalities, some of which were of extremely long standing, all guaranteed that. The events associated with the first draft plan of 1979 can be offered in evidence. In 1977, on the basis of enormously detailed technical studies, the commission's planners devised four possible growth management strategies (Edmonton Regional Planning Commission 1977). The choice of the dispersed growth alternative, however, was a thoroughly political decision that reflected the power structure of the commission at the time. Above all, it was a decision that the city of Edmonton was powerless to prevent under the regional planning system. City council therefore attempted to resolve the issue by turning to the annexation process instead. In this it was at least partially successful, both with respect to Edmonton's authorized growth share and, more significantly, in its stronger voice on the regional planning commission. These outcomes had political consequences of their own, of course, but that simply underlines the inescapably political character of regional planning—especially the metropolitan form of regional planning.

In terms of the case study, the real question is not why Edmonton's situation generated conflict but what that conflict reveals about the institution of regional planning under stress. By the early 1980s, when Edmonton's regional plan episode reached its climacteric, localism had become a force to be reckoned with in planning practice. Planning institutions had to adapt to this new reality, but the transition was not necessarily smooth or easy, or even well-understood. That was vividly illustrated in the Edmonton case. Underlying all the conflict was confusion and disagreement about the nature and purpose of regional planning and its appropriate role in a metropolitan setting. Should the regional plan be the policy-giving instrument, and hence an expression of regional will and authority, representing the overriding locality? Or should it be a coordinating device, a "compendium of local plans" as it was described during the Edmonton debates, with the real policy initiative coming from the individual municipalities? In more familiar language, should regional planning be top-down or bottom-up? Conventional planning theory, modernist theory, favoured the former, and so too did the planning staff of the EMRPC. The spirit of localism, on the other hand, demanded a bottom-up approach, and the Alberta planning system had actually moved in that direction in 1977. The significance of the legislative changes was not readily grasped, though; certainly not by municipal politicians and not even by professional planners.

The source of difficulty lay in the way the Alberta Planning Act was framed. Prior to 1977, the scope and contents of regional plans were closely prescribed, and the statute left no doubt that they were intended to be technical documents serving essentially functional ends. Among other things, they were to be prepared by "qualified planning officers"; they were to be based on scientifically conducted surveys and analyses; and they were to have overarching authority with respect to such matters as land-use regulation, population density, development phasing, and the provision of public works and infrastructure. All this disappeared in 1977, to be replaced by much briefer and vaguer statements that could be interpreted in various ways. That was the whole point, of course—the postmodernist point, although no one thought of it in just those terms. The role of the statute, in its new context, was to give regional planning commissions as much freedom as possible in determining for themselves how to approach their prescribed task, based on the wishes of their member municipalities. The statute could not state this explicitly, though. It required interpretation, which was not forthcoming until the Alberta Planning Board, troubled by the prescriptive nature of the plans it was receiving for review, issued its guidelines in 1982.

Given these circumstances, it is not surprising that confusion over the mandate for regional planning was a major source of conflict. Although the 1977 planning act established the ground for a radically different approach, it was only through the fire of practice that it could take on real substance. This also explains why the Edmonton regional planners were able to act as they did. Their view of the proper role of a regional plan was exactly the same after 1977 as it was before, and they approached the task of preparing the draft plans of 1979 and 1982 as though nothing had changed. For this reason, the key conflict in the regional plan process, and the one that truly indicated an institution in painful transition, was the clash of opposing visions between the staff planners, who stood for comprehensiveness and regional order, and the politicians on the regional plan committee, who stood for local initiative and decentralized control. Despite the committee's initial indecisiveness, it was a conflict the planners could not win, given the tenor of the times. Even the cabinet order, which confounded the whole process by introducing the complication of central interference in policy determination, could not stand against the spirit of localism at full flood. On the contrary, it intensified local feelings and so explains much of the aggressiveness with which the municipalities spoke out in defence of their autonomy.

The conflict between the two visions was clearly revealed as well in the *ex post facto* assessments of the staff planners and the members of the regional plan committee. The planners, who were embittered by the whole experience, had little good to say of it. With one exception they damned the process as ineffective, though agreeing that the plan was probably the best that could have been achieved under the circumstances—and the circumstance they particularly had in mind was the structure of the regional planning commission. In their judgment, the regional plan had foundered on the rock of local representation. No better outcome could be expected from a process in which decision-making authority was vested in people whose allegiance lay with the municipalities they had been elected to represent.

In part, the members of the regional plan committee agreed with this assessment. They admitted that their first loyalty was to their localities and that it was difficult to balance local and regional interests. They, like the planners, found much to criticize about the course the regional plan process had taken but considered it to have been redeemed by the fact that the local voice did ultimately prevail. In their view, the best regional plan is the one that interferes least with the prerogative of every municipality to make its own decisions and pursue its own growth aspirations. The dominant sentiment was most clearly expressed by a committee member who said, "Municipalities must control their fate. . . . If [regional planning] commissions have too much power, the electorate would lose control over decisions." To the planners, by contrast, most of whom remained wedded to their modernist ideals, effective regional planning required real power to be vested at the regional level. "The commission needs more clout," said one planner bluntly. "Regional planning will only work with a regional government that can enforce good regional design," suggested another.

On the basis of experience elsewhere in Canada, those opinions are debatable at best (see, for example, Cameron 1979; Robinson and

Webster 1985; Cullingworth, 1987). Larger questions nonetheless remain: Has an already weak institution been weakened still further, perhaps to the point of impotence, by the increased emphasis on local control? What role should regional planning play in the current climate? Does it have any value at all if the only acceptable purpose for a regional plan is to set policy in such broad terms that the constituent communities feel no constraint on their freedom of action? In Edmonton's case, there is no evidence yet that the plan as approved has had undesirable consequences, and there are no grounds for supposing that a more prescriptive plan would have had better effect on the form of the metropolitan area. The unease persists, however, certainly among professional planners, who fear that regional planning has indeed been diminished and may well have become impossible. The organization still exists but it functions primarily as a centralized service agency for the member municipalities, assisting them in the preparation and administration of their own planning instruments. Even that role is steadily being reduced as more and more municipalities are taking over planning responsibilities for themselves. Since most of them now have subdivision approval authority as well, a long shadow has been cast over the commission's future.

But that is to continue to think of regional planning in traditional terms. There is an alternative, more positive view, to which the Edmonton case study at least points. The most instructive aspect of the entire episode, for all who took part in it, was the attention it drew to the importance of *process*. For the first time, everyone involved in Edmonton's metropolitan planning system was learning that plan-making is not just a technical procedure, no matter how expert and dedicated the technical staff may be. They learned the hard way, unfortunately. The Edmonton case illustrated the planning process at its worst—divisive, embittering, and potentially destructive. Yet that did not in itself prove that regional planning is either unworkable or irrelevant. Localism and fragmentation are undeniably powerful forces. As one member of Edmonton's regional plan committee observed, "Any process not sensitive to municipal concerns is doomed from the start." But if it is accepted, as it surely must be, that the regional perspective is as vital today as it ever was, so too is the need for effective mechanisms for intermunicipal collaboration and collective decision making at the metropolitan scale. The challenge for regional planning, as one of these mechanisms, is to turn localism and fragmentation to constructive account. This, we believe, can happen only in a process controlled by the municipal governments themselves, as equal partners and equal participants—a process of negotiation and consensus-building that might best be thought of as a kind of diplomacy. If there is to be hope for a postmodern style of metropolitan planning, that would appear to be the key.

REFERENCES

AAMDC/AUMA. 1980. *Municipal Attitudes Towards Regional Planning in Alberta.* A Report by the Joint Working Committee of the Alberta Association of Municipal Districts and Counties and the Alberta Urban Municipalities Association. Edmonton.

Alberta. 1980. *Planning in Alberta: A Guide and Directory,* revised edition. Edmonton: Alberta Municipal Affairs.

_____. 1982a. *Revised Guidelines for Regional Plan Preparation and Review.* Edmonton: Alberta Planning Board.

_____. 1982b. *Framework for Application of Regional Plan Guidelines.* Edmonton: Alberta Planning Board.

Aron, J. 1969. *The Quest for Regional Cooperation.* Berkeley: University of California Press.

Batey, W. L., and P. J. Smith. 1981. "The Role of Territory in Political Conflict in Metropolitan Fringe Areas." In *The Rural-Urban Fringe: Canadian Perspectives,* ed. K. B. Beesley and L. H. Russwurm, Geographical Monographs No. 10, Downsview: Atkinson College, York University, 199-217.

Baum, H. S. 1980. "The Uncertain Consciousness of Planners and the Professional Enterprise." *Plan Canada* 20 (March): 39-53.

Bayne, P. E. 1986. "Regional Planning and Local Autonomy in the Edmonton Metropolitan Region, 1981-1984." Unpublished M.A. thesis, University of Alberta, Edmonton.

Beauregard, R. A. 1989. "Between Modernity and Postmodernity: The Ambiguous Position of U.S. Planning." *Environment and Planning D: Society and Space* 7(4): 381-95.

Bordessa, R., and J. Cameron. 1982. "Growth Management Conflicts in the Toronto-Centred Region." In *Conflict, Politics and the Urban Scene,* ed. K. R. Cox and R. J. Johnston, London: Longman, 127-45.

Bossons, J. 1978. *Reforming Planning in Ontario: Strengthening the Municipal Role.* Toronto: Ontario Economic Council.

Boyne, R., and A. Rattansi. 1990. "The Theory and Politics of Postmodernism: By Way of an Introduction." In *Postmodernism and Society,* ed. R. Boyne and A. Rattansi, London: Macmillan, 1-45.

Branch, M. C. 1988. *Regional Planning: Introduction and Explanation.* New York: Praeger Publishers.

Brooke, M. Z. 1984. *Centralization and Autonomy: A Study in Organizational Behaviour.* London: Holt, Rinehart and Winston.

Cameron, K. D. 1979. "Planning in a Metropolitan Framework: The Toronto Experience." In *Urban and Regional Planning in a Federal State: The Canadian Experience*, ed. W. J. Perks and I. M. Robinson, Stroudsburg, Penn.: Dowden, Hutchinson and Ross, 246-57.

_____. 1984. "Bill 9: The Day After." *CIP Forum ICU* (April): 1, 7.

Clark, G. L. 1984. "Theory of Local Autonomy." *Annals of the Association of American Geographers* 74 (June): 195-208.

Cullingworth, J. B. 1987. *Urban and Regional Planning in Canada.* New Brunswick, N. J.: Transaction Books.

Curry, M. R. 1991. "Postmodernism, Language, and the Strains of Modernism." *Annals of the Association of American Geographers* 81 (June): 210-28.

Dale, L., and T. L. Burton. 1984. "Regional Planning in Alberta: Performance and Prospects." *Alberta Journal of Planning Practice* 3: 17-41.

Dear, M. J. 1986. "Postmodernism and Planning." *Environment and Planning D: Society and Space* 4(3): 367-84.

Edmonton Metropolitan Regional Planning Commission. 1982. *Proposed Edmonton Metropolitan Regional Plan: A Draft for Public Review.* Edmonton.

_____. 1984. *Edmonton Metropolitan Regional Plan.* Edmonton.

Edmonton Regional Planning Commission. 1977. *A Choice of Growth Management Strategies.* Edmonton Region Growth Studies, Final Report. Edmonton.

_____. 1979. *Edmonton Regional Plan* (draft), 2 volumes. Edmonton.

Evenden, L. J. 1978. "Shaping the Vancouver Suburbs." In *Vancouver: Western Metropolis*, ed. L. J. Evenden, Western Geographical Series Vol. 16, Victoria: University of Victoria, 179-99.

Frisken, F. 1982. "Old Problems, New Priorities: Changing Perspectives on Governmental Needs in an Expanding Region." In *Conflict or Cooperation? The Toronto-Centred Region in the 1980s*, ed. F. Frisken. Proceedings of Urban Studies Programme Symposium, Downsview: York University, 7-13.

_____. 1990. *Planning and Servicing the Greater Toronto Area: The Interplay of Provincial and Municipal Interests.* Urban Studies Working Paper No. 12. North York: York University.

Gertler, L. O. 1972. *Regional Planning in Canada: A Planner's Testament.* Montreal: Harvest House.

Goodchild, B. 1990. "Planning and the Modern/Postmodern Debate." *Town Planning Review* 61 (April): 119-37.

Grant, J. 1988. "They Say 'You Can't Legislate Public Participation': The Nova Scotia Experience." *Plan Canada* 27 (January): 260-67.

Hall, P. 1970. *Theory and Practice of Regional Planning.* London: Pemberton Books.

Harvey, D. 1989. *The Condition of Postmodernity: An Enquiry into the Origins of Cultural Change.* Oxford: Basil Blackwell.

Hodge, G. 1986. *Planning Canadian Communities: An Introduction to the Principles, Practice and Participants.* Toronto: Methuen.

Hoggart, K. 1981. *Local Decision-Making Autonomy: A Review of Conceptual and Methodological Issues.* Occasional Paper No. 13. London: Department of Geography, King's College, University of London.

Howe, E. 1980. "Role Choices of Urban Planners." *Journal of the American Planning Association* 46 (October): 398-409.

Laux, F. A. 1990. *Planning Law and Practice in Alberta.* Toronto: Carswell.

Lim, G. 1983. *Regional Planning: Evolution, Crisis and Prospects.* Ottowa, N.J.: Allanheld, Osmun & Co.

Macdonald, H. I. 1984. "A Retrospective View from the Top." *Plan Canada* 24 (December): 92-99.

Magnusson, W. 1985. "The Local State in Canada: Theoretical Perspectives." *Canadian Public Administration* 28 (Winter): 575-99.

McDowell, B. D. 1986. "Regional Planning Today." In *The Practice of State and Regional Planning,* ed. F. S. So, I. Hand, and B. D. McDowell, Chicago: American Planning Association, 133-65.

Mumford, L. 1986. "The Regional Framework of Civilization." In *The Lewis Mumford Reader,* ed. D. L. Miller, New York: Pantheon Books, 207-16.

Perloff, H. S. 1957. *Education for Planning: City, State and Regional.* Baltimore: The Johns Hopkins Press.

Plunkett, T. J. and J. Lightbody. 1982. "Tribunals, Politics and the Public Interest: The Edmonton Annexation Case." *Canadian Public Policy* 8 (Spring): 207-21.

Rashleigh, T. 1983. "B.C.: Controversial Amendment." *CIP Forum ICU* (October): 1, 3.

Robinson, I. M. 1979. "Trends in Provincial Land Planning, Control and Management." In *Urban and Regional Planning in a Federal State:*

The Canadian Experience, ed. W. J. Perks and I. M. Robinson, Stroudsburg, Penn.: Dowden, Hutchinson and Ross, 204-37.

_____, and D. M. Webster. 1985. "Regional Planning in Canada: History, Practice, Issues and Prospects." *Journal of the American Planning Association* 51 (Winter): 23-33.

Sholberg, C. 1991. "Anarchism and City Planning." *City Magazine* 12 (Summer): 25-33.

Skelcher, C. 1982. "Planning Context and Planning Methodology in Regional Planning." In *Approaches in Public Policy*, ed. S. Leach and J. Stewart, London: George Allen and Unwin, 120-48.

Smith, P. J. 1982. "Municipal Conflicts Over Territory and the Effectiveness of the Regional Planning System in the Edmonton Metropolitan Area." In Kulturgeographische *Prozessforschung in Kanada*, ed. H. Becker, Bamberger Geographische Schriften 4, Bamberg, 207-33.

_____. 1991. "Community Aspirations, Territorial Justice and the Metropolitan Form of Edmonton and Calgary." In *Social Geography of Canada: Essays in Honour of J. Wreford Watson*, ed. G. M. Robinson, Toronto: Dundurn Press, 245-66.

_____, and H. L. Diemer. 1978. "Equity and the Annexation Process: Edmonton's Bid for the Strathcona Industrial Corridor." In *Edmonton: The Emerging Metropolitan Pattern*, ed. P. J. Smith, Western Geographical Series Vol. 15, Victoria: University of Victoria, 263-89.

Sussman, C. 1976. *Planning the Fourth Migration: The Neglected Vision of the Regional Planning Association of America*. Cambridge: The MIT Press.

Wichern, P. 1986. "Metropolitan Reform and the Restructuring of Local Governments in the North American City." In *Power and Place: Canadian Urban Development in the North American Context*, ed. G. A. Stelter and A. F. J. Artibise, Vancouver: University of British Columbia Press, 292-322.

Chapter 23

Industrial Decentralization and the Planned Industrial Park:
A Case Study of Metropolitan Halifax

Hugh Millward
St. Mary's University
Shelley Dickey
City of Halifax

This chapter is a Canadian case study of recent changes in the intrametropolitan location of industry, with particular emphasis on suburbanization and the rise of the planned industrial park. The decentralization of industry in the modern metropolis has been described as a fundamental long-run process (Scott 1982a, 129) in which industrialists respond to a variety of factors pushing them from the centre and attracting them toward the periphery. Centrifugal forces strengthened considerably after 1945, prompting governmental responses in the form of industrial zoning and, in many Canadian cities, publicly funded industrial parks. Metropolitan Halifax has been characterized by highly active provincial and municipal intervention in the market for industrial land, and this chapter assesses the locational impact of such intervention. Changes in industrial site requirements, the impact of new transportation technologies, and the increased role of urban planning are all examined, as is intermunicipal competition for new industrial plants. The Halifax-Dartmouth experience is compared with general models and

Comments in this chapter do not represent official positions or policies of the City of Halifax.

theories of evolving industrial location and with empirical studies drawn from Canada, the United States, and Britain.

Strictly speaking, all forms of employment are industry. The standard industrial classification used in the census includes, for example, retail trade, professional services, and construction. Yet in everyday parlance "industry" is associated with factories (though no longer with smokestacks), and thus primarily with manufacturing. Manufacturing (industry division E) involves fabrication, assembly, or blending of products, whether they be newspapers, clothing, or soft drinks, and is the focus of the analysis in this chapter. But purpose-built industrial buildings are increasingly warehouses and service buildings rather than factories, so much of the discussion will relate also to transportation and storage (division G), communication and other utilities (H), and wholesaling (I). This working description of industry accords with that used in municipal plans and zoning codes. It blurs at the edges, since services, offices, and retailing are increasingly found in so-called industrial parks.

Manufacturing industry is important in many Canadian metropolitan areas. It typically provided a major impetus for growth in the late nineteenth and early twentieth centuries and continues as the core of the basic (i.e., export) sector of the urban economy. Manufacturing industry is also important in that its locational requirements strongly influence urban land-use configurations, whether in the *laissez-faire* land market or in the increasingly planned and regulated land patterns of the post-1945 city. Industrialists are courted by municipal planners and politicians, since new industry generates tax revenue, basic employment, and (through the multiplier effect) additional service employment. In terms of "greenfield" planning, priority is given to setting aside large areas of suitable industrial land before allocating lands for residential development, service commercial activity, or recreation. Particularly where there is intermunicipal competition to attract new industry, industrial land is overzoned (more is set aside for this use than is actually required), which lowers its price relative to underzoned uses such as housing or commerce. In the pecking order of land uses, industry often gets the first bite at the lowest price.

At the local scale, manufacturing industries have traditionally been viewed as bad neighbours. Consequently they were initially segregated into industrial zones and later into planned suburban industrial parks. Concentrations of manufacturing firms, however, attract wholesaling, distribution, and business-service industries. Cheap serviced land, with the appropriate zoning, attracts sales/service outlets, warehouse retailers, and offices. In larger industrial districts, flows of business and commuter traffic attract conventional retailing and consumer services. Successful suburban industrial districts thus act as major nodes of both employment and commerce, becoming focal points for the entire suburbanization process.

METROPOLITAN HALIFAX: INDUSTRIAL DEVELOPMENT TO 1960

The Halifax metropolitan area is small enough (321,000 people in 1991) for a detailed study, yet large enough to display many typical features of urban development. There has been moderately rapid growth since 1945, and for the last two decades the metro economy has faithfully reflected the nation's unemployment and population growth rates. In addition, the metropolitan area comprises several municipalities that have been subject to a degree of regional planning while competing vigorously for industrial development; thus the important factors influencing industrial location are all represented.

The original townsite of Halifax, now the Central Business District (CBD), was founded in 1749 on the eastern side of a peninsula, adjacent to the deep and sheltered harbour (see Map 23.1). The sister community of Dartmouth was founded the following year (1750) on the opposite shore. The spatial growth of both communities was constrained and shaped by evolving transportation technologies, in the typical sequence (see Adams 1970; Muller 1981, 26-58). Early small-scale industry remained juxtaposed with other land uses, though with a tendency to locate at harbourside (Blakeley 1949; Raddall 1971; McCann 1979). This pre-industrial revolution pattern corresponds with initial stages of developmental models proposed by Pred (1964), Northam (1975, 300-05), and Yeates (1990, 228-32). In the early industrial revolution, the pattern remained oriented to the harbour, spreading northward a little, but not until the railway era did industrial suburbs grow up some distance from downtown. The first railway line, opened in 1854, skirted the northern perimeter of the peninsula and terminated three kilometres north of downtown at Richmond (Map 23.1).[1] This settlement rapidly became an industrial suburb, as did the north end of Dartmouth once a line was

---

[1]Downtown Halifax was connected to the rail system in the 1870s by an extension from Richmond to Water Street, just north of today's CBD.

Map 23.1. *Employment in Manufacturing Plants, 1967*

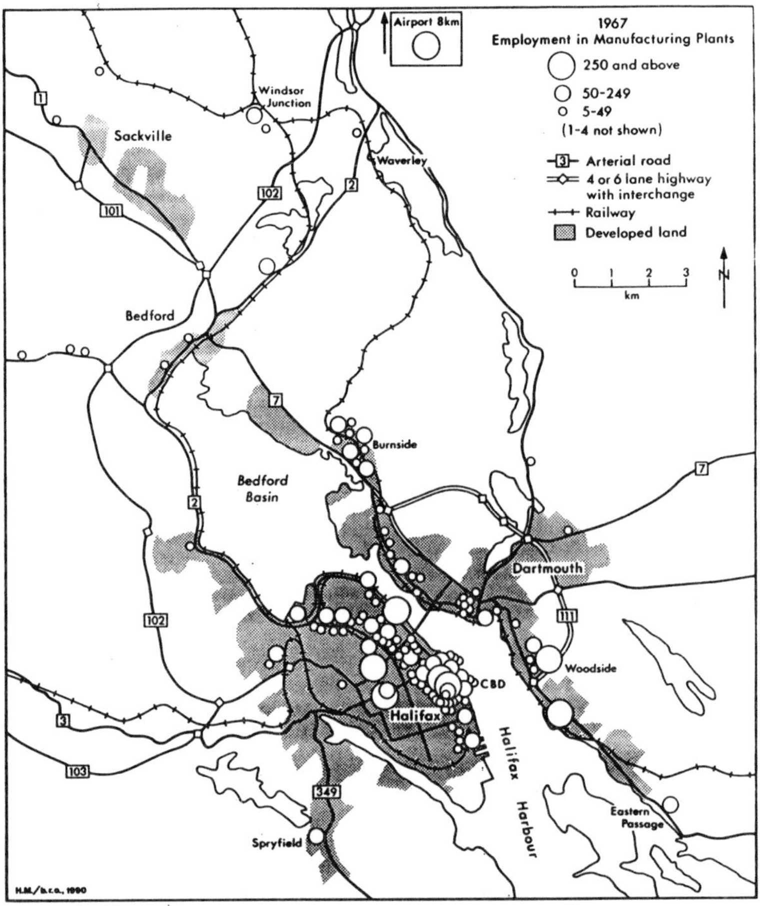

constructed across the Narrows in 1885.[2] A railroad spur led counter-clockwise from the Richmond terminus, parallelling the original line, but then striking south-east toward the centre of the peninsula. This "Cotton Factory siding" formed a partial belt-line[3] and like the other lines

---

[2]After the bridge collapsed twice, Dartmouth was re-connected to the rail network via Windsor Junction.

[3]Belt-lines were typical features in larger North American cities, and railroad companies often marketed industrial lands adjacent to these lines (Hartshorn 1980, 390-97).

promoted industrial development at "greenfield" sites on what was then the periphery of the built-up area (see Map 23.1).[4] The major exception was the CN line, built through the South End during the First World War. The deep cutting provided no room for adjacent industry, except where the line disgorged to the new ocean terminals south of the CBD.

The pattern of industry that had developed by the First World War changed little before 1960. Halifax suffered a prolonged depression in the 1920s and 1930s and even in the 1950s was experiencing industrial decline. Without new or expanding industries there was little response to the new possibilities afforded by trucking, which had produced noticeable decentralization in the United States as early as the 1920s (Hawley 1956; Zelinsky 1962; Pred 1964). In Canada, too, considerable suburbanization of industry occurred in major growth centres such as Toronto and Vancouver during the 1950s (Kerr and Spelt 1958; Steed 1973). But in Halifax inertia kept the industrial pattern constant: a large cluster in the downtown core and discontinuous ribbons around the harbour and along the railway lines (Map 23.1). Within the CBD were many small-scale enterprises, with printing and apparel prevalent. The largest plants were Moir's chocolate factory, the Schwartz spice factory, and the *Halifax Herald* newspaper building. Immediately north of the CBD, in the semi-slum of the North End, small-scale enterprises mingled with a few larger factories. Further north still, there were newer plants along the Cotton Factory siding and Murphy's clothing factory at the isthmus (on the CN South Shore line). Around the harbour, manufacturing plants included the Shipyard in Richmond, National Sea Products fishplant at the Ocean Terminals, the Marine Slipways in Dartmouth Cove, and the Imperial Oil refinery at Woodside. The latter was constructed in 1916, at the only site to meet all locational requirements: a large undeveloped tract adjacent to deep water, with rail access, and close to large lakes for freshwater intake. (The smaller Texaco refinery, built in the early '60s, was located at nearby Eastern Passage for similar reasons.) Outside the CBD, only two major plants were without rail access; Ben's bakery and the Co-operative dairy distributed their products locally by truck and were thus located centrally with respect to their market (i.e., in the middle of the peninsula).

---

[4]The built-up area was restricted to the peninsula and the Dartmouth waterfront until 1945 (see Millward 1981, Ch. 2).

CHANGES IN INDUSTRIAL LOCATION, 1960-1990

The year 1960 marks the beginning of a rapid process of industrial suburbanization. Although new industrial plants in earlier times had typically been built at the city's edge on "greenfield" sites, the process after 1960 was markedly different, for two reasons: (1) the development of planned industrial parks, specifically catering to the needs of industrialists, and (2) an accelerating exodus of industry from what had hitherto been its most favoured location, the central business district. These two processes are linked, in that industrial parks not only attracted new industry but also induced many established industries to relocate from the congested inner city.

Ideally, Map 23.1 would show the 1960 pattern. However, data on employment in manufacturing plants, published in the annual *Directory of Manufacturers* (Nova Scotia, Dept. of Industry, Trade, and Technology), are available only from 1967 onward. Already by 1967 some features of the modern pattern were beginning to emerge. The Woodside Industrial Park in south Dartmouth and Commodore Commercial Estates in north Dartmouth (later incorporated into Burnside Industrial Park) were already enjoying modest success. In addition, the Halifax International Airport, constructed in the late 1950s, had attracted a major manufacturer in the form of Fairey Canada (later renamed I.M.P.). Fairey, which serviced aircraft, had previously been located near the Shearwater airport.

The real shift from inner city to suburban industrial park, however, occurred in the 1970s and 1980s and is still underway. A comparison of Maps 23.1 and 23.2 demonstrates the magnitude of change, which is particularly striking when one considers the degree of inertia built into the pattern. The major focus of manufacturing firms has clearly shifted from the Halifax CBD to Burnside Industrial Park. In 1988 Burnside had a level of employment similar to the CBD in 1967 but spread over much more land. This reflects less competition from other land uses, lower land costs, and the shift from intensive to extensive use of land by modern industry.

Like the CBD, the inner-city zone of mixed land use in the Halifax North End has also lost employment, as has the Dartmouth downtown area. By contrast, new minor foci have arisen in the suburbs, notably Woodside Industrial Park and Hammonds Plains Road in west Bedford. The latter area not only contains an industrial park but has also attracted from inner-city Halifax a large free-standing plant, the Co-operative dairy.

Map 23.2. *Employment in Manufacturing Plants, 1988*

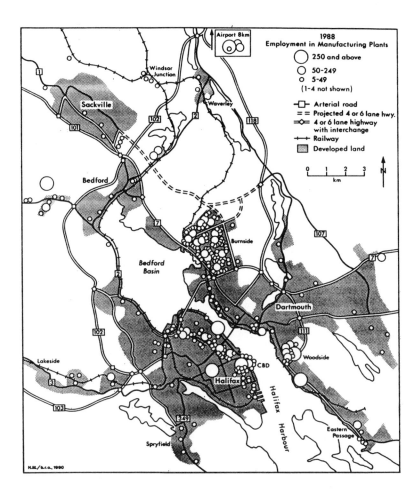

One other noteworthy change is the growth of manufacturing in Aerotech Industrial Park at the airport.

The changing industrial pattern conforms with and supports many generalizations about intra-urban industrial location. It reflects the impact of changing transportation technologies, notably the de-emphasis of railroads and the enhanced importance of peripheral freeways and highways (the latest stage in the models of Pred, Northam, and Yeates). It also reflects increased space needs of industry resulting from automation and assembly-line production methods, and the attraction of planned industrial parks. Industry was pulled toward the suburbs but also pushed out of the urban core. Not only were central premises outdated but they also lacked room for expansion and were incompatible with adjacent uses. In Halifax, planners began actively to discourage industry through downzoning in the North End, while urban renewal projects such as Scotia Square caused "economic extinction" of some CBD enterprises. Many of these push and pull factors were detailed in early essays by Colby (1933) and Haig (1927) that remain highly applicable to the recent Halifax experience. Haig's work in particular shows why printing clung tenaciously to the downtown area, since it requires access to its raw material (local news) and close contact with local markets (see also Groves 1971). Even so, the *Daily News* has already moved its plant to the suburbs and its larger competitor (the *Halifax Herald*) is preparing to do so.

The static model that most closely fits the current Halifax pattern was proposed by Cameron (1973) and portrayed graphically by Yeates (1990, 232-36). It defines and locates four major spatial groups of industry in an urban area: (1) central clusters (e.g., the Halifax and Dartmouth CBDs and the old North End), (2) decentralized clusters, typically appearing as industrial parks (e.g., Woodside and Burnside), (3) random spreads, comprising scattered plants serving the local market (e.g., Ben's bakery), and (4) peripheral patterns: large free-standing plants outside the built-up area (e.g., the refineries, Co-op dairy, and the airport industries). The Cameron-Yeates model describes an inland city and thus neglects (5) port-based industry (e.g., the Halifax shipyard, Dartmouth marine slips, and Dover flour mills at the Ocean Terminal). Herbert and Thomas (1982) note this typical group of industries in their model.

SITING AND DEVELOPMENT OF INDUSTRIAL PARKS

Map 23.3 is based on a map prepared for the latest updating of the Halifax-Dartmouth Regional Development Plan (Nova Scotia, Municipal Affairs 1988). Industrial parks are numbered and keyed to information in Table 23.1. Approximately half of all industrial land, whether developed or undeveloped, now lies within the official boundaries of industrial parks. In addition, undeveloped industrial lands lying adjacent to the parks generally are "holding" areas available for future park expansion. The major exceptions are areas zoned for expansion of the two refineries (Imperial Oil at Woodside and Texaco at Eastern Passage), and for expansion of major rock quarries (particularly Rocky Lake quarry east of Bedford).

Map 23.3. *Location of Industrial Lands, and Designated Industrial Parks*

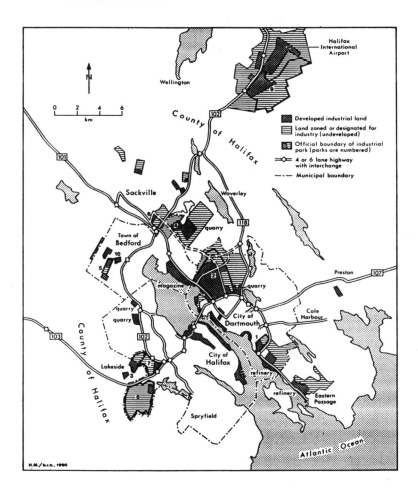

The growing dominance of industrial parks is typical. Bale (1977, 87) has commented that "today the most readily identifiable manufacturing sites within the urban region are industrial estates." Planners and economists have studied industrial parks as elements of land supply (e.g., Muncy 1970; Urban Land Institute 1976; Conway et al. 1979), and a small body of geographic literature focuses specifically on their locational aspects (Bale 1974, 1977; Cox 1966; Evans 1972; Hartshorn 1973; Northam 1965). All industrial parks are "organized districts with a com-

Table 23.1.   *Metropolitan Halifax: Industrial Parks, 1989*

Map No.	Name	Type (1)	Year Estbl.
1	Woodside Ocean	I/R	1959
2	Burnside		
	a) Commodore Estates	I	1960
	b) Burnside	I	1968
	c) City of Lakes	B	1985
3	Lakeside	I	1964
4	Bedford	I (heavy)	1972
5	Atlantic Acres	I (light)	1973
6	Sackville	I/B	1981
7	Bayer's Lake	I	1984
8	Ragged Lake	R/B	1984
9	Aerotech	I/R	1986
10	Hammonds Plains Rd.	I	1988

Notes:
(1)   Type codes: Industrial (i.e., fabrication-distribution-warehousing) = I; Business = B; Research and Science = R
(2)   NSBCC is the Nova Scotia Business Capital Corporation. This provincial crown corporation was formerly called Industrial Estates Ltd. (IEL). "Halifax," "Dartmouth," and "County," refer to the Industrial Commissions of the City of Halifax, City of Dartmouth, and County of Halifax, respectively.
(3)   Land presently occupied, or with a commitment for occupancy.
(4)   Total land area within the official boundary of the park. Excludes holding zones adjacent to parks.
(5)   Pending approval from N.S. Dept. of Environment.
Source: N.S. Muncicipal Affairs 1989, 2-11.

prehensive plan . . . for the regulation of lot sizes, land use, architecture and landscaping . . . " (Hartshorn 1973, 33) but three major functional forms may be identified. In order of both historical evolution and ubiquity, they are fabrication-distribution-warehousing parks, business parks, and research and science parks (Hartshorn 1980, 392-97). In addition, we may identify "fly-in" or airport parks as a special locational type (Muller 1981, 140).

Original Deverloper (2)	Present Owner (2)	Occupied Area (ha) (3)	Total Area (ha) (4)
IEL	NSBCC	52	146
private Dartmouth	Dartmouth	476	810
Dartmouth	Dartmouth	25	191
County	County	34	91
private	NSBCC	43	45
private	NSBCC	30	49
IEL	NSBCC	7	85
Halifax	Halifax	41	203
Halifax	Halifax	10	486
County	County	66	243
private	private	2	203 (5)

In Halifax, as elsewhere in North America, early industrial parks were intended for conventional industries. It was not until the 1980s that parks were specially designated for business or research (see Table 23.1). A prototype industrial park was laid out by the City of Halifax Industrial Commission in the early 1950s (Commission Street, beside the Cotton Factory siding), but the first officially designated park was developed by a provincial crown corporation in 1959. Dartmouth's Woodside Industrial Park has been only modestly successful, attracting two large manufacturers (electronics and chocolate). Its early slow growth was partly due to its lack of rail access: the shoreline track cannot be extended into the park. In 1979 the park's marketing orientation and name were changed to focus on ocean-related R and D industry (Norcliffe 1980, 538). As part of this strategy, a federal-provincial cost-sharing agreement provided funding for a common-user wharf. Little has come of this initiative to date, owing to downturns in both the fishing and offshore exploration industries.

Burnside Industrial Park was initiated in the late 1960s by the City of Dartmouth alongside the CN railway in north Dartmouth and adjacent to the earlier private development of Commodore Commercial Estates. There were numerous provincial subsidies to Burnside and many firms received tax incentives to locate there (City of Dartmouth 1976). Rail access was considered to be important in promoting growth (Canplan Consultants 1973), and three major spur lines were laid through Burnside and Commodore Estates. The two parks were amalgamated under city ownership in 1979, and in 1985 an extension was designated as the City of Lakes Business Park. The latter forms part of Burnside for planning and management purposes but is promoted separately as a "prestige natural environment . . . interlaced with a park and green space network." Its intended clients are "blue-chip" companies seeking a prestige business address.

Outside Dartmouth, the only industrial park designated in the 1960s lay in the municipality of the County of Halifax, at Lakeside (see Map 23.3). Developed by the county's industrial commission, it has both rail and highway access but is on the wrong side of the metropolitan area for regional distribution purposes, since most of the province's population is reached via routes 101 and 102. Only a small part of the park's potential area has been developed, and little future growth is likely.

In the early 1970s two small private parks were developed near the dormitory suburb of Bedford, which then lay in the county (it was incorporated as a town in 1980). In 1981, in response to recommendations in the Halifax-Dartmouth Regional Development Plan (Metropolitan Area Planning Committee 1975), the adjacent suburb of Sackville also acquired a small industrial park. All three of these parks are presently owned by a provincial crown corporation (Nova Scotia Business Capital Corporation, NSBCC). Bedford's municipal plan recommends distinct roles for Atlantic Acres (light industry) and Bedford Industrial Park (heavy and noxious industry), while Sackville's plan calls for more service and business uses in the Sackville Business Park. Development of a private park in Bedford, on Hammonds Plains Road, has been suspended pending approval of its water and sewer systems.

The City of Halifax entered the industrial park game late, owing to a lack of suitable sites. Harbourside locations had been developed for port activity; mainland areas with suitable rail and highway access were either "frozen" as water catchment areas, or lay outside city limits. Furthermore, the provincially sponsored 1975 regional plan recommended an industrial strategy based solely on locational and environmental suitability, without reference to municipal ambitions. In this plan, Halifax City was allocated no industrial park. Instead, major growth was to be in Burnside, with minor growth at Woodside, Eastern Passage, and Lakeside. Such a regional plan had unfavourable tax implications for Halifax, and the city overcame these recommendations in several ways. The most obvious approach was to acquire land in the vicinity of Lakeside Industrial Park. The city annexed extensive areas of virgin land in 1983, despite objections from the county, and designated them as industrial parks. Most of the Bayer's Lake area had been set aside for industry in the regional plan, but the extensive Ragged Lake Research and Business Park lay completely outside the plan's "development boundary" (see Map 23.3 and Table 23.1).[5] By this date regional planning had become largely ineffective since the province's 1983 Planning Act removed it from its preeminent position, leaving it powerless in the face of municipal aspirations.

Halifax City now has large parks on paper, but Burnside has already garnered the lion's share of suburbanizing industry. Like Lakeside, the Halifax parks lie on the wrong side of the metropolitan area. In addition one of them lacks rail access. A new interchange links Bayer's Lake to highway 102, however, and Bayer's Lake has gained a key tenant in the form of Volvo Canada.[6] Ragged Lake is attempting to compete head-on with the City of Lakes business park but lacks the established location and highway visibility enjoyed by the latter. Perhaps planned amenity features, such as walking trails and an on-site golf course, will redress the balance.

Another municipal venture has recently opened outside the development boundary of the 1975 plan and at considerable distance from downtown Halifax. The county's Aerotech Research and Manufacturing Park enjoys special locational advantages: a "fly-in" environment for managerial and sales personnel and ready access to the rest of the province via the freeway-standard 102 highway. It is promoted as a "high-technology park," providing a "campus-like setting." Major tenants to date are Pratt and Whitney, which manufactures aircraft-engine components, and Litton, which services avionic systems. Aerotech can draw on a huge area (1,000 ha) for expansion but its present boundaries

---

[5]The development boundary was intended to limit the spread of urban land uses and services. It was based primarily on environmental suitability for development.

[6]Volvo moved from a harbourside location in the Richmond area of Halifax. Its facility there had outdated buildings and inadequate storage space.

encompass 243 ha south of the airport and east of the highway (Map 23.3).

The process by which industrial parks were first established and operated owes more to the British than to the American example. In creating Industrial Estates Ltd. in 1957, the provincial government was consciously following the contemporary British model of top-down economic and land-use planning. Woodside Industrial Estate, IEL's first project, was the region's first planned industrial district. But almost from the beginning there were competing private and municipal ventures. A lack of coordination from the top and the failure to vigourously implement the recommendations of the 1975 regional plan have resulted in a proliferation of competing parks and agencies. The strong competition between uncoordinated developments is increasingly similar to the United States' case, though with the notable difference that almost all development of industrial sites remains directly controlled and heavily subsidized by local governments. The top-down planning model has been largely abandoned: provincial involvement in NSBCC is vestigial, and the regional planning process has been emasculated, leaving a free-for-all between competing municipal agencies.

THE SUCCESS OF BURNSIDE INDUSTRIAL PARK

As a group, the new industrial parks have clearly been attractive to industrialists. From Figure 23.1, we see that for 30 years nearly all growth in the manufacturing sector has been absorbed in these parks. From a low point in 1968, the number of manufacturing firms in the metropolitan area has grown by 143 percent. However, the number of firms outside industrial parks has grown by only 63 percent, while the number within industrial parks has grown by 1,173 percent. If we add nonmanufacturing industry, industrial parks have grown much more than Figure 23.1 suggests. The combined Burnside-City of Lakes park has a particularly large ratio of nonmanufacturing to manufacturing businesses (12:1), giving a total of 1,370 companies employing 21,350 people.[7] The nonmanufacturing enterprises are mainly wholesalers, distributors, sales/service outlets, and offices (Armdale Associates 1984).

Clearly, Burnside is by far the most successful park in absolute terms. It might be argued that recently developed parks are growing just as

---

[7] *The Burnside News*, quoted in the Sunday *Daily News*, Oct. 28, 1990.

Figure 23.1.   *Manufacturing Firms Within and Outside Industrial Parks, 1958-1988*

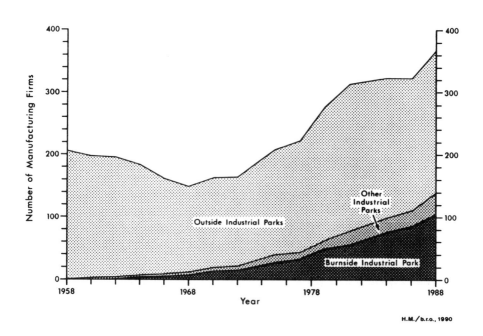

H.M./b.r.o., 1990

Source: derived from N.S. Directory of Manufacturing.

rapidly in relative terms but have simply not had time to attract many tenants. One way to assess this is to compute the average addition to occupied area, in hectares per year, since park inception. On this measure, only Aerotech Park has achieved a faster growth rate than Burnside-City of Lakes (22 ha/year versus 17), and all other parks have had much slower growth rates (Bayer's Lake is third, with 8 ha/year). It is highly unlikely that either Aerotech or Bayer's Lake can match Burnside's rate in the long run, since demand is too low: the recent take-up rate in all industrial parks has been only 36 ha/year (Nova Scotia, Municipal Affairs 1989, 16).

Why has Burnside been so successful? A questionnaire survey of Burnside firms reveals factors influential in attracting manufacturers to the park. The survey (Armdale Associates 1984) asked the firms, without suggesting responses, why they had located in the park. The 55 responding firms generally gave more than one reason. All advantages cited were grouped by Conrad (1986) into 25 specific reasons, under three broad headings (internal geographic features, external geographic features, and other factors).

Of the broad categories, *internal geographic features* were cited most frequently (84 percent of firms). Notably important were the availability of space to expand (i.e., a large inventory of developed lots, cited by 33 percent), the presence of customers (18 percent) or suppliers (11 percent) in the park, the availability of suitable buildings (15 percent), and attractive lot prices (15 percent). These factors, plus quality of premises/environment (7 percent), reflect the advantages of a mature and successful development. Access to trucking companies (5 percent) and ease of shipping and receiving (4 percent) were of less importance, while specific park services (2 percent) and parent company location (2 percent) were of little consequence.

Of the *external geographic features* (cited by 73 percent of firms), by far the most important was the central location within the metropolitan area (40 percent). Owing to the particular configuration of the coastline and transport network, the promotional brochure for this suburban development can rightly claim it to be "at the geographical centre of the entire Dartmouth/Halifax metropolitan area." More firms made specific mention of highway access (15 percent) than rail or water access (5 percent each), confirming that road transportation has become dominant. With proposed arterial connections to Sackville and highways 118 and 107, the park's highway advantages will be further enhanced (see Map 23.2). Of less importance were proximity to offshore exploration (7 percent), labour availability (7 percent), central regional location (5 percent), and access to air transportation (4 percent). Three unimportant factors were access to public transportation, proximity to owner's residence, and proximity to previous Halifax location (each mentioned by 2 percent of firms).

Only 25 percent of firms listed *other factors*. The most important of these was the prestige of the park, mentioned as influential by 18 percent of firms. Again, this is indicative of a mature and successful development. Tax agreements/incentives were specifically noted by only 4 percent of firms, while "superior capital asset" and "park promotion initiative" were mentioned by only 2 percent each.

More than any other metro development, Burnside embodies the full range of advantages cited in other surveys (Hartshorn 1973; Rusling 1975), summarized by Muller (1981, 139-40), and promoted in the standard manual on park design (Urban Land Institute 1976). Its early success was due to locational advantages combined with cost subsidies. Success bred success, in that many firms were attracted by the presence of suppliers and customers. Burnside has large land reserves to accommodate the growth and promotes itself on the basis of its track record ("Burnside: Atlantic Canada's *proven* location").

RELOCATION VERSUS SELF-GENERATED SUBURBAN GROWTH

Since 1945, and at an accelerating pace since 1960, older urban districts (in the Halifax area as elsewhere) have lost industry while the suburbs have gained a great deal. A natural assumption, made by writers such as Pred (1964), was that central firms were relocating to more attractive suburban sites. This theory views the outer ring merely as a reception area for companies moving from the core. Set against it is the notion that most new industries in the suburbs did not relocate from the centre but are "self-generated"; the suburbs, and particularly industrial parks, serve as incubator locations for new, local firms, or attract branch facilities of national corporations (Wood 1974). By this theory, central city losses reflect plant "deaths" more than plant relocations, while peripheral gains are mainly due to plant "births."

Before analyzing the Halifax situation, we should note that evidence from other studies is inconclusive. An early study of Toronto by Kerr and Spelt (1958) showed exactly two-thirds of new suburban firms had relocated from the central city, while more recently Steed (1973, 251) concluded that, for greater Vancouver, "by far the majority of plants appearing in the suburban periphery were new plants, not migrants." Self-generation also appears to be the dominant process in the United States and Britain (James and Hughes 1973; Bull 1978).

From the annual Directory of Manufacturers, the authors categorized Halifax-Dartmouth manufacturing firms into new versus pre-existing firms, and into industrial-park versus nonpark firms. Firms were traced from year to year for the period 1958 to 1984 to identify births, deaths, and relocations. Table 23.2 shows, surprisingly, that most new or relocating firms did not establish themselves in industrial parks; even in the later period, only 24 percent of such firms did so. For those locating in the parks, the dominant process in both early and late periods was "self-generation" rather than "relocation." Relocation was of some importance earlier (42 percent of additional firms) but of much less

Table 23.2.   *Destination of New and Relocating Firms in Metropolitan Halifax, 1958-1984*

	New Firms		Relocating Firms		Total of Additional Firms	
	In Parks	Elsewhere	In Parks	Elsewhere	In Parks	Elsewhere
1958-1970	14	129	10	64	24	193
1970-1984	87	295	29	81	116	376

Source: Derived from Conrad 1986, Tables 4 and 5.

importance recently (25 percent). The preponderance of new plants reflects the general background process of industrial restructuring, particularly the Halifax area's increasing role as a "branch-plant" centre serving the regional market (Norcliffe 1980, 540).

If so many new or relocating firms are added outside the parks, why has the number of firms outside remained almost static, while the number within has grown almost exponentially (see Figure 23.1)? The reason can only be that the survival rate for "nonpark" firms is much lower. Table 23.3 confirms this. In both the early and later periods, the chances of survival for firms outside parks, whether established or additional, were less than even. By contrast, firms within industrial parks seemed much more vital: 74 percent of those present in 1970 or added thereafter survived to 1984. Clearly, the industrial parks provide highly suitable environments for industry, but there may also be some filtering that deters marginal enterprises from locating in them.

MUNICIPAL RIVALRY: COMPETITION OR COORDINATION?

As noted earlier, most industrial parks in the metropolitan area were initiated by, and continue to be managed by, industrial commissions of the three larger municipalities. Bedford, the smallest municipality, did not feel able to promote and manage parks with its own resources and transferred them to NSBCC in the early eighties. The provincial crown

Table 23.3. *Survival Ratios of Firms in Metropolitan Halifax, 1958-1984*

| | Outside Industrial Parks | | | |
	Initial No. of Firms	No. of Incoming Firms	Final No. of Firms	Percent Surviving
1958-1970	205	193	141	35
1970-1984	141	376	220	43

| | Inside Industrial Parks | | | |
	Initial No. of Firms	No. of Incoming Firms	Final No. of Firms	Percent Surviving
1958-1970	0	24	20	83
1970-1984	20	116	100	74

Source: Derived from Conrad 1986, Tables 3, 4, and 5.

corporation's other ventures are also special cases that are unattractive to municipal commissions.

Municipalities are in strong competition to attract firms within their boundaries, primarily to increase their tax bases. As a result, all municipalities have several publicly owned industrial parks and compete vigorously to promote their locational and cost advantages. Because of the high level of government subsidization, privately developed parks have been unable to compete; at the present time, the only private venture is highly tentative and still awaiting planning permission.

Intermunicipal rivalry has several advantages. It provides each municipality with greater autonomy over industrial land-use planning and can lead to a pattern of many small industrial parks, scattered widely and equitably through the metropolitan area. In addition, it may help to attract industry that would not otherwise locate in the region. On the debit side, there are four main problems:

1. Most industrial parks are sited in nonoptimal locations. Careful research on environmental factors and transport links led the 1975 Regional Plan (Metropolitan Area Planning Committee 1975) to recommend only three major parks (Burnside, Woodside, and Lakeside). Many of the newer parks are at variance with Regional Plan policies.

2. Firms are induced to locate on the basis of short-term incentives, rather than the true or long-term locational and amenity advantages of the industrial park.

3. A large oversupply of industrial land results. Presently the metropolitan area has more than 300 ha of industrial park land serviced and ready for development (over nine years' supply), and a further 750 ha planned but not serviced (Nova Scotia Dept. of Municipal Affairs 1989, 16). A large oversupply means lengthier delays in recovering land development costs and therefore extra expense.

4. Competitive incentives lead to inordinate subsidization of industries locating in the less viable parks. Halifax Industrial Commission is presently looking for a legal way to give away land in its fledgling parks, where development costs range from $290,000 to $480,000 per hectare (*Mail-Star*, Feb. 15, 1990, 1-2). Not only is this a questionable use of municipal resources but also the subsidized land becomes highly attractive to nonindustrial uses, such as services, retailing, and offices.[8] These commercial activities are presumably being lured away from traditional downtown or shopping centre locations, a trend that conflicts with regional and municipal planning policies.

The need for coordination of municipal efforts was recognized in the early 1970s, and a regional agency responsible for industrial development was proposed (Metropolitan Area Planning Committee 1975). Unlike other regional initiatives in transportation and waste disposal, this body failed to materialize, perhaps because Halifax City felt it would not gain a fair share of benefits. Now that Halifax has its stakes in the industrial park competition the idea has been revived and several alternatives are under discussion (Nova Scotia, Department of Municipal Affairs 1989, 14-17). One proposal is for a Regional Industrial Commission for joint park promotion only. Each municipality would contribute funds, and the

---

[8] For a discussion of this phenomenon, see Shenkel (1972, 61-62).

commission would use these funds to promote the metropolitan region as a whole to outside firms. But there would be problems in assessing municipal contributions, and there is no guarantee that each municipality would attract industry commensurate with its contributions. The more successful parks, Burnside in particular, would still receive the lion's share of incoming industry, and huge incentives would still be offered at other parks.

A more ambitious proposal is for a Regional Industrial Commission to coordinate not only promotion but also park planning and the scheduling of development. A comprehensive intermunicipal agreement on costs and benefits would be necessary but would be extremely difficult where so much has already been invested in competing facilities. An equitable accounting would need to be made of the extent of federal and provincial funds already received and municipal funds invested for land acquisition, development, and servicing. The most successful parks might be penalized here. Burnside operates without subsidies at a small profit, whereas other parks have large operating losses. Yet if costs are to be balanced by benefits, new industry might well be redirected from this successful and cost-efficient location. To gain agreement on such matters will be an extremely challenging task.

The alternatives under discussion do not include tax-base equalization, whether achieved through intermunicipal tax sharing or through provincial equalization grants. This is in line with the "hands-off" approach that the province has adopted toward the metro municipalities during the 1980s; it is extremely reluctant to impose solutions on units of local government.

SUMMARY AND CONCLUSIONS

In the last 30 years, the metropolitan Halifax area has experienced significant shifts in the locational pattern of industry. Prior to 1960, industry was concentrated in the downtown area, in the area of urban blight lying north of it, along the harbourfront, and along railway lines. Since 1960, there has been a noticeable decline in these traditional areas and a marked growth in the outer suburbs. This suburban growth is largely in planned industrial parks, most of which are municipal ventures offering attractive sites at subsidized prices. Industries attracted to these parks initially relocated from the central areas but more recently have been "self-generated" (i.e., they are either new firms, or firms new to the region).

In many ways the recent Halifax experience is typical of changes occuring throughout the western world in response to an underlying process of "industrial restructuring" in the era of global capitalism. This phase of industrial restructuring is relatively recent, dating from the late 1960s (Soja *et al.*, 1983) to mid-1970s (Yeates 1990), and associated with the fifth long-wave of economic expansion (Hall 1985). The dates coincide remarkably with the take-off of manufacturing in the Halifax area's industrial parks (Figure 23.1). The era of global capitalism, however, is but an intensified phase of long-run changes in the organization of modern industrial production, which are the causative mainspring behind the equally long-run process of industrial decentralization. According to Scott (1982a, 1982b), decentralization is a response to capital accumulation, innovation in the techniques of production and transportation, and the substitution of capital for labour. Scott's analysis is important because it broadens our view of the urban production system to include "control" functions of management, sales, R and D, and producer services such as financing, accounting, advertising, and legal services. These labour-intensive control functions remain tied to the central city (and increasingly favour only the regional and national primate centres), while capital-intensive branch plants decentralize to the edge of the city (Scott 1982a, 125-34). In this way, the recent mushrooming of office buildings in downtown Halifax may be seen as part of the same process driving the decentralization of manufacturing and warehousing.

While industrialists have responded locationally to restructuring, governments have responded to locational shifts. In the Halifax case, the provincial government was initially heavily involved, espousing a top-down approach to economic planning and taking the leading role in developing industrial parks. Once municipalities became active in park development the province attempted to control decentralization through a vigourous regional planning process intended to steer development toward sites that balanced environmental concerns against the locational requirements of industry. The regional plan, however, was perceived by some municipalities as unfairly apportioning the tax benefits of industrial growth. It was strongly opposed by Halifax City in particular. The province retreated from regional planning, ceding more control to municipalities. The result has been a proliferation of competing industrial parks and huge municipal subsidies to develop a wasteful oversupply of industrial land.

Yet, in terms of the pace, scale, and character of industrial development, questions regarding who develops the industrial parks, the extent of subsidies, and land oversupply are largely irrelevant. Industrial and commercial firms continue to favour the optimum location, which in metro Halifax is Burnside. They continue to make rational locational choices, despite inducements to do otherwise. The proliferation of industrial parks and agencies is in a sense illusory, since two-thirds of all park occupants reside in Burnside's highly successful and central environment. For the rest, only Aerotech Park shows genuine signs of vitality, building on its special locational advantages. In this way, the Halifax case exemplifies the locational significance of responses to industrial restructuring at the intra-urban level. The economic response of industrialists, expressed as decentralization and the search for optimum locations, is clearly more influential than the political response of governments, expressed as competition among autonomous municipalities. The locational impact of governmental intervention in the industrial land market may be judged as minimal.

REFERENCES

Adams, J. S. 1970. "Residential Structure of Midwestern Cities." *Annals, Association of American Geographers* 60: 37-62.

Armdale Associates Ltd. 1984. *Occupancy and Facilities Survey of Firms in Burnside Industrial Park*. Halifax.

Bale, J. 1974. "Towards a Geography of the Industrial Estate." *Professional Geographer* 26: 291-97.

_____. 1977. "Industrial Estate Development and Location in Post-War Britain." *Geography* 62: 87-92.

Blakeley, P. R. 1949. *Glimpses of Halifax, 1867-1900*. Halifax: Public Archives of Nova Scotia.

Bull, P. J. 1978. "The Spatial Components of Intra-urban Manufacturing Change: Suburbanization in Clydeside, 1958-1968." *Transactions, Institute of British Geographers*, New Series, 3: 91-100.

Cameron, G. C. 1973. "Intra-urban Location and the New Plant." *Papers of the Regional Science Association* 31: 125-43.

Canplan Consultants. 1973. *Burnside Industrial Park Study*. Halifax.

City of Dartmouth. 1976. *Burnside Industrial Park: Applied Development Economics*. Dartmouth, N.S.

Colby, C. 1933. "Centrifugal and Centripetal Forces in Urban Geography." *Annals, Association of American Geographers* 23: 1-20.

Conrad, S. 1986. "The Impact of Industrial Parks on the Geography of Industrial Land in Metropolitan Halifax: Focus on Burnside Industrial Park." Halifax: Saint Mary's University, Department of Geography, unpublished B.A. thesis.

Conway, H., L. Liston, and R. Saul, eds. 1979. *Industrial Park Growth—An Environmental Success Story*. Atlanta: Conway Publications.

Cox, G. 1966. "Planned Industrial Districts." *Urban Land* 19: 3-5.

Evans, S. 1972. "Industrial Parks Restudied." *Urban Land* 31: 14-21.

Groves, P. 1971. *Towards a Typology of Intrametropolitan Manufacturing Locations*. Hull: University of Hull.

Haig, R. 1927. *Major Economic Factors in Metropolitan Growth and Arrangement*. New York: Arno Press reprint, 1974.

Hall, P. 1985. "The Geography of the Fifth Kondratieff." In *Silicon Landscapes*, ed. P. Hall and A. Markusen, Boston: Allen and Unwin, 1-19.

Hartshorn, T. 1973. "Industrial/Office Parks: A New Look for the City." *Journal of Geography* 72(3): 33-45.

_____. 1980. *Interpreting the City*. New York: John Wiley.

Hawley, A. 1956. *The Changing Shape of Metropolitan America: Deconcentration Since 1920*. Glencoe: The Free Press.

Herbert, D., and C. Thomas. 1982. *Urban Geography*. Chichester, U.K.: John Wiley.

James, F., and J. Hughes. 1973. "The Process of Employment Location Change: An Empirical Analysis." *Land Economics* 49: 404-13.

Kerr, D., and J. Spelt. 1958. "Manufacturing in Suburban Toronto." *Canadian Geographer* 12: 11-19.

McCann, L. 1979. "Staples and the New Industrialism in the Growth of Post-Confederation Halifax." *Acadiensis* 10(2): 29-64.

Metropolitan Area Planning Committee. 1975. *Halifax-Dartmouth Regional Development Plan*. Halifax: MAPC.

Millward, H. 1981. *The Geography of Housing in Metropolitan Halifax, Nova Scotia*. Halifax: Saint Mary's University, Atlantic Region Geographical Studies, No. 3.

Muller, P. 1981. *Contemporary Suburban America*. Englewood Cliffs, N.J.: Prentice-Hall.

Muncy, D. 1970. "Planning Guidelines for Industrial Park Development." *Urban Land* 29: 3-10.

Norcliffe, G. 1980. "Industrial Development and Port Activity in Halifax-Dartmouth." *Canadian Public Policy* 6: 533-41.

Northam, R. 1965. "The Planned Industrial District in Anglo-America." *Yearbook of the Association of Pacific Coast Geographers* 27: 39-48.

_____. 1975. *Urban Geography*. New York: John Wiley.

Nova Scotia Department of Municipal Affairs. 1988. *Industrial Land Use Map, Halifax-Dartmouth Regional Development Plan Update*. Halifax: Community Planning Division.

_____. 1989. *Halifax-Dartmouth Regional Plan Review: Industrial Parks Update, 1989*. Halifax: Community Planning Division.

Pred, A. 1964. "The Intra-Metropolitan Location of American Manufacturing." *Annals, Association of American Geographers* 54: 165-80.

Raddall, T. 1971. *Halifax: Warden of the North*, rev. ed. Toronto: McClelland and Stewart.

Rusling, J. 1975. "Factors Influencing the Location of Manufacturing Activity in Southern Ontario." In *Industrial Development in Southern Ontario*, ed. D. Walker and J. Bater, Waterloo: University of Waterloo, Department of Geography Series No. 3, 145-66.

Scott, A. 1982a. "Locational Patterns and Dynamics of Industrial Activity in the Modern Metropolis." *Urban Studies* 19: 111-42.

_____. 1982b. "Production System Dynamics and Metropolitan Development." *Annals, Association of American Geographers* 72: 185-200.

Shenkel, W. 1972. "The Economic Consequences of Industrial Zoning." In *Urban Land Use Policy: The Central City*, ed. R. Andrews, New York: The Free Press.

Soja, E., R. Morales, and G. Wolff. 1983. "Urban Restructuring: An Analysis of Social and Spatial Change in Los Angeles." *Economic Geography* 59: 195-230.

Steed, G. 1973. "Intrametropolitan Manufacturing: Spatial Distribution and Locational Dynamics in Greater Vancouver." *Canadian Geographer* 17: 235-58.

Urban Land Institute. 1976. *Industrial Development Handbook*. Washington, D.C.: U.L.I.

Wood, P. 1974. "Urban Manufacturing: A View from the Fringe." In *Suburban Growth: Geographical Processes at the Edge of the Western City*, ed. J. Johnson, London: Wiley, 129-54.

Yeates, M. 1990. *The North American City*, 4th edition. New York: Harper and Row.

Zelinsky, W. 1962. "Has American Industry been Decentralizing? The Evidence for the 1939-1954 Period." *Economic Geography* 38: 251-69.

Chapter 24

Municipal Government and Residential Land Development:
A Comparative Study of London, Ontario, in the 1920s and 1980s

Andrew Sancton
Byron Montgomery
The University of Western Ontario

The transformation of vacant land into ordered rows (or crescents) of houses is one of the most complex, interesting, and important functions of our political-economic system. Unfortunately, we seem to know remarkably little about how it actually works. Economists, geographers, and sociologists study the various factors shaping our residential areas, but their search is generally for aggregate data and for theories that explain whatever broad patterns of behaviour are buried therein. Land-use planners concern themselves with how residential areas should be developed but have left us with few accounts of what actually happens, even though many of them are key actors in both government and the private sector. Developers understand the process all too well, but if they had a penchant for written analysis of their own activities they would probably not be developers in the first place. Political scientists know about structures of local government and, in some cases at least, about how the nature of community power structures affects patterns of down-

We gratefully acknowledge the financial support of the Social Sciences and Humanities Research Council of Canada, the helpful cooperation of officials in the planning and engineering departments of the city of London, initial advice from Ross Paterson, and detailed commentary on the conference version of the paper from George Fallis, Frances Frisken, and CMHC research staff.

town development (Stone 1989). Urban historians are remarkably helpful in explaining how residential development actually occurred in decades and centuries past (Linteau 1982; Weaver 1982; Paterson 1985) but almost by definition are much less involved in analyzing current processes.

This chapter briefly describes and analyses the creation of two subdivisions in London, Ontario: one in the 1920s and the other in the 1980s. There are a great many obvious differences in the ways in which they came into being. The main object of the chapter is to determine to what extent these differences are significant. Has the way in which new residential land is created changed fundamentally over the past 60 years, or is the basic process still roughly the same? What, if anything, does the nature of the changes tell us about the fundamental issues involved in the outward expansion of Canadian metropolitan areas? What are the mechanisms by which sewers, water supplies, and roads are extended to newly created neighbourhoods? Who makes the initial investment? Who bears the burden of paying back the loans? Does it matter?

In approaching these questions, three important types of change in the subdivision-approval process will be considered: changes in the relative role of participants (municipal governments, developers, and the general public); changes in the legislative context; and changes in the way services are financed. This last issue is especially relevant in light of the recent implementation of Ontario's new Development Charges Act. The potential impact of the act on many declared objectives of Canadian housing policy—such as affordability and intensification, for example—has not been adequately debated.

London, Ontario, may or may not be representative of other Canadian cities.[1] Its only importance for this chapter is that it provides the setting for an attempt to capture some of the subtleties and complexities in the process of residential land development that would not be apparent in collections of aggregate data. Before examining the two cases, however, we must have some familiarity with the evolution of the legal processes for subdividing land and for providing municipal services to the newly created areas. A discussion of these issues in the London, Ontario, context comprises the first half of the chapter.

---

[1]Armstrong (1986, 165) and Bloomfield (1989, 140) cite the statement made by the Dominion Statistician in the 1920s that "London is a microcosm of Canadian life, one of the most typical of Canadian cities."

THE SUBDIVISION AND SERVICING OF LAND

For there to be private ownership of land there must be an effective system for keeping track of who owns what. At the heart of the system of land ownership is some form of registry office. In theory, original grants of land could be registered in such an office, and the owner could then proceed to make purely private arrangements—including outright sale—for its disposition. Subsequent owners would rely on proof of purchase to trace their ownership back to the original grant. Such a system is fraught with uncertainty—both for owners and governments. Rogers points out that "Because of the failure to register plans consequent upon subdivision of land for sale and because of the confusion arising in land registration, title certification, and municipal administration in general, it became, over a century ago in Ontario, mandatory to register such plans in the registry office" (Rogers 1973, 75). The key point seems to be, however, that there was originally no attempt at substantive regulation. Anyone who went through the correct administrative process at the registry office could subdivide his or her land.

Since the subdivision of land, particularly in urban areas, inevitably led to new demands for such local public services as sewers and roads, municipalities were seen to have a direct interest in the subdivision process. The 1910 Ontario Registry Act "provided that the Registrar should not register a plan of subdivision unless accompanied by the approval of the municipal council or order of a judge approving such a plan" (Rogers 1973, 76). Judges could hear appeals from negative municipal decisions. In 1918 the Ontario Planning and Development Act provided that cities, towns, and villages could declare "urban zones" in areas up to five miles outside their boundaries and that, for such zones, they would have to approve any new subdivision. Under the same law, the Ontario Railway and Municipal Board (ORMB) became the agency for appeals of municipal subdivision decisions. The 1946 Ontario Planning Act made subdivision control a direct provincial responsibility, although the municipal advisory role was extremely important. In recent years the province has begun delegating the legal authority back to some of the larger municipalities, particularly regional governments.

Another important feature of the 1946 Planning Act was that it strongly encouraged municipalities to adopt "official plans," one objective of which was to relate their developmental aspirations to their servicing needs or intentions. For the purposes of this chapter it is important to realize that the 1920s case study predates the statutory existence of official plans, while the 1980s one takes place four decades after their introduction.[2]

Local Improvement Taxes

The Ontario Local Improvement Act of 1914 established a system whereby urban municipalities could construct new installations such as water mains, sewers, curbs, gutters, sidewalks, and paved streets and pass on the cost through a special local improvement tax levied on property owners of abutting land. Where municipalities laid sewers of larger capacity than was necessary for the land immediately abutting, other land that could derive use could also be assessed. Where the work dealt with street improvements and council felt it unfair that abutting land should be fully assessed, council could have the municipality pay a "just portion." If council considered an improvement to benefit equally nonabutting land, such land could be taxed at the same rate. If nonabutting land benefited, but not equally, council could choose an appropriate proportionate rate for the nonabutting land.

Local improvements could be initiated either by the municipal council or by property-owners. If a council supported residential development in a particular area, it would initiate the local improvement process. If, by a two-thirds vote, city council declared a particular road, sidewalk, or bridge to be a local improvement, then the assent of affected property owners was not needed. However, if the majority of owners representing half the value of the specially assessed property opposed the improvement, they could petition the ORMB to intervene. If a two-thirds majority of council supported a sewer extension recommended by the provincial or local board of health, property owners had no such right of appeal.

Property owners could initiate local improvements by petitioning the local council. If two-thirds of owners, representing half the value of the properties liable to be assessed, directed the city to act, council was forced to comply. However local improvements were initiated, borrowing was the responsibility of the municipality. When the work was finished, debentures were issued to cover the entire cost of the improvements.

---

[2]A new Ontario Planning Act was legislated in 1983, but there was little significant difference from the old one with regard to the nature and purpose of official plans. Unless otherwise noted, all direct quotations and specific information pertaining to these subdivisions derive from Housing Commission of London (1919-22).

Property owners were assessed whatever amount was required to cover the debenture payments. If in any year the fund collected an amount insufficient to pay the owners' portion of principal and interest, the municipal corporation was liable to make up the shortfall. To do so the council could increase each owner's assessment in the remaining years. The main features of this system for local improvements are still in place in Ontario to this day. New arrangements for financing infrastructure in residential subdivisions have been added, but the older ones have not been repealed. In most major municipalities, however, only relatively minor installations in established areas are financed through local improvement taxes. A typical example might be the building of a sidewalk where one had not existed before. Affected property owners present the required petition; the city builds the sidewalk and, for 20 years, the property owners' taxes are increased accordingly.

From the municipality's point of view there was one major flaw in financing infrastructure in new subdivisions by local improvement taxes: if the properties did not sell, the developer would likely be bankrupt and the taxes would not be paid. The municipality would end up owning, at best, some vacant houses or, at worst, an entire partially completed subdivision, with roads, sewers, and water mains leading nowhere. The tax burden for financing the useless installations would shift to the taxpayers of the city as a whole. In exceptionally difficult economic circumstances, such as those experienced in the 1930s, financial disasters of this kind could push the municipality to the edge of bankruptcy and beyond (Steele 1956, 88).

Subdivision Agreements

Just as with World War I, the aftermath of World War II brought great pressure on municipalities to provide new housing. Notwithstanding their experiences in the Great Depression, most were willing, with federal and provincial help, to finance major expansions in trunk sewers, water mains, and major roads. In so doing, their debt levels shot upward. In such circumstances, how were the more local installations normally associated with local improvement taxes to be financed?

It was the private developers who came to the rescue. Knowing that their new houses were certain to be purchased, they (initially at least) had few reservations about entering into "subdivision agreements" with municipalities, under which they undertook to build the public infrastructure themselves according to municipal specifications. Their costs would normally be passed on to the home purchasers, who would now face higher mortgage payments instead of local improvement taxes. Given that residential mortgage rates are generally higher than interest rates paid on municipal debentures, total financing costs under this system were higher (Milner 1967, 74). The perceived societal benefit was the removal of the constraints on subdivision production caused by real or apparent limitations on municipal borrowing capacities.

The Ontario Committee on Taxation has described the historical origin of subdivision agreements as follows:

> The early development of direct financing of municipal service installations has not been well documented. But it is clear that the practice of requiring developers to agree to take responsibility for providing certain services or meeting certain costs which would otherwise fall upon the municipality first gained importance in the years immediately following World War II. Among the earliest municipalities to impose such conditions were the three major recipients of Toronto's metropolitan expansion—the large townships of Etobicoke, North York, and Scarborough. Initially, the legality of subdivision agreements . . . was in doubt. These agreements none the less multiplied in a setting where, given the pace of urban growth and the demand for housing, neither developers nor municipalities were overly concerned with legal refinements (Ontario 1967, ii, 310).

By the time the legal status of subdivision agreements was clarified in the late 1950s and early 1960s (Ontario 1967, ii, 313-14), they were being used for all major residential subdivisions throughout the province. Under this new system, there could be no approved subdivision unless the applicant had access to sufficient capital resources to finance and build the infrastructure. The result was that local speculators and small building companies were forced out by larger concerns, usually major construction companies that had begun acquiring farmland for eventual subdivision so as to insure their own supply of developable land (Ontario 1973, 35).

Many subdivision agreements contained provisions obliging the developer to pay "cash imposts," "lot levies," or "development charges" for unspecified costs associated with the new subdivision (Amborski 1988). Such monies could pay for improvements to major installations outside the subdivision if they could be shown to be needed as a direct or indirect result of the subdivision's being built. In London's case, the city's chief administrative officer described the "system" for determining development charges in these highly critical words:

With each new subdivision development lengthy negotiation procedures were necessary before approval was given to such development. This process entailed bargaining at great length with the [council's] Public Works Committee, with the committee members acting as arbitrators between the Engineer's Department and the Developer and sometimes the Urban Development Institute. The result of this process was that usually the most experienced and forceful bargainer obtained the best deal from the Council, thus it was evident that the process was most unfair and in all likelihood economically unsound to the Corporation (London 1980, 1).

According to the deputy city engineer, the system of development charges prior to 1972 was confusing and complex because it comprised a plethora of charges and payments, from sewer outlets and boundary charges, to "preferred" methods of calculation, to Local Improvement and Municipal Act charges—all of which were even more difficult to understand because of a wide number of statutory limitations and procedures (London 1978, 5).

London's Major Sewerage and Road Works Capital Reserve Fund

In November 1970 the local chapter of the Urban Development Institute (UDI)—the developers' interest group—formally requested city council to establish a flat-rate charge to cover the costs of improvements to major roads and sewers associated with new residential subdivisions. After a year of negotiation between UDI representatives and city officials, such an arrangement was worked out. In 1971, as a result of private provincial legislation, London became the first municipality in the province to have explicit legislative authority to levy development charges. The Major Sewerage and Road Works Capital Reserve Fund came into existence in April 1973 (London 1978, 3). The main change in the new arrangements was that henceforth anybody (even someone creating a new, legal apartment in his or her own dwelling) would have to pay a flat-rate per-unit charge to the reserve fund. Initially the charge was $366 for each single-family or semi-detached unit, $319 for each unit of row housing, and $227 for each apartment (London 1980, 2). Developers would still negotiate with the city to determine responsibility for building improvements to major roads and sewers and to work out mutually agreeable allowable costs for the developer's portion. When the work was complete, the developer would submit a claim to the city's finance commissioner to have such costs refunded from the reserve fund.

If the flat-rate charges had been set at an appropriate level, the system should have worked. Unfortunately, mainly as a result of lobbying from the UDI, they were set too low. The result was that obligations mounted much faster than revenues. By 1979 the fund was $18.6 million in arrears, and developers were having to wait between 21 and 31 months for the payment of claim (London 1984, App. G). Ironically, the only way a developer could speed up repayment was to keep building; when a developer was owed money by the fund, he could use such assets as credits on development charges payable for new units. The result was that developers who were not continuing to build had to wait even longer for repayment. Individual unpaid developers had no right to insist on earlier payment because part of each subdivision agreement with the city included provisions stating that repayments were due only when sufficient monies were available in the fund. Perhaps this explains why, initially at least, few city officials seemed aware of or concerned about the fund's growing problems.

Despite the legal niceties, such a situation could not persist. In late 1979 the state of the fund became a matter of open public debate. Understandably, some council members and media commentators questioned the competence of city officials who somehow seemed to have allowed an unanticipated deficit of $18.6 million. In March 1980, city council accepted the resignation of the chief administrative officer, demoted the city engineer, and fired the finance commissioner. To improve the cash flow of the reserve fund, the city injected $2.6 million (which was repaid without interest by 1985), increased the per-unit flat-rate charge, and eliminated the procedure whereby developers could receive credit for outstanding development charges by using monies owed them by the fund. By 1984 waiting periods for repayment were reduced to between one and three months and all seemed to be working smoothly (London 1984, App. G).

In 1989 city council added a Capital Works Growth Reserve Fund to help finance capital projects that otherwise would have been paid for through the city's normal capital budget. Charges for it and the original fund (now called the Urban Works Reserve Fund) were identical. Effective January 1, 1990, total funds payable per unit for the two funds were $5,024 for single-family and semi-detached units, $4,190 for row housing units, and $2,793 for apartments.

The legal underpinnings, if not the substance, of the city's development charges will be changed dramatically in 1991 when the new Development Charges Act, approved by the provincial legislature in 1989, comes into force. The new law provides a common legal framework for municipal development charges and extends the right to impose them to school boards. Clearly such charges are seen by policymakers at both provincial and municipal levels as an especially appropriate way of financing the high costs associated with new residential development.

TWO CASE STUDIES

Residential Subdivision in the 1920s:
Garfield Street and Pine Lawn

The first case study in this involves two subdivisions developed by the city of London shortly after World War I. Following the return of Canadian soldiers, housing became a major national issue. In late 1918, under the authority of the War Measures Act, Robert Borden's Unionist government loaned $25 million to the provinces for 25 years at five percent interest. The money was to be granted mainly to municipalities willing to construct new housing for sale at cost, but limited-dividend housing societies and lot-owners building houses for their own personal occupancy could also benefit. Other relevant federal restrictions were that: land should be purchased "without regard to speculative value" and not more than 10 percent of the cost of any house should derive from the cost of the land; 10 percent of all land purchased should be reserved for playgrounds; water and sewerage should be supplied before construction; and all houses should meet specified minimum standards of construction (Canada 1919, 55).

Ontario's response to the federal initiative came in April 1919, when the Ontario Housing Act was approved by the provincial legislature. It provided that, in order to participate in the provincial program, municipalities must either appoint a housing commission or incorporate a separate housing company. London city council opted for a three-man commission. According to the legislation, the commission had the authority to buy land and to sell it to ex-servicemen and residents "of moderate means" either as vacant lots or as lots already containing built houses. In London, honourably discharged soldiers were required to "furnish satisfactory collateral security by way of bond of employer, or a friend. . . ." The bond had to provide for a minimum 20 percent deposit and reference to the character, health, and probable future earnings of the applicant. The commission loaned money to purchasers on the same terms as the province's agreement with the federal government. Legislation passed in 1920 (the Municipal Housing Act) injected more funds into the program by providing for provincially guaranteed municipal debentures, but this time the interest rate charged to municipalities was six percent.

In his inaugural address as chair of the Housing Commission of London (HCL) in January 1920, E. R. Dennis appealed for action in terms remarkably similar to those of persons seeking action on homelessness in the 1990s.

> At the present time, we know that the supply of houses is decidedly inadequate. No houses are to rent. Practically no houses are being built to rent. New families coming to the city are obliged to live in rooms, housed with one or more other families. Realizing the significance of these facts, the commission should adopt and prosecute as quickly as possible far-sighted, sound, and vigorous policy to provide this year a substantial worthwhile addition to our housing accommodation.

After receiving insufficient response from appeals to owners of vacant property to make their land available for development, the HCL decided that the only way it could meet the overwhelming demand for housing was to become directly involved in the creation of what were now becoming known as subdivisions, i.e., newly built residential neighbourhoods. Two areas were chosen for such development.

The first was on Garfield Street in south London. In 1920 the commission purchased for $7,850 sufficient property for the building of 17 houses. The only problem with the municipally built houses on Garfield Street was that, at a retail price of $5,700 a unit, they were rather expensive for people of moderate means.

The Pine Lawn subdivision was larger and more complex. Fourteen acres in a newly annexed area of southeast London were purchased from two separate owners for a total cost of $14,182. For Pine Lawn, rather than developing the land itself as it did on Garfield Street, the HCL hired a private company. Forty-two houses were built on time and at a cost more suitable for the intended beneficiaries.

Difficulties in Pine Lawn related to municipal services. Being at the city's southeast extremity, the area could not easily connect to existing municipal infrastructure. In the summer of 1920, the city council, claiming financial constraints, declined to make the necessary extensions to the trunk sewer. Similarly, the Public Utilities Commission refused to install water supply lines until the houses were occupied. This action was apparently part of a significantly larger dispute about exactly who was responsible for the financing of municipal services in new subdivisions.

Since the HCL had a broad interest in stimulating housing construction of all kinds, it had little sympathy for the penny-pinching tactics of those charged with responsibility for roads, sewers, and water mains. But having no jurisdiction over such matters itself, there was little it could do except complain. As a temporary measure in Pine Lawn the HCL installed septic tanks and, with the permission of the Ontario Housing Commission, rented many of the new houses instead of selling them, the justification being that potential purchasers could not be expected to commit their life savings to houses for which there was no guarantee that municipal services would be forthcoming.

About one year later, when a violent wind and rain storm hit London, many of the roofs in Pine Lawn leaked. This drew the wrath of the mayor, who claimed that the houses were ramshackle and were falling down. Apparently objective reports from building inspectors proved the mayor wrong, but the subdivision's already shaky image was tarnished further. It did not help that the roofs were not repaired for several months.

By January 1922, after the municipal sewers were in place in Pine Lawn, the HCL was still having difficulty selling its houses in both subdivisions. The Garfield Street houses were being advertised at $4,698 and the Pine Lawn ones at between $3,193 and $3,399 (*The London Free Press*, March 25, 1922, 39). Private subdivision developers had now emerged and were able to provide stiff competition. To counteract expected financial losses, the HCL started selling off its pool of 104 vacant lots. Meanwhile, it continued to rent the houses it could not sell. The last one was not sold until 1949.

The city's experience with Garfield Street and Pine Lawn was not a happy one and perhaps helps explain the lack of any kind of municipal involvement in family-housing provision that has persisted in London to this day. These cases have not been presented because they were typical of residential development in the 1920s. Obviously the vast majority of new houses in London were being built entirely by the private sector. The cases were chosen because, unlike the situation with private developments, there is at least some available documentation about how they came to be. The Pine Lawn subdivision, even though sponsored by a public authority, also illustrates the kinds of problems that emerge when there is little or no connection between the building of a subdivision and the provision of the required municipal services.

Residential Subdivision in the 1980s: Stoneybrook

Unlike Garfield Street and Pine Lawn, the Stoneybrook subdivision was developed by the private sector. With only one potential exception, such was always the case throughout the 1980s. Even at times of severe housing shortages, such as the early years of the decade, the city resisted any temptation to try to provide family housing. A second difference in the two cases is that by the 1980s London had established a comprehensive land-use planning system, complete with an official plan and zoning bylaws—all prepared and administered by a professional planning staff.

The 69 hectares of farmland at the extreme northern periphery of the city on which Stoneybrook was built became part of the city in 1960 when London more than doubled its territory as the result of a massive annexation. By 1974 it had been acquired by the Matthews Group, one of London's two major residential developers. In that year Matthews applied for permission to subdivide the land so as to build approximately 570 single-family houses and 200 units of row housing.

London's planning department recommended approval, but the city received dozens of complaints from existing residents on the other side of the area's major east-west arterial road. The complainants argued that the developer's plans to build three-storey row housing along the road would reduce property values in the area. Town houses of this kind were called "monstrosities." It was alleged that their occupation by families with young children would lead to traffic congestion and safety problems, as well as overcrowding in the local schools. Local aldermen argued that such high-density development was too expensive because it would mean increased expenditures for sewers, watermains, and streets (*The London Free Press*, August 10, 1976, 25).

The developer's response was that the main reason for including the row housing was so that it could act as a sound barrier between the single-family houses and noise coming from the main road. Despite such a telling admission, the developer backed down in the face of continued local opposition. The plans were changed to provide for 635 single-family houses only.

Final approval of Stoneybrook's first phase did not take place until 1979, five years after the original application. Delays were caused by the need to upgrade the nearby pollution control plant, to rezone the land from farmland to residential to bring it into accord with the city's official plan, to acquire the necessary approval from various provincial agencies, and to work out all the details of the servicing arrangements. However, after 1979 it was the developer who wanted delay. During the 1980s city council granted various extensions to its original approvals. The plan of subdivision for the first phase was registered in 1982; the plan for the fifth and final phase in 1987.

Subdivision agreements between the city of London and the Matthews Group were signed for each of Stoneybrook's five phases. The agreements set out the standards for all infrastructure construction. They also specified the land that would be conveyed to the city on completion, as well as the various utility easements that would be required. While construction was underway, city engineers had the authority to make periodic inspections to insure that work was being carried out as provided for in the agreement.

Prior to beginning construction or registering the plan of subdivision, whichever came first, the developer was obligated to provide certain financial guarantees that the necessary infrastructure would indeed be built. These took the form, for the first phase at least, of a cash deposit with the city of $231,000 and a bond for $2,080,000. In the event that facilities built by the developer had not been satisfactory, the city could have used these funds to make the necessary improvements. After each phase was completely built to the city's satisfaction, council approved an "assumption" bylaw, thereby establishing municipal ownership of all the appropriate land and facilities as specified in the subdivision agreement.

As far as development charges were concerned, the developer paid the per-unit cost as established at the time building permits were issued for each unit. The charge for units built as part of the first phase was $1,843; for the fifth it was $3,615. Total revenue to the city's development fund from Stoneybrook must therefore have been approximately $1.5 to $2 million. City records show that the developer was paid $700,000 for roadworks and sewers associated with Stoneybrook. The most visible evidence of such work can be seen along the east-west arterial: new intersections leading into the subdivision and a new sidewalk along its length. The amount of money represented by the difference between the total development charges paid and the amount claimed back by the developer was available to the city to use for other growth-related capital costs, such as making the required improvements to the pollution control plant. To determine whether or not the real costs of the Stoneybrook subdivision were met by the development charges would be virtually impossible.

Comparing the 1920s and 1980s

How did the municipal role in creating residential subdivisions change between the 1920s and the 1980s? One difference is that, in the early 1920s at least, the municipality itself, acting through its housing commission, actually built houses for sale on the open market. The Garfield Street and Pine Lawn developments in London might not have been typical, but their direct municipal sponsorship is an historical fact. There are no such examples in London in the 1980s. If anything, the decade was one in which the city retreated from its already limited involvement in the provision of family housing. In the creation of the Stoneybrook subdivision—and dozens like it—the city waited passively for developers' requests. The notion that the city itself should provide housing was quite outside the realm of local political discourse.

On the regulatory front, there can be little doubt that the municipality of the 1980s is infinitely more involved in almost all aspects of subdivision development. However, it would be wrong to suggest that there was a regulatory void in the 1920s just because official plans and comprehensive zoning bylaws did not exist. Municipal approval for subdividing was mandatory, although there were extramunicipal avenues of appeal, as there still are in Ontario today. Some areas were subject to municipal zoning bylaws, and all new buildings required permits so as to ensure that they were properly built.

Municipal regulation undoubtedly has a significant impact on the building of residential subdivisions. On the negative side, it slows down the process, thereby increasing costs and/or reducing the number of producers. Arguably, such regulation encourages uniformity and stifles architectural creativity. But it brings benefits as well. It ensures that surface water will drain to some approved, predetermined location; that roads will be suitable for use by garbage trucks, snowplows, and buses; that underground utilities will be accessible for repair; and that at least some land will be made available for such public facilities as schools and parks.

The early advocates of land-use planning expected more. They argued that the "community master plan," as enforced by comprehensive zoning, could shape urban development in accordance with some agreed upon notion of an overriding public or city interest (Hodge 1986). It is in this sense that the complex planning apparatus of London, Ontario—and other Canadian cities—falls short. Even most planners themselves recognize that their real task in municipal government is to facilitate the cost-effective development of our cities by major companies rather than to inspire new visions for our built environment.

The financing of infrastructure for new residential subdivisions has progressed from local improvement taxes to subdivision agreements and development charges. Whatever the virtues of the modern arrangements might be, they are not a mechanism for increased municipal control of the development process. They have been supported by the development industry—in London at least—precisely because they help free developers from municipal financial constraints. Such constraints derive from the limitations—either self-imposed or as determined by the province and/or the financial marketplace—on a given municipality's capacity to incur long-term debt. As a municipality approaches its upper limit for debt, it must begin to make difficult decisions about allocating scarce resources, in this case funds for the building of new infrastructure. In such circumstances, the need to make these decisions empowers the municipality to shape the nature of its outward physical expansion. Such empowerment is precisely what private developers wish to avoid; hence their support for a mechanism enabling them effectively to purchase the necessary infrastructure for their own projects by paying some specified per unit charge in advance.

IMPLICATIONS OF DEVELOPMENT CHARGES

In recent years in Ontario the principle of higher and more comprehensive development charges has rarely been questioned, except recently as it applies to the financing of new schools. As revenues from the charges grow, there must inevitably be a tendency among municipal councillors to believe that building infrastructure for new residential subdivisions is a costless, if not profitable, proposition. In such circumstances, the role of the planner in providing policy advice to council becomes increasingly irrelevant. Why should any proposal ever be turned down if there appear to be no costs or risks for the city? Once the city has established a level of development charges that is capable of financing all new infrastructure within its territory, then the only role for the municipal council is to wait for the subdivision applications to arrive and to turn them over to the planners to make sure that the provisions for infrastructure are up to the city's standards.

Determining the real costs of a new subdivision is, of course, extremely problematic. In Ontario we have now reached the point where municipalities and school boards have the legal authority to levy development charges so as to cover just about any kind of new capital cost imaginable, including "rolling stock, furniture and equipment and . . . materials acquired for circulation, reference or information purposes by a library board" (Ontario 1989). Conscientious municipal officials are already combing capital budgets searching for items to be financed from development charges. Few expenses are likely to escape their net. But, as J. B. Milner pointed out in 1967, even with development charges ". . . it by no means follows that . . . the municipality can afford the current operating costs of the urban development after the capital costs have been assumed, first by the developer and then by the house buyers" (Milner 1967, 74).

It is true that property-tax revenues from the new subdivision would cover normal costs for maintenance and repairs of the new facilities. However, there are much larger, more long-term issues involved in determining the real cost of servicing a new subdivision. For example, providing public transit in a new peripheral subdivision is likely to require public subsidies at a considerably higher level than the average for the system as a whole (Sewell 1978; Frankena 1982, 173). The cumulative impact of a number of new subdivisions in a given area will lead not just to the widening of existing arterials but to demands for new ones, possibly for expressways near or through existing neighbourhoods. The construction of new shopping malls to service the new residential development might well have deleterious effects on the downtown commercial area, leading to the expenditure of public funds on parking facilities and/or beautification programs to help keep it competitive. None of these observations about underlying connections and interdependencies will come as any surprise to land-use planners or to anyone who thinks seriously about how cities work. But they do undermine the notion that, as a practical objective of public policy, development charges can be set at such a level that they can be made to cover the real costs of new development.

Even if we assume that it is possible to determine the real average cost of the infrastructure required to support a new unit of a particular type of housing, it is still not at all obvious that such an amount should be the common charge for each new single-family dwelling or each new apartment. As we have seen, development charges in London have applied both to the developer of a new subdivision on the suburban periphery and to the owner of a large home downtown who is creating a new, legal apartment within what was originally a single-family dwelling. A more serious difficulty is that the development charge for a large house on a large suburban lot is exactly the same as for a small house on a small lot in a more central part of the city that might be undergoing redevelopment. Such a policy leads to regressive taxation as well as discouraging the building of more compact, densely developed cities.

If it is assumed that increasing residential densities in the developed parts of our cities is a much cheaper way of providing municipal infrastructure for new residents than is the building of new subdivisions, then the levying of a common development charge in both circumstances makes little sense. However, any move to vary the charge depending on the apparent real costs would lead to the situation that the common charge was supposed to eliminate: protracted negotiations between the municipality and the developer, the various outcomes of which could well be inconsistent and unfair. A possible solution might be to eliminate development charges altogether in predetermined parts of the city for which residential intensification seems especially desirable. Such determinations could presumably become part of the process involved in revising a municipality's official plan.

Any alternative to development charges involves municipalities taking on more debt. Because of reckless capital borrowing in the past, both for railways in the nineteenth century and for new infrastructure immediately prior to the Great Depression, Ontario municipalities seem exceptionally sensitive to the evils of borrowing. But over the last 50 years much has changed. Provincial supervision of both subdivision approvals and municipal financial practices has increased dramatically, as have the professional skills and qualifications of municipal employees. Although most municipal councils might still be dominated by prodevelopment forces, there is now usually some form of opposition within the council or the community that is at least capable of ensuring that proposals for new development are subject to open public debate. In short, the notion that municipal councils could bankrupt their city governments by approving financially irresponsible plans for infrastructure to accommodate new development is no longer realistic.

If municipalities were themselves to finance new suburban infrastructure, they would become much more involved in deciding exactly how and when new development takes place. In so doing they would likely reduce the overall supply of serviced land, thereby potentially providing windfall profits to the developer whose land was chosen for development at any particular time. This in turn would inevitably lead to calls for "betterment levies" or taxes on the increased value of land resulting from municipal decisions to allow development. Such taxes are notoriously difficult to administer. Although introduced at various times by Labour governments in Britain, for example, they have failed to survive the last decade of Margaret Thatcher's Conservative administration. Although talked about from time to time (Milner 1967, 75), betterment levies have never been seriously considered in Canada. Now that development charges are so prevalent, there is even less likelihood than before that provincial governments will ever decide to follow Labour's example.

The great virtue of development charges is that they enable large developers to use their own financial resources to maintain an abundant supply of new housing. They are based on the admirable principle that developers should not reap the financial benefits of investments and risks that they do not themselves undertake. Unfortunately, the implementation of this principle is far from easy. To the extent that development charges act as a disincentive to intensification of already developed residential areas while at the same time reducing the likelihood that councils will carefully consider long-term costs of new subdivisions, it might well be that their unintended consequences are quite harmful.

CONCLUSIONS

To understand how subdivisions are created we need to know about the respective roles of the municipal government, the general public, and the developers. For the two cases examined here, the evolution of the municipal role has already been discussed. In the early 1920s an agency of the municipal government itself acted as the developer. In the 1980s such a municipal role was virtually unthinkable; instead the city saw its task as ensuring that privately developed subdivisions met predetermined engineering standards and were not in flagrant violation of planning policies aimed at encouraging some form of orderly development. Significant as they might be, changes in the municipal role seem not nearly as important as those involving the general public and the developers.

How can we characterize the public's role in relation to Pine Lawn and Garfield Street? First, there is no evidence that any members of the general public were involved in, or concerned about, the selection of the two sites. There was no legislative requirement that such consultation take place and no apparent questioning of the municipality's right to use its land for what would now be called low-income housing. Public pressure on local authorities in relation to this initiative seemed much more concerned with ensuring that local tax rates not be raised as a result of having to finance the required infrastructure. Interestingly enough, it was precisely this kind of cumulative public pressure that led over the years to local improvement taxes, subdivision agreements, and development charges: in short, anything to minimize the impact of new development on general municipal tax rates and/or debt burdens.

In the case of the Stoneybrook subdivision in the 1980s, public pressure from adjoining residential property owners caused the elimination of all higher-density units likely to be in a price range suitable for families with low and moderate incomes. This phenomenon has been widely observed and has caused the Ontario government recently to insist that 25 percent of all housing units in new subdivisions be suitable for low or moderate income-earners. The extent to which this new policy will be successful is still unclear. Another way to help bring about the same outcome might be to *reduce* the current emphasis on encouraging the participation of property owners in decisions about exactly how nearby vacant land is to be developed, assuming there is to be no change in what has already been laid out in official plans or their equivalents.

As far as developers are concerned, there can be no doubt whatever that changes in the subdivision process over the years have forced smaller operations out of the business and have led to the large integrated development companies that are now responsible for so many of the new housing starts in major Canadian metropolitan areas (Canada 1976, 189-90; Lorimer 1978). Although it is undoubtedly the case that these development companies have been able to pass on to their customers most or all of the costs of subdivision agreements and development charges, it is also clear that, in order to survive the time lag between the payment of the charges to the municipality and the ultimate selling of the houses, developers must be well capitalized and have access to hefty lines of credit. On a much smaller scale, a similar point can be made about the purchasers of the new houses. They too must have ready access to large amounts of capital so as to finance, among other things, the costs of the infrastructure associated with their new neighbourhood. In relative terms, the burden of debt on developers and individuals has increased while that of municipalities has decreased.

When municipalities are not themselves bearing the financial costs of new development and when they feel constrained to accommodate all or most of the wishes of adjoining property owners, they can scarcely be considered important actors in the process by which outward urban expansion takes place. To the extent that their refusal to intervene in the process leads to the absence of moderately priced housing and continued trends toward low-density urban sprawl, it is inevitable that there will be ongoing skepticism about the utility of municipalities in efforts to solve one of the most significant of our urban problems.

REFERENCES

Amborski, David P. 1988. "Impact Fees Canadian Style: The Use of Development Charges in Ontario." In *Development Impact Fees: Policy, Rationale, Practice, Theory and Issues*, ed. Arthur C. Nelson, Chicago: Planners Press, 52-64.

Armstrong, F. H. 1986. *The Forest City: An Illustrated History of London.* Northridge, Calif.: Windsor Publications.

Bloomfield, Gerald T. 1989. "No Parking Here to Corner: London Reshaped by the Automobile, 1911-61." *Urban History Review* 18 (October): 139-58.

Canada. 1919. Commission of Conservation. *Conservation of Life* 5-1 (January). Ottawa: The King's Printer.

_____. 1976. Royal Commission on Corporate Concentration. *Cadillac-Fairview Corporation: A Corporate Background Report,* Study No. 3. Ottawa: Supply and Services Canada.

Frankena, M. W. 1982. *Urban Transportation Financing: Theory and Practice in Ontario.* Ontario Economic Council Research Studies 26. Toronto: University of Toronto Press.

Hodge, Gerald. 1986. *Planning Canadian Communities.* Toronto: Methuen.

Housing Commission of London. 1919-22. *Minutes.*

Linteau, Paul Andre. 1982. "The Development and Beautification of an Industrial City: Maisonneuve, 1883-1918." In *Shaping the Urban Landscape: Aspects of the Canadian City-Building Process*, ed. Gilbert A. Stelter and Alan F. J. Artibise, Ottawa: Carleton University Press, 304-20.

London, Ontario, City of. 1920-49. *Estimates.*

London, Ontario, City of. 1978. "History of the Development Fund."

London, Ontario, City of. 1980. Chief Administrative Officer. "Development Charges and Developers' Claim Liquidation Fund," p. 1.

_____. 1984. "Review of Development Charge By-law No. C.P.985-533." June.

The London Free Press.

Lorimer, James. 1978. *The Developers.* Toronto: James Lorimer.

Milner, J. B. 1967. *Tentative Proposals for the Reform of the Ontario Law Relating to Community Planning and Land Use Controls.* Toronto: Ontario Law Reform Commission.

_____. 1967. Ontario Committee on Taxation. *Report.* Toronto: The Queen's Printer.

_____. 1973. Ontario Economic Council. *Subject to Approval: A Review of Municipal Planning in Ontario.* Toronto: Ontario Economic Council.

_____. 1989. *Development Charges Act.* Toronto: The Queen's Printer.

_____. 1991. Ministry of Municipal Affairs. *A Guide to the Development Charges Act, 1989.*

Paterson, Ross. 1985. "The Development of an Interwar Suburb: Kingsway Park, Etobicoke." *Urban History Review* 13 (February): 225-36.

Rogers, Ian MacF. 1973. *Canadian Law of Planning and Zoning.* Toronto: Carswell.

Sewell, John. 1978. "Public Transit in Canada: A Primer." *City Magazine* 3 (May): 40-55.

Steele, Donald R. 1956. "Municipal Controls on Subdivisions." *Law Society of Upper Canada Special Lectures,* 88.

Stone, Clarence N. 1989. *Regime Politics: Governing Atlanta, 1946-1988.* Lawrence, Kan.: University Press of Kansas.

Weaver, John C. 1982. "From Land Assembly to Social Maturity: The Suburban Life of Westdale (Hamilton), Ontario, 1911-1951." In *Shaping the Urban landscape: Aspects of the Canadian City-Building Process,* ed. Gilbert A. Stelter and Alan F. J. Artibise, Ottawa: Carleton University Press, 321-55.

Chapter 25

Local Taxation as an Instrument of Policy

David M. Nowlan
The University of Toronto

INTRODUCTION

The mandate of local government is generally conceived to be the efficient provision of services and programs in response to the preferences of local residents. If local jurisdictions are small, and if the actions of one jurisdiction have little effect on another, then the implementation of this mandate can be relatively straightforward. By functioning as a price to be paid by residents for local services received, local taxation has an important role to play in this implementation. Local tax prices provide an incentive to which residents may respond by indicating their preference for higher or lower service and tax levels, or by moving to a jurisdiction with a more attractive mix of taxes and services. This aspect of local taxation was well understood by Kenneth Eaton in the 1960s, who said of the property tax: "It is one of the relatively rare kinds of tax that is levied on the so-called benefit principle, meaning that there is a fairly close relationship between tax paid and tangible benefits received

This is a revised version of a paper, originally entitled "Changing Perspectives on Municipal Taxation," that I presented in October 1990 at a York University workshop on *The Changing Canadian Metropolis*. I thank those who commented on that earlier version, especially George Fallis who discussed the paper at the workshop, Frances Frisken who organized the workshop, Peter Spurr and Graham Murray from CMHC, one of the sponsoring organizations for the workshop, and Richard Bird, a colleague at the University of Toronto.

through the expenditure of the proceeds by the taxing authorities. In a sense the tax is merely a bill for services" (Eaton 1966).

In local jurisdictions with residents who differ little in their economic circumstances and who share a common preference for some mix of local government services, the type of tax used to pay for local government will not much matter. Whether a property tax, a poll tax, user charges, or a local income tax, each tax will impose about the same burden on each of the similar households, and each household will gain about the same benefit from the local tax-supported spending. Unluckily for any simple theory of local taxation, increasing urbanization and the growth of Canada's metropolitan areas have resulted in complex structures of local government with jurisdictions that have characteristics that are almost the opposite of these. Our city and regional governments serve residents who are immensely heterogeneous in their economic and social circumstances, and, no doubt, in their preferences. Moreover, the geography shared by all residents of any given metropolitan region results unavoidably in a high degree of interdependence among the jurisdictions within the region.

In spite of these complicating factors, the efficient servicing of local needs is still a reasonable characterization of the role we assign to local governments, but the implementation of this mandate is anything but straightforward. In our growing metropolitan areas, local-government efficiency means a lot more than choosing the best-valued fire truck or building a school of the right size; it means managing efficiently our local environments of land, water, and air; it means structuring land use to overcome the inevitable inefficiencies of the private land market; and it means bringing to bear on local residents the true costs of such activities as garbage production, water consumption, and automobile over-use. As well, a local government may have to recognize that the preferences to which it must respond are those of people who range from low-income tenants to wealthy home owners, and from inner-city dwellers to residents of the outer suburbs.

As the burden of local government becomes heavier, especially in metropolitan areas, and as the role of this level of government becomes more complex, we need to think more creatively about the use of local taxation as an instrument of local policy. Properly structured local taxes function as signals to residents and property owners, signals that can lead to more efficient levels of government output and to changes in land use, travel behaviour, development timing, building densities, and city size, all of which are policy matters of increasing concern to metropolitan municipalities. However, outside the technical literature on local public finance, interest in local taxation is focused not on these policy effects but rather on issues of administration and distributive fairness, and on the adequacy of local revenue sources. These issues are important, of course, but their importance should not cause us to ignore the potential that exists to use taxation as an instrument to link the costs of public services with their benefits or to correct distortions in the market price of urban resources or amenities; nor should it cloud an awareness of undesirable resource-use and land-development effects that may unwittingly result from existing tax practices. To emphasize redistributive effects rather than allocative or incentive effects is to adopt a perspective more suited to the analysis of a national tax structure than the structure of local-area taxes.

At a national level, there exists more of a separation between taxation and expenditure than at the local level. One indication of this difference is the restriction imposed on local governments that current expenditures not exceed current revenue, a restriction that has no counterpart at other levels of government. Nationally, we tend to regard a desirable tax structure as one that respects the principle of equal treatment of equals, and one that follows an ability-to-pay principle of progressive taxation. Expenditures are decided upon according to processes, bureaucratic or political, that are linked only minimally, if at all, to their tax implications. Considerable effort is spent analysing the distorting effects of national taxes, which are considered undesirable. Neutral taxes, those with minimal allocative effects and maximal distributive effects, are the paragons of national taxes.

If this perspective is transferred to municipalities, it precludes any consideration of the use to which taxes might be put to further local goals. Local taxes become viewed simply as funding sources needed to meet the revenue requirements of local spending programs, and neutral taxes, quite naturally, are favoured for this purpose, in spite of the fact that neutrality itself has proven to be a more elusive quality than expected. Local taxes especially are less likely to approximate the requirements of neutrality than provincial or national taxes, because there is more opportunity at the local level to avoid or minimize the tax burden.

To the extent that benefits and tax costs are not well correlated, on a household-by-household or business-by-business basis, taxes will result in a redistribution of income or wealth among local-area residents. But there is no reason to think that this redistribution will be neutral, i.e., that it will not have allocative effects. Higher property taxes without improved benefits may, for example, worsen the well-being of some people or businesses and lead them to change locations, or it may reduce the capital value of some properties and alter the timing and type of development that occurs on those sites. Allocative effects of this sort may be desirable in some circumstances and not in others. The point is that local taxes do have these effects, and it is better to understand and to use them for policy purposes than to ignore them.

In this chapter, the effects of different types of local tax in different settings are reviewed and commented upon. The merit of one type of tax over another is shown to depend largely on whether the use of local government services, or the exposure to local taxes, can readily be varied by households and businesses. An ability to vary one's exposure to a local tax or user charge allows benefits to be brought into line with service costs, and it is this adjustment mechanism that underlies arguments for the broader application of cost-based taxes, the most obvious examples of which are user charges for some local services like water consumption or transit use. Many theories of local taxation presume that individuals can vary their exposure to any kind of local tax, a property tax perhaps, or a poll tax, by moving about among jurisdictions in an efficient search for the best combination of tax rates and service levels. Mobility of this sort will be encouraged by cost-based taxes and will tend to lead to greater homogeneity within municipal jurisdictions.

If mobility is low or if for other reasons households or businesses cannot vary their use of or exposure to local services, then cost-based taxes are less efficient than benefit taxes. Benefit taxes distribute tax burdens among the population in the same manner as the benefits of tax-supported programs are distributed. As my subsequent discussion indicates, there are reasons for thinking that this benefits approach to taxation may be more suitable for larger, heterogeneous, regional municipalities, and it leads to the suggestion that local income taxes may be one of the most efficient methods of taxation for metropolitan-scale local governments.

Part of my analysis deals with the effect of the property tax in altering the timing and extent of urban development. This is not an aspect of local taxation that is customarily considered, but the increasing importance of using land efficiently in metropolitan areas, which generally means using it more compactly, suggests that these development effects should play a more prominent role in the design of local taxes. Development charges and lot levies are another increasingly popular form of local tax with implications for land use. The efficiency of this type of levy is discussed in the penultimate section of the chapter.

In the next section, I begin my analysis by discussing the basis for supposing that we want local governments to pursue an objective of operating efficiently; that is we want to encourage the efficient supply of government services and the efficient use of land and local environmental resources. This provides a context for examining in detail in subsequent sections the role of local taxes as instruments to help achieve these goals.

What Do We Want From Local Governments?

If local taxes are to be used as policy tools because of their resource effects, we need to know how they work and what to look for in their use. Even before that, we need to raise the question of what, or whose, goals are to be served by the structure and level of local taxation. Since metropolitan areas consist of urban jurisdictions within larger political entities—the provinces and the country as a whole—policies in metropolitan jurisdictions, including taxation policy, are likely to have to respond to a rather complex set of goals.

Simply conceived, municipal governments exist to provide local public services, the costs of which are expected to be borne locally. In this rudimentary model, local services and local taxes affect only those who live or do business in some geographically limited area; the level and quality of spending reflects the preferences of these residents.

As frequently happens, the real world has conspired to complicate matters considerably, thereby limiting the applicability of this simple view of municipal public finance. Not only do the effects of local spending programs or local land-use regulations often reach well beyond the population of the municipality in which they take place, but, since we live principally in urban areas and move about among them, our national and provincial problems and goals have a strong urban dimension. These facts have made local governments sometimes the partners of senior governments for the delivery of such services as education, health, welfare, housing, policing, or transportation, and sometimes the subordinates of those governments. Metropolitan issues reaching beyond the geography of individual municipal governments have also led to complex structures of regional government.

In this more complicated reality, the conceptual linkage of the simple model that equates the amount of revenue raised from the local population with the costs of municipal services is broken. In contrast with the simple model, the quality of some urban programs is established by a broader public than the inhabitants of a particular city, and the cost of these services is borne by that broader public through taxes levied in ways that are consistent with public distributive goals. To the extent that municipal governments deliver these broadly conceived programs, we would expect their expenditures to be greater than locally generated revenue, which is exactly what has happened in this country and elsewhere as urbanization has advanced and as problems requiring provincial and national solutions shift increasingly to urban areas.

The data in Table 25.1 illustrate this point with respect to the sources of local government revenue in Canada from 1958 to 1988. The proportion of local government revenue transferred from other governments—virtually all of it from provincial governments—increased over the years until by the late 1970s transfers provided almost 50 percent of all municipal revenue. It is also clear from the data that tied transfers, those related to specific items of municipal spending, have accounted for almost all the increase. The percentage of total transfers did not continue to rise during the 1980s, partly because significant spending responsibilities shifted from the municipal to the provincial level in some provinces and partly because provinces responded to fiscal pressures by attending less to urban needs. This has contributed to a continued sense of financial crisis at the municipal level.[1]

How, faced with this complex mixture of own-source revenue, tied transfers, and untied grants, might one go about analyzing municipal tax policy? The most common approach is to begin by attempting to disentangle those municipally provided services or programs that have some clearly local geographic dimension, and that exist to serve local preferences, from those with broader implications. Programs with broader implications include those with direct benefits that reach well beyond the boundary of a municipality (such as harbours, airports, hospitals, and through roads) plus such things as social services or housing assistance to low-income families or disadvantaged people whose well-being is of concern to more than just the residents of the local municipality in which they reside.

Given this distinction between local and nonlocal services, it can be argued that those services with broader, nonlocal effects should be pro-

---

[1]Concern over a mismatch between spending responsibilities and revenue sources is longstanding. For an earlier discussion, see Eric Hardy's paper of 30 years ago (Hardy 1961).

Table 25.1.   *Sources of Local Government Revenue*

	1988	1978	1968	1958
Own-source	51.0%	50.5%	59.4%	69.9%
Tied transfers	41.6%	41.6%	35.4%	25.6%
General Transfers	5.4	7.9%	5.2%	4.5%
	100.0%	100.0%	100.0%	100.0%

Sources: Canadian Tax Foundation 1990 for the years 1988 and 1978; Gillespie 1973 for the year 1968; and Bird 1970 for the year 1958.

vided in response to the goals and values of the province or the country as a whole (as reflected by the policies of provincial and federal governments), and that they should be paid for by revenue raised across the whole affected jurisdiction: the province or the country, as the case may be. Residents of any municipality that delivers such a broad-based program will of course pay their share, but their share will be determined by the distributional rules governing taxation over the whole of the broader constituency. The remaining local services would be supported by locally raised revenue. If municipal residents wanted more of a local service, they would pay more; no other community need be involved. This approach essentially embeds a simple municipal model, with local services decided upon and paid for by local residents, within a more elaborate model of urban government.

Not all programs fall neatly into one or other of these categories,[2] but the separation of types of expenditure according to their focus on local or nonlocal services, and the differentiation between revenue sources designed to support each, have been persistent themes in Canadian writing on municipal public finance. This thinking has influenced the

---

[2]For example, reducing the use of automobiles in urban areas might be an objective of all three levels of government—local, provincial, and national. Taxation, regulation, land-use policies, and transportation spending at all three levels might be used to support this objective. A mixed-jurisdiction issue of this type is obviously easier to deal with if, as in the automobile example, the values of all jurisdictions have the same orientation.

changing pattern of municipal revenue sources over the last several decades and is particularly noticeable in the field of primary- and secondary-school education where, in some provinces, total financial responsibility has been shifted to the provincial level. General welfare assistance and subsidized housing are other examples of extended services, delivered largely by municipalities although paid for principally by the provinces and the federal government.

Robin Boadway and Harry Kitchen have drawn the dividing line between local services and extended services with the argument that "property-related services (including water supply, sewage, roads, and fire protection) would be financed from property tax revenue. . . .   On the other hand, people-related services (health, education, and welfare, for example) should be financed through taxes based on the ability-to-pay principle (personal income tax)." They go on to suggest that, "since local governments do not have access to personal income taxation, these functions ought to be funded by provincial or federal governments" (Boadway and Kitchen 1984, 237). Paul Hobson (1987, 72; 1991, 235) and the Economic Council of Canada (1987, 99) are among others who support the relevance of this distinction, and it underlies the division of spending and taxing responsibilities advocated in the recent *Report of the Advisory Committee* on provincial-municipal financial relationships in Ontario (Ontario 1991).[3]

It is a standard feature of multilevel government models that the more broadly based, higher levels of government should handle the redistributive side of public finance, in response to national or provincial goals, while the lowest level of government, the municipal governments, should

---

[3]While recognizing the need to differentiate between local and more broadly based spending, some commentators have been skeptical about the use of property- versus people-related services as a way of defining the dividing line. The influential 1967 Ontario (Smith) Committee on Taxation had serious reservations about using local taxes to finance only those services that are directly related to property (Ontario Committee on Taxation 1967, Vol. I, 47) and the 1977 (Blair) Commission on the Reform of Property Taxation in Ontario called the distinction between property-related and people-related services "facile," and went on to say that "Upon even perfunctory examination, it is evident that the differentiation between so-called services to land and services to people is wholly irrelevant; there is, in any perspective whatsoever, no such thing as 'services to land'; there are only services demanded by people" (Ontario 1977, 2-3).

seek simply to provide services and programs efficiently.[4] Clearly, the provision of local services in accordance with the rudimentary model of municipal public finance is quite consistent with this sought-after division of responsibilities. Since the costs of local programs are borne by the local municipal taxpayers, with their quality or size determined by local preferences, no redistribution will occur among municipalities; each local jurisdiction gets what local services it pays for, and it pays for those of no other municipality. Redistribution of income or wealth could similarly be avoided within municipalities if each local resident or business were taxed or otherwise charged an amount that was directly related to the value of benefits received by that resident from local services. All the redistributive effects of taxing and public spending would then be the responsibility of levels of government above the municipality. Those nonlocal programs or services delivered within and possibly by municipalities would have their program standards and revenue sources established by other levels of government in response to the political values of a broader public. In this dichotomous model, efficiency need be the only public-finance criterion at the local level.

Efficiency and Taxes

If this model of local government is accepted, then the question becomes whether local taxes can be used to encourage efficiency. To do this, taxes (and related charges such as levies and user fees) have to work

---

[4]For an elaboration of this point see the canonical work on fiscal federalism by Wallace Oates (1972). It is, however, possible to contemplate models in which redistribution through spending and taxing can more efficiently be accomplished by local governments than by higher level governments. Mark Pauly has shown that if there is a spatial dimension to equity issues; if, for example, a community is more concerned about its own poor than about the poor in other communities; then, under some circumstances, it is better for local governments than for higher levels of government to take complete responsibility for redistribution. Under a wider set of circumstances, it is efficient for local government to be at least a partner in establishing locally differentiated redistribution policies (Pauly 1973). This is a point that is likely to be especially relevant in larger, metropolitan-oriented municipalities that are either the upper tier of a federated regional governing system or the single municipality in a large, urbanized region.

to help bring together the costs and benefits of urban activities, including government-provided services and programs.

For example, if the cost of increasing the quality of the water supply in a metropolitan area is $10 million annually, it would be efficient to proceed with the project if residents taken together were willing to pay that much or more for the improvement. Asking everybody individually how valuable the higher-quality water is to them, with the intention of summing the results, is not likely to yield useful information. If people have to pay an amount equal to their stated personal valuation, they will be inclined to give an answer that is less than their true valuation; and if they don't have to pay, they will lose nothing by falsely answering with a high valuation. Suppose, however, that the project is to be funded by increasing the property-tax rate and that people are asked to indicate their preference for proceeding or not. If property taxes are distributed among residents in exactly the same way as the valuation of the water-quality improvement is distributed, then there will be either unanimous endorsement of the project, if the total annual valuation exceeds the annual cost of $10 million, or unanimous rejection, if the aggregate valuation falls short of this cost. This example shows that, in theory at least, a property tax can give local governments the information they need to be efficient, if the tax base is distributed just as benefits are distributed.[5]

An easier example might be the following. Suppose a municipality has a policy of shovelling snow from the sidewalks of elderly residents free of charge and offers to extend this service to any household for a fee that reflects the extra cost of the extra shovelling. If a household values the benefit from the public snow removal above the fee, that household will sign up for the service; otherwise not. This fee, which might be thought of as a special form of tax, will clearly relate benefits to costs and so support the efficiency goal of local government, just as the well-distributed property tax base did in the previous example.

The taxes in these two examples encourage efficiency by linking benefits to costs. For this linkage to occur, two conditions must be met.

---

[5] In this example, I have not distinguished between residents who are tenants and those who are owner-occupiers. The residents whose views are being sought are assumed to be those who will bear the burden of any increase in the property tax. With renters and owners distinguished, and with the suffrage embracing residents generally, whether property owners or not, the example will be valid under some circumstances but not others. This matter is explored in subsequent sections.

First, the tax must reflect as accurately as possible the true social cost of the project or activity that gives rise to the tax;[6] and second, individual taxpayers must be able to adjust their benefits to this cost by taking more or less of the proposed activity or project. In the example of the water-quality improvement project, the first of these conditions might be met by ensuring that the $10 million annual price tag includes a reasonable estimate of the social or environmental costs of any environmental problems associated with it. By the assumption that valuations of water-quality benefits are distributed in the same way as the tax base and that these taxpayers can vote to proceed with the project or not, the second condition has been satisfied. Both conditions are more obviously met in the snow-removal example.

If these two conditions are met, local taxes will function very much like prices in a competitive market, mediating between the social cost of services (or other activity subject to taxation) and their private valuation by the taxpaying residents, with costs equated to value at the margin. Local spending under these circumstances will be efficient.[7] In essence,

---

[6]This notion of cost could be expanded upon by noting that if a local municipal service benefits people outside the tax-paying locality, then the service should be subsidized by other levels of government. In this case, it is efficient to charge local taxpayers less than the full cost of the service. If a program or service has negative effects, the taxpaying users should pay amounts that exceed the cost of its provision. These standard rules for subsidies or penalty taxes are valid only if the second efficiency condition is also met.

[7]The idea that an efficient outcome is one with costs equated to value at the margin is subject to qualification. Just as competitive markets in private goods may not achieve or hold efficient allocations under some circumstances, so too the efficient use of local taxes may require departures from the simple equation of marginal costs and marginal values. The most likely circumstance in local public finance under which some alternative efficiency condition arises is when local services and programs are produced subject to decreasing average costs as size expands. If local governments are required to balance their operating budgets, as indeed they are in Canada, then the presence of even one decreasing-cost program or service will generally lead to efficiency conditions in which marginal tax costs are different from marginal values across all programs. Some authors get around this matter and retain the simple marginal efficiency conditions by assuming that lump-sum taxes can be used in addition to taxes that allow for benefits or value adjustments. For purposes of this chapter, I consider the equalization of costs and individual valuations at the margin as the basic efficiency concept and assume that when efficiency requires a departure from this

the benefits of local services, household-by-household and business-by-business, will be efficiently matched to the true social costs of the services. Distributive issues will not arise. It is evident that these two conditions are very strong and will be met in practice only imperfectly, but they do provide a basis for assessing the actual effects of local taxes and so constitute a useful reference framework for subsequent discussion.[8]

Interestingly, there seems in fact to have been an expansion in the use by municipalities of some types of tax that are especially well suited to meet these efficiency conditions required by the standard model. This has probably been less by design than simply as the outcome of a continuing search for new revenue sources. An example is the local improvement tax. This tax, which has been used in Canada for many years, brings the cost of local public improvements to bear directly on the local beneficiaries. In this way, the tax acts as an instrument that itself helps determine the desirability of undertaking the spending. Development levies or impact fees are one-time equivalents of local improvement taxes, with the potential to affect municipal development patterns.

User fees are another example of an increasingly popular type of municipal charge that can be designed specifically to encourage the

---

standard it can be thought of as a refinement and not a rejection of the standard. It should be understood, however, that there are circumstances in which these refinements could dramatically alter the nature of efficiency taxes. It should also be understood that the marginal conditions for efficiency are appropriate principally for the evaluation of small changes and cannot readily be generalized for application to large changes. For large departures from the status quo, a comparison of total changes in benefits and costs is needed, not just a comparison of marginal quantities. With large changes, distributional effects cannot in general be avoided, even when everyone benefits from the change, and the notion of a pure benefits tax needs to be substantially qualified (see Foley 1967).

[8]Some authors argue that the efficiency of local taxes should be assessed within the broad context of the national tax structure (see, for example, Thirsk 1982, 394, and Damus, Hobson, and Thirsk 1987). From this perspective, local taxes are evaluated according to the extent to which they appear to improve or to worsen distortions caused by national taxes such as personal or profits taxes. While this may be an understandable focus for national agencies to take, it is more logical to evaluate the efficiency properties of local taxes from the perspective of local economies and then to evaluate the need to adjust the structure of higher-level taxes to achieve national goals, given the best possible structure of local taxes.

efficient consumption of some types of publicly provided services. If the fee reflects the cost of service, then the first condition will be met, while the second will be met if the consumption of a service financed through user charges can be varied on a consumer-by-consumer basis. The desirability of using such charges when feasible is clearly grounded in the conceptual model outlined in the previous section, which assigns to local government allocative and not redistributive goals, and it has been strongly urged upon local governments by authors such as Richard Bird.[9] Whether because of these conceptual arguments or simply as a result of a desire to relieve the property tax of further pressure,[10] municipal own-source fees and other nontax revenues have risen rapidly over the past several decades, as Table 25.2 shows. Correspondingly, revenue from the property tax and related taxes has fallen from close to 90 percent of own-source revenue in the 1950s to approximately 70 percent in the late 1980s.

The principal reason that taxes such as user fees, development levies, and local-area improvement charges are believed to encourage efficient resource allocation is that the beneficiaries can adjust their consumption or use of the taxed service or program so as to bring their margins of valuation into line with costs, which will be reflected in a properly set tax. The mechanism by which this can happen is quite transparent in the case of marketable public services such as water, electricity, or transit, the use of which may be adjusted as tax prices change, but it exists in essentially the same form in the case of development charges or impact fees, as developers alter the size or timing of proposed developments in response to the charges. This ability to vary one's exposure to a tax is much more problematic when, as in the case of a property tax, a local

---

[9]Bird argued a number of years ago in his widely cited book on user charges that ". . . the appropriate ideal for local public finance is to approximate as closely as possible to the efficient pricing of government-provided services. With regard to property, what this means is more reliance on specific benefit financing such as assessments and less on the general property tax, while with regard to other sources of local revenue, it obviously means more emphasis on user and service charges of various sorts" (Bird 1976, 103).

[10]The common use of flat-rate water charges rather than metered consumption fees and the virtual absence of time-of-use residential electricity fees or transit fares suggest that improved resource allocation has not been the primary motivation for the introduction of user fees, but the potential is nonetheless apparent.

Table 25.2. *Distribution of Municipal Own-Source Revenue*

	1988	1978	1968	1958
Taxes	71.3%	75.6%	84.2%	87.5%
Fees	19.3%	16.6%	15.8%	12.5%
Other	9.4%	7.8%		
	100.0%	100.0%	100.0%	100.0%

Sources: Canadian Tax Foundation 1990 for the years 1988 and 1978; Leacy (ed.) 1983 for the years 1968 and 1958.

income tax or a poll tax, the tax is applied in some consistent manner across a whole jurisdiction and used to support a broad range of municipal services or programs that are available equally to all residents, like urban parkland or fire fighting services. Except in the stylized example of the water-quality project, where individual and collective views were the same, it is not immediately apparent in such cases how each person individually could avoid some tax cost by reducing consumption of local services, or alternatively how they could choose individually to pay more because they wanted more public service.

This is a matter that deserves careful attention, since property taxes, and business taxes related to property value, even though diminishing in relative importance, are still the principal local source of municipal revenue. Although varying greatly in significance from province to province, property-related taxes generate revenue for municipalities that approximates the aggregate value of tied transfers from the provincial and national governments. In total, they are as large a source of government revenue as the profits tax on business, which makes their use high by international standards. A 1988 OECD survey estimated that, on average for OECD countries, taxes on property constituted 2.0 percent of GDP and 5.4 percent of total tax revenues; for Canada the comparable figures were 3.2 percent and 9.3 percent.[11] Given this significance, and the fact that user fees and similar charges are feasible in only a limited range of

---

[11]As reported in Perry 1990, 1329.

circumstances, the extent to which compulsory, jurisdictionwide taxes like the property tax can play a role in encouraging local efficiency is clearly an important question and one that has been subject to considerable scrutiny and analysis in recent academic literature.

As a major revenue source for many local governments, property taxes contribute heavily to the funding of local services and thus serve in a general way to associate overall costs with overall benefits in municipalities. While property-tax costs and the benefits of tax revenue may be linked in this way jurisdiction-by-jurisdiction, the coupling of benefits to tax costs for individual households or businesses within each jurisdiction depends on the distribution of the burden of property taxes and on its relationship to the distribution of the benefits received from municipal spending. If the burden falls more heavily on some and the benefit on others, then municipal taxing and spending will have distributional effects that are unwanted from the point of view of the standard model of municipal finance. If the burdens and the benefits of a property or other jurisdictionwide tax are distributed similarly among the residents, the tax is a "benefit" tax, resident-by-resident. Within the context of the efficiency model of local government, benefit taxes are desirable because they encourage processes by which optimal amounts of local services are provided, and they can help produce efficient patterns of land use.

In the next two sections, I discuss mechanisms by which a property tax might function more-or-less as a benefits tax. The ability of residents to move in order to avoid the tax liability turns out to be a critical consideration, but one that has peculiar side-effects on the nature of municipal politics. In the subsequent sections, I expand the discussion by recognizing that, in addition to providing incentives for residents to move, the property tax can alter the uses to which land is put and therefore the structure of urban and metropolitan areas.

The Property Tax as a Benefit Tax: Mobility and Politics Lost

The land area of a municipality is partitioned into a number of proprietary lots, many or perhaps most of which will have been built upon. Buildings are used for either commercial or residential purposes, and they may be occupied by tenants or owners. Each rented property will have some annual gross rental income from which costs, including any taxes the owner has to pay, are deducted to arrive at a net revenue flow. The market value of the property is given by the capitalization of the expected future net revenue flows. If the building is occupied by its owner, then the net revenue flow may be thought of as the minimum net annual amount that the owner would take to vacate the property and rent it to someone else; this is the owner's annual "reservation price."

Consider now property taxes, which are set as a proportion of a property's market value (setting aside any administrative questions about the relationship of assessed values to market values—see Bossons 1981; Denny 1981). Suppose the property tax rate is increased. If the gross rental flow for the property is unchanged, then the net rental flow must decline, which will reduce the market value of the property. Similarly, the higher liability associated with the tax increase may reduce an owner-occupier's reservation price. Tax rates and property values are inversely related in these circumstances.

Clearly, the effect of the higher property tax on the market value of the property depends on whether or to what extent the owner can raise gross rents to tenants in order to cover the higher tax costs. If rents can be raised then some or all of the higher tax liability can be shifted to the tenants. If higher rents drive tenants or would-be tenants away, there can be no forward shifting of the tax to tenants, and the property owner will feel the full burden of the higher tax. (If the property is owner-occupied, then the owner will obviously bear responsibility for the tax. Whether this constitutes a burden depends on whether the reservation price mentioned above is lowered or not, as will presently become apparent.)

Without forward shifting, higher taxes will reduce the market value of a piece of property. If this were the end of the story, the effect of tax changes would be purely distributive, and property taxes would be unable to fulfill the role assigned to the local component of the general municipal finance model outlined previously. Such a tax could neither link local costs to local benefits, nor could it be used to achieve efficient resource use. But how plausible is the complete absence of forward shifting?

Suppose that a municipality levies higher taxes but spends the tax revenue on activities or infrastructure that improve the well-being of those who reside there. Perhaps additional taxes are spent on cleaner water supplies or better public transit, or on new schools or parkland. If this occurs and the residents of any given property perceive some benefit associated with the enhanced, publicly provided services, then, for rental properties, rents can be increased without driving the tenants away, and the net revenue will not fall by as much as the additional tax burden. With respect to owner-occupied properties, the added value of benefits will buffer the tax-induced fall of the reservation price.

Although theoretically possible, the likelihood that the benefits of new spending are distributed in precisely the same way as the associated property taxes seems small, but the extent to which the two distributions are typically correlated is an open and important question to which we will return. If the benefits and the tax charges are unrelated, then the question is, who bears the burden of the resulting redistribution? The answer to this depends partly on the mobility of the residents, and in this connection the distinction between owner-residents and tenants assumes particular significance.

Consider those residents who are tenants. If property taxes are increased in order, say, to add or improve some local service, then the ability of the property owners to shift these new tax costs forward to the tenants depends not just on the benefits of the new spending, as perceived by the tenants, but on the tenants' ability or willingness to move elsewhere to avoid any rent increase in excess of the benefit value. If tenants were more-or-less indifferent before the tax hike between their present accommodation and some equally satisfactory alternative in a locality unaffected by the tax increase, then the property owners will be unable to increase rents by more than the value of the tenant-perceived benefits associated with the new spending. Any remaining tax cost would appear in the form of lower net rents that would lead to lower market values for the properties. Of course, if the value of the benefits exceeded the magnitude of the property tax, then the owners could raise rents by more than the tax increase and the value of the properties would rise.

Suppose indeed that residents, both people and businesses, have a very precise view of the value to them of living or locating where they are. This view might well be formed on the basis of service levels, property rents (or property prices), and tax costs in other jurisdictions. If the costs of living in their present municipality were to rise, or the level of benefits to go down, then these residents would move, or threaten to move, to an alternative jurisdiction. In these circumstances, any difference between the tax costs of new municipal spending and the benefits to the residents of that spending will be capitalized in the market value of the property. Existing residents may not actually move, but their potential to move leads to the capitalization effect.

Figure 25.1 shows what would happen with this capitalization effect at work. Nine properties are shown with initial, before-tax property values from $100,000 to $500,000. These values have fully adjusted to the existing level of taxes and service benefits. Suppose an additional 10

Figure 25.1. *Capitalization Effect*

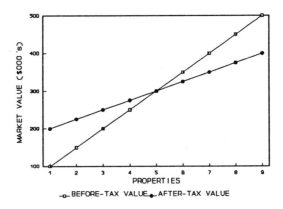

-o- BEFORE-TAX VALUE -•- AFTER-TAX VALUE

percent annual property tax is imposed (an exaggerated amount, but one that has an easy-to-see effect in the diagram) and that the benefits from this tax have a constant value of $30,000 annually for every resident (since this amount is exactly the average tax collected, one can think of the local government as simply handing back the revenue from the new tax by giving $30,000 to every resident). For residents in the $300,000 property, new taxes equal new benefits so they break even. Those renting the more highly valued properties have to pay more in new taxes than they receive in benefits. Because of the mobility assumption, this means that the owners of the higher priced properties have to lower their rental rates and the capital values of the properties fall. For cheaper properties the reverse occurs: spending benefits in excess of the new tax extractions lead to high demand, with consequential rent hikes and property value increases.

Suppose that the 10 percent tax rate increase, with its corresponding $30,000 annual benefits to each resident, was not in place but only a proposal. Local government might consider testing the merit of the proposal by asking for resident opinion, perhaps through a referendum. It turns out that the government will be able to get very little useful information in this way, if the tenant-residents are mobile. Mobile tenants would have no reason to be for or against any tax or spending proposal, since they can avoid any net costs by moving, or threatening to move, and they will gain no net benefits because demand by in-bound residents will cause rents to increase by amounts that offset any potential gains. In short, the mobility of tenant-residents greatly reduces the amount of information about the efficiency of government actions that can be gained through normal political means. With tenant demand determining the market level of property rents, only property owners will have any interest in government spending and taxing decisions, and only those owners who are actual residents, or otherwise entitled to vote in the municipality, will be politically active. This could mean that a local government seeking opinion even on a proposal providing highly correlated benefits and tax costs, property-by-property, would be able to gain little useful information from its voting residents. The information signalled by the votes of owner-occupiers might be an accurate reflection of the property-by-property net benefits associated with the proposal, but even if there were a consensus among property owners, the number of voters might be such a small portion of the eligible voters that the result would not be persuasive.

If resident mobility is significant, then any political mechanism for determining efficient patterns of local spending and taxing is likely to be much weakened. However, there is a considerable body of local public finance literature based on the view that, although not political, mobility itself constitutes a mechanism that will produce a much higher degree of correlation between tax payments and service benefits than would be expected in a municipal population of randomly heterogeneous residents. The argument is that if people or businesses can freely move among jurisdictions with different taxing and spending patterns they can choose better their preferred combinations of either lower taxes and fewer services or higher taxes with better services. This could moderate the capitalization effect of mismatched tax costs and spending benefits in the following way. If landlords cannot pass on a new tax charge to existing residents because those residents do not value highly enough the spending benefit associated with it, they may nonetheless be able to raise rents and still attract new tenants from elsewhere who place a higher value than the original residents on the spending benefits (obviously they couldn't do this if the benefit was a simple per-property payment of $30,000 as in the example underlying Figure 25.1, since the value of this payment will be the same for everybody; but for most new or expanded service benefits, the personal values to different households or businesses will be different).

If this type of sorting by tenant preference takes place as different municipal jurisdictions provide different mixes of tax rates and spending benefits, then municipal units will become more homogeneous. In the limit, with everyone completely mobile, each separate tax and spending jurisdiction would be populated with residents having identical preferences, living in identically priced properties and paying the same taxes. If indeed homogeneous municipalities of this sort did emerge, whether the tax scheme was a property tax or a household poll tax would be a matter of indifference, since everyone would pay the same amount in any case. Either tax would certainly be efficient; all residents would share a common view toward the preferred level of taxation and services.

Whether this model with its assumption of costless mobility could lead to an efficient system of municipalities, even in theory, depends heavily on the nature of the costs of local-government services and programs. If, for example, a police department of some given size and cost could serve any number of people with equal ease, with no diminution of service levels, then clearly the most efficient city size to police, i.e., the one with the least costly police services per resident, would be the largest possible city. Each additional resident would add nothing to the cost of policing and could help share the burden of cost. If all city services had this structure of costs, then having the population broken down into smaller communities each with its own police department and other service units would be very inefficient. But if the cost of municipal services typically rises or falls *pari passu* with a change in the size of the residential population, so that the average cost of the service per resident stays more-or-less constant, then there is no particular advantage to larger or to smaller jurisdictions, and the sorting process envisaged by the model would not, on that account, be inefficient.[12]

---

[12]In the literature on club theory, which is one of the building blocks of the municipal mobility model, it is a standard result that homogeneous clubs are more efficient than mixed clubs, a result that depends importantly on the structure of service costs and the extent of production or consumption interdependencies among the residents. In the local public finance literature it has been recognized that one implication of this result, if property taxes are used as the source of revenue, is that residents with high marginal service evaluations will want to set up zoning constraints to maintain high property values in order to reduce "freeloading" by residents in low-value properties who would have equal access to high quality services but pay lower taxes (see Hamilton 1975). In fact, some authors maintain that the mobility model results will break down unless there exists this form of restrictive zoning (Hobson 1987, 24; Mieszkowski and Zodrow 1989, 1108). This need for zoning constraints depends, however, on the

The essential features of this mobility model were first set out by Charles Tiebout many years ago (Tiebout 1956) and have become associated with his name. While many economists remain skeptical about its empirical relevance, it has gained adherents over the years. (See Hamilton 1983 for a favourable review of some of the evidence that can be adduced in its support, and Mieszkowski and Zodrow 1989 for a more negative review.) At best, the efficient outcome envisaged in the model[13] is most likely to be approximated when municipalities are small suburban taxing jurisdictions, the sort of fragmented municipalities common in the metropolitan areas of the United States where much of the academic literature originates. The Tiebout mechanism is unlikely to be as significant in Canada's metropolitan areas, with their extended unitary or hierarchical metropolitan government structures.

Land-Use Effects of the Property Tax: Politics Regained

The distinguishing feature and principal attraction of the benefits perspective on local taxation is the recognition that tax receipts are used to provide beneficial programs or services for residents. The Tiebout model has used that perspective to argue that, if our urban population is mobile, a preference for any particular combination of tax rates and spending programs may be expressed by moving to a preferred jurisdiction. Residential political opinion toward municipal spending has no role

---

assumption that the benefits of municipal services to a resident would be of equal value no matter how valuable a property that person resided in. If benefits are related to the value of the property, then restrictive zoning is not necessary.

[13]Implicit in my discussion is the assumption that municipalities provide services or programs at the lowest cost for the particular offerings. Taken to its conceptual limit, the Tiebout model would predict that any municipality offering services inefficiently, i.e., at tax costs higher than this minimum, would lose population and possibly disappear as adjacent, efficient jurisdictions encroached on the land area of the inefficient jurisdiction. This is the outcome of Vernon Henderson's model (Henderson 1985), which yields efficient patterns of municipal spending with a long-run Tiebout mechanism and without normal politics (property owners and developers make decisions usually made by governments). While some supporters of the Tiebout model see the absence of politics as a strength of the mechanism, others, such as Susan Rose-Ackerman, have been persistently critical of the model precisely because it does not deal with the politics of municipal public finance (see, e.g., Rose-Ackerman 1983).

to play in this model; walking replaces talking.[14] From this perspective, any difference between incremental tax payments and incremental local service benefits has a purely redistributive effect. The value of the difference is capitalized in the market value of the affected properties, with the whole of the cost or the advantage being borne by the property owners. If tax rates were to rise with no corresponding increase in benefits, then property values would fall by an equivalent, capitalized amount.

The mobility of modern urban populations, business and residential, is at the heart of the Tiebout model, but mobility alone can produce results such as the complete capitalization of net tax payments and the absence of political interest on the part of tenant residents only in one of two circumstances: either mobility is complete, in the sense that every resident is freely mobile and indifferent between residing where they do or some place else, or there is no structural adjustment of properties—no development and no change in building size or use.

The first of these possible assumptions, complete mobility, entails demand curves for tenancy in any jurisdiction that are completely elastic, i.e., horizontal, so the capitalization and no-politics results occur whether property redevelopment occurs or not. But if not all residents in a tax jurisdiction are completely mobile, the demand curves for tenancy will have some inelasticity; they will not be horizontal. In this case, complete capitalization of net taxes and the irrelevancy of politics will occur only if there is no property development, no change in building densities or building types in response to the tax changes. In these circumstances, the supply of structures will be completely inelastic and, given any degree of elasticity of tenant demand, there can be no forward shifting to tenants of tax increases (except to the extent that the increases are matched by spending benefits).

The circumstances necessary to get the Tiebout results are extreme, and at best, the model might be of interest in the very long run, when everyone could adjust to some preferred pattern of taxes and service levels.[15] Most policy has a less distant focus in time; it is therefore of

---

[14]This is the "exit" rather than the "voice" option of Hirschman 1972.

[15]In the very short run, structures might be regarded as being in fixed supply and so the Tiebout model might appear to be applicable. But, in the very short run, mobility is also very low. With an inelastic supply of structures and an inelastic demand for accommodation, the very short-run effect of a tax change is indeterminate.

practical as well as theoretical interest to see what happens if resident demand for accommodation has some inelasticity and building supply some elasticity.

Suppose some property or set of properties is faced with an increase in the property tax rate, an increase that is not offset by an equivalent benefit value. If demand is completely elastic or supply of structures completely inelastic—the Tiebout variant of the benefits model—the rental value net of taxes is reduced by the whole of the tax increase and the property value falls. If, however, we allow the building structure on the property to be changed over time, then the tax increase will likely provoke some allocative or resource effects. Since a bigger building adds to the value of the tax base for property tax purposes, an optimally sized building with a higher tax rate is smaller than the best-size building with a lower tax rate. With the tax increase, there will therefore be a tendency to reduce building repairs that would retain the value of the property and ultimately to reduce the size and value of the building on the property. In this way, the property owner will have minimized the capitalization loss associated with the tax increase; the resource result is that the supply of rentable space will fall.

The tax-induced reduction in rentable space will lead to a price increase for accommodation in the area affected by the tax increase, if the demand is anything other than completely elastic. The unit rental price will rise, and some of the reduction in property value will be mitigated at the expense of the remaining tenants. This price rise would also reduce the extent of the change in the optimal building size.

These land-use effects allow us to reconsider the role of the property tax within a benefits framework. Both the Tiebout model and a model with land-use effects lead to the result that a tax increase matched property-by-property with a spending benefit equal in value to the tax increase will have neither allocative nor redistributive effects. Those who benefit, pay; and there is no tax-induced adjustment to building size or use.

Beyond that superficial similarity, there is a vast difference in the implications of the two approaches. Under Tiebout assumptions, residents who are tenants will not be faced with rent increases beyond the value of the spending benefits, no matter what the tax cost; they have, therefore, no reason to be interested in voting for or against any tax-spending proposal. The alternative assumptions, that building size and use will adjust in response to the capitalization of net tax costs, will place some of the burden of those costs back on those who rent accommodation or office space.

Consider assumptions that are just the reverse of those in the Tiebout model. Suppose that the demand for space by tenants is completely inelastic, while the supply of space is responsive to the capitalization effect. Under these polar assumptions, all of the cost of a tax increase net of the value of benefits is shifted forward to tenants. In such circumstances, the distinction between owner-occupiers and tenants is unimportant; the model regains its politics, as both tenants and owners have a vital interest in the relationship of tax costs to program benefits for any new proposal. The merits of any tax and spending change will now be reflected in the voting patterns of the residents, who now care about the outcome, and politics will again be an important part of the process.

If, contrary to the Tiebout results, tax costs are all shifted forward, then the best tax schemes will be those that best match tax costs to resident benefits. Is this something that the property tax can do? Although it seems unlikely, it is not a relationship that can be dismissed out-of-hand.[16]

The frequency of streetside garbage collection, the size of the public library collection, the quality of transit service, the capacity of the roadways, the amount of space devoted to parkland, the equipment available to the fire department, the number of police, and so on are all service characteristics that once decided upon are equally available to every resident. However, in a heterogeneous jurisdiction, as most municipalities are, different residents undoubtedly will value differently the benefits of adding to or subtracting from the quality or frequency of each of the services. It is not implausible that the value of some of these services, such as fire protection and policing, may indeed bear some direct relationship to property value. There may also be an indirect

---

[16]Some authors, see especially Thirsk (1982), have been critical of the nonresidential property tax. The argument is that it may impose a distorting charge on capital and business, and thus lower the economic welfare of society, and it may be possible for the tax to be "exported" from one municipality to the residents of another through tax-induced higher prices on the commercial goods or services that originate in the taxing municipality. However, as Roger Smith has pointed out, these undesirable side effects of the nonresidential property tax need not exist if the tax is "tied more closely to benefits received" (Smith 1982, 406).

relationship between residential benefit values and property values if, in any given jurisdiction, higher-income households both value government services more highly and live in property with higher market values.

Realistically, property value and property taxation may be well correlated with the benefits of some kinds of local-government services, but poorly correlated with many others. John Bossons has been among the authors who have argued that taxes and benefits could be more closely matched if property taxes were not based "uniformly on market value." He has proposed that property taxes be divided into a "property services tax" and a "municipal general revenue tax." The property services tax, to be used to pay for "protective and property services . . . and local roads and parks," would reflect the different costs of "providing municipal services to properties of varying uses, characteristics, and location" while the general revenue tax would be more like a standard property tax and used for general administrative and other municipal services less directly related to property (Bossons 1981, 75-77). Harry Kitchen and Melville McMillan seem to have in mind something similar in suggesting that the distinction between "people-related and property-related services" might lead to a two-part property-tax system (1985, 237), and the idea is commented upon favourably by Thirsk (1982). The Economic Council of Canada has also raised the possibility of reforming the property tax so that it would become "a pure benefits tax" reflecting "the cost of property-related services" (1987, 104).

Given the efficiency goal that underlies our conception of municipal public finance, reform aimed at achieving a better matching of tax payments to benefits is clearly desirable. The notion of linking property taxes to the municipal costs of servicing property needs to be approached with some caution however, since the efficiency condition we seek requires that taxes be related to benefits, resident-by-resident, not necessarily to costs. In the aggregate, of course, tax revenue must equal program costs, but it is only if residents can vary their consumption or use of municipal services that cost-based taxes will encourage benefits and costs to be equated.[17]

---

[17]If local services are subject to congestion, as most are, and if residents can vary the amount of use they make of a service in response to a user fee, then a cost-related user fee may be efficient even with immobile residents. In some circumstances, a properly set user fee may generate enough revenue to pay the full costs of the service. In other circumstances, user-fee revenues may have to be supplemented with benefits-related taxes.

If the Tiebout mechanism is effective, then cost-based taxes are appropriate since, by moving, people and businesses can relate benefits to costs through the intermediation of municipal taxes. But if this mechanism is ineffective then taxes should be benefit-related, not cost-related. For this conclusion to be valid, it is not necessary to make polar opposite assumptions to Tiebout; it is not necessary to assume, that residents are completely immobile. Any combination of some immobility on the part of residents and some building-space supply response on the part of property owners and developers will impose some net tax burden on both tenant and owner residents, if tax increases and spending benefits are not equal. Since there will be an incentive to vote for or against any particular tax proposal whether the full or only a part of the net tax burden falls on the resident-voter, politics will re-enter the process with any weakening of the extreme Tiebout-model assumptions. Since the Tiebout assumptions seem very unlikely to underpin any realistic response to tax and spending proposals, the search for local taxes that match tax burdens with spending benefits is central to the quest for an efficient local-tax structure.

In the snow-shovelling example used previously, the key element was the ability of residents to choose individually between having the shovelling service and paying the cost or not having the service and not paying the cost. If the proposed program had been one of mandatory shovelling, then constant tax costs for each property would be unlikely to match benefits to costs, since each resident will undoubtedly have a unique view of the value of the service. Of course, there's no reason why these valuations would correlate nicely with the market value of the properties either.

Wayne Thirsk has observed that "since the residential property tax is tied to the consumption of housing rather than the consumption of public services, the tax can be considered to be a benefit tax only if these two types of consumption are highly correlated across different households" (1982, 394). In municipalities with a large, heterogeneous, residential population, it might be easier to believe that household income is better correlated than property value with the consumption of public services. This association suggests that a municipal income tax may relate tax payments to service benefits more directly than a market-value property tax. This appears to be a direction that the reform of municipal finance has taken in other countries and may well deserve more exploration here than it has so far received. There has been some interest in financing "people-related" municipal services through a local income tax (see, for example, Economic Council of Canada 1987, 104), usually on the ground that such services are best financed on the basis of ability to pay. It is less understood that there is also an argument for using a local income tax as the source of revenue for "property-related" services. This argument is likely to be especially strong for regional governments in metropolitan areas, and for central-city governments, where the range of income groups is typically larger than the range in suburban municipalities, and where the relationship of household income to property value is weaker. In more homogeneous jurisdictions with less variation in housing values and income levels, whether property values or income is taxed may be a matter of less significance.

Land-Use Policy and the Property Tax

With demand for accommodation neither fully elastic nor completely inelastic, property tax increases (net of benefits) in some localities will result in an increase in rents, a reduction in property values, and a reduction in the amount of available, rentable space. These results Aaron calls the "traditional" view of property taxes (Aaron 1975). The significance of this traditional view is that a tax-rate change unaccompanied by offsetting benefit changes has a clear effect on the amount of development or building space, and it thus encourages one to think of the strategic role that property taxes could play in guiding metropolitan development.

The traditional view focuses on tax changes in one locality, and from that perspective quite reasonably uses the assumption that the rate of return required on building capital is given. In the mid 1970s, Mieszkowski and Aaron (Mieszkowski 1972; Aaron 1975) explored the implications of an alternative assumption, that over the whole economy the supply of building capital, not its price, is fixed. This assumption underlies the "new" view of property taxation (Aaron 1975). Investment, according to the new view, augments the capital stock at a rate that is unaffected by capital's rate of return. From the perspective of any individual municipality, the supply of building capital may be variable, but taken over all municipalities the supply is fixed.

For tax changes (net of benefits) in any one jurisdiction, the implications of the new view are almost the same as those of the traditional view. A net tax increase will lower the optimal capital to land ratio, reduce the rate of building investment, and probably raise rental prices. Under the new view, there may be an additional effect, a reduction in the economywide return to capital. This occurs because, given the fixed capital supply assumption, the building investment driven out of the new taxing jurisdiction must be absorbed elsewhere. In general, this absorption can occur only if the rate of return on capital is lowered. Since any given municipality that raises its tax rate will be small relative to the whole economy, this reduction in the return to capital may be scarcely noticeable However, if all municipalities raise their property tax rates simultaneously, then capital cannot scoot off to another more favourable jurisdiction, and capital as a whole has to absorb the loss in returns.[18] If those who occupy building space reduce their demands for space if prices rise, then the only way for the given amount of building capital to remain occupied is for rental prices to stay put. This means that the burden of economywide property tax increases (net of benefits) must fall entirely on capital and on land values.[19]

For purposes of analyzing the structure of national taxes and its effect on factor returns, the new view of property taxation is highly significant (see, for example, Damus, Hobson, and Thirsk 1987); but for purposes of understanding the role of local taxes within individual municipal or metropolitan areas, the new view adds little to the traditional view outlined above. Both views lead to the conclusion that localized property-tax changes, unless matched property-by-property with benefit changes, will likely have allocative (as well as redistributive) effects that, over time, will alter the pattern of building development and land use.[20]

---

[18]Interestingly, this very point was made by the British economist F. Y. Edgeworth in an 1897 article on tax theory: if "the investments which are open as an alternative to an intending builder are not indefinitely extensive in comparison with the house-building industry," then capitalists may be "obliged to submit in consequence of the house-tax to some permanent reduction in profits" (Edgeworth 1897, 68). He credited the idea to a work of Pantaleoni's, *Traslazione dei Tributi*, and he repeated it in a subsequent discussion of evidence presented to a turn-of-the-century Royal Commission on Local Taxation (Edgeworth 1900, 184).

[19]Paul Hobson (Hobson 1986) has a nice discussion of the factors affecting the way in which changes in both the national average property tax rate (net of benefits) and local differentials in the rate are distributed among renters, capital owners, and land owners.

[20]Most authors who have studied the effect of property tax changes on land use have not used models that allow them to say anything about the timing of land-use and building changes. Typically, only the equilibrium situation before and after the tax change is analyzed. But there is a growing interest in using dy-

There have been a growing number of studies of the effects of changes in property tax rates on building densities and municipal size, some using analytical models and others based on numerical simulations of urban areas. With respect to building densities, Donald Shoup has used post-1945 construction-cost data for Los Angeles office buildings to calculate that imposing an annual rate of tax on property value of 2 percent would reduce the optimal size of an average building by about 14 percent below the size that would be built if there were no property tax (Shoup 1978). (He cautions that this may not be a widely applicable result and that another study done of Honolulu hotels shows "much more" sensitivity to the tax rate.) An earlier study by Ronald Grieson using 1970 housing data in the United States reported that housing density would increase an estimated 23 percent if a 3 percent property tax were replaced by some nonproperty-related tax (Grieson 1974).

With respect to municipalwide effects, Donald Haurin has analyzed the effect of a change in the property tax in any one municipality relative to rates elsewhere. Within the context of a standard model of an urban area, with a labour market and with residents freely mobile to and from the municipality, a rate increase will in general reduce the size of the municipality, reduce its population, and reduce its residential building density; a rate decrease, or increases elsewhere with no change in this municipality's tax rate, will of course have the opposite effects (Haurin 1981). Robert Steen, building on the pioneering earlier work of Richard Arnott and James MacKinnon (Arnott and MacKinnon 1977), has studied property-tax effects by modelling numerically a multijurisdiction metropolitan area with a fixed, income-differentiated residential population (Steen 1987a, 1987b). His simulations provide an extremely interesting set of results, one of which is that moving from a lump-sum head tax to a property tax leads to much reduced inner-city population densities and increased metropolitan sprawl, as the urbanized area pushes

---

namic models to show more explicitly the process of land conversion from one use to another. Different models handle the market for building space differently, but when property taxes based on market value are introduced into the models, they all have the common feature that the timing of property development and (usually) the size of the development interact with the tax rate. A typical result is that a higher property tax will reduce the size of future developments, i.e., there is less building capital used per unit of land (Nowlan 1976a; Kanemoto 1985) but that it may advance or delay the conversion of property to a new use (Nowlan 1976a, 1976b; Kanemoto 1985; Anderson 1986).

out into previously undeveloped land. Steen also finds that changing from a multiple-government to a single-government structure in the metropolitan area, with property and not head taxes used both before and after the change, will result in increased central densities and a reduced metropolitan land area (in his model, within each jurisdiction residents receive a common level of benefits from local services).

Land-use effects of the sort just described are sometimes said to entail "deadweight" losses. These losses occur because of a presumed allocative inefficiency caused by an inefficient tax structure, one that has not served to equate private benefits to tax costs. There may be situations, however, in which the equating of private benefits to tax costs will not lead to efficient land uses. If, for example, some patterns of metropolitan land use involve much higher public infrastructure costs than other patterns, or if there are unpriced costs of congestion and environmental deterioration associated more with some land uses than others, then taxes that aim simply to equate private benefit valuations to the monetary costs of government services may themselves encourage land-use inefficiency. To the extent that property taxes net of benefits can alter land uses, they may be regarded as a planning instrument, a suggestion made in Bossons (1981) and elegantly explored a number of years ago by Harvey Brazer (1961), who envisaged a tax on commercial property as, in part, a charge for the unpriced cost of environmental damage. Such a role for taxes on commercial property has also been elaborated by William Fischel (1975). With unpriced costs or benefits, efficient property taxes will be those that equate, at the margin, social benefits to social costs.

In practice, the information needed accurately to adjust local taxes to achieve efficient local economies in this broader sense is likely to be unrealistically large, but the potential role of property taxes to help accomplish existing metropolitan and local land-use goals should not for this reason be ignored. Suppose a local planning region has established as a goal a more compact urban form, or suppose it wants to promote a secondary commercial subcentre. Then, as the above examples show, differential property taxes could clearly be used to help achieve the desired outcome. Higher property taxes will likely slow down development; lower taxes will speed up development. If municipal policy called for the development of commercial nodes away from downtown, as it does under the current Official Plan for Metropolitan Toronto, then lower tax rates at the nodes and higher tax rates downtown would be called for. If policy seeks to speed up residential development near the central commercial area in order to reduce commuting, as it does in Vancouver, then lower residential taxes would be set for downtown residential properties.

Development Charges, Linkage Fees, and Other Special Levies

Although traditional property and business taxes remain the mainstay of municipal finance in Canada, additional levies on property are being increasingly used as supplementary sources of revenue. Many of these levies are one-time (or sometimes multi-year) development charges the purpose of which is to raise revenue to cover infrastructure costs directly associated with the development of the taxed property. Some, such as local improvement taxes, are continuing levies established to cover the costs of special expenditures that benefit a defined local improvement area. Lot levies, water and sewer imposts on new developments, and local improvement taxes have existed in one form or another for many decades, but the office-housing linkage fee, currently imposed by some U.S. cities on new downtown commercial developments (Nelson 1988), is a new type of tax being contemplated by some municipalities. The province of Ontario broke new ground in 1990 when it instituted an annual commercial concentration levy of $1.00 a square foot on all commercial property in excess of 200,000 square feet in the Greater Toronto Area (Ontario 1989).

Under the fund-accounting approach used by municipalities, special-purpose levies are usually taken into municipal reserve funds rather than revenue funds and are not, therefore, included in Statistics Canada's definition of local-government revenue. Although this makes it difficult from published data to establish the precise extent to which such extractions are used in Canada, their growing importance is confirmed by authors such as David Amborski (1988) and Enid Slack and Richard Bird (1991) who have looked into the matter. Some indication of the increasing significance of these special levies in Ontario in recent years is contained in the data underlying Figure 25.2. For the province as a whole, the magnitude of reserve-fund revenue in relation to the size of the normal revenue funds rose from 10 percent to over 15 percent between 1980 and 1987, the last year for which data are available, and that proportion was growing exponentially at the end of the period. Contributions from reserve funds to capital funds, through which most capital expenditures are made, rose to 25 percent in 1987 from only 10 percent 10 years earlier.

Figure 25.2.   *Significance and Use of Reserve Fund Revenue*

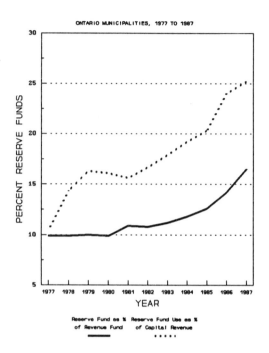

ONTARIO MUNICIPALITIES, 1977 TO 1987

Reserve Fund as % Reserve Fund Use as %
of Revenue Fund   of Capital Revenue

Source: Ontario 1988 and Ontario 1990.

Because the conceptual basis of development charges and similar levies is seldom articulated, those upon whom they fall tend to regard them simply as expedient revenue-raising devices for financially strapped municipalities; indeed, many municipalities may view the charges in this way themselves. The explicit justification usually given for development charges is that they, like sewer and water imposts, provide funds to cover the costs of additional municipal infrastructure needed to service the new developments. For example, Ontario's *Development Charges Act,* 1989, was introduced in order "to permit both municipalities and school boards to impose development charges on all types of development that will increase the need for municipal services or school facilities."[21] But this justification, on its own, ignores the fact that properties subject to development charges or lot levies also pay normal property and business taxes that, under ordinary circumstances, might reasonably be expected to cover the additional public expenses.

To be defended as a tax that helps a municipality achieve its goal of efficient land development, a development charge should be regarded as a charge for public costs that will not be covered by the extension of the usual property tax to the new development. From this perspective, a proposed development charge or special levy should be subjected to a simple test, a question: if a property is developed and begins paying normal property and business taxes, will the general tax rate in the municipality increase because of the development? This might be called the "expansion" test. If the normal rate will not change in the face of the development, then the test will fail, and the proposed development fee should not be levied. The cost of expanding public services and infrastructure to accommodate the development will be covered by ordinary tax revenue generated by the property; development levies would constitute a double charge.

Suppose, however, that this test is passed, and the development charge appears to be justified because tax rates overall would rise even with the additional assessment base generated by the new development. A second test must then be applied to determine the appropriate structure of the special levy. The second test, also in the form of a question, is to ask whether the additional public costs and higher tax rates would exist if the increase in municipal population or employment generated by the new development were exactly offset by a decrease in population or employment elsewhere in the tax jurisdiction. This is an "anonymity" test. If indeed the costs of growth associated with the new development would continue to exist even if they were offset by population or employment decreases elsewhere, then these costs are specific to the new development; they are not anonymous. The second test is therefore

---

[21]From the "Explanatory Notes" in Bill 20, *An Act to Provide for the Payment of Development Charges*, Ontario, 38 Elizabeth II 1989. This *Act* provides for an extension of the development-charges concept to include soft-service expenses directly associated with new developments and applies explicitly to previously urbanized as well as newly urbanizing areas; previous authority for lot levies under the *Planning Act* was at best ambiguous on both counts.

passed and special levies to cover the costs would be efficient and appropriate.[22]

Whether costs related to new development pass or fail the first of these tests will depend in part on the prevailing structure of normal property taxes.[23] Thus, if costs such as service roads, sewer connections, and schools are typically covered through property taxes, then the expansion test applied to these costs will fail, indicating that these are not appropriate costs to be recovered through special levies in addition to the regular taxes that the development will pay. But if such items are not typically covered, then they will pass the expansion test; if the anonymity test is also passed, the costs should properly be covered through a development levy.

If proposed development charges pass the expansion test but fail the anonymity test, this must mean that there are increasing costs associated with expansion in this municipality, but that these costs are not uniquely related to the new development (the anonymity test tells us this). Suppose, for example, that a development charge is proposed to pay for additional transit capacity in a municipality, capacity that is deemed necessary because of additional demand associated with the new development; and suppose as well that the expansion test is passed, meaning that taxes would rise throughout the municipality if this development did not pay the proposed development charge. The anonymity test is equivalent to asking whether the additional transit costs exist because of some peculiarity in the location or layout of this new development, or whether an addition of a similar number of people or jobs elsewhere within the municipality would cause the same increase in

---

[22]Both of these tests presume that the question of changes in normal tax rates or of population and employment offsets is asked in the context of a constant quality of public service or municipal living standards. Also, although the discussion is written in terms of additional costs, there may be circumstances in which development leads to reduced public tax rates, perhaps because of more efficient land-use configurations. In this case the proposed tests may be applied symmetrically to cover development subsidies rather than development charges.

[23]For example, costs that might efficiently be recovered through development charges in Ontario might not appropriately be funded by development charges in Quebec. "[In Quebec], many of the costs of urban infrastructure—for example, sewer and water connections—are recovered through the property tax instead of being included in the initial price of a residential lot, as occurs in other provinces" (Thirsk 1982, 387).

transit costs. If growth anywhere else in the municipality would have the same cost effects as this particular development, then the anonymity test will not be passed. The costs of growth still need to be recognized in the tax structure, but that recognition should consist of a special charge levied across the whole municipality, or at least over that part with respect to which the new development is anonymous. If the costs of growth are special to this development, then the anonymity test will pass, and a development charge against the new development will be efficient.

To make the example more concrete, suppose some metropolitan municipality has a strong central employment area, and new residential development is proposed in the suburban fringe. Given the commuting needs to the central area, the required public infrastructure costs of transit and road capacity associated with the fringe development are expected to be high. The anonymity test asks whether these costs would still exist if the population increase envisaged in the fringe development were offset by population decreases elsewhere, say in the central area. The answer in this case is likely to be "no"; the costs of transportation infrastructure are higher if the areas of population expansion are more distant from the centres of employment. In this case, a development charge on residential growth on the periphery of the taxing jurisdiction is efficient.

If the costs of expansion are not uniquely related to property proposed for development, i.e., if the anonymity test for a property-specific development charge fails, then grounds for a growth levy may still exist, but such a levy, if it is to be used efficiently, should apply to all similarly situated property, existing and proposed. Such a general levy will be appropriate normally in circumstances where there are external effects, such as environmental costs or inefficient land-use patterns, associated with growth and development in a particular metropolitan area or part of a metropolitan area. The general levy would become a general subsidy where efficient land use calls for increasing density or intensification in order to reduce public infrastructure costs. The basic logic of applying the charge across all property and not just on new development is that incentives in the form of taxes or subsidies have to be in place as much for existing households and businesses as for potential residents of new developments.

Such a broad-area development charge is exactly what the provincial government in Ontario has implemented with its commercial concentration levy, which is a tax on all commercial property above a minimum size in the Toronto metropolitan area. Building area and not assessed value has been chosen as the tax base, presumably on the grounds that the tax is meant to provide a disincentive for Toronto-focused employment expansion because of excessively high infrastructure costs. Because the tax applies to existing as well as new property, it provides both an incentive for existing businesses to move out of the area as well as a disincentive to new businesses thinking of moving in. Given the purpose of the tax, this dual set of incentives is appropriate, since the effect on infrastructure costs is the same whether an existing business is encouraged to leave or a new one deterred from entering. It is this symmetry between the two types of effect that underlies the anonymity test.

Office-housing linkage fees may similarly be regarded as a form of development charge that recognizes the additional public and private costs associated with commercial development in the central area of a city, and the fact that some of these costs can be mitigated if housing is built closer to jobs (for an estimate of the magnitude of this effect, see Nowlan 1989; Nowlan and Stewart 1991). Linkage fees of this sort are being considered in Toronto and in other Canadian cities. If indeed excessively concentrated commercial development is costly, and if housing in proximity to such development can serve to reduce public infrastructure costs, then commercial levies and housing subsidies are appropriate because the expansion test outlined above is passed. But, these costs and subsidies will fail the anonymity test. This means that "linkage" fees and housing subsidies, if they are to be efficient, should be applied not just to new commercial developments and new housing, but to all commercial space and all housing in the designated area.

Proposed development charges that have passed both the expansion and the anonymity tests and are therefore appropriately levied against new development will have associated with them the benefits that flow from the services they are used to finance. If the services would not exist without the development charges, and if the magnitude of the charges and the value of the benefits is more-or-less the same, then the development charges will simply be shifted forward into the market value of the developed property. If the services would have existed in any case, with or without the development charges, then some part of the charges will be capitalized back into the initial value of the property, which will serve to deter the amount of development that takes place, an allocative effect of the charge that is presumably unintended. A development levy (or subsidy) that, to be efficient, is applied not just to new development but to all properties in some designated area has essentially the same role in encouraging local government efficiency as property taxes that are used as planning instruments to help achieve efficient land uses. This was discussed at the end of the last section. Such levies will discourage growth in the targeted area, or encourage it if a subsidy rather than a charge is applied. This, of course, is exactly the response that is wanted in the face of the increasing costs that gave warrant to the charge in the first place, or the decreasing costs that justify a subsidy.

CONCLUDING COMMENTS

If municipalities are regarded principally as administratively convenient ways of delivering infrastructure and services that, in effect, have been established by custom or by provincial fiat, then there is little point in discussing the efficiency properties of local taxes. With output standards established, the distributive rather than the allocative role of taxes will necessarily be of primary interest. Since, as the preceding discussion has shown, neutral local taxes playing only a distributive role are more imaginary than real, this perspective must lead either to local government funding that consists entirely of transfers from the general revenue of senior governments, or to local taxation with allocative effects that are simply ignored.

If, by contrast, local governments are envisaged as more active and independent levels of government with responsibility for service provision that could vary substantially from place to place, and with authority to guide the development of urban form, then we are likely to want a flexible local tax structure, one that will permit costs to be targeted more closely to those who benefit and one that will allow municipalities to provide the appropriate encouragement for desired developments and discouragement for the less desired.

Local jurisdictions in Canada of course play both roles. In part, they are the government level through which provincial and sometimes national programs and services are delivered; and in part they must rest on their own fiscal bottoms in providing local and regional services. It is with respect to the latter role that the desirability of bringing the costs of government spending to bear as directly as possible on those who benefit is an especially solid foundation from which to analyze the role of local taxation.

With respect to local taxation, this desired relationship between costs and benefits can be achieved in either of two ways. If residents can adjust their use of costly services, then taxes that reflect costs are efficient. This is the basic logic underlying the promotion of user charges, but it is a logic that can apply as well to the overall tax structure of small urban jurisdictions with mobile populations. The ability to move readily into or out of such municipalities allows household or business benefits from municipal spending to be adjusted to the tax costs per resident of those benefits. If, however, residents cannot, or cannot easily, adjust their consumption of local services, then a tax that mimics as closely as possible the distribution of the value of these services to residents is desirable—a benefit tax. The desirability of a benefit-oriented tax structure will likely be greatest when the taxing jurisdiction is large and heterogeneous, a metropolitanwide jurisdiction, for example. Within metropolitan municipalities, user charges will be efficient in circumstances where residents can vary their individual use of the service to which charges apply; otherwise, the best tax structure will be one that best correlates taxes with resident benefits.

The local tax structure that is necessary to help a municipality respond efficiently to local preferences and achieve efficient uses of land and other resources is likely to be more complicated the larger and the more heterogeneous the taxing jurisdiction. For smaller, more homogeneous municipalities, there may be little practical difference between, say, a residential tax based on property value and one based on household income. If the jurisdiction is extremely homogeneous, even a flat-rate tax per household or per person (a poll tax) might have distributional and allocative consequences that are not much different from a property or income tax. But, for urban areas having the characteristics of regional economies and for governing structures that are metropolitan in scope, these one-tax alternatives are no longer appropriate. If metropolitan areas have federated local-government structures, like those of southern Ontario, with relatively high intraregional mobility but lower interregional mobility, then simpler tax structures at the local levels of government may be adequate, but the regional municipalities will need more sophisticated tax structures.

It is tempting in the face of growing metropolitanism to think of our urban governments as little provincial or national governments, with spending and taxing decisions taken independently and with taxes playing largely a distributive role. There is of course no hard and fast dividing line that can tell us when some regional governing entity should look more like a traditional municipal government and when it should look like a higher-level government, but it is inconsistent to regard a regional, metropolitan government as an agent of redistribution through its tax structure while restricting that structure to the rigid alternatives prescribed by provincial statutes.

The argument for a more flexible local tax structure is even more compelling if we regard metropolitan governments not as minor provincial governments but, more traditionally, as governments charged with a mandate to respond to the interests of local residents in the provision of services and in the guidance of land and other resource use. Metropolitan-scale governments especially are increasingly called upon to address with their own financial resources issues that range from poverty, crime, and health through to land-use planning, waste management, and regional transportation needs. The property tax may have a role to play in funding some of these local needs, but for large-scale local governments there is also a strong argument for a local income tax. A differentiated property tax could be used, as we have seen, as a policy instrument to help guide land into efficient uses, as could properly formulated development charges or subsidies. These are issues that deserve more policy attention. The complex relationship between local taxes and their allocative effects should not become a reason for paralysis and frozen policies; rather, it should stimulate our interest in understanding better the ways in which taxes can help municipalities of all sizes accomplish their service, their resource use, and their social goals.

REFERENCES

Aaron, Henry J. 1975. *Who Pays the Property Tax? A New View.* Washington: The Brookings Institute.

Amborski, David P. 1988. "Impact Fees Canadian Style: The Use of Development Charges in Ontario." In *Development Impact Fees: Policy Rationale, Practice, Theory and Issues*, ed. Arthur C. Nelson, Chicago: Planners Press for the American Planning Association.

Anderson, John E. 1986. "Property Taxes and the Timing of Urban Land Development." *Regional Science and Urban Economics* 16, 483-92.

Arnott, R. J., and J. G. MacKinnon. 1977. "The Effects of the Property Tax: A General Equilibrium Simulation." *Journal of Urban Economics* 4: 389-407.

Bird, Richard M. 1970. *The Growth of Government Spending in Canada.* Toronto: Canadian Tax Foundation.

_____. 1976. *Charging for Public Services: A New Look at an Old Idea.* Canadian Tax Papers No. 59. Toronto: Canadian Tax Foundation.

Boadway, Robin W., and Harry M. Kitchen. 1984. *Canadian Tax Policy.* 2d edition. Canadian Tax Paper No. 76. Toronto: Canadian Tax Foundation.

Bossons, John. 1981. "Property Tax Reform: What is Desirable." In *Municipal Fiscal Reform in Ontario: Property Taxes and Provincial Grants,* ed. John Bossons, Michael Denny, and Enid Slack, Toronto: Ontario Economic Council.

Brazer, Harvey E. 1961. "The Value of Industrial Property as a Subject of Taxation." *Canadian Public Administration* 4: 137-47.

Canadian Tax Foundation. 1990. *Provincial and Municipal Finances 1989.* Toronto.

Damus, Sylvester, Paul Hobson, and Wayne Thirsk. 1987. "The Welfare Effects of Property Taxation in an Open Economy." Discussion Paper No. 320. Ottawa: Economic Council of Canada.

Denny, Michael. 1981. "Property Tax Reform in Ontario: An Economic Assessment." In *Municipal Fiscal Reform in Ontario: Property Taxes and Provincial Grants,* ed. John Bossons, Michael Denny, and Enid Slack, Toronto: Ontario Economic Council.

Eaton, A. Kenneth. 1966. *Essays in Taxation.* Canadian Tax Papers No. 44. Toronto: Canadian Tax Foundation.

Economic Council of Canada. 1987. *The Taxation of Savings and Investment.* Ottawa: Supply and Services Canada for the Economic Council of Canada.

Edgeworth, F.Y. 1897. "The Pure Theory of Taxation." *Economic Journal* 7: 46-70.

_____. 1900. "Incidence of Urban Rates." *Economic Journal* 10: 172-93.

Fischel, William A. 1975. "Fiscal and Environmental Considerations in the Location of Firms in Suburban Communities." In *Fiscal Zoning and Land Use Controls,* ed. Edwin S. Mills and Wallace E. Oates, Lexington, Mass.: Lexington Books, 119-69.

Foley, Duncan K. 1967. "Resource Allocation and the Public Sector." *Yale Economic Essays* 7: 45-98.

Gillespie, W. Irwin. 1973. "An Examination and Analysis of Municipal Financial Problems." In Canadian Tax Foundation, *Report of the Twenty-fifth Tax Conference,* 1973: 561-90.

Grieson, Ronald E. 1974. "The Economics of Property Taxes and Land Values: The Elasticity of Supply of Structures." *Journal of Urban Economics* 1: 367-81.

Hamilton, Bruce W. 1975. "Zoning and Property Taxation in a System of Local Governments." *Urban Studies* 12: 205-11.

_____. 1983. "A Review: Is the Property Tax a Benefit Tax?" In *Local Provision of Public Services: The Tiebout Model after Twenty-five Years,* ed. George R. Zodrow, New York: Academic Press, 85-107.

Hardy, Eric. 1961. "The Serious Problems of Municipal Finance." *Canadian Public Administration* 4(2): 154-63.

Haurin, Donald R. 1981. "Property Taxation and the Structure of Urban Areas." In *Research in Urban Economics,* Vol. 1, ed. J. Vernon Henderson, Greenwich, Conn.: JAI Press Inc., 263-76.

Henderson, J. Vernon. 1985. "The Tiebout Model: Bring Back the Entrepreneurs." *Journal of Political Economy* 93(2): 248-64.

Hirschman, A. O. 1972. *Exit, Voice, and Loyalty.* Cambridge: Harvard University Press.

Hobson, Paul A. R. 1986. "The Incidence of Heterogeneous Residential Property Taxes." *Journal of Public Economics.* 29: 363-73.

_____. 1987. "The Economic Effects of the Property Tax: A Survey." Discussion Paper No. 317. Ottawa: Economic Council of Canada.

_____. 1991. "Local Government in Canada: Creature, Chameleon, Consort." In *Provincial Public Finances: Vol. 2, Plaudits, Problems, and Prospects,* ed. Melville McMillan, Canadian Tax Paper No. 91. Toronto: Canadian Tax Foundation, 215-40.

Kanemoto, Yoshitsugu. 1985. "Housing as an Asset and the Effects of Property Taxation on the Residential Development Process." *Journal of Urban Economics.* 17: 145-66.

Kitchen, Harry M., and Melville L. McMillan. 1985. "Local Government and Canadian Federalism." In *Intergovernmental Relations* (Richard Simeon, Research Coordinator), Royal Commission on the Economic Union and Development Prospects for Canada, Research Studies Vol. 63, 215-61.

Leacy, F. H. (ed). 1983. *Historical Statistics of Canada, 2d Edition.* Ottawa: Statistics Canada.

Mieszkowski, Peter. 1972. "The Property Tax: An Excise Tax or a Profits Tax?" *Journal of Public Economics* 1: 73-96.

_____. 1989. "Taxation and the Tiebout Model: The Differential Effects of Head Taxes, Taxes on Land Rents, and Property Taxes." *Journal of Economic Literature* 27: 1098-1146.

Nelson, Arthur C. 1988. "Downtown Office Development and Housing Linkage Fees: An Introduction to the Symposium." *Journal of the American Planning Association* 54: 197-98.

Nowlan, David M. 1976a. "Land Conversion and Land Policy in the Central City." Paper presented to the Canadian Economics Association, June.

_____. 1976b. "Value and Use of Land: The Public Connection." *Urban Forum/Colloque Urbain* 2(3): 13-22.

_____. 1989. "Commercial Growth and the New Toronto Plan." In *Proceedings of the Cityplan '91 Forum on the Future of the City of Toronto* (May 1989). Toronto: City of Toronto Department of Planning and Development.

_____, and Greg Stewart. 1991. "The Effect of Downtown Population Growth on Commuting Trips: Some Recent Toronto Experience." *Journal of the American Planning Association* 57(Spring): 165-82.

Oates, Wallace E. 1972. *Fiscal Federalism.* New York: Harcourt-Brace.

Ontario Committee on Taxation. 1967. *Report Volume I: Approach, Background and Conclusions; Report Volume II: The Local Revenue System.* Toronto: Queen's Printer.

Ontario. 1977. *Report of the Commission on the Reform of Property Taxation in Ontario.*

_____. 1988. *Summary of Ontario Municipal Statistics: 1977-1986.* Toronto: Ministry of Municipal Affairs.

_____. 1989. *1989 Ontario Budget.* Ministry of Treasury and Economics. Toronto: Queen's Printer for Ontario, May 17.

_____. 1990. *Municipal Financial Information 1987.* Toronto: Ministry of Municipal Affairs.

_____. 1991. *Report of the Advisory Committee to the Minister of Municipal Affairs on the Provincial-Municipal Financial Relationship.* Toronto: Ministry of Municipal Affairs.

Pauly, Mark V. 1973. "Income Redistribution as a Local Public Good." *Journal of Public Economics* 2: 35-58.

Perry, David B. 1990. "Fiscal Figures." *Canadian Tax Journal* 38(5): 1326-36.

Rose-Ackerman, Susan. 1983. "Beyond Tiebout: Modeling the Political Economy of Local Government." In *Local Provision of Public Services: The Tiebout Model After Twenty-five Years*, ed. George R. Zodrow, New York: Academic Press, 55-83.

Shoup, Donald C. 1978. "The Effect of Property Taxes on the Capital Intensity of Urban Land Development." In *Metropolitan Financing and Growth Management Policies*, ed. George F. Break, Madison, Wis.: The University of Wisconsin Press, 105-32.

Slack, Enid, and Richard Bird. 1991. "Financing Urban Growth Through Development Charges." *Canadian Tax Journal* 39(5): 1288-1304.

Smith, Roger S. 1982. "Comment." Comment on a paper by Wayne R. Thirsk. In *Tax Policy Options in the 1980s*, ed. Wayne R. Thirsk and John Whalley, Canadian Tax Paper No. 66. Toronto: Canadian Tax Foundation, 403-07.

Steen, Robert C. 1987a. "Effects of the Property Tax in Urban Areas." *Journal of Urban Economics* 21: 146-65.

Steen, Robert C. 1987b. "Effects of Governmental Structure in Urban Areas." *Journal of Urban Economics* 21: 166-79.

Thirsk, Wayne R. 1982. "Political Sensitivity Versus Economic Sensibility: A Tale of Two Property Taxes." In *Tax Policy Options in the 1980s*, ed. Wayne R. Thirsk and John Whalley, Canadian Tax Paper No. 66, Toronto: Canadian Tax Foundation.

Tiebout, Charles M. 1956. "A Pure Theory of Local Expenditures." *Journal of Political Economy* 64: 416-24.

Contributors

Caroline Andrew teaches political science at the University of Ottawa. She has written on questions relating to women and local politics and on the intergovernmental context of urban development. Her current research deals with emerging policy areas in municipal government, giving particular attention to the links between community organization and municipal policy.

Michel Barcelo teaches and does research on urban planning and housing issues at l'Institut d'urbanisme of the Faculté de l'aménagement at the University of Montreal.

Patricia E. Bayne completed M.A. and Ph.D. degrees in geography at the University of Alberta in 1986 and 1992. Her research has dealt with the preparation of Edmonton's regional plan and with the generation of alternatives in the planning process. She is currently a sessional lecturer in geography and urban planning at the University of Alberta.

François Charbonneau is a member of l'Institut d'urbanisme of the Faculté de l'aménagement at the University of Montreal. His research and teaching interests include urban political economy, urban history, and urban data bases, particularly as these relate to rental housing and urban social development. He has recently carried out research in Montreal, Abidjan and Peubla (Mexico).

Theodore Cohn is Professor of Political Science at Simon Fraser University, where his research and teaching areas include international political economy and Canadian foreign policy. His current research focuses on the North American Free Trade Agreement and the General Agreement on Tariffs and Trade, on global cities, and on subnational governments and international relations.

Gerald Daly is a member of the Faculty of Environmental Studies at York University. His research interests include housing, urban planning, and comparative social policy. He is currently engaged in a project to assess social policies dealing with poverty alleviation in Kenya.

Wayne Davies is Professor of Geography at the University of Calgary, where he also coordinates the undergraduate Urban Studies Program. He has written and published widely on a large range of topics in urban geography.

Shelley Dickey received her masters degree in planning from the University of Toronto in 1988. She currently works as a professional planner in the Department of Development and Planning of the city of Halifax.

Jerome Durlak is Associate Professor of Mass Communications and Director of the Interactive Multimedia Lab at York University. He is also Associate Director of CulTech, an autonomous, not-for-profit collaborative research centre sited at and supported by York University with initial funding from the federal Department of Communications.

George Fallis is Chair of York University's Department of Economics and a member of the Urban Studies Program. He has published several books on housing economics and housing policy, and many articles and reports on rent control, the optimal role of government in housing, and Canadian housing policy. He has been a consultant on housing and urban economics to local, provincial, and national governments and international agencies.

Frances Frisken is a member of York University's Urban Studies Program and Undergraduate Program Director in the Division of Social Science. Her research and publications have dealt principally with the political development of the Toronto area and with Canadian urban policy. She has done extensive academic and applied research on Canadian urban transit policy.

Pierre Hamel is a professor at l'Institut d'urbanisme of the Faculté de l'aménagement at the University of Montreal. He is currently a visiting professor at the Urban and Regional Studies Unit of the University of Kent in Canterbury. His teaching and research interests include planning theory, urban policies, and social movements.

Andrew S. Harvey is Professor and Chair of Economics, Saint Mary's University, Halifax. He has authored numerous monographs and articles in a number of areas, including leisure studies, urban and regional economics and planning, time-use methodology, evaluative research, women's studies, and secondary data analysis. Currently he is coordinating an international time-use research project for the UN Institute for Research and Training for the Advancement of Women (INSTRAW).

Christopher Leo is Professor of Political Science and Coordinator of Urban Studies at the University of Winnipeg. He has published books and articles in the areas of urban politics and African political economy. His current research focuses on the politics of downtown redevelopment in Vancouver, Edmonton, Winnipeg, and Toronto.

David Ley is Professor of Geography at the University of British Columbia, Vancouver. His research has emphasized the social and political geography of the city, particularly inner-city issues.

Sara L. McLafferty is Associate Professor of Geography at Hunter College of the City University of New York. She conducts research on geographical access to human services, urban labor markets, and health and employment problems in inner-city neighborhoods.

Warren Magnusson is Associate Professor of Political Science at the University of Victoria, where he teaches political theory and participates in the Interdisciplinary Program in Social and Political Thought. He has written extensively about social movements, urban politics, and the state in Canada and elsewhere.

John Marshall is Professor of Geography at York University and a founding member of the undergraduate Urban Studies Program. His principal fields of interest are urban geography and the history of geography. His current research involves transatlantic comparisons of the frequency distribution of city size.

Hugh Millward is Professor of Geography at Saint Mary's University in Halifax, where he has taught since 1975. His research deals primarily with urban development issues and with aspects of the geography of Nova Scotia.

Fathali M. Moghaddam is Associate Professor of Psychology at Georgetown University. He has previously taught at McGill University in Montreal and Tehran University, Iran, and has worked for the United Nations Development Program (UNDP). His research and publications deal principally with the influence of culture on social behaviour.

Byron Montgomery is an M.A. graduate in political science from the University of Western Ontario and for five years was a research assistant in its Local Government Program.

Robert Murdie is Associate Professor of Geography at York University and a member of the Urban Studies Program. His research interests are in urban social geography and housing analysis. He has also developed a framework for measuring quality of life in Canadian metropolitan areas. He is currently involved in studies of social housing in Canada and Sweden and of the housing experiences of immigrants and refugees in Greater Toronto.

David Nowlan is Professor of Economics and former Vice President of Research at the University of Toronto. He has published extensively in a variety of fields, including development planning, growth and technical change, the economics of higher education, transportation economics, urban and regional economics, the economics of federalism, land economics, and the economics of regulation. His current research is on the theory of regulation and planning, metropolitan and regional tax policies, and urban transportation pricing.

Robert Paehlke teaches at Trent University in Peterborough, Ontario. He has published a book and numerous journal articles on environmental politics and policy. He is currently editing *The Encyclopedia of Conservation and Environmentalism* for Garland Publishing.

Valerie Preston is Associate Professor of Geography at York University and a member of the Urban Studies Program. Her past research has dealt with the affordability of rental housing, consumer demand for condominiums, and individual variations in residential preferences. Currently she is investigating the way spatial and social processes affect women's participation in local labor markets during a period of rapid economic restructuring.

Louise Quesnel is Professor of Political Science at Laval University and a member of the Centre de recherche en aménagement et en développement. In 1992-93 she served as president of the Social Science Federation of Canada. Her recent publications deal with party politics at the municipal level and with the planning and development of central city cores.

Joanne M. Sabourin holds an M.A. from the University of Ottawa and a Ph.D. from York University. She currently lives in Ottawa.

Andrew Sancton is Director of the Local Government Program and Professor of Political Science at the University of Western Ontario. His research and publications have dealt primarily with municipal and metropolitan politics and governance.

John Sewell, a lawyer by training, has had a varied career as a community organizer, writer, teacher, journalist, and politician. Most recently he has served as chair of the Metro Toronto (Public) Housing Authority (1986-88), and as chair of the Commission on Planning and Development Reform in Ontario (1991-93). He has also published books on citizen participation in urban politics, on urban policing and, most recently, on urban planning.

Alan Smart is Associate Professor of Anthropology at the University of Calgary. He has conducted field research in Hong Kong and Guangdong province, China. He is currently investigating the character and impact of Hong Kong investment in Guangdong, and conflicts over the use of space between Hong Kong immigrants and Anglo-Canadians in Canada.

Patrick J. Smith is Associate Professor and former Chair of Political Science at Simon Fraser University. His research and publications deal with local/municipal government, planning, global cities, comparative metropolitan and regional governance, local democracy, constitutional reform, and labor market policy.

Peter J. Smith is Professor of Geography at the University of Alberta, a past president of the Canadian Association of Geographers and past editor of *The Canadian Geographer*. His research interests include the implications of metropolitan fragmentation, both administrative and territorial, for planning procedures and urban form.